7/92

WITHDRAWN

Dracula
The Vampire and the Critics

Studies in Speculative Fiction, No. 19

Robert Scholes, Series Editor

Andrew Mellon Professor of Humanities

Other Titles in This Series

Dracula
The Vampire and the Critics

Edited by
Margaret L. Carter

UMI Research Press

Ann Arbor / London

Copyright © 1988
Margaret Louise Carter
All rights reserved

Produced and distributed by
UMI Research Press
an imprint of
University Microfilms Inc.
Ann Arbor, Michigan 48106

Library of Congress Cataloging in Publication Data

**Dracula : the vampire and the critics / edited by Margaret L.
Carter.**
p. cm—(Studies in speculative fiction ; no. 19)
Bibliography: p.
Includes index.
ISBN 0-8357-1889-1 (alk. paper)
1. Stoker, Bram, 1847-1912. Dracula. 2. Dracula, Count
(Fictitious character) 3. Vampires in literature. I. Carter,
Margaret L. (Margaret Louise), 1948- . II. Series.
PR6037.T617D783   1988
823'.8—dc19

88-17244
CIP

British Library CIP data is available.

Contents

Foreword

Foreword, in the sense of forward . . . What can *Dracula* criticism look forward to now that Margaret Carter has brought together many of the best essays on Stoker's novel? Where do we go from here?

This question announces itself whenever a milestone is reached in the reception of a text or an author or a tradition. *Middlemarch* . . . John Donne . . . pastoral . . . These and other happy subjects of literary study have known many critical milestones. The Gothic tradition, however, is—in this instance as in so many others—eccentric. Milestones here are critical in the other sense of the term. They are crucial, because so rare. Gothic fiction has lived out a reception history appropriate to the crazy self-divisions that it chronicles. Amazing power to transfix readers immediately and for generations is accompanied by a silence from the academy that also spans generations. Critical milestones for Gothic are therefore all the more crucial.

Frankenstein has known such a critical moment. In 1979, George Levine and U. C. Knoepflmacher culminate a decade of serious study and inaugurate another with *The Endurance of Frankenstein*. Mary Shelley and her masterpiece pass once and for all into serious consideration. Recently, Gordon Hirsch and I undertook a comparable project on the occasion of the centenary of *Strange Case of Dr Jekyll and Mr Hyde*. New essays with diverse methodologies explored the diversity of Stevenson's masterpiece. Now it is *Dracula*'s turn. Margaret Carter has gathered together a body of critical work that indicates why Stoker's masterpiece has held readers in the same willing thrall that marks Dracula's "victims" in the novel. Range and depth, cultural sweep and psychological and formal intricacy: these qualities of the greatest art in every epoch are established for *Dracula* in *The Vampire and the Critics*.

Carter's Introduction is so expeditious in its survey of Stoker scholarship that I can forego any redundant summary and return to my initial question. Where do we go from here? Three areas of study seem particularly promising.*

---

*From the students in my 1988 seminar on Late Victorian British Gothic Fiction I received considerable help in defining areas of promise within these fields. I want to thank for their intelligence,

One is the political. Though Wasson's essay is inevitably chilled by Cold War anxiety, it does lay out the way in which empires as well as psyches are opposed in *Dracula*. West vs. East. What is lacking in Wasson is any detailed grounding of this imperial opposition in Stoker's own time. Senf takes a step in the right direction when she notes that Jonathan Harker "fears a kind of reverse imperialism, the threat of the primitive trying to colonize the civilized world" (97). That Britons felt this increasingly in the Late Victorian period is shown by both a specific phenomenon like the hysteria over Kipling's arrival from India in 1890 and the more general sense of "autumnal chill" that marked the last years of the old Queen's reign. Late Victorian theories of Empire and the new science of anthropology are direct avenues to our recovery of Britain's anxiety at this time.

John Allen Stevenson devotes his recent essay to these subjects. Westmark's *History of Human Marriage* leads to revealing analysis of *"Dracula*'s insistence on the terror and necessity of racial struggle in an imperialist context."* Much more study needs to be done, however. Stevenson's principal focus is not upon the immediate milieu of Late Victorian discourse. "My emphasis . . . is on Stoker's novel as a representation of fears that are more universal than a specific focus on Victorian background would allow. . . . The anthropologist [Westmark] was expressing nothing not on the mind of the Deuteronomist millennia before." Dozens of Late Victorian anthropologists, ethnographers, politicians, and journalists created an intricate discourse in which fears of devolution struggled with themes of racial purity, in which economic concerns were masked by and opposed to claims for Britain's civilizing mission, in which fears of decline in literary puissance evoked appeals for a new infusion of talent even as they fueled and were fueled by apprehensions about Britain's decline in the Darwinian struggle of global politics. Exploration of these discourses as they weave together in Stoker's epoch will help us to read *Dracula* in context and thus in character.

Comparable exploration will show how politics relates to class in the novel. Hatlen is admirably adventurous in attempting to transcend the limitations of Lukácsian Marxism—its exclusion of the "romance" from discussions of narrative fiction—by drawing upon Jameson and Frye. In the process, Hatlen effects what seems to me one of the conjunctions most important for criticism today. He links politics and psychology. "The real subject of the book [*Dracula*] is, I submit, the *relationship between* psychological repression and social oppression. . . . The point at which sexuality and politics meet—that is the point at which Stoker's book locates itself" (133). In exploring this intersection of class

kindliness, and wit: Carol Jagielnik, Amy Kessel, Carolyn Russell, Diance Schwemm, Douglas Sun, and Elizabeth Trembley. I want to record a special debt to Stephen Arata whose excellent work on the politics and anthropology of empire will some day enrich readers of Stoker, Kipling, Conrad, and James as it has me and my colleagues.

and sex, Hatlen, however, takes up positions—about both women and men—which subsequent critics will probably diverge from. For example, he defines Lucy and Mina as "female members of the ruling class . . . two delicately bred young ladies who lead lives of (apparently) total leisure" (121). To blur Lucy and Mina into a single type—the leisured daughter of hegemony—is to occlude basic differences between the two women and thus to blunt class analysis. Unlike Lucy who does indeed travel idly with her wealthy mother, Mina is anything but leisured. Her first words in the novel open a letter to Lucy which distinguishes the two women immediately.

> Forgive my long delay in writing, but I have been simply overwhelmed with work. The life of an assistant schoolmistress is sometimes trying. I am longing to be with you, and by the sea, where we can talk together freely and build our castles in the air. I have been working very hard lately, because I want to keep up with Jonathan's studies, and I have been practicing shorthand assiduously. When we are married I shall be able to be useful to Jonathan. (chap. 5)

Not only is Mina not leisured, but her hard work is as an "assistant." She must work hard at a relatively subordinate position on the employment ladder. From this fact arise various questions.

Does the class difference between Mina and Lucy help explain the different sexuality that each displays? "Work" appears twice in Mina's passage—with her impending marriage as well as her present employment. "Useful" is what Mina wants to be to both her husband and her pupils. Though Stoker makes it clear that Mina as well as Lucy is attracted to the subversive sexuality of Dracula, is he also suggesting that subversive sexual involvement varies inversely with involvement in the work force? To what extent does Lucy's leisure, her disengagement from economic relations, predispose her to the predaceous attacks that she makes on children whose accents ("bloofer lady") and grubby faces indicate their lower class status? Does the fact noted by many critics—that Lucy is less than absolutely enraptured by her fiancé, Lord Godalming—derive at least in part from the fact that being "useful" to *anyone*, husband or children or whomever, has never been required of her?

Class and sex generate a different set of questions about women when Hatlen remarks that "women born outside the magic circle of the ruling elite (the only concrete examples in *Dracula* are perhaps the three vampire women at Castle Dracula) were instead generally *hyper*sexualized by the same society" (133). On the one hand, Dracula's three women are apparently part of the "the ruling elite," for Jonathan expressly establishes them as "ladies." Critics have speculated about their specific relation to Count Dracula (are they his wives or sisters or daughters or some combination thereof?), but fairly clearly their predaceous sexuality correlates with their place among the ruling elite and thus associates them with Lucy rather than with proletarian women. What about *these* women in *Dracula*? Are they hypersexualized? Useful analysis could be devoted to the Westenra servants who succumb to the drugged wine. Is their stupor, in effect, a post-coital response to Dracula's visit? While they are not of course consciously of the devil's party, their slumber surely does facilitate Dracula's attack upon Lucy. Related questions might be asked about: the servant who steals the cross from Lucy's body and thus fosters Dracula's post-mortem designs upon her; the servants who cannot be trusted as blood donors; the mortuary woman who treats Dr. Seward familiarly in a "brother-professional way." Lower class women are numerous and important in *Dracula*. They have suffered occlusion at the hands not of Stoker but of his critics.

Lower class *men* are discussed by Hatlen in terms of traits bodied forth by Count Dracula. "An odd accent, a 'dark' aura, an irresistible sexual potency, a powerful smell. . ." (129). Hatlen goes on to add that of course Dracula is also evidently aristocratic, since the Count represents everything, upper and lower, that is not middle class. But the principal anxiety embodied in *Dracula* is "the threat of a revolutionary assault by the dark, foul-smelling, lustful lower classes upon the citadels of privilege" (130). To what extent this is indeed the principal threat in *Dracula* each reader will decide. What I want to suggest now is where else in the novel a politically oriented criticism can find class issues associated with men. One place is old Mr. Swales, whose marginal role in the plot of *Dracula* is reflected in critics' ignoring of him (Johnson is a positive exception here), but whose role in Stoker's critique of patriarchy is important indeed. Swales constitutes a counterforce to Dr. Van Helsing, since he indicts the hollowness of the patriarchal structures that Van Helsing enlists the Army of Light to preserve. Swales is the one who establishes, for example, that the graves of the sailors in Whitby Churchyard are all empty, and thus that the tombstones' pieties are all hollow rhetoric.

Like the sailors who die by drowning, the laborers who drink liquor throughout the workday are another neglected subject (though Leatherdale has done useful work here). To what extent does a class joke—you know how bibulous those proles are!—cover a deeper dilemma, an oral fixation that marks the proletariat as regressive and may well constitute a more powerful link to Count Dracula than odor (which has no class association in the novel)? Finally, the co-option of lower-class men can be explored in the person of the locksmith who is brought in to help the Army of Light perpetrate one of its felonies. To what extent is legality itself a class issue? Apparently any means is permissible to and even imperative for patriarchs once they define the destruction of Dracula as a national priority. Surely these men would be singing a different tune if the locksmith were employing his skills to invade *their* property—especially if he justified the felony as a means to that redistribution of wealth which Karl Marx defined as *his* national priority.

Psychoanalytic and feminist approaches have proven particularly effective with *Dracula*. The misogynistic treatment of Lucy and Mina and the evident presence of the New Woman are by now topics at once firmly established and ripe for further speculation. Likewise, now that the oedipal structure of father (Dracula), son (Van Helsing's Army of Light), and mother (Lucy-Mina) is well recognized, we can go beyond the fact of this triangle to its function. To what extent is the Oedipus less a deep structure expressing our most secret desires than a relatively evident screen for desires still more threatening? To what extent, in other words, is the Oedipus a culturally sanctioned way to repress mother and the pre-oedipal? In her influential essay, Roth has shown effectively how matricidal drives underlie patricidal ones in *Dracula*. Her discussion of the novel's deployment of defenses, of projection and denial, plus Byers's own attention to defenses and Bierman's to the "oral triad," enable us to go on and question the role of Dracula himself in the dramatization of pre-oedipal anxieties. If we see the Count as the articulation of polymorphously perverse sexuality, then textual indications of his role as woman and child—as well as phallic predator—can be brought into play. Bentley, for example, has stressed that blood in *Dracula* represents both milk and menstrual discharge, and that vampirism itself displays tendencies to "infantile erotic regression" (29). From here we can go on to the manifold indications of the Count's roles as mother, wife, and child—the fact, for example, that his two ships are the (mythic mother) *Demeter* and the (sexually voracious) *Czarina Catherine*, and that his return to the coffin is a decidedly womb-oriented motion.

Considering Dracula in terms of the mother-child dyad will, in turn, lead us to the other mothers in the novel, especially Mrs. Canon and Mrs. Westenra. Why is Mrs. Canon in *Dracula* at all? Is her marginalization in terms of the plot a defense against her centrality in terms of male anxiety about motherhood? Surely Mrs. Canon preys so predaceously upon her son that he can escape only by committing suicide. Mrs. Canon seems especially symptomatic of bad motherhood if we take Mrs. Westenra seriously. Unlike most critics who ignore her entirely or dismiss her readily ("Lucy's mother dies too early in the book to be much of a character" [Weismann, p. 73]), Johnson recognizes how intensely Lucy's rebellion against Victorian orthodoxy is directed against her mother. This interpretation captures only part of the complexity, however, because Johnson goes on to repeat the patriarchy's treatment of Mrs. Westenra in *Dracula*. Though he credits Lucy with repressed unconscious emotions, Johnson restricts her mother to the conscious. She is simply "repressive, outdated, selfish . . . dominated by the past." Seward does much the same thing when he says that "in a case where any shock may prove fatal, matters are so ordered that, from some cause or other, the things not personal—even the terrible change in her daughter to whom she is so attached—do not seem to reach her. . . . If this be an ordered selfishness, then we should pause before we condemn anyone for the vice of egotism" (chap. 10). If we recognize in Mrs. Westenra what Seward and his fellow patriarchs cannot face—an unconscious as potentially subversive as a man's—we can begin to explore her many bizarre actions in *Dracula*. Does she really take down the garlic from Lucy's window simply because she judges it harmful to her daughter's health? And how do we explain her final actions— stripping the garland from Lucy's neck and then cutting off her daughter's last defense, flight, by knocking her unconscious? To what extent, in other words, does Mrs. Westenra have a "bad heart" because she is unconsciously in league with Dracula? And why?

Another important occlusion in the psychic life of Stoker's characters has been singled out by Christopher Craft in his excellent essay—the homoerotic attractions of patriarchy. In light of Craft we can return to Griffin's view of Lucy as "Dracula's tool . . . a pipeline from one set of victims to another" (140) and see Lucy also as patriarchy's tool, a pipeline connecting the men who transfuse her. They exchange bodily fluids in a Girardian triangle that makes woman only the conduit of desire between rivals, thereby allowing these men to manage the rivalry they cannot acknowledge (Roth, p. 60). A comparable service is provided by Mina at the time of her ravagement by Dracula. Though Jonathan's ineffectuality here can be seen as a detumescent swoon resulting from his wife's conjugal demands, the moment is made overdetermined by Stoker's phrasing—"breathing heavily *as though in a stupor*" (chap. 11, my italics). If Jonathan is *not* in a stupor, if he is participating voyeuristically in Dracula's subversion of Mina (as he did when, attacked directly by the vampire *women* and "afraid to raise my eyelids," he nonetheless "looked out and saw perfectly under the lashes"), he has become the passive victim experiencing the dominant male's puissance.

Among expressly literary issues, two seem particularly promising—the formal and the traditionary. Close analyses by Senf, Seed, and Johnson have been sufficiently persuasive that a certain embattled, defensive posture can, I hope, be foregone by subsequent students of *Dracula*'s form. Defensiveness was an inevitable response to the tendency of psychologically-oriented critics to stress unconscious over conscious forces in the production of Stoker's narrative and thus to reinforce the patronizing view—traditional with Mary Shelley as well— that he was less an artist than an automatic writer. "They deny that Stoker really knew what he was doing as he wrote" (Johnson, p. 231). Defensiveness has been made unnecessary by recent work of both formalist and psychological critics. Senf, Seed, and Johnson establish beyond question that Stoker was a careful architect who built with a conscious eye for determined effects. In turn, the best recent work from psychological perspectives (Craft, and Johnson [1984], for instance) pays close attention to details obviously intended by Stoker. Getting beyond defensive/aggressive postures will enable critics to get on to important formal questions still unanswered.

To what extent, for example, are the letters, journals, etc. in the first half of *Dracula* characterized, as Senf maintains, by "a constancy of style . . . [that] further diminishes any individualizing of traits" (121), and to what extent is Seed correct that "the journals' styles reflect character. . . . Each [is a] partial and individual account" so that "the stylistic gap between these letters and Harker's journal implies a moral gap between two worlds that cannot have contact" (232, 229)? The full consequence of the critics' disagreement here appears when Senf and Seed reach diametrically opposed views of the end of *Dracula*. To what extent are the novel's ambiguities resolved? Senf, who sees the characters' styles as homogeneous, sees Stoker eliding all these characters in order to finally deny any easy attribution of virtue to the Army of Light. Seed, on the other hand, sees stylistic differences gradually melting away so that the last quarter of *Dracula* allows "no gap between their accounts, only a shift in perspective. This is crucial. As the gaps between individual accounts close, so Dracula becomes better known, better defined, and therefore the easier to resist" (235–36). Clearly readers cannot decide how ironic *Dracula* ultimately is until they evaluate the components of Stoker's narrative.

Another important formalist question is: what information gets told by whom? The crisis moment in Mina's life when Dracula makes her drink from the slit in his chest is recounted from *Seward*'s viewpoint, and is then followed by a section from Jonathan. We never find out what *Mina* felt. That Jonathan asks *Seward* what happens (339) repeats the exclusion of Mina which the novel itself practices. Jonathan doesn't ask Mina about her feelings for the same reason that Stoker doesn't let her provide a journal entry. Such repressiveness in turn leads to the larger question of genre within *Dracula*. Ordinarily different genres can be read as emanations from different levels of consciousness. We tend to be less intimate in letters to our employers than in love notes to spouses, and we may be more intimate still in diaries resolutely private. Since everything in *Dracula* is eventually made public, however, since the diarists soon know that the group will read their words, how intimate will anyone risk being? As fear of the unconscious leads characters to proliferate details in an obsessive attempt to control the unknown, so the obsessive homogenization of genres does more than Van Helsing expressly proposes—more than equip each member of the Army with all possible information. It encourages the repression of whatever might prove disconcerting to the diarist and thus subversive of the Army's mission. Critics in their stylistic analysis will have to be both delicate and aggressive if we are to improve our sense of all that is not being said.

The literary traditions that *Dracula* derives from have been referred to by many scholars, but there remains much sustained, careful work to be done here.

This work is especially important because of the (apparently permanent) dearth of material on Stoker's life. Since we seem stymied in our desire to know more about where he comes from psychologically—the apparent childhood trauma with Mrs. Stoker, his mother, and the probable adult difficulties with Mrs. Stoker, his wife—we need to know all we can about where Bram Stoker came from literarily. We might begin with the texts that *Dracula* expressly foregrounds. *The Rime of the Ancient Mariner,* for example. In addition to following out recent leads by Seed and Varma and to charting new courses through the poem, scholars might also examine a second Coleridge narrative, a drama of predation and role shifting and the frustration of both heterosexual and homosexual passion—*Christabel.* Another text foregrounded by *Dracula* has received no critical attention. Cued by "the children [who] were playing nothing but Red Riding Hood" in the week after the "wolf got out" of the zoo (chap. 15), we might well explore the role of the wolf in the bedroom of Lucy and her old mother, especially since menstruation is an issue for both Perrault's resolutely admonitory fairy tale and Stoker's ambiguously admonitory cultural fable.

Carmilla is an evident source of *Dracula,* but no full-scale comparison of the stories has been undertaken. There are many intriguing similarities at the local level, like the fact that both tales introduce Shakespeare passages which they misquote revealingly. More basic, and more intricate than critics have indicated, is the derivation of Dr. Van Helsing, who comes not only from the supervening authority, Dr. Hesselius, but also from the imported vampire killer, Baron Vordenburg. These associations will be particularly helpful in revealing the moral obliquities of Stoker's patriarch if critics will also explore how richly compromised Le Fanu's own patriarchs are. And finally, there is *Dracula*'s large-scale debt to *Carmilla* at the level of narration, where deception and repression are more consistently at play than in another obvious influence, *The Woman in White.* Like Stoker's narrators, Laura ends *Carmilla* without ever admitting the extent of her implication in the monstrous other.

Among literary influences from the decade immediately prior to *Dracula,* two texts seem particularly promising. *Strange Case of Dr Jekyll and Mr Hyde* foregrounds an issue central to *Dracula*—the role of professionalism in cultural life. "Henry Jekyll, M.D., D.C.L., L.L.D., F.R.S., etc" . . . "Abraham Van Helsing, M.D., D.Ph., D. Litt., etc., etc." (chap. 9). The more we see Van Helsing in the Henry Jekyll line of men embodying the initials and thus the ideals of a culture where erudition and hard work are the paramount virtues, the more we can see that the bourgeois world of *Dracula* is formed by the same self-division which prompts Henry Jekyll to tear himself in two and then murder the embodiment of the law, Sir Danvers Carew, M.P. Van Helsing's Hyde is Dracula himself, as Stoker carries on Stevenson's concern with the physician gone wrong (a tradition that harkens back to *Frankenstein,* although Victor, despite popular lore, is *not* a physician and has no degrees, since professionalism and the whole question of an expressly *bourgeois* patriarchy are less important to Mary Shelley at the beginning of the nineteenth century). Another important link to *Jekyll and Hyde* is *Dracula*'s concern with devolution. As Hyde is the archaic, simian creature who eventually takes over the urbane Jekyll and terrorizes his elegant world, so Count Dracula with his tendency to grow ever younger embodies the threat of reverse colonization, of the more primeval Carpathian culture taking over the most "highly developed" technocracy in Western Europe.

A second novel from the mid-1880s is so important to Stoker that *Dracula* (and *The Lair of the White Worm*) could not, I believe, exist without it. The novel is *She*. In addition to the pervasive anxiety about women that Haggard shares with Stoker, there are the same specific sources of threat to Britain. Ayesha, like Mina, is androgynous, a man-woman whose mind must be subordinated to her heart at all cost. Stoker follows Haggard's peremptory strategy: as Ayesha is made to deny her "masculine" mind by admitting that she really is only an emotional female who wants to be dominated ("Forgive me my weakness. . . . Thou seest after all I am a very woman. . . . At last my deliverer came—he for whom I had watched and waited through the generations"), so Mina is made to abet in that exclusion from the Army of Light which effectively reduces her to a Girl Friday with sibylline credentials. Knowledge is so threatening in both *She* and *Dracula* because it derives from the deep past. The queenly Ayesha and the Transylvanian Count go back centuries as embodiments of the archaic force of returned repressions. That this return is a reverse colonization is made express in *She* when Ayesha plans a westward "journey to this England of thine" to depose and replace Queen Victoria. For salvation, Haggard looks to the source of strength traditional in British patriarchy and central to *Dracula*— Oxbridge gentlemen. Horace Holly and Leo Vincey, like Van Helsing and his Army, represent different generations who share common loyalties—to nation and the male enterprises sanctioned by and devoted to her. *She* and *Dracula* would not be late Victorian, however, if they could avoid acknowledging that their Oxbridge optimism rests on somewhat shaky ground. Haggard's patriarchy, like Stoker's, is characterized by absent fathers. As Mr. Hawkins, Mr. Swales, Lord Godalming, and Mr. Westenra are all dead either before *Dracula* opens or soon after, so *She* posits for Leo Vincey a father whose life is a failure and whose death is a suicide. Paternal dysfunction makes reverse colonization all the more threatening. Like Stoker, however, Haggard determines that his novel can be read as the thorough triumph of traditional virtue. What Haggard will not do, what enables *Dracula* to transcend *She* and become one of the great British novels of the late Victorian period, is to call this triumph into question. Stoker cannot rest easy with the facility of Haggard's politics. However mightily

Stoker is drawn to the resonances of fraternal solidarity, he appends to *Dracula* a final Note that confirms all the novel's ambiguities and unsettles any certitude about the future.

That is why Margaret Carter today is collecting essays on *Dracula* rather than on *She*. And that is why we can look forward and ask so promisingly about Stoker—where do we go from here?

WILLIAM VEEDER

Preface

This anthology has grown out of a lifelong admiration for Bram Stoker's definitive tale of vampirism. When I first began to research vampirism in English literature, relatively few secondary sources on *Dracula* existed. In the mid-seventies, however, an explosion of academic interest in the novel occurred. It is a privilege to be able to bring together this comprehensive collection of thirty years of *Dracula* scholarship. This volume could not exist without the generosity of all the individual authors who have allowed me to reprint their work. In gathering materials, I received indispensable help from Henry K. Vester, Marlene Wood, the University of Maryland, College Park, the Nimitz Library of the United States Naval Academy, and the Anne Arundel County Public Library. I am indebted to all my predecessors in *Dracula* research, especially to Clive Leatherdale's bibliography in *Dracula: The Novel and the Legend*. I hope this collection will be as enlightening to other *Dracula* specialists as the process of compiling it has been to me.

Bram Stoker, 1906

Introduction

Margaret L. Carter

"Jolly good blood and thunder—with perhaps a little more blood than usual" (Harry Ludlam, *A Biography of Dracula*, 107), or "a novel that lurches toward greatness, stumbling over perceived and unperceived mysteries" (Leonard Wolf, *A Dream of Dracula*, 222)? Or perhaps a political transmutation of the life of Elisabeth Bathory (Gabriel Ronay, *The Truth about Dracula*)? Or raw material for a case study of the sexual neuroses of Bram Stoker in particular or late Victorian culture in general (a host of critics—including Bierman, Bentley, Byers, Craft, Griffin, and Weissman, among others—presenting various interpretations)? Less than thirty years ago, few scholars would have bothered asking such questions about Bram Stoker's *Dracula*.

Though vampirism in folklore has attracted scholarly attention since the early twentieth century, most notably in the work of Montague Summers, only in recent decades has vampirism in literature undergone close scrutiny. Aside from a few articles published from 1956 through the 1960s, serious study of *Dracula* and vampire fiction in general began in the early 1970s. In 1970 the first modern edition of *Varney the Vampyre; or, The Feast of Blood* was released under the editorship of Devendra P. Varma. The introduction and preface to that edition discussed the work's influence on Stoker. In 1972 Wolf published *A Dream of Dracula*, a multifaceted reflection on Stoker's novel from the viewpoints of psychology, literature, and popular culture. Soon afterward followed his *Annotated Dracula*. Almost simultaneously two studies of Vlad the Impaler, the historical Dracula, *In Search of Dracula*, by Raymond McNally and Radu Florescu, and Ronay's *The Truth about Dracula*, appeared. A flood of articles on *Dracula* accompanied and followed this upwelling of scholarly interest in a tale of horror formerly ignored by the academic community. The secondary literature on *Dracula* now comprises so much material that a retrospective survey is appropriate. Clive Leatherdale undertakes such a survey, also touching on Stoker's life, the book's publication history, the career of Vlad the Impaler, and folklore sources. However, no previous volume has brought together, for easy reference, a selection of secondary material dealing with *Dracula*. The present collection offers a sample of articles, covering about three decades in chronological order, approaching Stoker's novel from a variety of critical viewpoints. (The bibliography also supplies updated information on criticism produced since 1985, the date of Leatherdale's study.) *Dracula* specialists and students of supernatural fantasy and nineteenth-century fiction in general will all benefit from having these sources readily available in a single volume.

Contemporary reactions to the archetypal vampire tale at the time of its publication did not look deeper than its generic identity, in common with Stoker's biographer Ludlam, who characterizes the book accurately but incompletely as the "last of the great Gothic romances" (179). Seeking superlatives with which to praise Stoker, the *Daily Mail* reviewer enshrined him with Poe, Radcliffe, Mary Shelley, and the Brontës. The *Pall Mall Gazette* bestowed equally lavish compliments, while *The Bookman* and *Punch* delivered mixed reviews. The *Athenaeum* (26 June 1897) is typical of the latter, censuring the novel as "wanting in the constructive art." Though *Dracula* contains, amid its "grotesquely incredible events . . . better moments that show more power . . . even these are never productive of the tremor such subjects evoke under the hand of a master." The critic asserts, in common with most later readers, that "The early part goes best, for it promises to unfold the roots of mystery and fear lying deep in human nature." The grudging conclusion, "his object, assuming it to be ghastliness, is fairly well fulfilled," leaves *Dracula* straitly confined within its generic boundaries, as sensational entertainment. Since the early 1970s, however, along with the revitalization of vampires in popular fiction there has arisen considerable scholarly interest in the definitive vampire novel. Most studies of *Dracula* may be categorized as either historical, political, psychosexual, metaphysical, or structural (i.e., focusing on narrative technique, not necessarily adhering to a "structuralist" school of criticism). I shall offer an overview of *Dracula* studies with examples of each of these approaches.

Stoker's masterpiece received virtually no academic attention before 1956, except for brief references connected with studies of vampirism in folklore. One of Montague Summers's sources, Dudley Wright, confines himself to the remark, "Mr. Bram Stoker has made the vampire the foundation of his exciting romance *Dracula*" (186). Summers's monumental *The Vampire: His Kith and Kin* concludes with a chapter entitled "The Vampire in Literature." Here Summers devotes three pages to *Dracula* of which he acknowledges "there is no sensational romance which in modern days has achieved so universal a reputation" (333). While praising the novel as "a book of unwonted interest and fascination" (335), the eminent Gothicist condemns *Dracula* for a defect that has since become a stock criticism, its length and "prolixity" (333). (Curious, considering this point, that Summers *prefers* the near-plotless blood-feast of the 868-page *Varney the Vampyre*!) He is rather hard on the "tedious courtships of Lucy Westenra" and dismisses all the characters as "lay figure[s]" and "labels rather than individuals" (334). The overshadowing of mundane details of nine-teenth-century life by things creeping out of Hell, Summers praises as the novel's special virtue. His critique may be summarized in the statement that "there are passages of graphic beauty, passages of graphic horror, but these again almost entirely occur within the first sixty pages" (334–35). It is intriguing that he attributes most of *Dracula's* excellence to Stoker's choice of subject—a tribute to the subliminal power of the vampire motif often echoed in later *Dracula* criticism, as is the implication that the book has little artistic merit in itself.

Another early source of commentary on *Dracula*, still briefer, comprises three sentences in H. P. Lovecraft's *Supernatural Horror in Literature* (begun in the 1920s but not copyrighted until 1939). Lovecraft remarks that Stoker "created many starkly horrific conceptions in a series of novels whose poor technique sadly impairs their net effect." *Dracula* is acknowledged as the best of these, "almost the standard modern exploitation of the frightful vampire myth . . . a tale now justly assigned a permanent place in English letters" (78). Today we would omit the "almost"! The first extended commentary on the tale after Summers's, Ludlam's discussion in his biography of Stoker (1962), is more summary than criticism. He provides valuable information about Stoker's re-search and draws attention to the novelist's use of the historical Dracula, Vlad Tepes ("The Impaler"), but airily dismisses any notion of "deep psychological motives" underlying the novel (107).

Serious study of *Dracula* begins in earnest six years before Ludlam's biography, with *"Dracula, the Monastic Chronicles and Slavic Folklore"* (1956), by Bacil Kirtley. This article is the earliest English source, though the connec-tion is drawn in a 1929 Russian work cited by Kirtley, to discuss the fictional Dracula's derivation from the historical Vlad, Prince of Wallachia. Besides recording many of the legends attached to Vlad Dracula's name, Kirtley cata-logues all Stoker's important debts to folklore—the Scholomance near Lake Hermannstadt, the hazards of the Eve of St. George, the vampire's appearance in a glowing mist, his assumption of animal forms, the efficacy of garlic and impalement. Kirtley, moreover, is the first to identify Van Helsing's friend Arminius with the Hungarian linguist Arminius Vambery.

Kirtley's article, surprisingly, seems to have sparked no interest at the time. The next critical contribution falls into the psychosexual category rather than the historical. In "The Psychoanalysis of Ghost Stories" (1959), psychiatrist Maurice Richardson analyzes three tales, including *Dracula*, in Freudian terms. Unlike Joseph Bierman, who later uses Stoker's childhood as the key to *Dracula*, Richardson treats the novel as a self-contained unit. Applying the "primal horde" hypothesis of Freud's *Totem and Taboo*, Richardson casts Count Dracula as the evil father who wants to keep all the women for himself. The four young men, Harker, Holmwood, Seward, and Morris, correspond to the sons who kill the father to end his sexual monopoly. Their leader, Van Helsing, is the "good father" who defeats his evil counterpart and gives the "sons" permission to satisfy their sexual desires legitimately. To Richardson we owe the unforgettable summary of *Dracula* as "a kind of incestuous, necrophilous, oral-anal-sadistic all-in wrestling match" set in "a sort of homicidal lunatic's brothel in a crypt" (427). His assertion that *Dracula* does not make sense from any viewpoint other than the Freudian one, however, is disproved by the numerous and varied treatments that follow.

On a more popular level, science fiction author Anthony Boucher's introduction to a 1965 edition of *Dracula* endorses the Freudian approach and echoes the perennial scholarly puzzlement about exactly why this piece of "blood and thunder" so captivates the imagination. Boucher calls *Dracula* "assuredly a masterpiece of a kind, if not a literary one" (p. v). Of vampirism in general, he says, "No other supernatural theme typifies so implicity that lethal alliance of love and death . . . dominant in our popular literature" (p. viii). Noting Stoker's mastery of horror amid the familiar, Boucher emphasizes the central importance of science and detection in *Dracula*. Dominated by the personality of Van Helsing, "a hard-headed scientist of the only century to believe that science knew everything" (p. ix), the novel represents the final bastion of confidence in the powers of the human mind and in sharp antitheses between Light and Dark, Good and Evil. Though later critics cast doubt on how firmly Stoker, as implied author within the text, holds this confidence, the overt acts and words of the heroes seem to convey just such a world view.

An unambiguous distinction between Good and Evil underlies Richard Wasson's reading in "The Politics of *Dracula*" (1966). In Wasson's interpretation, however, the heroes are not battling the forces of Hell. Instead of a demon incarnate, the Romanian Count becomes a symbol of barbaric Eastern European expansionism, opposed by a Western alliance. Holmwood represents British aristocracy, while Morris, the American, supplies the heavy armament. The battle focuses upon Lucy Westenra, allegorized as "The Light of the West." Wasson ingeniously supports his case by citing Van Helsing's remarks about the enigmatic antiquity of Dracula's native land. This essay, however, does not mention Vlad Dracula's historical existence, a point that would have greatly strengthened the argument. It is unsettling that the text refers to the Romanian Count as "the Austrian"—perhaps an unconscious association with Hitler?

Contemporaneous with Wasson's article, "The Historical Dracula" (1966), by Grigore Nandris, treats Vlad's background and career at greater length than does Kirtley's article. Like Kirtley, Nandris also delves into the folklore upon which Stoker drew in converting the Wallachian warlord into a vampire. Devendra Varma's 1970 essay, though nominally an introduction to the first twentieth-century edition of the mid-Victorian thriller *Varney the Vampyre; or, The Feast of Blood*, focuses mainly on the folklore vampire—Oriental as well as European—and places Dracula in that context with a poetically phrased appreciation of the vampire Count as a literary and legendary figure. In "The Genesis of Dracula: A Re-Visit" (1975), Varma surveys the novel's roots in folklore, history, and Stoker's own life. A frequent lecturer on *Dracula* and vampirism, Varma later delivered an address, "Dracula's Voyage" (1986), which provocatively interprets the Count's pilgrimage from Transylvania to England in terms of Coleridge's *Rime of the Ancient Mariner*.

Historical study of Vlad and his connection with the fictional Dracula first became available to the general public, however, with *In Search of Dracula* (1972) by McNally and Florescu. Besides unfolding the career of Vlad, this book surveys legends of vampirism, shows how Stoker followed and deviated from various facts of Vlad's life, outlines the authors' "search" for the historical Dracula, locates the real Castle Dracula, and explores the mysteries of the Impaler's post-mortem career (for instance, the disappearance of his body). Some irrelevancies creep in, such as an account of Elisabeth Bathory, the "Blood Countess" of Hungary. Though flawed by such extraneous material and by the absence of footnotes or index, this book contains many useful features, such as numerous illustrations, an extensive bibliography and filmography, and the first English translations of two manuscripts about Vlad and of a series of Romanian folk tales. McNally and Florescu also collaborated on *Dracula: A Biography of Vlad the Impaler* (1973), a more detailed, chronologically straightforward study of the Impaler's life, in which they conclude, "Behind the mythical Dracula image lies hidden not only symbolic significance but the tactics of terror as means of social integration and political control" (180–81).

A similar conclusion had already been reached by Gabriel Ronay in *The Truth about Dracula* (1972). Relatively superficial in his treatment of the vampire concept, Ronay seems interested only in the political uses of the mythos surrounding Vlad Tepes. "The truth about Dracula," according to Ronay (who, fittingly, served as advisor to the filming of *Countess Dracula*, loosely based on Elisabeth Bathory's career), is that Stoker must have been guided in his portrayal of Dracula by Bathory's bloody crimes. The Countess, Ronay points out, was far more overtly vampiric than Vlad. This author takes a stance toward vampirism similar to Voltaire's: the superstition, in its present form, originated as a tool in the hands of ideological oppression. The life of Vlad the Impaler, admired in his own time as a ruthlessly just ruler and defender of his nation, was used in the same way. Ivan the Terrible, who justified his own despotism as emulation of the heroic Impaler, is characterized as "The Russian Dracula." In the twentieth century Hanns Heinz Ewers employs the vampire in fiction as a symbol of the Nazi spirit. Up to this point Ronay's analysis is provocative and plausible. Less plausible is his final chapter, citing Hitler, Mussolini, and Stalin as modern heirs of Dracula, and still more tenuous is the attempt to place John F. Kennedy in the same company—especially when Ronay credits Kennedy with Barry Goldwater's famous "extremism in the defense of liberty" slogan!

But something about *Dracula*, it seems, has the power to evoke extravagant reactions. Wolf, who has made the close study of the novel that Ronay apparently did not, finds echoes of the vampire myth in cultural phenomena as diverse as the Hell's Angels and the popular sex manual, *The Sensuous Woman*. Wolf's highly successful *A Dream of Dracula* (1972), in addition to relating the novel to Stoker's life, subjects the book to close analysis and, applying Jungian theory, explores the nature of vampirism and its symbolic value for contemporary culture. Wolf's interpretation focuses on the repressed sexuality of Victorian England and characterizes Stoker as dominated by "the fascination, and the fear of woman" (257). For the twentieth century, this critic suggests, the vampire represents not only sexuality but power, albeit of a curiously directionless and futile kind. Dracula becomes "the willing representative of the temptations, and the crimes, of the Age of Energy. . . . Granted that he has energy without grace, power without responsibility, and that his will is an exercise in death. . . . He has collected on the devil's bargain, the infinitely stopped moment" (302). Wolf later edited *The Annotated Dracula* (1975), a facsimile reprint of the first edition's text, with modern illustrations by Satty. This volume's introduction briefly recapitulates the evolution of the nineteenth-century literary vampire, the life and works of Bram Stoker, and Wolf's views on vampirism previously expressed in *A Dream of Dracula*. For its exhaustive historical notes and translation of the dialect employed by some of Stoker's Yorkshire characters, if nothing else, this edition is indispensable to the student of *Dracula*. Wolf points out Stoker's occasional factual errors and internal inconsistencies, as well as tracing patterns of imagery through the text. In addition to a bibliography of sources the editor consulted in composing the annotations, other critical apparatus includes maps, a partial filmography, a list of the principal English and foreign-language editions of the novel, a tally of Dracula's appearances in the story, and a calendar of the novel's events. This last item demonstrates the care with which Stoker constructed his plot—in spite of Wolf's own regrettable tendency to treat Stoker as, not a maker consciously working at his craft, but a wellspring of neuroses overflowing onto the page.

Close reading of *Dracula* in terms of its author's psychology is undertaken more rigorously by Joseph Bierman in "*Dracula:* Prolonged Childhood Illness, and the Oral Triad." Also published in 1972 (a pivotal year for *Dracula* criticism), Bierman's article shows the novel as arising directly from Stoker's life experiences. Stoker's childhood illness, keeping him bedridden until the age of seven, along with the probable treatment of "bleeding," is linked to rivalry with his younger brothers. These repressed feelings, Bierman suggests, were brought to a head by the knighting of Henry Irving and Dr. William Stoker (Bram's older brother) in 1895, the year Stoker began *Dracula*. The "oral triad," a concept borrowed from Bertram D. Lewin's *The Psychoanalysis of Elation*, consists of the unconscious connection among sleeping, eating, and being eaten. The vampire's sucking of blood, Renfield's obsession with eating "lives," and abnormal sleep states are, of course, dominant motifs in *Dracula*. A scene especially important to this reading is Mina's "Baptism of Blood" at the Count's hands, in which Harker falls into an unnatural stupor while Dracula first eats and then is "eaten." Bierman also traces Stoker's use of the imagery of sickness, sleep, eating, regurgitation, death, and resurrection in two earlier tales from *Under the Sunset* (1882), "How Seven Went Mad" and "The Wondrous Child." While revealing *Dracula's* roots in Stoker's psyche, Bierman hints at the sources of the tale's universal fascination. His ongoing research into Stoker's working methods led to publication of a second article, "The Genesis and Dating of *Dracula* from Bram Stoker's Working Notes" (1977).

Bierman's psychoanalytic approach foreshadowed a plethora of psychosexual treatments of *Dracula* in the seventies and eighties. One prevalent theory holds that Stoker's portrayal of female vampires symbolizes male fear of women's sexuality. Phyllis A. Roth and Judith Weissman each advance this thesis (1977). To Roth the destruction of the woman-turned-vampire represents the destruction of the devouring mother in favor of the good mother (Mina). Weissman illuminates the vampire's role as sexually voracious female by a comparison with Bertha Rochester, the mad wife in *Jane Eyre*. Earlier (1972) Carrol Fry identifies Count Dracula with the aristocratic rake in the tradition of Richardson's Lovelace, transforming pure ladies into fallen women, and Christopher Bentley explores the overall sexual implications of vampiric predation in *Dracula*, drawing heavily on the Freudian insights of Ernest Jones and touching upon homoeroticism. Gail Griffin (1980) also sees the primary threat in Stoker's novel as, not the Count himself, but the threatening sexuality and aggression he unleashes in women. Atypical among psychosexual readings is Thomas B. Byers' focus upon Dracula himself and his relationship to the heroes, an interaction based on fear of male dependency, which muse be eradicated by destroying the vampire (1981). Burton Hatlen (1980), combining psychological with Marxist interpretation, presents the Count as both sexually and socially "other." Christopher Craft (1984) views the novel's conflict in homoerotic terms. John Allen Stevenson (1988) analyzes vampiric intercourse as a parody of ordinary human sexuality. After Bierman, critics make little attempt to find direct links between the story's psychosexual overtones and Stoker's own life and character. An exception is Wolf, who places heavy emphasis on Stoker's supposed ambivalence, combining fascination and fear, toward women. Wolf draws upon Stoker's bizarre *Lair of the White Worm* (1911) to support this position— without, strangely, mentioning that tale's more obvious resemblances to *Dracula*, such as the Byronic villain, the preoccupation with a supernatural being's unnatural longevity, the practice of hypnotism and psychic predation, and the pairing of a dark and a fair heroine (even the names are similar to those of *Dracula's* heroines). Daniel Farson, Stoker's great-nephew, hints, in *The Man Who Wrote Dracula* (1975), at sexual aberrations underlying Stoker's fiction.

Fascinating as the novel's psychosexual implications may be, Stoker himself would probably have vehemently denied any such subtext in his fiction. More work needs to be done with the elements of *Dracula* that its author seems to have consciously deemed important. Fontana's article analyzes one such element, Stoker's shaping of the Count's appearance and personality according to the scientific criminology of Lombroso. Charles Blinderman (1980) and Geoffrey Wall (1984) also deal with Stoker's response to the science of his day. Blinderman's picture of Dracula in terms of scientific materialism, as a Darwinian superman, is particularly unusual and offers a fresh look at the sometimes neglected Renfield. Advances in technology pervade *Dracula*, throwing into relief the vampire's numinously archaic traits. Several critics have amplified upon the erotic overtones of blood transfusion, but we should also recognize that plot device's function as an instance of the "nineteenth-century up-to-date" armament arrayed against the vampire. Relatively little has been written about Stoker's immediate sources—particularly his fictional sources, aside from the oft-mentioned *Carmilla*—and the specific stages through which *Dracula* evolved from its inception to its published form. (One exception is Hennelly's 1982 study of Stoker's debt to Wilkie Collins's *The Woman in White*.) Publication of Stoker's working papers, now in preparation under the editorship of Bierman and Patricia Willis, Curator of American Literature at Yale's Beinecke Library, will greatly facilitate analysis of that process. We may thereby develop a more accurate picture of Stoker as literary craftsman, constructing a highly complex plot.

The sexual and the historical/political overlap in Stephanie Demetrakopoulos's "Feminism, Sex Role Exchanges, and Other Subliminal Fantasies in Bram Stoker's *Dracula*" (1977), Carol Senf's "*Dracula*: Stoker's Response to the New Woman" (1982), and the chapter on Stoker in Weissman's *Half Savage and Hardy and Free* (1987). Senf, in "*Dracula:* The Unseen Face in the Mirror" (1979), is one of the few critics to give much attention to the novel's multiple-narrator structure. Suggesting how this narrative strategy undercuts the reliability of the various reports by emphasizing their subjective nature, she holds that the "heroism" of the protagonists is a mask for their own sexual and aggressive impulses. She also draws attention to the novel's pervasive, yet oddly neglected, motif of madness. Since Royce MacGillivray (1972) had already asserted that *Dracula*'s narrative complexity is its greatest strength, it seems strange that few scholars have chosen to pursue this line of inquiry. Only David Seed (1985) devotes a complete article to Stoker's use of the diary as a narrative device. Analyzing *Dracula* in narrative order, Seed demonstrates how the form of each section facilitates Stoker's purpose of first plunging characters and reader into mysteries that defy rational explanation, then fragmenting the characters' perceptions and distancing them from the truth of their experience, and finally filling the gaps in their perception to make possible the vampire's overthrow.

Relatively unexplored, too, are the novel's philosophic and religious implications. Mark M. Hennelly, like Senf, connects *Dracula*'s moral conflict with its narrative structure. He sees Stoker's central theme as an epistemological conflict between the vampire's world view and the heroes'. A resolution between the two may produce "a gnosis which will rehabilitate the Victorian wasteland" (13). Hennelly may be the only critic to hint at positive values in the character of the vampire, drawing upon the Grail legend and casting the vampire Count as the Fisher King. Strangely, Stoker's use of Christian imagery has been little discussed, aside from Christopher Gist Raible's brief account of the ways in which Dracula's behavior parodies Christian doctrine and sacraments (1979) and Brian Murphy's discussion of Dracula as Satanic hero (1976). Leatherdale's chapter on that topic explores in more detail Count Dracula's role as Antichrist, as well as pointing out the liberties Stoker, in his portrayal of Van Helsing, takes with Roman Catholic belief and practice. Gwenyth Hood (1987) brings a fresh outlook to the material by comparing Dracula, as demonic tyrant, to J. R. R. Tolkien's Antichrist figure, Sauron.

Comments on *Dracula* in recent books on supernatural fiction in general are too numerous to catalogue here. Rosemary Jackson (1981), notably, applies Marxist criticism and the theories of Tzvetan Todorov in suggesting that *Dracula* summons up subversive energies to control them through the heroes, representing the social and religious establishment. William P. Day (1985) analyzes Stoker's novel in terms of androgyny, the double, and the self as Outsider. Two recent critics have dealt extensively with *Dracula* in book-length studies. James B. Twitchell's *The Living Dead* (1981) surveys vampirism throughout the nineteenth century as a Romantic motif, with particular attention to the theme's function as a symbol of the relationship between artist and art. Devoting part of a chapter to *Dracula*, Twitchell interprets the story in terms reminiscent of Maurice Richardson, as a battle between a band of brothers, led by the "good" father, and the "bad" father who attempts to possess their mothers/sisters/wives. This critic sees the novel as essentially an adolescent male fantasy, with the Count both feared and envied for his limitless exercise of power without responsibility. Twitchell seems convinced that "*Dracula*'s claim on our attention is not . . . its artistic merit" (135). Like so many previous readers, he attributes the novel's power to extra-literary factors. He elaborates his theory in the vampire chapter of his later book, *Dreadful Pleasures* (1985), a study of horror motifs in popular culture, with special emphasis on Dracula, Frankenstein, and the Wolfman.

Also in 1985, Leatherdale published *Dracula: The Novel and the Legend*, a survey of vampire folklore, Stoker's career, the historical Dracula, the writing of the novel, and twentieth-century *Dracula* scholarship. To his review of criticism, including chapters on sexual, psychological, political, religious, and metaphysical interpretations, he adds his own comments in each category. To any reader interested in further exploring the study of *Dracula* up to 1985, I recommend Leatherdale's bibliography. Rather than attempting to duplicate it, I offer a representative sample of various critical approaches. Leatherdale has recently edited *The Origins of Dracula* (1987), a collection of nonfiction essays on vampirism consulted by Stoker while researching the background for *Dracula*. Richard Dalby, specialist in Stoker bibliography, briefly cites in his introduction to *Dracula's Brood,* an anthology of rare vampire fiction, a selection of Stoker's lesser-known contemporary folklore and fictional sources. Multimedia bibliographies by Martin Riccardo and Donald F. Glut survey materials concerning the vampire in legend, history, and literature on a more popular level.

Study of *Dracula* on its own terms, as a self-contained achievement of literary craftsmanship, seems to be firmly established in contemporary scholarship. I hope the present volume will stimulate further innovative forays into the realm of the Lord of Vampires.

1

Dracula, the Monastic Chronicles and Slavic Folklore

Bacil F. Kirtley

Bram Stoker's *Dracula*, that somewhat belated apparition from the sub-literary pits of Gothic horror fiction, has enjoyed a continuous notoriety since its first printing in 1897. Not only has the novel been republished numerous times, but its adaptions to the stage[1] and to the cinema have repeatedly attracted crowded audiences. In the United States the story's impact has been sufficiently pervasive to furnish popular speech with a connotative tag in the figure of the vampire Dracula, whose mere name is evoked to suggest a stereotype of that shuddery, but not uncozy, fright purveyed by certain types of class-"C" motion pictures.

As might be expected, the materials out of which Bram Stoker put together his shocker were largely the stock-properties of Victorian supernatural fiction. Yet, certain of his themes—especially if the uncritical reader at which the novel was aimed be considered—have a curiously recondite origin and his *decor* possesses a surprisingly deliberate authenticity. Not only was the central figure of the novel, Dracula, ultimately historical, his exploits being preserved in the Russian monastic chronicles, but many of the supernatural beliefs and practices which provide the narrative both with its rationale and its emotional climate are rather faithful reproductions of superstitions which have undergone their most distinctive elaboration in the area of Southeastern Europe where the novel is set.

In the course of Stoker's novel, Dr. Van Helsing—whose several roles include wise counselor, shaman, and distinguished medical doctor—reveals the following information about the vampire Dracula's origin:

> I have asked my friend Ariminius, of Buda-Pesth University, to make his record; and from all the means that are, he told me of what has been. He must, indeed, have been that Voivode [English "Waywode"] Dracula who won his fame against the Turks over the great river on the

This article originally appeared in *Midwest Folklore* 6 (1956), No. 3.

Hie facht sich an gar ein graussen

liche erschröckenliche hystorien von dem wilden wütrich.
Dracole wayde. Wie er die leüt gespißt hat. vnd gepraten.
vnd mit den haußtern, yn ainem kessel gesoten. vñ wie er die
leüt geschunden hat vñ zerhacken lassen als ein kraut. Jtez
er hat auch den mütern ire kind gepraté vnd sy habes müs-
sen selber essen. Vnd vil andere erschröckenliche ding die in
disem Tractat geschriben stend. Vnd in welchem land er
geregiret hat.

Vlad the Impaler Surrounded by His Victims

very frontier of Turkeyland. If it be so, then he was no common man; for in that time, and for centuries after, he was spoken of as the cleverest and the most cunning, as well as the bravest of the sons of the 'land beyond the forest.' That mighty brain and that iron resolution went with him to the grave, and are even now arrayed against us. The Draculas were, says Arminius, a great and noble race, though now and again were scions who were held by their coevals to have had dealing with the Evil One. They learned his secrets in the Scholomance, amongst the mountains over Lake Hermanstadt, where the devil claims the tenth scholar as his due. In the records are such words as 'stregoica'—witch, 'ordog,' and 'pokol'—Satan and hell; and in one manuscript this very Dracula is spoken of as 'wampyr,' which we all understand too well.[2]

This is not altogether the wild and pseudo-erudite talk of horror fiction. Stoker put in Van Helsing's speech details of a legend which have documentary confirmation.

In the monastery at Kirill-Belozersk, in northern Russia near the Finnish border, was found a manuscript which dates from the year 1490 and which is a copy of a document originally penned in 1486.[3] The manuscript relates the story of Dracula (Rumanian for "devil"), which is the name bestowed in horror by monkish chroniclers upon Vlad Tsepesh, Governor of Wallachia from the years 1456 to 1462 and again in the year 1476. The material of the Kirill-Belozersk manuscript was widely circulated among the monasteries of the Eastern Slavs, and by the middle of the 16th century had reached as far as Germany, a fact attested by the appearance of the Dracula story in the vernacular edition of Sebastian Münster's *Cosmographia universa* in 1541 (Latin edition, 1550).[4]

Dracula's exploits form a rough cycle of twelve incidents—incidents which for preposterous and whimsical cruelty challenge comparison with the outrages of young Caligula—and in the oldest manuscripts they are presented in the following order: (1) the Turkish ambassadors sent to Dracula's court in Wallachia failed to remove their fezzes in his presence. To Dracula's question about this impropriety, the emissaries replied that such was their custom. The witty governor had their fezzes nailed to their heads in order to "fix them in this observance."[5] (2) Dracula offered to join forces with the Turkish sultan upon the condition that his army be granted immunity from attack. The sultan accepted. After marching his army five days into Turkish territory, Dracula wheeled his host toward home. On the return march his men ravaged the countryside and killed, impaled, or tortured all the land's inhabitants. (3) All offenders against Dracula's laws were put to death, whatever their offense. In his domain was a spring of cool, sweet water by which he placed a golden drinking cup. No one ever dared steal this, so great was the fear he aroused. (4) Once Dracula had the aged, sick and poor of his domain summoned. He invited his guests into a large, specially made apartment and there fed them and gave them wine. He then asked the assembled unfortunates if they wished to be freed from all earthly care. They answered that they did; whereupon Dracula burned the building down upon them. (5) Two Catholic monks from Hungary visited Dracula in order to beg alms. Dracula took each separately, showed him the numerous wretches impaled upon stakes in his courtyard and asked him whether he had acted rightly. The first monk said no; the second monk said that a ruler was appointed by God to execute the wicked and reward the righteous. Dracula had the first monk impaled; the second monk he gave fifty gold ducats and dismissed with honor. (6) A merchant who had 160 gold ducats stolen from a cart appealed to Dracula for justice. Dracula had a similar quantity of gold, with the addition of one extra ducat, replaced in the cart. The merchant reported to Dracula the restoration of his money, as well as the presence of the additional ducat, at the very moment the captured thief was brought in. Dracula let the merchant go, telling the latter that had he not reported the extra ducat, he would have impaled him along with the thief. (7) Dracula was particularly cruel to lazy and unchaste women, as exemplified by this story. Once he met a poor peasant wearing a torn shirt. The peasant was asked if he had a wife, and next, if he had flax. When he replied affirmatively, Dracula had the hands of the peasant's lazy wife cut off and then ordered her to be impaled. (8) A peasant attending Dracula while he dined among the corpses of his courtyard held his nose against the stench. Dracula had him impaled in order to elevate him above such annoying odors. (9) Dracula continually set traps in the form of subtle questions for foreign envoys. If they failed to elude these, he impaled them, saying that he was not responsible for the punishment, but their master, who chose unsuitable emissaries. (10) Dracula had workmen make him iron casks which he filled with gold and lowered into a river. Afterward he had the workmen killed so that his secret would not be known.[6] (11) King Matthias of Hungary defeated Dracula and imprisoned him at Vyshegrad on the Danube for twelve years. Even in prison Dracula managed to act with customary cruelty. He caught mice and impaled them, bought birds and plucked them alive. (12) In return for embracing Catholicism, the king freed Dracula and restored him to his former eminence. Ten years later, after defeating the Turks in a battle, Dracula rode to the top of a hill in order to survey his victory and was mistakenly killed by one of his own men in the failing light.[7]

Unquestionably the historical past that Van Helsing in his speech (quoted above) assigns the fictional vampire Dracula is that of Vlad Tsepesh, Voivod of Wallachia. Did Stoker, however, incorporate in the story any further particulars from the chronicle, beyond his identification of the character with the sinister governor and his utilization of the locale mentioned in the documents? Did he know the specific details of the Dracula legend or did he merely have a general impression of its content? Indeed, one circumstance in the story's plot indicates that he may have had more than a hazy idea of the chronicles' Dracula. In his novel Stoker seems to have adapted the legend of Dracula's imprisonment (incident no. 11 above) and to have attached it to the figure of Renfield, the zoöphagous (life-eating) maniac. Renfield, imprisoned in an asylum, devotes his energies to trapping flies. With his bag of flies he lures spiders; and with spiders, he attracts birds. "The blood is the life,"[8] Renfield announces; and he values each species according to the number and complexity of life-forms it destroys and consumes. He eats flies and spiders alive, but perfers birds because they have imbibed more richly of the "life principle."

Stoker's knowledge of Dracula may have come from any of several sources. He may have actually met with the chronicles in a little-known translation; he may have encountered a mention of the Voivod in some history of the Hungarian empire; or he may have learned about the figure from a personal communication with a continental *savant*. Van Helsing in his speech mentions that his information about Dracula derived from a letter written him by Arminius, who may be identified as Armin (or, Latinized, Arminius) Vambery, the great Hungarian linguist, historian, explorer (Southeastern and Central Asia), folklorist and professor (at Buda-Pesth). Though Vambery mentions no Vlad Tsepesh in the English translation of his popular history of Hungary, it is not inconceivable that Stoker obtained this knowledge from him through some more intimate mode. Stoker mentions on various pretexts throughout the novel several distinguished people with whom he was acquainted (for example, Ellen Terry, the famous actress, whose theatrical manager he was), and his reference to Arminius similarly may have been an effort to lend the novel verisimilitude by the inclusion of a factual circumstance. However, this is mere speculation.

If Stoker limned the outline of his novel's central figure from a model found in legendary history, he touched in many features of his story from details he discovered in modern folklore—specifically, in the folklore of Southeast Europe. The Draculas attended Scholomance, the devil's school, in the mountains over Lake Hermannstadt, where every tenth scholar became the devil's victim.[9] The following passage upon Rumanian folklore may have been the source of Stoker's information.

> As I am on the subject of thunderstorms, I may as well here mention the *scholomance*, or school, supposed to exist somewhere in the heart of the mountains, and where the secrets of nature, the language of animals, and all magic spells are taught by the devil in person. Only ten scholars are admitted at a time, and when the course of learning has expired, and nine of them are released to return to their homes, the tenth scholar is detained by the devil as payment, and, mounted upon an *ismeju*, or dragon, becomes henceforward the devil's aide-de-camp, and assists him in "making the weather"—that is, preparing the thunderbolt.[10]

In *Dracula*, on the Eve of St. George "all the evil things in the world will have full sway."[11] This belief is also borrowed from folklore, for one work mentions that "this is a great night to beware of witches" and speaks of "occult meetings taking place,"[12] while another states that on St. George's Eve vampires go abroad to obtain their power.[13]

Stoker also used Southeast European forms of the vampire superstition rather consistently. The belief in these demons, about which the action of the novel pivots, is found in a wide variety of cultures, but nowhere else has it preoccupied a people to the extent that it did in the Slavic parts of the old Austro-Hungarian empire, the area from which the superstition diffused in modern times to revitalize a belief which had begun to wane in more westerly areas of Europe.[14] Indeed, in 1756 Maria Theresa felt compelled to dispatch a commission to Wallachia for the purpose of investigating a vampire panic and reassuring the populace.[15] Lower Hungary, even in the 18th century, became associated in popular thought with vampirism much in the same fashion as Haiti has become linked with *vodun* in the 20th century mind.[16] Consequently, Stoker's placing Dracula's lair in the Carpathian Mountains between Moldavia, Bukovina, and Wallachia was eminently appropriate, though in itself no proof that he utilized the forms of belief indigenous to that region. However, there is much substantiating evidence which indicates that he did know the forms of belief local to the Transylvanian regions.

Dracula sometimes appears in the form of phosphorescent specks (Stoker, pp. 156–57, p. 238); the *striga,* or Rumanian vampire, often comes as points of light shimmering in the air (Murgoçi, p. 321, p. 345). As a vampire, Dracula "can, within limitations, appear at will when, and where, and in any of the forms that are to him; he can within his range, direct the elements . . . he can command all the meaner things: the rat and the owl, and the bat—the moth, and the fox, and the wolf; he can grow and become small; and he can at times vanish and come unknown" (Stoker, pp. 260–62). Murgoçi (p. 332) writes that Rumanian folk belief ascribes to vampires the powers of self-transformation. Another author confirms this statement.[17] And folklore furnishes precedents for associating certain animals, as did Stoker, with vampirism. The Transylvanian Saxons (Szeklers) couple the bat with acts of vampirism.[18] In Volcea, Rumania, it is recorded that vampires are reincarnated as death's-head moths (Murgoçi, p. 322). *Ianga Creanga,* the Rumanian folklore journal, records the incident of an exorciser of vampires being eaten by wolves (Murgoçi, p. 324), an episode which the protagonists only narrowly avert in the final chapters of *Dracula.* In the novel, as in folklore (Murgoçi, p. 328, 333), garlic has the power to protect against vampires; and Stoker's method of slaying these demons by decapitation and stake impalement is likewise widely recognized in folk belief.[19]

The above examples of Stoker's utilization of folk themes are by no means exhaustive, but they are sufficient to show that he approached his materials with a certain conscientiousness. Few with a developed critical sense would claim that *Dracula* is a "successful" novel; yet, the fact that it is still in print and is still read proves it has a kind of vitality, provokes a kind of interest. It would seem the story's vitality and interest, such as these are, must be attributed to its atmosphere, to the stature of its villain and to the spirit of the chase which permeates it. The story's atmosphere is Gothic, the legacy of more than a century of stylized literary treatment; its villain is in conception medieval, a product of mythopoeic imagination's entranced horror with a cruel but competent figure at a time when the few successful military leaders who maintained unbroken the thin outer rim of European sovereignty were allowed to cultivate strong and bizarre feelings without interference; the spirit of the chase, and the resulting suspense, which pervade the novel, however, has its conventions not in literary precedent, but in the canon of superstition. The manner in which the vampire is run to ground is in complete accord with the rules of folk belief.

Notes

1. Montague Summers, *The Vampire, His Kith and Kin* (London, 1928), 335–36.

2. Bram Stoker, *Dracula* (New York, Modern Library ed., n.d.), 264–65.

3. A.D. Sedelnikov, "Literaturnaya istoriya povesti o Drakule," *Istoriya po russkomu yazyku i slovesti,* II (1929), 623ff.; N. K. Gudzy, *History of Early Russian Literature* (New York, 1949), 273–74.

4. Sedelnikov, 623ff. A genealogy of Dracula manuscripts is listed on p. 651 of the work.

5. This tale is later told about Ivan the Terrible (Sedelnikov, p. 644).

6. This is, of course, quite similar to stories recounting the burial of pirate gold in which all members, save one, of the burying party are killed.

7. The Kirill-Belozersk version of the above material is reprinted in Sedelnikov, pp. 652–59; a summary in English may be found in Gudzy, pp. 269–74.

8. Stoker, p. 154.

9. Stoker, p. 265.

10. Emily de Laszowska-Gerard, *The Land Beyond the Forest* (New York, 1888), 198.

11. Stoker, p. 5.

12. Gerald, p. 193.

13. Anges Murgoçi, "The Vampire in Rumania," *Folk-Lore* 37 (1926), 325.

14. Stefan Hock, *Die Vampyrsagen und ihre Verwertung in der deutshen Literatur* (Berlin, 1900), 30–31.

15. Hock, p. 40.

16. Hock, pp. 42ff.

17. Friederich S. Krauss, "Vampyre im südslawischen Volksglauben," *Globus* 61 (1892), Nr. 21, 327.

18. Heinrich von Wlisocki, *Volksglaube und Volksbrauch der Siebenbürger Sachsen* (Berlin, 1893), 163.

19. A. L. Jellinek, "Zur Vampyrsage," *Zeitschrift des Vereins für Volkskunde* 14 (1904), 234.

2

The Politics of *Dracula*

Richard Wasson

From the time of its appearance in 1897, Bram Stoker's *Dracula* has never been out of print, has been translated into several languages (including Gaelic) and has been transformed into several versions for the theatre and movie-going public.[1] No doubt numerous psychological and sociological explanations for the novel's popularity might be offered; among these possibilities is a political theme (perhaps "undertone" might be more exact) which would appeal to audiences throughout the series of crises presented by the two world wars and the cold war. Count Dracula, if not always in the plays and movies, at least in the novel represents those forces in Eastern Europe which seek to overthrow, through violence and subversion, the more progressive democratic civilization of the West.

This claim might seem facetious to those inclined to regard the book as a hack job designed to titillate its audience. But even writers of popular novels have political opinions and Stoker is no exception. When elected to the chief office of the historical society at Trinity College, he attracted widespread attention in the Dublin newspapers by pleading for "a united nations."[2] His first published book was on the duties of Irish court clerks and he wrote a pamphlet pleading for home rule for Ireland. In his biography of Henry Irving, whose secretary Stoker was, he tells of his repeated failures to interest the Englishman in that cause.[3] In *Lady of The Shroud* (1909), one of the most entertaining bad novels ever written, he uses the vampire theme to present a fantastic solution to the Balkan situation. Under the leadership of the heir of an English capitalist, "The Land of the Blue Mountains," a tiny state on the Adriatic, rings itself with cannon and battleships, protects its skies with "aeros," the then ultimate weapon, and leads its neighbors into a confederation of states called "Balka," thus order-

---

This article first appeared in *English Literature in Transition* 9 (1966).

ing the cháos which tempts the imperialistic ambitions of both the Turkish and the Austro-Hungarian empires. In that book Stoker abandons the vampire-horror techniques about halfway through to write what he undoubtedly thought was a political novel.

In *Dracula* the political theme is more covert and certainly less urgent; but it is nevertheless there and in the same peculiar way as in *Lady of the Shroud*. The locale of the novel, near the border of three Balkan territories in the center of Romania, is suggestive enough. Jonathan Harker, whose journal begins the tale, describes it as a distinctly eastern portion of Europe where the laws and customs of the West do not apply. Harker describes the area as "certainly an imaginative whirlpool of races . . . where hardly a foot of soil has not been enriched by the blood of men, patriots, invaders."[4] While the rest of Europe has been free to develop a culture, this area has been a bloody battleground.

More interesting than the location is Dracula's ancestry—he is a direct descendent of Attila the Hun: "What devil or what witch was ever so great as Attila, whose blood flows through these veins," the Count rhetorically asks Harker. "Is it any wonder," he continues in language far too familiar in the twentieth century, "that we were a conquering race?" (p. 27) The Count sees himself as having performed an important political function for the West: through war and diplomacy he and his "race" kept the Turks at bay and finally defeated them: "Who was it crossed the Danube and beat the Turk on his own ground?" (p. 28) He later acts the part of the betrayed and the sacrificed by telling Mina that "hundreds of years before they were born", he had intrigued and "fought" for the very men who were now seeking to destroy him (p. 268), a fact which Van Helsing, who, as we shall see in a moment, represents the assorted powers of the West, grudgingly acknowledges (p. 224). But his victory has rendered him historically obsolete and left his people exhausted: "The warlike days are over; blood is a precious thing in these days of dishonorable peace," he continues in language similar to that of other leaders associated with the decline of Austro-Hungarian power; "the glories of the great races are as a tale that is told" (p. 28). The people are exhausted and "the walls of my castle are broken," he tells Harker. The Count, descendent of the Hun, feels himself cheated and deprived, and like his ancestor, who, in a moment of victory over the Turks turned Westward, decides to move on England. His land a place of wars' excrement, he seeks his just rewards by reviving the Westward push of the "hooded hordes."

But the political motif becomes more complicated, for Stoker sees the Count as a threat to progress, which he conceives in terms of increasing democracy and improved technology. One line of thematic development asserts that whereas in the old days the Count had to exist on the primitive frontier of Western culture, his best chance for survival is now in England, the most progressive, rational and democratic nation in Europe. On another level, Stoker points out that modern victories can be better won by subversion than by invasion and that modern war depends upon the conversion of the citizens of democracy to a vampirish bloodlust. These themes add up to the idea that technological progress, having cut humanity off from the old superstitious, dark knowledge, makes itself increasingly vulnerable to the demonic powers like the vampire, for, having written them off as unreal, civilized man has no defense against them. Since only doctors of the mind, Seward and Van Helsing, can cope with such monsters the novel carries the implication that demonish forces have been unloosed in the human psyche by technological and political progress.

Count Dracula's motives for coming to England make these themes clear. Becoming a vampire through his great lust for slaughter and his knowledge of alchemy, he seeks to perpetuate himself by changing his locale and his mode of operation.[5] Van Helsing, in the unintentionally comic dialect Stoker gives him, provides an excellent summary of Dracula's plan: "He find out the place of all the world of most promise to him. . . . He learn new social life, new environment of old ways, the politic, the law, the finance and the science, the habit of a new land and new people" (p. 229). England is the "place of most promise" because "its law, its social life, its politics and science will serve to protect him" (p. 79), will be "his sheath and armor, his weapon to destroy us" (p. 300).

For example, in his old territory the Count must cope with a suspicious, superstitious peasantry which carries garlic and crosses to defend itself. In contrast, the peasantry of England (what little there is left of it) is rationalist and skeptical. When Mr. Swales, the hard-bitten old seafarer who turns out to be an easy and early victim of the Count, hears rumors of strange goings-on, he argues, "It be all fool talk, lock, stock and barrel. These bands an' wafts an' boh-ghosts and batguest an' bogles an' all anent them is fit to set bairns an' dizzy women a-belderin'. Thy be nowt but air-blebs" (p. 61). Stoker demonstrates this point through Dr. Seward, the psychologist who tries to combat Lucy Westenra's strange illness. Completely baffled, he is forced to call in his continental friend, Dr. Van Helsing, who tells him, "You are a clever man, friend John; you reason well and your wit is bold; but you are too prejudiced. You do not let your eyes see nor your ears hear, and that which is outside your daily life is not of account to you. Do you think that there are things which you cannot understand, and yet which are; that some people see things that others cannot. . . . Is it not the fault of our science that it wants to explain all and if it explain not, then it says there is nothing to explain?" (p. 178).

Initially the Count's plan meets with success. He gets into England, spreads the coffins (with the bloody dirt in which he must nightly lie) carefully around London and establishes contact with the mad Renfield. Moreover, he selects as his first victim Lucy Westenra (appropriately, as her name implies, she is the light of the West), a typical Victorian upper-middle-class woman who has known no evil. But though he turns her into a vampire, a group forms to save her and thwart his evil power.

If the Count's motives are political, the group's are even more so. They see themselves as an alliance of free men, qualified "by nationality, by heredity, or by possession of natural gifts" (p. 227) and dedicated to setting the world free (p. 300). The group forms around Lucy Westenra's three lovers: Dr. Seward, the appropriately named Lord Godalming, Quincy P. Morris, an American; and Lucy's friend, Mina Harker. Coming to their aid are Dr. Van Helsing, Mina's husband, and Seward's patient, Renfield. Each contributes something specific. Lord Godalming, for example, gets favors unextended to commoners (p. 278). Van Helsing as a Catholic has an unlimited supply of the Host, a fine seal for door and window cracks through which the Count must vaporize himself (pp. 195, 196). Harker's legal knowledge enables the group to evade the law (p. 243). Madam Mina manages to get bitten by the vampire, but instead of deserting to the Count, she uses her new-found sympathy with his un-British East European habits to help the allies track him down.

More interesting perhaps is Quincy P. Morris, who is popular literature's archetypal Texas millionaire. Though the dialect Stoker has him speak is as bad as Van Helsing's, he serves an important political function. As we might suspect, the American is the most pragmatic campaigner. While Van Helsing is in charge of the long-range plans, it is Morris who is always there with practical suggestions and who on the spur of the moment can make the best decisions. Once, when the group is surprised by the Count, Morris concocts a plan of action which almost traps him. More importantly, when the Count is on the run and Van Helsing is directing his efforts to trapping him, Morris points out that while the group is well prepared to exorcise evil spirits, they are virtually defenseless against more material threats from wolves and gypsy partizans. He therefore volunteers to supply the necessary military aid in the form of Winchesters. "I propose we add Winchesters to our armament. I have a kind of belief in a Winchester when there is any trouble ... " (p. 303). Stoker not only suggests that America become the armorer of the West but argues that she cannot live up to her full promise until she gives up the Monroe Doctrine's restrictive measures against her participation in European affairs (p. 216).

Perhaps the most interesting character in the group is the madman Renfield, through whom Stoker builds up the pseudo-scientific theory of vampirism. The man theorizes that by eating live flesh and consuming blood from living bodies he can stay alive forever (p. 218). Yet Renfield, unlike the Eastern European Count, recognizes the horror of his dream. He has himself committed and though it costs him his life, he resists the Count's bribes of a repast of live rats and bats in order to warn the others of Dracula's strategy (pp. 260, 261). English reason is strong enough to counter Eastern European bloodlust, even in a lunatic.

This group proves that though progress makes England vulnerable, it also provides the means by which Dracula can finally be destroyed. While the Count can manipulate elements of English society to his advantage, he ultimately has to rely on tradition and habit. The defenders, however, "have the sources of science" and "are free to use them." They have "self devotion in a cause and an end to achieve which is not a selfish one" (p. 300). The Austrian is limited by the narrowness of his purpose; he cannot operate during daylight hours; he cannot move freely over water; he cannot enter rooms or seduce a victim unless the person allows him to. Though he has the stubborn cunning of a secret purpose and superior powers of political and military maneuvering, he is limited by his lack of freedom.

The allies quickly rout the Austrian. Together they track him to his Transylvanian lair and ambush him on the road. Covered by American Winchesters in the hands of Seward, Godalming, and Van Helsing, Harker and Morris push through the army of defending gypsies and simultaneously plunge knives into Dracula's heart and sever his head, killing the Count forever. This act frees Mina from her own vampirism and restores peace to the world.

Thus the Count is controverted and his threat to the progress of Western civilization brought to an end. While on the surface Stoker's Gothic political romance affirms the progressive aspects of English and Western society, its final effect is to warn the twentieth century of the dangers which face it, both in the years following *Dracula*'s publication and in the present. It is Dracula's menace that is most memorable, and that menace is only increased by the progress of the civilized world. One of the things Van Helsing most fears is that the Count will come to learn more of Western life, come ultimately to adopt a kind of scientific approach and to learn that he has freedom of choice. If blood lust of the vampire once links itself to modern politics, to modern science, there will be little if any defense against it, a fact which has been too vividly proven in our violent century. The popular imagination so stirred by the political horrors of our time, which turns again and again to the nightmares of the Nazi era and which reads the warnings of science fiction with great attention, cannot help but be stirred by the political implications of *Dracula*.

Notes

1. Harry Ludlam, *A Biography of Dracula* (London: Fireside Press, 1962), pp. 150–70.

2. Ibid. p. 25.

3. Bram Stoker, *Personal Reminiscences* (London: Heinemann, 1906), pp. 343, 344.

4. Bram Stoker, *Dracula* (New York: Grosset & Dunlap, 1897). All page references are to this first American edition and hereafter indicated in parentheses in the text.

5. Dracula did not become a vampire by being bitten but by studying the black arts and by waging war. Thus, will and intellect led him to vampirism. See *Dracula*, pp. 233ff.

3

The Monster in the Bedroom: Sexual Symbolism in Bram Stoker's *Dracula*

Christopher Bentley

By far the best-known literary treatment of the vampire myth is Bram Stoker's novel *Dracula*. First published in 1897, this belated Gothic romance has eclipsed the fame of earlier vampire stories such as John Polidori's *The Vampyre* (1819) and Thomas Prest's *Varney the Vampire* (1847). It has been reprinted many times, and has also been translated into other European languages. A play based on the book was produced in the nineteen-twenties, became a West End success in 1927, and remained for some years a popular attraction at theatres in Britain and North America, being occasionally revived today. An even large public knows *Dracula* through several film versions of the novel, beginning with a classic of the German silent cinema, *Nosferatu* (1922). Because of Stoker's novel the name of a fifteenth-century Rumanian prince, relatively unknown outside his own country, has become a familiar word,[1] but *Dracula*'s great success cannot be attributed to conventional literary strengths, in which the work is deficient.[2] The possibilities in a psychoanalytical approach to *Dracula* have been noted,[3] but no attempt has been made to investigate in detail the sexual implications of the story.

Ernest Jones, in the section entitled "The Vampire" in his monograph *On the Nightmare*, states that the vampire superstition "yields plain indications of most kinds of sexual perversions,"[4] and it would seem that such perversions, concealed by symbolism, are the dynamic of *Dracula*, and may largely account for the initial success and continued popularity of the work. Nothing in Stoker's other writings or in what is known of his life suggests that he would consciously write quasi-pornography, and it must be assumed that he was largely unaware

This article first appeared in *Literature and Psychology* 22 (1972), No. 1.

of the sexual content of his book.[5] In common with almost all respectable Victorian novelists, Stoker avoids any overt treatment of the sexuality of his characters. The obscenity laws, the tyranny of the circulating libraries, and the force of public opinion were, throughout the greater part of the nineteenth century, powerful constraints on any author who wrote for the general public; but it is probably that for many writers, including Stoker himself, an even stronger reason for avoiding sexual matters was a personal reticence amounting to repression. Stoker's "living" characters (that is, those other than vampires) are, both the women and the men, models of chastity. One male-female relationship, that of Jonathan Harker and Mina Murray, is of primary importance to the story, and they marry at an early stage of the plot, but the sexual elements that presumably exist in their relationship are never revealed, much less discussed. However, what is rejected or repressed on a conscious level appears in a covert and perverted form through the novel, the apparatus of the vampire superstition, described in almost obsessional detail in *Dracula*, providing the means for a symbolic presentation of human sexual relationships.

A close examination of certain episodes in the work shows that Stoker's vampires are permitted to assert their sexuality in a much more explicit manner than his "living" characters. One of the three vampire women who attempt to attack Jonathan Harker at Dracula's castle assesses the potency of her intended victim with a surprising directness: "He is young and strong; there are kisses for us all." Although their nominal intention is to suck Harker's blood, the advances of the women and Harker's responses are, throughout this significant episode, consistently described in sexual terms:

> All three had brilliant white teeth, that shone like pearls against the ruby of their voluptuous lips. There was something about them that made me uneasy, some longing and at the same time some deadly fear. I felt in my heart a wicked, burning desire that they would kiss me with those red lips. It is not good to note this down, lest some day it should meet Mina's eyes and cause her pain; but it is the truth. . . . The fair girl shook her head coquettishly, and the other two urged her on. . . . I lay quiet, looking out under my eyelashes in an agony of delightful anticipation. The fair girl advanced and bent over me till I could feel the movement of her breath upon me. . . . There was a deliberate voluptuousness which was both thrilling and repulsive. . . . I closed my eyes in a languorous ecstasy and waited—waited with beating heart.[6]

The ambivalence of Harker's response, combining both "longing" and "deadly fear," is especially revelatory, as is his concern over the feelings of his fiancée, Mina: the vampire women offer immediate sexual gratification, though on illicit and dangerous terms, a tempting alternative to the socially imposed delays and frustrations of his relationship with the chaste but somewhat sexless Mina. The entire episode, including Harker's subsequent doubt as to whether he was awake or dreaming, has the unreal quality of a masturbatory fantasy or erotic dream.

Ernest Jones's remarks on the widespread folkloristic belief in vampire attacks support this interpretation:

> The explanation of these phantasies is surely not hard. A nightly visit from a beautiful or frightful being, who first exhausts the sleeper with passionate embraces and then withdraws from him a vital fluid; all this can point only to a natural and common process, namely to nocturnal emissions accompanied with dreams of a more or less erotic nature. In the unconscious mind blood is commonly an equivalent for semen.[7]

With the exception of Dracula's brief and abortive assault on Harker when momentarily aroused by the sight of blood from a shaving cut trickling down the latter's chin, the prominent vampire attacks in the novel are always on members of the other sex; the female vampires attempt to make Harker their prey, and Dracula attacks Mina Harker and Lucy Westenra, suggesting that vampirism is a perversion of normal heterosexual activity. The relationships between the vampires themselves are rather more complicated; of the three vampire women, two resemble Dracula and so presumably are related to him, while the third is spoken of as their sister. Therefore it would appear that they are either Dracula's daughters or sisters, but when one of them taunts Dracula with the accusation: "You yourself never loved; you never love!," he rejoins meaningfully: "Yes, I too can love; you yourselves can tell it from the past. It is not so?," implying that an incestuous relationship has existed between them.[8] In this interchange Stoker seems to be consciously endowing his vampires with a sexual freedom that would be unthinkable in his "living" characters. A remarkable heightening of sexuality occurs in the formerly virginal Lucy when she becomes a vampire, and, as in the episode of the three vampire women, "languorous" and "voluptuous" are two of the terms that Stoker chooses from his rather limited vocabulary of the erotic to describe the new freedom of her behaviour.[9]

The blood of the living, which the vampire craves, also has strong sexual undertones. Ernest Jones, in the passage quoted above, equates the loss of blood to a vampire with the emission of semen, and this is undoubtedly what underlies the attempted attack on Harker by the vampire women; but even when no vampire is present, the giving and receiving of blood may still be charged with sexual meaning. Lucy Westenra, weakened by Dracula's nocturnal attacks, receives blood transfusions from, successively, Arthur Holmwood, John Seward, Dr. Van Helsing, and Quincey Morris; of these men, one, Holmwood, is her fiancé; two, Seward and Morris, are rejected suitors who remain on friendly terms with her, while the fourth, Van Helsing, is of course well-disposed towards the young woman. This sequence of blood transfusions symbolizes sexual intercourse, with Lucy of necessity acquiring a freedom and promiscuity that could not possibly be described in actual terms, especially when the central figure is a girl whose behaviour is as chaste and respectable as that of her friend Mina. Stoker himself is a least partly aware of the sexual implications in those transfusions. After Seward has given blood to Lucy, Van Helsing, who has conducted the transfusion, warns the young man: "Mind, nothing must be said of this. If our young lover should turn up unexpected, as before, no word to him. It would at once frighten him and enjealous him, too. There must be none. So!"[10] Van Helsing's many scholastic accomplishments do not include the ability to speak idiomatic English, but it is evident that he fears Lucy's fiancé will be sexually jealous of the man who has been privileged to give her his blood. After Lucy's burial Seward writes in his diary:

> When it was all over, we were standing beside Arthur, who, poor fellow, was speaking of his part in the operation where his blood had been transfused to his Lucy's veins; I could see Van Helsing's face grow white and purple by turns. Arthur was saying that he felt since then as if they two had been really married, and that she was his wife in the sight of God. None of us said a word of the other operations, and none of us ever shall. Arthur and Quincey went away together to the station, and Van Helsing and I came on here. The moment we were alone in the carriage he gave way to a regular fit of hysterics.[11]

Later Van Helsing explains to Seward the reason for his unseemly amusement:

> "Said he not that the transfusion of his blood to her veins had made her truly his bride?"
> "Yes, and it was a sweet and comforting idea for him."
> "Quite so. But there was a difficulty, friend John. If so that, then what about the others? Ho, Ho! Then this so sweet maid is a polyandrist, and me, with my poor wife dead to me, but alive by Church's law, though no wits, all gone—even I, who am faithful husband to this now-no-wife, am bigamist."[12]

Again the sexual content of the blood transfusions is made abundantly clear.

The same symbolism would seem to be present in a curious episode later in the story, when Dracula has invaded the bedroom of Harker and his wife Mina.

> On the bed beside the window lay Jonathan Harker, his face flushed, and breathing heavily as though in a stupor. Kneeling on the rear edge of the bed facing outwards was the white-clad figure of his wife. By her side stood a tall, thin man, clad in black. His face was turned from us, but the instant we saw we all recognised the Count—in every way, even to the scar on his forehead. With his left hand he held both Mrs. Harker's hands, keeping them away with her arms at full tension; his right hand gripped her by the back of the neck, forcing her face down on his bosom. Her white nightdress was smeared with blood, and a thin stream trickled down the man's bare breast which was shown by his torn open dress. The attitude of the two had a terrible resemblance to a child forcing a kitten's nose into a saucer of milk to compel it to drink.[13]

This description should be compared with Mina's own account of her experiences in which she relates that after first sucking her blood Dracula

> "pulled open his shirt, and with his long sharp nails opened a vein in his breast. When the blood began to spurt out, he took my hands in one of his, holding tight, and with the other seized my neck and pressed my mouth to the wound, so that I must either suffocate or swallow some of the—Oh my God! my God! what have I done?" . . . Then she began to rub her lips as though to cleanse them from pollution.[14]   Rape

The episode contains a strange reversal of the usual relationship between vampire and victim, as Dracula is forcing Mina to drink his blood. Stoker is describing a symbolic act of enforced fellatio, where blood is again a substitute for semen, and where a chaste female suffers a violation that is essentially sexual. Of particular interest in the earlier passage is the striking image of "a child forcing a kitten's nose into a saucer of milk to compel it to drink," suggesting an element of regressive infantilism in the vampire superstition.[15]

The symbolic meanings of blood in *Dracula* are rendered more complex by an incident that occurs later in the same chapter. Mina, bleeding after Dracula's attack on her, is being comforted by her husband:

> She shuddered and was silent, holding down her head on her husband's breast. When she raised it, his white night-robe was stained with blood where her lips had touched, and where the thin open wound in her neck had sent forth drops. The instant she saw it she drew back, with a low wail, and whispered, amidst choking sobs:—
> "Unclean, unclean! I must touch him or kiss him no more. Oh, that it should be that it is I who am now his worst enemy, and whom he may have most cause to fear."[16]

Although the reaction of horror, and its accompanying exclamation of "Unclean," comes from Mina, and although Jonathan firmly refuses to share it ("Nonsense, Mina. It is a shame to me to hear such a word. I would not hear it of you; and I shall not hear it from you"). Mina's description of herself while the "thin stream of blood" trickles from her recalls ancient primitive fears of menstruation. The mention of a "thin open wound" is especially noteworthy: in *Dracula* the mark of the vampire's bite is usually described as two round punctures caused by the elongated canine teeth, whereas this phrase suggests a cut or slit similar to the vaginal orifice. Some of Freud's observations on menstrual taboos are relevant to this episode:

> The primitive cannot help connecting the mysterious phenomenon of the monthly flow of blood with sadistic ideas. Thus he interprets menstruation, especially at its onset, as the bite of a spirit-animal, or possibly as the token of sexual intercourse with this spirit. Occasionally the reports reveal this spirit as one of an ancestor and then from other knowledge we have gained we understand that it is in virtue of her being the property of this spirit-ancestor that the menstruating girl is taboo.[17]

"Spirit-animal" is a curiously apt term for a vampire, and, though Dracula can scarcely be an ancestor of Mina's, he does claim as his "property" both her and Lucy ("Your girls that you all love are mine already"),[18] and of course he has actually bitten Mina, causing the "unclean" flow of blood, and symbolically he has forced her to undergo sexual intercourse with him. In this incident veinous blood symbolizes not semen but menstrual discharge, suggesting that blood as a symbol has multiple meanings in *Dracula,* but that sexual significances predominate.

The methods used to destroy vampires also contain sexual implications, and, revealingly, are modified according to the sex of the vampire. Lucy, who becomes a vampire after succumbing to Dracula's attacks, is released from her "undead" state into true death by her erstwhile fiancé, Arthur, who drives a hardened and sharply pointed wooden stake through her heart. The phallic symbolism in this process is evident, and Lucy's reactions are described in terms reminiscent of sexual intercourse and orgasm, and especially the painful deflowering of a virgin, which Lucy still is:

> The Thing in the coffin writhed; and a hideous, blood-curdling screech came from the opened red lips. The body shook and quivered and twisted in wild contortions; the sharp white teeth champed together till the lips were cut, and the mouth was smeared with a crimson foam. But Arthur never faltered. He looked like a figure of Thor as his untrembling arm rose and fell, driving deeper and deeper the mercy-bearing stake, whilst the blood from the pierced heart welled and spurted up around it. His face was set, and high duty seemed to shine through it; the sight of it gave us courage, so that our voices seemed to ring through the little vault.
> And then the writhing and quivering of the body became less, and the teeth ceased to champ, and the face to quiver. Finally it lay still. The terrible task was over.[19]

On the other hand, when Dracula himself is to be destroyed, although a stake driven through the heart remains part of the method, the emphasis is shifted to decapitation of the vampire. Now it has long been recognised that the head is a very common penis-substitute in dreams concerning the fear of castration.[20] Dracula is rendered powerless, symbolically castrated, by having his head cut off; a sexual revenge is taken on the creature whose depredations have been basically sexual in character. Van Helsing, the novel's expert on vampirism, sometimes uses the term "sterilize" when discussing means of defeating and destroying Dracula, implying that he entertains a castration fantasy based on fear and envy of the vampire's powerful sexuality.

Although vampirism is ostensibly presented as a supernatural phenomenon of evil, to be combated with the weapons of religion, such as the Cross and the Host, and those of superstition, such as garlic, it is in actuality treated as a shameful and terrible disease. Two physicians, Seward and Van Helsing, the former an authority on mental illness and the latter a polymath who has made a special study of vampirism, are omnipresent, and their medico-scientific techniques, including blood transfusions, hypnotism, and sedatives, are an important part of the fight against Dracula. The traditional view of vampirism as a species of demonic possession to be cured by spiritual means survives in the novel, but it has been partly displaced by a more modern attitude which sees vampirism as a disease and a perversion possibly amenable to medical treatment, recalling the Victorians' horror of masturbation and nocturnal emissions.

Details of the vampire's existence are rich in psychological implications: the stench of decay around Dracula and places associated with him would seem to contradict the very basis of vampirism, namely that the vampire corpse is not subject to natural decay like ordinary corpses, but Ernest Jones writes: "Bearing in mind the anal-erotic origin of necrophilia . . . we are not surprised to observe what stress many writers on the subject lay on the horrible stink that invests the Vampire."[21] Stoker describes the smell in the chapel at Carfax, Dracula's deserted lair, as being "composed of all the ills of mortality" and "as though corruption had become itself corrupt."[22] The atmosphere of sin and guilt is as strong as the mephitic odour. Dracula's wooden coffins filled with earth, as necessary as blood for sustaining the vampire's life in death, since he must return to one of them during each day, are an obvious womb-substitute, and together with Van Helsing's repeated assertions that Dracula has a "child-mind" or a "child-brain," confirm the suggestion already advanced, namely that there is an element of infantile erotic regression in vampirism.

Though the vampire's attack symbolizes sexual intercourse, or more precisely, in view of the presumed chastity of the two female victims, loss of virginity, there is one important difference. Unlike actual defloration, the process is reversible, for the victim can be redeemed by the death of her seducer, the vampire; the burn-mark on Mina's forehead, caused by the touch of the Host when she was "unclean," disappears as soon as Dracula is destroyed. The physical and spiritual degradation incurred by the victim of a vampire need not be permanent, and in any case to fall victim to a vampire does not, in this novel, involve social degradation; the vampire women who attack Harker at Dracula's castle are described as "ladies by their dress and manner," and Dracula himself, though presented as a creature of infinite wickedness, is, as Stoker emphasizes, a European nobleman with an ancestral home, a distinguished lineage, and a "courtly" manner. On occasions he displays thoroughly aristocratic contempt for his somewhat *bourgeois* antagonists, while they, with a proper sense of his rank, customarily refer to him in their diaries and journals as "the Count." Dracula has much in common with the corrupt but gentlemanly seducers of popular fiction and drama whose archetype is Lovelace in Richardson's *Clarissa*. Just as they can attempt and sometimes succeed in the seduction of innocent females without forfeiting their claim to be gentlemen because of the freedom given them by society's double standard, and because of a received definition of the gentleman that includes licentiousness as one of his qualities, so Dracula appears curiously guiltless in his vampirism, for he is merely obeying the dictates of his corrupt nature, and, in choosing beautiful young women as his victims, is only exercising an admittedly perverted *droit de seigneur*. In particular his nocturnal visits to Lucy, pre-empting the claims of her fiancé, have a distinct echo of the medieval *jus primae noctis*, the more so as Dracula, who is several centuries old, once was a feudal lord, and certainly retains the outlook and behaviour of one.

Dracula received a number of reviews in the popular journals of the period. *Punch* offers a determinedly jocular notice in which "ingenious" is the strongest word of the praise.[23] The *Spectator* summarizes the plot of "Mr. Stoker's clever but cadaverous romance" and concludes:

> Its strength lies in the invention of incident, for the sentimental element is decidely mawkish. Mr. Stoker has shown considerable ability in the use that he has made of all the available traditions of vampirology, but we think his story would have been all the more effective if he had chosen an earlier period. The up-to-dateness of the book—the phonograph diaries, typewriters, and so on—hardly fits in with the mediaeval methods which ultimately secure the victory for Count Dracula's foes.[24]

The *Athenaeum* finds *Dracula* "highly sensational," but

> wanting in the constructive art as well as in the higher literary sense. It reads at times like a mere series of grotesquely incredible events; but there are better moments that show more power, though even these are never productive of the tremor such subjects evoke under the hand of a master. An immense amount of energy, a certain degree of imaginative faculty, and many ingenious and gruesome details are there. At times Mr. Stoker almost succeeds in creating the sense of possibility in impossibility; at others he merely commands an array of crude statements of incredible actions. . . . The people who band themselves together to run the vampire to earth have no real individuality or being. . . . Still Mr. Stoker has got together a number of "horrid details," and his object, assuming it to be ghastliness, is fairly well fulfilled. Isolated scenes and touches are probably quite uncanny enough to please those for whom they are designed.[25]

Earlier in the same decade English reviewers had abused Ibsen's *Ghosts,* in terms more literally appropriate to Gothic fiction, as "Absolutely loathsome and fetid . . . Gross, almost putrid indecorum . . . Literary carrion . . . Morbid, unhealthy, unwholesome and disgusting . . . Morbid horrors of the hideous tale . . . Just a wicked nightmare . . . Noisome corruption" and had described the author as "A gloomy sort of ghoul, bent on groping for horrors by night,"[26] but the reviewers of *Dracula*, while they may find artistic flaws in the novel, detect nothing that is morally objectionable. Ibsen, of course, had dared to be explicit about sexual relationships in contemporary society and had treated such a forbidden topic as hereditary venereal disease. Stoker's work, in spite of its modern setting, is a fantasy using the materials of folklore, and its chief character is therefore permitted to force his way into the bedrooms of respectable young women and to exercise freedoms that would be surprising even in the avowedly "fast" novelists of the day. The reviewers' comments suggest that the sado-masochistic accounts of human suffering and violent, premature death that are the nominal subject matter of *Dracula* caused little or no offence to contemporary readers, while they were apparently oblivious to the novel's covert treatment of perverted sexuality.

Notes

1. See Grigore Nandris. "The Historical Dracula: The Theme of His Legend in the Western and in the Eastern Literatures of Europe," *Comparative Literature Studies,* III, 4 (1966), 367–96.

2. A representative scholarly view of *Dracula* is to be found in a modern history of the English novel, which describes it briefly as "a vampire story rendered plausible by documentary devices imitated from Collins," and acknowledges that it was an "immense popular triumph," (Lionel Stevenson, *The English Novel: A Panorama* (Boston, 1960), p. 428).

3. Maurice Richardson, "The Psychoanalysis of Ghost Stories," *The Twentieth Century,* CLXVI, 994 (December 1959), 426–30.

4. Ernest Jones, *On The Nightmare* (London, 1931), p. 98.

5. Bram Stoker (1847–1912) was educated at Trinity College, Dublin, and worked for ten years in the Irish Civil Service. In 1878 he became Henry Irving's business manager. With the exception of some of his short stories Stoker's other works of fiction are markedly inferior to *Dracula.* His first book was *The Duties of Clerks of Petty Sessions in Ireland* (1879), and his most substantial literary production is *Personal Reminiscences of Henry Irving* (1906), a biography of his employer and lifelong friend.

6. Bram Stoker, *Dracula* (London, 1897), pp. 38–39 (Ch. 3).

7. Jones, op. cit., p. 119.

8. *Dracula,* p. 40 (Ch. 3).

9. Ibid., p. 216 (Ch. 16).

10. Ibid., p. 130 (Ch. 10).

11. Ibid., p. 177 (Ch. 13).

12. Ibid., p. 179 (Ch. 13).

13. Ibid., p. 289 (Ch. 21).

14. Ibid., p. 296 (Ch. 21).

15. Cf. Jones, op. cit., p. 120: "When the more normal aspects of sexuality are in a state of repression there is a tendency to regress towards less developed forms. Sadism is one of the chief of these, and it is the earliest form of this—known as oral sadism—that plays such an important part in the Vampire belief."

16. *Dracula,* pp. 291–92 (Ch. 21).

17. Freud, "Contributions to the Psychology of Love, The Taboo of Virginity (1918)," *Collected Papers*, IV (London, 1934), pp. 221–22.

18. *Dracula*, p. 315 (Ch. 23).

19. Ibid., pp. 220–21 (Ch. 16).

20. Freud, "A Connection between a Symbol and a Symptom (1916)," *Collected Papers*, II (London, 1924), pp. 162–63.

21. Jones, op. cit., p. 122.

22. *Dracula*, p. 257 (Ch. 19).

23. *Punch*, 26 June 1897, p. 327.

24. *Spectator*, 31 July 1897, p. 152.

25. *Athenaeum*, No. 3635, 26 June 1897, p. 835. *Dracula* was also reviewed in the *Daily Mail*, the *Pall Mall Gazette*, the *Lady*, and the *Bookman*.

26. Cited from William Archer in George Bernard Shaw, *The Quintessence of Ibsenism* (London, 1891), pp. 89–91.

4

Fictional Conventions and Sexuality in *Dracula*

Carrol L. Fry

To the general reading public, Bram Stoker's *Dracula* is one of the best known English novels of the nineteenth century. It was an immediate best seller when it appeared in 1897, and the frequent motion pictures featuring the machinations of Count Dracula since the 1931 film version of the novel have helped make vampire folklore very much a part of the English and American popular imagination. The work's fame is in part attributable to its success as a thriller. The first section, "Jonathan Harker's Journal," is surely one of the most suspenseful and titillating pieces of terror fiction ever written. But perhaps more important in creating the popular appeal of the novel is its latent sexuality.

This feature of the work is most apparent in Stoker's use of disguised conventional characters, placed in new roles but retaining their inherent melodramatic appeal for a sexually repressed audience. The most apparent of these characters is the "pure woman," the staple heroine of popular fiction from Richardson to Hardy. In dozens of novels of the eighteenth and nineteenth centuries, this pure woman is pursued by a "rake," a seducer who has designs on her virtue. The melodrama is based on the reader's suspense regarding whether or not he will succeed. Those women who lose their virtue become "fallen women," outcasts doomed to death or secluded repentance. In *Dracula*, there are two "pure women," Lucy Westenra and Mina Harker, the former of whom actually does "fall." The role of "rake" is played by Count Dracula, and vampirism becomes surrogate sexual intercourse. The women who receive the vampire's bite become "fallen women,"

Stoker establishes Dracula as a rake in large part by making him a "gothic villain," a derivative of the rake in English fiction. Like most gothic villains, Dracula lives in a ruined castle, remarkably like Udolpho, Otranto, Grasmere

---

This article first appeared in *Victorian Newsletter* 42 (1972).

Abbey, and dozens of other sublimely terrifying structures in English fiction. It even has subterranean passages, slightly modified to serve as daytime resting places for the vampires. Moreover, Dracula's physical appearance is that of the rake-gothic villain. He has a "strong—a very strong" face and "massive eyebrows." His face shows the pallor typical of Radcliffe's Schedoni, Maturin's Melmoth, and Lewis's Ambrosio, and, most impressively, he possesses the usual "glittering eye" of the villain. Stoker returns to this feature over and over. When Harker first sees him, he immediately notes "the gleam of a pair of very bright eyes, which seemed red in the lamplight"[1] and the Cockney zookeeper interviewed by the reporter for the *Pall Mall Gazette* describes the Count's "'ard cold look and red eyes" (p. 120).

The rake and the gothic villain pursue and "distress" the pure woman in melodramatic popular fiction of the eighteenth and nineteenth centuries, and Dracula sets out in pursuit of Lucy Westenra and later of Mina Harker in the best tradition of this character type. First, however, Stoker firmly establishes his heroines in their roles. Lucy gets three proposals (a frequently used method of establishing worth in women) from thoroughly admirable men, and when she tells the heroic Quincy Morris that she has a prior attachment, he says: "It's better worth being late for a chance of winning you than being in time for any other girl in the world" (p. 56). Dr. Van Helsing says of Mina: "She is one of God's women, fashioned by his own hand to show us men and other women that there is a heaven where we can enter, and that its light can be here on earth. So true, so sweet, so noble, so little an egoist—and that, let me tell you, is much in this age" (p. 161). But perhaps the most important aspect of Stoker's presentation of Lucy and Mina is that the description of both, before Dracula preys on them, completely omits physical detail. One gets only an impression of idealized virtue and spirituality. They are like Rose Maylie in *Oliver Twist,* who is "cast in so light and exquisite a mould; so mild and gentle; so pure and beautiful; that earth seemed not her element, nor its rough creatures her fit companions."[2]

Stoker had apparently done some research on the folklore of vampirism,[3] and most of the detail he gives is verified by the work of Montague Summers.[4] The vampire's inability to cast a reflection, his fear of daylight, and the stake in the heart as a means of killing him are all part of the folklore of eastern Europe. But one element of this folklore is particularly appropriate for melodramatic fiction: the contagious nature of vampirism. Both the rake of the popular novel and the vampire of folklore pass on their conditions (moral depravity in the former and vampirism in the latter) to their victims. In fiction, it is conventional for the fallen woman to become an outcast alienated from the rest of mankind, or to die a painful death. If she lives, she often becomes a prostitute or the chattel of her seducer. The bawdy house to which Lovelace takes Clarissa

in Richardson's novel is staffed by the rake's conquests, and in
Romance of the Forest, Adeline, the heroine, is abducted by
kept in a house occupied by his numerous kept women.

Similarly, Dracula's castle is occupied by his "wives," who
earlier time his victims. At the outset of the novel, when the fair
about to drink the blood of Jonathan Harker is stopped by the Coun
"a laugh of ribald coquetry," and says to her lord: "You yourself ne
you never love!" (p. 40). Dracula replies: "Yes, I too can love; you y
can tell it from the past. Is it not so?" (p. 40). He has loved them
vampire's phallic bite, and they have become outsiders, Un-Dead, and,
fallen woman, not part of the human race. The frequent references to "lov
to "kisses" and the type of physical description of the lady vampire make
parallel between seduction and vampirism apparent. The wives are consiste
described in terms of erotic physical beauty, but they are hard and wanton
their attractiveness. Moreover, in Victorian fiction, prostitutes, like cockroache
most often appear at night (one thinks, for instance, of Esther in Mrs. Gaskell'
Mary Barton), just as vampires, in folklore, must avoid the daylight.

The change in Lucy Westenra's appearance after she receives Dracula's
attention is marked. Physically, her features are altogether different. Dr. Seward
describes her in her tomb when the group goes there to destroy her: "The
sweetness was turned to adamantine, heartless cruelty, and the purity to wantonness" (p. 179). Instead of the "pure, gentle orbs we knew," her eyes are "unclean and full of hell fire" (p. 180). She approaches Arthur with a "languorous,
voluptuous grace," saying "My arms are hungry for you" (p. 180). In all, "The
whole carnal and unspiritual appearance" seems "like a devilish mockery of
Lucy's sweet purity" (p. 182). Throughout, the description of female vampires
underscores their sexuality, and the words "voluptuous" and "wanton" appear
repeatedly in these contexts, words that would never be used in describing a
pure woman. Clearly, Lucy has fallen, but in the end she is saved from herself
in rather conventional fashion. Her death and the smile of bliss on her face as
she passes satisfy the reader's desire for a happy ending to her story and fulfill
his expectation regarding the fate proper to a fallen woman.

Much of the interest of the novel from this point lies in the fate of Mina
Harker, who begins to take on the character of the fallen woman. After the
vampire has mixed his blood with hers and has been routed from her bedroom,
she cries: "Unclean, unclean! I must touch him [Jonathan, her husband] or kiss
him no more" (p. 240). Later, after she is burned by the holy wafer used as a
weapon against the Count, she exclaims: "Unclean! Unclean! Even the Almighty shuns my polluted flesh" (p. 250). During the journey to Dracula's
castle, she has begun to take on the "beauty and fascination of the wanton
Un-Dead" (p. 309). But when Dracula is killed, all of the physical effects are

ersed, and she again becomes a pure woman, fit for motherhood and a happy
e. She never quite becomes a fallen woman and hence can be saved at the end
the novel.

There are a good many other parallels drawn between vampirism and
exuality in addition to the melodramatic effects achieved through the manipulation of conventional characters. The fact is that vampire lore has much in
common with human sexuality. The vampire's kiss on the throat and the lover's
kiss are easily made one in the reader's mind, and the Nosferatu's bite can be
made parallel in the popular imagination with the love bite or the phallic thrust.
In the novel, the very act of biting is made highly erotic. In describing Dracula's
embrace, Mina says: "Strangely enough, I did not want to hinder him" (p. 250).
But perhaps the most suggestive passage in the novel occurs when Jonathan
Harker describes his experience while in a trance induced by Dracula's wives.
As the fair bride approaches him, he finds in her a "deliberate voluptuousness
which was both thrilling and repulsive," and he feels "a wicked, burning desire
that they would kiss me with those red lips" (p. 39). After a certain amount of
coquettish argument as to who would begin, the fair bride bends over his throat,
and Harker describes his sensations:

> Lower and lower went her head as the lips went below the range of my mouth and chin and
> seemed to fasten on my throat. Then she paused, and I could hear the churning sound of her
> tongue as it licked her teeth and lips, and I could feel the hot breath on my neck . . . . I could
> feel the soft shivering touch of the hard dents of two sharp teeth, just touching and pausing
> there. I closed my eyes in a languorous ecstasy and waited—waited with beating heart. (p. 39)

One can hardly wonder that the novel was enormously popular.

Notes

1. Bram Stoker, *Dracula* (New York, 1965), p. 38. Further page references appear in the text.

2. Charles Dickens, *The Adventures of Oliver Twist,* The Oxford Illustrated Dickens (London, 1949), p. 212.

3. In *A Biography of Dracula: The Life Story of Bram Stoker* (London, 1962), Harry Ludlam states that much of the author's information came from Arminium Vambery, a professor of oriental languages at the University of Budapest. Also, there was a historical Dracula. Stoker was aware that one of the fifteenth-century leaders of the fight against the Turks, Vlad V, was called Dracula; and the Count's lecture to Johnathan Harker in Chapter 3 of the novel shows that Stoker knew a little about the history of eastern Europe. But according to Professor Grigore Nandris, there is "no association in Rumanian folklore between the Dracula story and the vampire mythology" ("The Historical Dracula: The Theme of His Legend in the Western and in the Eastern Literatures of Europe," *Comparative Literature Studies*, III [1966], 366–96).

4. See *The Vampire in Europe* (New Hyde Park, N.Y., 1962) and *The Vampire: His Kith and Kin* (New Hyde Park, N.Y., 1960).

5

The Genesis of Dracula: A Re-Visit

Devendra P. Varma

I could a tale unfold whose lightest word
Would harrow up thy soul, freeze thy blood
Make thy two eyes, like stars, start from their spheres. . . .
Shakespeare

Dracula was killed in 1477 while defending Christendom on this side of the Danube, and the Turks carried away his head as a gift to the Sultan of Constantinople, where it was openly exhibited on a stake. Dracula's "headless body" was buried in Snagov, the island monastery, twenty miles north of Bucharest. The tomb, when opened in 1931 by two archaeologists, Dinu Rosetti and George Florescu, was found empty. The body was gone! A couple of avenues of conjecture opened up as to what could have happened. One, and by far the most delightfully ghoulish and chilling, is that he turned into a vampire, preying on young men and women. The women, by legend, wear the traditional uniform of a diaphanous nightgown, sometimes in black or sense-titillating pink, but always diaphanous. The second and more prosaic explanation is that the monks at an early date may have burnt his body and scattered the ashes to the winds. Or did he turn into mist and slip away, a talent which vampires alone possess? There have been documented proofs that Dracula, the caped count who spent his evenings tippling on the blood of beautiful women, was a real person. He did die and was buried. What happened to his body? Robert Bloch wrote to me:

This article originally appeared in *The Vampire's Bedside Companion*, ed. Peter Underwood, London: Leslie Frewin, 1975.

Castle of Death from Stoker's *Under the Sunset*

How wonderful to learn of your Transylvanian trip! A friend of mine, Alan Dodd, made the pilgrimage about a year or so ago, and sent me a packet of grave-earth; for sentiment's sake, I suppose. He too, commented on the omnipresent mist of evening, and the sense of being under surveillance by the eyes of an unseen presence . . .

We know *why* the grave is empty, don't we?

Today a strange calm broods over the tranquil setting of the Snagov monastery, but legend has it that shortly after Dracula's burial a violent hurricane swept over the countryside. The monastery built by Dracula's grandfather was uprooted from its very foundations, steeple, bell-tower and all, and submerged into the lake. Superstitious peasants to this day affirm that they have seen Dracula's ghost rise from the waters, and whenever the lake is ruffled by winds, one can hear the muffed sound like tolling of a distant bell. Who know, perhaps the spirit of Dracula, the great undead, still sojourns there awaiting retribution.

The supernatural terrors and fascination with creatures feasting on human blood, recreated with poetic licence in the fiction of the nineteenth century, have their roots in true events. The fear engendered by the broken bodies of hundreds of pretty maidens, found drained of their blood in the neighborhood of a Gothic castle in the foothills of the Carpathians in the first decade of the seventeenth century, was real enough. The peasants, wondered, worried and frightened, fixed on Dracula as the villain, saying he had turned into a vampire to prowl the countryside.

Superstition and legend are deeply rooted in this beautifully wild and savage country, where the tenor of life has not changed in a thousand years. In the valley of the Carpathians, peasants still hang garlic blossoms on their doors and solemnly warn visitors to the castle: "Return before nightfall," and cross themselves. For generations peasants in the surrounding valley have whispered sinister tales of horror enacted within those castle walls. And although they talk about it they rarely muster up courage to visit the ruins. In the prevailing superstitious beliefs, the spirit of Stoker's "undead hero" still seems to dominate the spot. The night watchman guarding the precincts at night clutches an old Bible as if to ward off the evil spirits that hover around. A decade ago the castle's female caretaker gave birth to a demon babe.

Frustrations and mysterious accidents have occurred to several expeditions. In 1969, two American filmmakers ventured there, but were soon rushed to hospital with inexplicable internal bleeding. The atmosphere of the ruins was so eerie, said Professor McNally, that he felt faint and could not bring himself to enter the portals. Professor Florescu came down with a mysterious illness and another member of the team fell into a ravine and broke his hip. A photographer who took the photograph of Castle Dracula died within three days! "A broken hip and six months in hospital for one of our members" was the fate of another expedition. McNally wonders if it was "Dracula's way of saying that despite the ruins of his castle, he still rules in some other, unearthly domain?" Were these accidents just coincidences, or bad luck? I grew more curious and wished to explore for myself.

I had seen the antique sixteenth-century oil painting of Dracula which hangs in Castle Ambras near Innsbruck, Austria. He wears a Hungarian noble-man's tunic, an ermine cape and his Turkish-style fur headdress is richly en-crusted with jewels. But is does not hide the cruel and malignant glint of his wide-open green eyes under thick bushy eyebrows; his thin, reddish up-curled lip and black moustache on a pallid shaven face are impressive, and so are the curly locks of jet hair dangling on his wide shoulders. But Stoker's *Dracula* is different: he is a misunderstood anti-hero, a demon-lover, with an aching long-ing in his heart and the same hypnotic gleam of the eye. He too has vivid red lips, and a mien full of "lonesome sadness." The concept of the undead subsist-ing on the life-blood of its victims remains a voluptuous idea, for what an experience it must be to be embraced by a female vampire? Professor Walter Storkie of California, an authority on vampire lore in Hungary, Romania, Yugo-slavia and Greece, had once written to me: "We certainly have the subject of Vampires in common, for I too, have been interested in them for many years since my first visit to Hungary in 1929 where I had a vampire experience."

In the spirit-haunted wild Carpathian mountains still stand, gaunt and lonely, the ruins of Castle Dracula, as if beckoning from the realm of death and oblivion through the dark passage of centuries. There is something grandiose and plain-tive in those sinister ruins perched upon a jagged mountain peak, the entire sight emphasized by sheer granite cliffs dropping precipitously no less than a thou-sand feet on three sides, as the Arges river curls below in wisps of mist rising almost continually.

The road to Castle Dracula winds through the green and brown foothills past stone huts painted pink, pale green, or yellow, around churches with curved steeples, shepherds in sheepskin cloaks and peaked caps and grandmothers in headkerchiefs and black skirts over stiff white petticoats. The road passes through Curtea de Arges, site of an ancient cathedral, and occasionally one sees shep-herd boys on their carts and roving bands of gypsies. The climb begins from the village Capatineni where one encounters the horrified looks and also blessings of the superstitious local people.

The stern commanding air of the great pile, the majesty of its strategic, desolate location, and the wild beauty of its landscape are a sure invitation to any poet or artist. There could not possibly be a more apt setting for fearful crimes or mysterious hauntings. The upper portion of the trail is covered with wild flowers, luxuriant greenery and fungi; three quarters of the way down the valley, the black sweep of forest greets the eye. To its south the ruins command a panoramic vista of the Wallachian plain; to the north stand the snow-covered peaks of Fagaras mountains. Isolated thus on a remote precipice, Castle Dracula must have been virtually impregnable. The spirit of Dracula seems to be best preserved in those sunken stones, Alpine weeds, snake holes and trails of masonry pebbles falling down to the river Arges. No other sound of life disturbs the quiet except the melancholy hooting of the owl, or the footfalls of a strayed and daring traveller. Within those ramparts rats and mice abound, while the Romanian mountain bear is an occasional trespasser, as is the mountain lynx. The most dangerous visitor is the wolf; wild dogs often howl at night during the full moon—sending a shiver down the spine. The singular geography and bizarre design of the castle ruins make the wayfarer aware of its bloody past. Perhaps no other castle is filled with such awful memories. They say that evil spirits still haunt those ruins and the peasants of the valley speak of strange flickers, as of candlelight, being visible from a distance on dark nights.

I stared in a trance-like fashion in a cold, eerie mood; remembered the vampire count and felt as if he had been waiting for us. A curious unease pervaded my soul as I gazed at the relic. I was overcome by a mysterious wistfulness, a sense of dreadful emptiness. This mood of foreboding was created by an intolerable gloom which engulfed my spirit. Time seemed to have stood still; a dense and impenetrable silence fell with an oppressive hush. There was something unutterably overpowering and disquieting about the place so weird and awesome. A dreadful fear overwhelmed me. I remembered Stoker: "Supernatural, as if it had been transported from another world and planted stone by stone on this towering peak." And the sense of the uncanny reminded me of Coleridge's:

> A savage place, holy and enchanted
> That ever beneath a waning moon was haunted,
> By woman wailing for a demon lover.

A few birds, not many, glided by the front wall, otherwise there was no sign of life, and nothing stirred. I looked around me: no cottages, no glimmer of lights, no blue smoke rising from chimneys, no sounds; the very stillness was frightening. To the south one beheld only the deep, twisting gorges of the Arges valley.

We felt as if we were being watched all the time. No one else was there, of course, but we could sense an unearthly presence of evil. You could feel there was someone just around the corner. We were very, very scared. Truly, the shades of evil pervade this place even today, like an icy breath from the past. Stoker had already captured the atmosphere: "The shadows are many and the wind breathes cold through the broken battlements, from whose tall windows came no ray of light."

Architecturally the castle once combined the best characteristics of Teutonic and Byzantine fortifications. The walls, a patchwork of brick, stone and concrete, were an astounding six feet thick. The foundation was barely distinguishable from the granite rock on which it perched. Three ruined towers on the north wall and two deep dungeons seem to speak of a grim turbulent past and vanished glories. Those untidy heaps of stones, the crumbling towers where now only the nocturnal birds find refuge, were once doubly reinforced to resist the Turkish cannons, a proud and steadfast symbol of resistance to the outside invader.

As I stood there I could well imagine Jonathan Harker's attempt to escape from this dreadful prison, from this haunted fortress where he experienced many strange things, its atmosphere of magic, terror and horror, which drove him well to the verge of insanity. I recalled in Stoker's novel, Harker's peering out of his bedchamber window to ascertain whether some tremendous form might be ascending the sheer wall as the vampire count did. Or was that a trick of moonlight, or some weird effect of shadow? "I saw the fingers and toes grasp the corners of the stones, just as a lizard moves along a wall." Harker saw Dracula's head coming out of the window and he began to crawl down the castle wall over that dreadful abyss, *face down*, with his cloak spreading out around him like great wings. I stood rapt and amazed in the chamber where Harker may well have stayed and I too saw through the roofless window, the leaning wall, which still stands to this day with all its jutting stones.

The sight of the ruined turret reminded me of the tragic folktale concerning Dracula's wife who rushed up the winding staircase and hurled herself from the minaret into the river below: how her body must have rolled down the precipice into the flowing Arges! Professor McNally had told me that to this day that point of the river is called *Riul Doamei* or "The Princess' River," a spot where the waters are reddened by a vague subterranean object, and the peasants say they have often heard the plaintive wailings of Dracula's wife rise from the gurgling waves.

> Deep into the darkness peering
> Long I stood there, wondering, fearing
> Doubting, dreaming dreams,
> No mortals ever dared to dream before.

Dracula's figure rises like a grim spectre from the past: how he sacked cities, decimated villages into ashes, and impaled thousands of Turks, Saxons, Germans and disloyal Romanians. "The memory of bad princes," writes Voltaire, "is preserved like that of fires, plagues and inundations." Dracula's contemporaries dreaded him as the living embodiment of Satan come as a scourge upon the earth; or like Faustus who sold his soul to the Devil in return for unlimited power, for surely he knew the secrets of life and death. He had known astrologers, alchemists and necromancers, and pursued his thirst for the unbounded occult.

Dracula is not the mythical product of a Victorian Irishman's lurid imagination. There was a factual basis for those fantasies. The legend of the vampire count and his mysterious nocturnal life relate to documented history, for Dracula did exist. He has been identified as Vlad Tepes the Impaler, who during the fifteenth century, after his mysterious escape from Turkish captors, ascended the throne as Prince of Wallachia. A full account of his life, acts of cruelty and reign of terror, are contained in McNally and Florescu's fascinating study *In Search of Dracula*. Both authors have probed the folklore concerning this fearsome real-life prince and vampire, and established the true identity of this mysterious man and legend by researching into cracked and chipped fifteenth-century records, blurred manuscripts locked in the dust-laden vaults of ancient European monasteries, crudely lettered pamphlets mouldering in antique archives, and by charting the folktales whispered in Slavic countries.

Philologists agreed at the sixth congress of onomastic sciences in Munich in 1958 that Stoker's *Dracula* can easily be identified with the historical personality of Vlad the Fifth of Wallachia, called the Impaler for his cruelties. He ruled from 1456 to 1462 and was briefly restored to his throne in 1476. Stoker only embroidered upon the historical Vlad Tepes and associated it with the local superstitions; his descriptions of the country and the castle, and of the river curling below the granite mountains, are amazingly accurate. And that's strange, because Stoker never visited Transylvania.

But before I investigate the sources and genesis of Stoker's *Dracula*, it would be apt to tell of an incident at the end of my expedition. The sun was low over the mountain-filled horizon, and there was not a breath of air when I began to retrace my steps down the valley to the highway below. Did I fancy that I heard something? I listened and there was the distinct sound of footfalls following me, but there was no one to be seen! Other members of my party had preceded me an hour before, while I had lingered on in the ruins to complete my notes. I have never been able to explain the echo of those footfalls, or the unseen, everwatchful presence, and I hurried on my way.

> Like one, that on a lonesome road
> Doth walk in fear and dread,
> And having once turned round walks on
> And turns no more his head
> Because he knows, a frightful fiend
> Doth close behind him tread.

The dark, blood-curdling vampire superstition is not a quaint folklore of Eastern Europe alone. The vampire is of dateless antiquity. In the dim corridors of time there is no more sinister figure than the living dead which prowls from its grave at night to drink the blood of the innocent and the beautiful. I have furnished a detailed history of the vampire-myth elsewhere. Although this myth has been much embellished in its poetic manifestations by literary artists, the vampire remains an embodiment of the Faustian quest to conquer eternity, a symbol and an image which transcend time and space.

The vampire stories have a hideous ring of realism. Hundreds of young maidens were found dead and drained of their lifeblood in the Carpathian valleys and lowlands of Hungary as the seventeenth century dawned. Public records reveal that in 1732, in Serbia and Wallachia, vampirism spread like pestilence causing numerous deaths. There had been a notorious case of vampirism near Belgrade in 1731. As the century drew to its close, reports of dead returning from the grave multiplied alarmingly.

Such incidents coincided with church-inspired bulletins that "vampires were excommunicated persons whom the Earth is said to cast up." The church also documented complex rituals for protection against vampires: the weapons of attack were garlic, the Cross and communion wafers. Excommunication from the church was an infallible method of turning into a vampire. A case of suicide inevitably guaranteed "the sleep of the undead." Those who were denied full and proper burial rights, or passed away apostate or unbaptised, or persons who had feasted upon the meat of a sheep killed by a wolf, or even those who had lived an immoral, evil life, were supposed to turn into vampires.

Dracula lived at a time when there was a widespread belief in vampires. Outbreaks of plague and premature burials were quite prevalent. It was not uncommon to see a body rise from a cart while being driven to the cemetery. Catalepsy often resulted in premature burial and "corpses" would stir and revive in a shallow grave. The peasants practised the ritual of exhuming the dead. Twisted bodies in crypts and coffins would provide proof that the body had been possessed by a vampire. Even to this day, in Transylvania, stakes are driven through the hearts of the dead to keep them in their graves.

Vampire bats are a common phenomenon in the Carpathians, and their victims exhibit symptoms of rabies. People with bat wounds become demented and wish to bite others, and usually die within weeks. Such symptoms of hydrophobia concord well with the Dracula vampire myth. On the authority of Montague Summers, cases of vampirism seem to happen every day, but they are hushed up. As recent as 1970, there have been reported cases from England, Sumatra and elsewhere.

There has not yet been any valid or thoroughgoing research upon the sources of Stoker and the genesis of *Dracula*. He had, of course, seen the torture tower of the old castle at Nuremberg. His brother George, once a surgeon in London, had in Turkey gained experience in handling human corpses. Irving, whom Stoker served, himself had been vampire-like, draining those who worked with him. But Stoker's fascination with vampirism, already stimulated by Sheridan Le Fanu's *Carmilla*, was rekindled in the 1890s by his meeting in the Beefsteak Room with a professor from the Hungarian University of Budapest who had the exotic name Arminius Vambery. It has been surmised that he elaborated to Stoker some details of Transylvanian superstitions and mentioned the strange Wallachian Prince "Voivode Drakula" who had ruled in 1456 and was called "The Impaler" because of his ravenous activities. Vambery showed Stoker a fifteenth-century manuscript which referred to him as a "Wampyr."

Daniel Farson, a prolific writer and broadcaster, and a grandnephew of Bram Stoker, has stated that the opening chapters of *Dracula* were written at Cruden Bay, a small fishing village north of Aberdeen, where Stoker stayed during a walking tour in 1893, then returned each year during the off seasons from the Lyceum Theatre to relax. Cruden Bay is much the same today and has not been caught up in modern progress; there are still small fishermen's cottages dotting the seashore and fishing-nets stretched on high poles like a series of black tents. And there is even a ruined castle lashed by the sea! To the north of Cruden Bay rise great rocks of red granite, jagged and broken, and the stormy sea often blasts upon the rocks in grand fury. We can fancy Stoker striding across the sands of Cruden, and as Harry Ludlam notes: "To the sound of the sea on the Scottish shore, Count Dracula made his entry." But there were other influences.

The carved vampire fangs and canine teeth of Tibetan and Nepalese images of gods shed strange light on the origin of vampire legends. Did the tales of weird beings who subsisted by drinking the blood of sleeping persons originate in Transylvania, or with the Hindus of ancient India? Clues concerning the Indian origin were provided by a prominent orientalist, Sir Richard Burton, the nineteenth-century translator of the *Arabian Nights*. In 1870, Sir Richard had translated eleven vampire tales of apparent Indian origin from a thoroughly Hindu legend composed in Sanskrit, the ancient and sacred language of India. Sir Richard thought that these tales inspired future writing of "facetious, fictitious literature."

Tibetan manuscripts concerning vampires were "held in such high regard that they were embalmed in images to increase their sanctity." My findings on these researches are contained in my Introduction on "The Vampire in Legend, Lore, and Literature," prefixed to the 1970 Arno edition of T. P. Prest's *Varney the Vampire; or The Feast of Blood*.

On 13th August 1878, Sir Henry Irving arrived by train at the Westland Row Station, Dublin, accompanied by Richard Burton. It was on that railway platform that Irving introduced Stoker to Burton who had been to Mecca. Stoker writes: "The man riveted my attention. He was dark and forceful, and masterful and ruthless. I have never seen so iron a countenance . . . He is steel! He would go through you like a sword!" In January 1879, Stoker saw Burton again in

London with Irving in the Green Room Club. The first supper at Irving's rooms in Grafton Street on Saturday night, 8th February has thus been recorded by Stoker: "The subdued light and the quietude gave me a better opportunity of studying Burton's face; ... I sat opposite to him and not beside him. The predominant characteristics were the darkness of the face—desert burning; the strong mouth and nose, and jaw and forehead—the latter somewhat bold—and the strong, deep, resonant voice. My first impression of the man as of steel was consolidated and enhanced." That night Burton talked about many things including the translation of the *Arabian Nights*, a task of extensive magnitude and demanding research.

During the next meeting on Saturday, 15th February, the evening chat veered round Burton's experiences on the west coast of Africa, the Gold Coast, where he was consul and where he sustained his good health by *never going out in the mid-day sun* and by drinking *a whole flask of brandy every day*! But the third supper on 21st February, at Bailey's Hotel, South Kensington, arranged by Mr. Mullen the publisher, was most interesting, especially when Burton mentioned experiences, or expounded grounds for some theory which he held. Burton narrated "some of his explorations amongst old tombs." While posted as consul in Damascus, Burton had developed a new passion for archaeology, and he seemed to lavish upon the ancient dead all the inquisitiveness he had devoted to the living in India and Africa. He had spent weeks in the Syrian mountains, searching for skulls, bones and inscriptions while mapping ruins. Stoker writes: "Burton's face seemed to lengthen when he laughed; the upper lip rising instinctively and showing the right canine tooth. This was always a characteristic of his enjoyment."

After a lapse of nearly six years Stoker met Burton again. On 9th July 1886, Irving invited Sir Richard and Lady Burton to supper in the Beefsteak Room after the staging of *Faust*. Burton described his clandestine and dangerous visit to Mecca in the disguise of an Arab. A lad recognised him and quietly slipped away to pass on information, but Burton took the situation in hand and having pursued the lad to a solitary corner suddenly drove a poniard into his heart! When Burton described this incident at dinner, there fell a hush and muffled silence; then some guests got up from the table and walked out of the room. Burton continued in his resonant voice: "The desert has its own laws, and there—supremely of all the East—to kill is a small offense. In any case what could I do? It had to be his life or mine!" Stoker notes that as Burton spoke "the upper lip rose and his canine tooth showed its full length like the gleam of a dagger."

Indeed Burton had a most vivid way of narrating incidents, especially of the East. He was gifted with a fine imaginative power and a memory richly stored by study and bizarre experiences. Stoker asserts that: "Burton *knew* the East. Its brilliant dawns and sunset; its rich tropic vegetation, and its fiery arid deserts; its cool, dark mosques and temples; its crowded bazaars; its narrow streets; its windows guarded for outlooking and from in-looking eyes; the pride and swagger of its passionate men, and the mysteries of its veiled women; its romances; its beauty; its horrors." And it was on 18th September 1886, as night wore on, that Burton's fancy seemed to run riot in all its alluring power, and the whole world of thought seemed to flame with gorgeous colour. He talked of unknown places of the earth and of some unspeakable mysterious secrets. This excellent swordsman and archaeologist who had revelled in *Arabian Nights* and translated several volumes of the oriental erotica, had surely heard the story of the strange Prince of Wallachia and the Carpathian legends from the descendants of those merchants and carpet-sellers of Damascus who had supplied rugs and furs and decorative motifs to Vlad Dracula for his castle. It was Burton who further passed on those whispered folktales and legends to Bram Stoker. And the image of Dracula caught the fancy of Stoker—the image of a handsome, bloodthirsty, outlandish prince in his embroidered shirt, ermine cape, and a headgear plumed with ostrich feathers!

Professor Oswald Doughty, writing his book on Gabriel Rossetti, makes the point that "Exhumation of the passionately loved dead had become quite a literary fashion," and quotes instances from Victorian life and society. In 1862, Rossetti's wife Lizzie committed suicide by taking an overdose of laudanum. On the second and third days following her death, so lifelike was her appearance— perhaps because of some preservative ingredient of the drug—that Gabriel refused to believe her dead and insisted upon a last opinion of the coroner before she could be buried in Highgate Cemetery. There is a touching story that tells of Rossetti placing a little red-edged manuscript book of verses, bound in rough grey calf, poems that were inspired and addressed to his wife, in the coffin near the face of the dead beloved, wrapped round in the flowing tresses of her beautiful golden hair. Seven and a half years after her burial, he exhumed her body to recover the manuscript which he had sealed in her grave.

That early October evening of 1869 in Highgate Cemetery must have been a scene at once macabre and strange: Lizzie's open coffin reflected in the light of a great fire made beside the grave as protection against infection. Lizzie's body, it is reported, was still wonderfully preserved, perhaps still the effect of the drug which had proved fatal. Hall Caine writes: "the body was apparently quite perfect on coming to the light of the fire on the surface, and when the book was lifted, there came away some of the beautiful golden hair in which Rossetti had entwined it." The manuscript glowing in the red light of the fire, emerged from the sealed doors of the tomb.

Those who were present must have gazed with an intense elation upon the form of an almost legendary figure, and wondered at the famed golden hair which was to become a source of so much pre-Raphaelite inspiration. News gradually leaked out that Lizzie's hair had continued to grow after her death, long, beautiful and most luxuriant, so as to fill the coffin with its burning gold! And was Stoker, a friend of Hall Caine, unaware of all this happening during his life and times?

6

The Genesis and Dating of *Dracula* from Bram Stoker's Working Notes

Joseph S. Bierman

The questions of when and how Bram Stoker started to write *Dracula*, became acquainted with an historical Dracula, and selected the Transylvanian setting for his vampire novel have been the subject of speculation. No reference to these questions is to be found in Stoker's work, but a number of hypotheses have been put forward in recent years by interested scholars.

Ludlam,[1] Stoker's first biographer, writes that Stoker began *Dracula*[2] in 1895 or 1896, following a nightmare about a "vampire King rising from the tomb to go about his ghastly business," and that this information came from his son, the late Noel Thornley Stoker. Ludlam also states that Arminius Vambery, a distinguished Professor of Oriental Languages at the University of Budapest, traveller, and author (and who was to become the professor Arminius of Stoker's novel) told him about Transylvania in 1890. Yet Stoker's account of the Vambery meeting of 30 April 1890, in a work which is substantially autobiographical,[3] says nothing of Transylvania. Without describing circumstances or indicating a source for the information, Ludlam relates also that at an unspecified time, Stoker learned that the Voivode Drakula or Dracula had earned for himself the title of Impaler, "and that Stoker had read" two fifteenth-century manuscripts in an unspecified language, one of which spoke of him as a "wampyr,"[4] and that subsequently "Bram sought the help of Arminius Vambery in Budapest."

It appears that neither Stoker's knowledge of the fifteenth-century manuscripts nor the role of Professor Vambery, as they are put forward by Ludlam, can be substantiated. Ludlam's assertions about the conversations must be seen as mere transfers from fiction to fact. What Professor Arminius says in Chapter

---

This article originally appeared in *Notes and Queries* 24 (1977).

18 of *Dracula* about Transylvania and its superstitions, about Voivode Dracula, and about "wampyrs" cannot be taken to represent what Professor Arminius Vambery actually told Bram Stoker.

McNally and Florescu[5] also date the writing of *Dracula* at 1895–97[6] and evidently draw their biographical detail from Ludlam. To the description of Stoker's meeting and correspondence with Vambery, they add detailed material without reference to source. "The two men dined together and during the course of their conversation Bram was impressed by the Professor's stories about Dracula 'the impaler.' After Vambery returned to Budapest, Bram wrote to him requesting more details about the notorious 15th-century prince and the land he lived in. Transylvania, it seemed, would be an ideal setting for a vampire story."[7] Yet Stoker's account of the meeting mentions neither Dracula, vampires, "the impaler," nor, as noted, Transylvania. As to the correspondence, McNally and Florescu themselves say: "Unfortunately, no correspondence between Vambery and Stoker can be found today. Moreover, a search through all of the professor's published writings fails to reveal any comments on Vlad (the impaler), Dracula, or vampires."[8]

Farson, Stoker's grand-nephew, writes in his biography of Stoker that "there is good reason to assume that it was the Hungarian professor who told Bram, for the first time, of the name of Dracula."[9] However, Farson gives no direct proof as the basis for this statement.

Some clarification of the origins of these elements in *Dracula* now is possible. The Collection of the Philip H. & A. S. W. Rosenbach Foundation in Philadelphia is the repository of manuscripts of Stoker's notes for *Dracula*.[10] They shed light, not only upon the inception date for the novel, but also on when and how Stoker learned of the historical personage Dracula, decided upon Transylvania as the setting for the novel, and introduced them into the outline for his vampire novel.

The Stoker material in the collection consists of handwritten and typewritten notes, dated and undated, about numerous subjects of central or tangential interest to a writer who was thinking of settings, characters, and plot for a story of the supernatural; descriptions of topography, landscape and customs from the work of contemporary travellers in Danubian countries; notes on a theory of dreams; transcriptions of tombstone inscriptions; accounts of conversations with old sailors and coastguardsmen; and notes for the novel itself.

The earliest date on any manuscript is 8 March 1890. This date is on manuscript in Stoker's distinctive and almost illegible handwriting that is an outline for a first section of the novel which differs from the final version in only a few details. It is an outline for a novel in epistolary form like *Dracula*, and consists mainly of one line summaries of letters describing the action. Some of the letters are from an as-yet-unnamed Count to his Solicitor. The location of the Count's Castle is shown as Styria. The word "vampire" is not mentioned, but there are phrases, such as "describe old dead man made alive . . . waxen color." Although Jonathan Harker is not yet called by name, he is without doubt the male character in a sketch of the scene in the novel with the vampiresses in the Castle: "Young man goes out sees girls one tries to kiss him not on lips but throat Old Count interferes—Rage and fury diabolical—This man belongs to me—I want him—a prisoner for a time. . . . "

Another of the dated manuscript notes (14 March 1890) is an outline of four books of a novel. A number of lines in the outline have been altered by deletions and substitutions. In one line, part of "Book I—London—Midsummer," the word Styria has been deleted and Transylvania substituted. At other lines, in "Book II—Tragedy," numerous substitutions have been made, such as:

> . . . [The Auctioneer *deleted*]—Whitby—argument uncanny things
> [The Doctor *deleted*]—Whitby—the storm-ship arrives
> [The lawyers Clerk *deleted*] Lucy walks in sleep . . .

A substitution on the following line of the outline of the same Book contains the first reference to Dracula in dated notes. It is followed by another, in "Book III—Discovery":

> . . . [A Medical Impasse *deleted*]—A Night of Terror (wolf missing) Dracula visits asylum . . .
> [Discoveries *deleted*] Mina suspects Dracula Texan to go to Transylvania . . . [11]

When did Stoker alter those notes? There are a number of possible answers. He might have done so at any time between the day they originally were made, 14 March 1890, and 29 February 1892, the date of a manuscript note in which Whitby, Dracula, Bistritz, and the Borgo Pass (Transylvania) appear, as original entries rather than as substitutions. The alterations could have been made as the outcome of his meeting with Vambery on 30 April 1890, if they spoke of Dracula and Transylvania at that time. Stoker might also have altered the outline for reasons not connected with the Vambery meeting at any time between March 14 and the end of February 1892.

The notes in the Rosenbach Collection disclose that during a Whitby holiday in August 1890 Stoker gathered a mine of information, almost all of which he was to use in *Dracula*. Descriptions from the notes appear nearly verbatim in Chapters 6 and 7. On 11 August he recounts a conversation with a coastguard, who told him "of various wrecks. A Russian Schooner 120 tons from Black Sea ran in with all sail main stay foresail jib nearly full tide Put out two anchors in harbor I look and she slewed round-against-pier—Another ship got into harbour Never knew how all hands were below praying. . . . Above Russian vessel was light ballasted with silver sand." In another note he adds, "On 24 October 1885 the Russian schooner 'Dimetry' about 120 ton was sighted off Whitby about 2 p.m. Wind northeast Force 8 (fresh gale) strong sea on coast (cargo silver sand—from mouth of Danube) ran into harbour by pure chance avoiding rocks. The following is extract from Log Book of the Coast Guard Station." For his novel, Stoker changed the details of the tale somewhat, but Dracula enters Whitby harbour in a violent storm on the ship "Demeter."

The range of Stoker's investigations at Whitby can be gauged from the subject matter of his notes. Although Whitby seems an unlikely place for him to have learned of the historical personage Dracula, there is evidence in the same set of notes that this is so. Among them, a typewritten page of excerpts from a volume in "Whitby Library O.1097" headed, *"Account of the Principalities of Wallachia and Moldavia, Etc,* Wm Wilkinson, late consul of Bukorest, Longmans, 1820" contains the following:

> P. 19. DRACULA in Wallachian language means DEVIL. Wallachians were accustomed to give it as a surname to any person who rendered himself conspicuous by courage, cruel actions or cunning. P. 18.19 The Wallachians joined Hungarians in 1448, and made war on Turkey, being defeated at battle of Cassova in Bulgaria and finding it impossible to make stand against the Turks submitted to annual tribute which they paid until 1460, when Sultan Mahomet II, being occupied in completing conquest of island in Archipelago gave opportunity of shaking off yoke. Their VOIVODE (DRACULA) crossed Danube and attacked Turkish troops Only momentarily success. Mahomet drove him back to Wallachia where pursued and defeated him. The VOIVODE escaped into Hungary and the Sultan caused his brother Bladus received in his place. He made treaty with Bladus binding Wallachians to perpetual tribute and laid the foundations of that slavery not yet abolished. (1820)

Stoker's encounter with the Wilkinson book in Whitby Library also permits an hypothesis about the circumstances that led him to replace Styria with Transylvania as the vampire's homeland. Stoker's handwritten notes show that at some time, he made himself familiar with "Transylvanian Superstitions,"[12] by Mme. E. de Laszowska Gerard, which appeared in the July 1885 *Nineteenth Century* magazine, which was then edited by Stoker's acquaintance, Sir James Knowles. The article contains a rich collection of folk belief, much of which Stoker was to use in his novel; included were references to "Vampires," "Drakuluj" (defined as Devil), and "Roumeniens." It is not certain, however, how Stoker's borrowings from Gerard occurred.

It is possible that Stoker, impressed by the tale of the wreck of the Black Sea schooner Dimetry, and already in the midst of constructing a vampire story, found Wilkinson's volume in Whitby Library while in search of information about Black Sea and Danubian countries. He may, in turn, have been reminded of—or motivated to search out—Gerard's more colourful account of five years earlier with its reference to Transylvanian vampires and Draculuj-devils, and thus to make the change in locale which the deletions and additions in his notes reflect.

Whether or not Stoker ever spoke or corresponded with Arminius Vambery about Dracula and Transylvania may never be known. However, all of the significant material attributed to Professor Arminius in the novel can be found in Gerard's article, Wilkinson's book, and two other books from which Stoker excerpted notes.[13,14]

Notes

1. Harry Ludlam, *A Biography of Dracula: The Life Story of Bram Stoker* (London, 1962), 99–100.

2. Abraham (Bram) Stoker, *Dracula* (London, 1897).

3. Abraham (Bram) Stoker, *Personal Reminiscences of Henry Irving* (New York, 1906), 371–72.

4. Ludlam, op. cit., 100.

5. Radu Florescu and Raymond T. McNally, *Dracula: A Biography of Vlad the Impaler* (New York, 1973), 160.

6. In my article "*Dracula*: Prolonged Childhood Illness, and the Oral Triad," *American Imago*, 29 (1972), 186–98, I, too, followed Ludlam in dating the inception of *Dracula*.

7. Raymond T. McNally and Radu Florescu, *In Search of Dracula* (Greenwich, 1972), 178.

8. McNally and Florescu, op. cit., 178.

9. Daniel Farson, *The Man Who Wrote Dracula: A Biography of Bram Stoker* (London, 1975), 126.

10. Material from these manuscripts is quoted by permission of the trustees of the Philip H. & A. S. W. Rosenbach Foundation, Philadelphia.

11. Like numerous characters and subplots that appear, disappear or are changed in the early outlines of Dracula, the Texan's name goes through several changes before Quincey Morris is chosen, and his trip to Transylvania is dropped.

12. Gerard expanded this article into her better-known book, *The Land Beyond The Forest* (New York, 1888).

13. A Fellow of the Carpathian Society, *Magyarland* (London, 1881), and E. C. (Major) Johnson, *On The Track of the Crescent* (London, 1885).

14. I wish to express my thanks to Helen H. Jaszi for bringing to my attention information about Bram Stoker and Arminius Vambery, and for assisting in the preparation of this note.

7

Suddenly Sexual Women in Bram Stoker's *Dracula*

Phyllis A. Roth

Criticism of Bram Stoker's *Dracula*, though not extensive, yet not insubstantial, points primarily in a single direction: the few articles published perceive *Dracula* as the consistent success it has been because, in the words of Royce MacGillivray, "Such a myth lives not merely because it has been skillfully marketed by entrepreneurs [primarily the movie industry] but because it expresses something that large numbers of readers feel to be true about their own lives."[1] In other words, *Dracula* successfully manages a fantasy which is congruent with a fundamental fantasy shared by many others. Several of the interpretations of *Dracula* either explicitly or implicitly indicate that this "core fantasy"[2] derives from the Oedipus complex—indeed, Maurice Richardson calls *Dracula* "a quite blatant demonstration of the Oedipus complex . . . a kind of incestuous, necrophilous, oral-anal-sadistic all-in wrestling match"[3] and this reading would seem to be valid.

Nevertheless, the Oedipus complex and the critics' use of it does not go far enough in explaining the novel: in explaining what I see to be the primary focus of the fantasy content and in explaining what allows Stoker and, vicariously, his readers, to act out what are essentially threatening, even horrifying wishes which must engage the most polarized of ambivalences. I propose, in the following, to summarize the interpretations to date, to indicate the pre-Oedipal focus of the fantasies, specifically the child's relation with and hostility toward the mother, and to indicate how the novel's fantasies are managed in such a way as to transform horror into pleasure. Moveover, I would emphasize that for both the Victorians and twentieth-century readers, much of the novel's great appeal derives from its hostility toward female sexuality. In "Fictional Conventions and

This article originally appeared in *Literature and Psychology* 27 (1977).

Sexuality in *Dracula*," Carrol Fry observes that the female vampires are equivalent to the fallen women of eighteenth and nineteenth century fiction.[4]

The facile and stereotypical dichotomy between the dark woman and the fair, the fallen and the idealized, is obvious in *Dracula*. Indeed, among the more gratuitous passages in the novel are those in which the "New Woman" who is sexually aggressive is verbally assaulted. Mina Harker remarks that such a woman, whom she holds in contempt, "will do the proposing herself."[5] Additionally, we must compare Van Helsing's hope "that there are good women still left to make life happy" (207) with Mina's assertion that "the world seems full of good men—even if there *are* monsters in it" (250). A remarkable contrast![6]

Perhaps nowhere is the dichotomy of sensual and sexless woman more dramatic than it is in *Dracula* and nowhere is the suddenly sexual woman more violently and self-righteously persecuted than in Stoker's "thriller."

The equation of vampirism with sexuality is well established in the criticism. Richardson refers to Freud's observations that "morbid dread always signifies repressed sexual wishes."[7] We must agree that *Dracula* is permeated by "morbid dread." However, another tone interrupts the dread of impending doom throughout the novel; that note is one of lustful anticipation, certainly anticipation of catching and destroying forever the master vampire, Count Dracula, but additionally, lustful anticipation of a consummation one can only describe as sexual. One thinks, for example, of the candle's "sperm" which "dropped in white patches" on Lucy's coffin as Van Helsing opens it for the first time (220). Together the critics have enumerated the most striking instances of this tone and its attendant imagery, but to recall: first, the scene in which Jonathan Harker searches the Castle Dracula, in a state of fascinated and morbid dread, for proof of his host's nature. Harker meets with three vampire women (whose relation to Dracula is incestuous[8]) whose appeal is described almost pornographically:

> All three had brilliant white teeth that shone like pearls against the ruby of their voluptuous lips. There was something about them that made my uneasy, some longing and at the same time deadly fear. I felt in my heart a wicked, burning desire that they would kiss me with those red lips.

The three debate who has the right to feast on Jonathan first, but they conclude, "He is young and strong; there are kisses for us all" (47). While this discussion takes place, Jonathan is "in an agony of delightful anticipation" (48). At the very end of the novel, Van Helsing falls prey to the same attempted seduction by, and the same ambivalence toward, the three vampires.

Two more scenes of relatively explicit and uninhibited sexuality mark the novel about one-half, then two-thirds, through. First the scene in which Lucy Westenra is laid to her final rest by her fiancé, Arthur Holmwood, later Lord Godalming, which is worth quoting from at length:

> Arthur placed the point [of the stake] over the heart, and as I looked I could see its dint in the white flesh. Then he struck with all his might.
>
> The thing in the coffin writhed; and a hideous, blood-curdling screech came from the opened red lips. The body shook and quivered and twisted in wild contortions; the sharp white teeth champed together till the lips were cut, and the mouth was smeared with a crimson foam. But Arthur never faltered. He looked like a figure of Thor as his untrembling arm rose and fell, driving deeper and deeper the mercy-bearing stake, whilst the blood from the pierced heart welled and spurted up around it. (241)

Such a description needs no comment here, though we will return to it in another context. Finally, the scene which Joseph Bierman has described quite correctly as a "primal scene in oral terms,"[9] the scene in which Dracula slits open his breast and forces Mina Harker to drink his blood:

> With his left hand he held both Mrs. Harker's hands, keeping them away with her arms at full tension; his right hand gripped her by the back of her neck, forcing her face down on his bosom. Her white nightdress was smeared with blood, and a thin stream trickled down the man's bare chest which was shown by his torn-open dress. The attitude of the two had a terrible resemblance to a child forcing a kitten's nose into a saucer of milk to compel it to drink. (313)

Two major points are to be made here, in addition to marking the clearly erotic nature of the descriptions. These are, in the main, the only sexual scenes and descriptions in the novel; and, not only are the scenes heterosexual,[10] they are incestuous, especially when taken together, as we shall see.

To consider the first point, only relations with vampires are sexualized in this novel; indeed, a deliberate attempt is made to make sexuality seem unthinkable in "normal relations" between the sexes. All the close relationships, including those between Lucy and her three suitors and Mina and her husband, are spiritualized beyond credibility. Only when Lucy becomes a vampire is she allowed to be "voluptuous," yet she must have been so long before, judging from her effect on men and from Mina's descriptions of her. (Mina, herself, never suffers the fate of voluptuousness before or after being bitten, for reasons which will become apparent later.) Clearly, then, vampirism is associated not only with death, immortality and orality; it is equivalent to sexuality.[11]

Moreover, in psychoanalytic terms, the vampirism is a disguise for greatly desired and equally strongly feared fantasies. These fantasies, as stated, have encouraged critics to point to the Oedipus complex at the center of the novel. Dracula, for example, is seen as the "father-figure of huge potency."[12] Royce MacGillivray remarks that:

> Dracula even aspires to be, in a sense, the father of the band that is pursuing him. Because he intends, as he tells them, to turn them all into vampires, he will be their creator and therefore "father."[13]

The major focus of the novel, in this analysis, is the battle of the sons against the father to release the desired woman, the mother, she whom it is felt originally belonged to the son till the father seduced her away. Richardson comments:

> The set-up reminds one rather of the primal horde as pictured somewhat fantastically perhaps by Freud in *Totem and Taboo,* with the brothers banding together against the father who has tried to keep all the females to himself.[14]

The Oedipal rivalry is not, however, merely a matter of the Van Helsing group, in which, as Richardson says, "Van Helsing represents the good father figure,"[15] pitted against the Big Daddy, Dracula. Rather, from the novel's beginning, a marked rivalry among the men is evident. This rivalry is defended against by the constant, almost obsessive, assertion of the value of friendship and *agape* among members of the Van Helsing group. Specifically, the defense of over-compensation is employed, most often by Van Helsing in his assertions of esteem for Dr. Seward and his friends. The others, too, repeat expressions of mutual affection ad nauseum: they clearly protest too much. Perhaps this is most obviously symbolized, and unintentionally exposed, by the blood transfusions from Arthur, Seward, Quincey Morris, and Van Helsing to Lucy Westenra. The great friendship among rivals for Lucy's hand lacks credibility and is especially strained when Van Helsing makes it clear that the transfusions (merely the reverse of the vampire's blood-letting) are in their nature sexual; others have recognized, too, that Van Helsing's warning to Seward not to tell Arthur that anyone else has given Lucy blood, indicates the sexual nature of the operation.[16] Furthermore, Arthur himself feels that, as a result of having given Lucy his blood, they are in effect married. Thus, the friendships of the novel mask a deep-seated rivalry and hostility.

Dracula does then appear to enact the Oedipal rivalry among sons and between the son and the father for the affections of the mother. The fantasy of parricide and its acting out is obviously satisfying. According to Holland, such a threatening wish-fulfillment can be rewarding when properly defended against or associated with other pleasurable fantasies. Among the other fantasies are those of life after death, the triumph of "good over evil," mere man over super-human forces, and the rational West over the mysterious East.[17] Most likely not frightening and certainly intellectualized, these simplistic abstractions provide a diversion from more threatening material and assure the fantast that God's in his heaven; all's right with the world. On the surface, this is the moral of the end of the novel: Dracula is safely reduced to ashes, Mina is cleansed, the "boys" are triumphant. Were this all the theme of interest the novel presented, however, it would be neither so popular with Victorians and their successors nor worthy of scholarly concern.

Up to now my discussion has been taken from the point of view of reader identification with those who are doing battle against the evil in this world, against Count Dracula. On the surface of it, this is where one's sympathies lie in reading the novel and it is this level of analysis which has been explored by previous critics. However, what is far more significant in the interrelation of fantasy and defense is the duplication of characters and structure which betrays an identification with Dracula and a fantasy of matricide underlying the more obvious parricidal wishes.

As observed, the split between the sexual vampire family and the asexual Van Helsing group is not all clear-cut: Jonathan, Van Helsing, Seward and Holmwood are all overwhelmingly attracted to the vampires, to sexuality. Fearing this, they employ two defenses, projection[18] and denial; it is not we who want the vampires, it is they who want us (to eat us, to seduce us, to kill us). Despite the projections, we should recall that almost all the on-stage killing is done by the "good guys": that of Lucy, the vampire women, and Dracula. The projection of the wish to kill onto the vampires wears thinnest perhaps when Dr. Seward, contemplating the condition of Lucy, asserts that "had she then to be killed I could have done it with savage delight" (236). Even earlier, when Dr. Seward is rejected by Lucy, he longs for a cause with which to distract himself from the pain of rejection: "Oh, Lucy, Lucy, I cannot be angry with you. . . . If I only could have as strong a cause as my poor mad friend there [significantly, he refers to Renfield]—a good, unselfish cause to make me work—that would be indeed happiness" (84). Seward's wish is immediately fulfilled by Lucy's vampirism and the subsequent need to destroy her. Obviously, the acting out of such murderous impulses is threatening: in addition to the defenses mentioned above, the use of religion not only to exorcise the evil but to justify the murders is striking. In other words, Christianity is on our side, we *must* be right. In this connection, it is helpful to mention Wasson's observation[19] of the significance of the name "Lord Godalming" (the point is repeated). Additional justification is provided by the murdered themselves: the peace into which they subside is to be read as a thank you note. Correlated with the religious defense is one described by Freud in *Totem and Taboo* in which the violator of the taboo can avert disaster by Lady Macbeth-like compulsive rituals and renunciations.[20] The repeated use of the Host, the complicated ritual of the slaying of the vampires, and the ostensible, though not necessarily conscious, renunciation of sexuality are the penance paid by those in *Dracula* who violate the taboos against incest and the murder of parents.

Since we now see that Dracula acts out the repressed fantasies of the others, since those others wish to do what he can do, we have no difficulty in recognizing an identification with the aggressor on the part of characters and reader alike. It is important, then, to see what it is that Dracula is after.

The novel tells of two major episodes, the seduction of Lucy and of Mina, to which the experience of Harker at Castle Dracula provides a preface, a hero, one whose narrative encloses the others and with whom, therefore, one might readily identify. This, however, is a defense against the central identification of the novel with Dracula and his attacks on the women. It is relevant in this context to observe how spontaneous and ultimately trivial Dracula's interest in Harker is. When Harker arrives at Castle Dracula, his host makes a lunge for him, but only after Harker has cut his finger and is bleeding. Dracula manages to control himself and we hear no more about his interest in Harker's blood until the scene with the vampire women when he says, "This man belongs to me!" (49) and, again a little later, "have patience. Tonight is mine. To-morrow night is yours!" (61) After this we hear no more of Dracula's interest in Jonathan; indeed, when Dracula arrives in England, he never again goes after Jonathan. For his part, Jonathan appears far more concerned about the vampire women than about Dracula—they are more horrible and fascinating to him. Indeed, Harker is relieved to be saved from the women by Dracula. Moreover, the novel focusses on the Lucy and Mina episodes from which, at first, the Jonathan episodes may seem disconnected; actually, they are not, but we can only see why after we understand what is going on in the rest of the novel.

In accepting the notion of identification with the aggressor in *Dracula*, as I believe we must, what we accept is an understanding of the reader's identification with the aggressor's victimization of women. Dracula's desire is for the destruction of Lucy and Mina and what this means is obvious when we recall that his attacks on these two closest of friends seem incredibly coincidental on the narrative level. Only on a deeper level is there no coincidence at all: the level on which one recognizes that Lucy and Mina are essentially the same figure: the mother. Dracula is, in fact, the same story told twice with different outcomes. In the former, the mother is more desirable, more sexual, more threatening and must be destroyed. And the physical descriptions of Lucy reflect this greater ambivalence: early in the story, when Lucy is not yet completely vampirized, Dr. Seward describes her hair "in its usual sunny ripples" (180); later, when the men watch her return to her tomb, Lucy is described as "a dark-haired woman" (235). The conventional fair/dark split, symbolic of respective moral casts, seems to be unconscious here, reflecting the ambivalence aroused by the sexualized female. Not only is Lucy the more sexualized figure, she is the more rejecting figure, rejecting two of the three "sons" in the novel. This section of the book ends with her destruction, not by Dracula but by the man whom she was to marry. The novel could not end here, though; the story had to be told again to assuage the anxiety occasioned by matricide. This time, the mother is much less sexually threatening and is ultimately saved. Moreover, Mina is never described physically and is the opposite of rejecting: all the men become her sons, symbolized by the naming of her actual son after them all. What remains constant is the attempt to destroy the mother. What changes is the way the fantasies are managed. To speak of the novel in terms of the child's ambivalence toward the mother is not just to speak psychoanalytically. We need only recall that Lucy, as "bloofer lady," as well as the other vampire women, prey on children. In the case of Lucy, the children are as attracted to her as threatened by her.

I have already described the evidence that the Van Helsing men themselves desire to do away with Lucy. Perhaps the story needed to be retold because the desire was too close to the surface to be satisfying; certainly, the reader would not be satisfied had the novel ended with Arthur's murder of Lucy. What is perhaps not so clear is that the desire to destroy Mina is equally strong. Let us look first at the defenses against this desire. I have already mentioned the great professions of affection for Mina made by most of the male characters. Mina indeed acts and is treated as both the saint and the mother (ironically, this is particularly clear when she comforts Arthur for the loss of Lucy). She is all good, all pure, all true. When, however, she is seduced away from the straight and narrow by Dracula, she is "unclean," tainted and stained with a mark on her forehead immediately occasioned by Van Helsing's touching her forehead with the Host. Van Helsing's hostility toward Mina is further revealed when he cruelly reminds her of her "intercourse" with Dracula: "Do you forget," he said, with actually a smile, "that last night he banqueted heavily and will sleep late?" (328) This hostility is so obvious that the other men are shocked. Nevertheless, the "sons," moreover, and the reader as well, identify with Dracula's attack on Mina; indeed, the men cause it, as indicated by the events which transpire when all the characters are at Seward's hospital-asylum. The members of the brotherhood go out at night to seek out Dracula's lairs, and they leave Mina undefended at the hospital. They claim that this insures her safety; in fact, it insures the reverse. Furthermore, this is the real purpose in leaving Mina out of the plans and in the hospital. They have clear indications in Renfield's warnings of what is to happen to her and they all, especially her husband, observe that she is not well and seems to be getting weaker. That they could rationalize these signs away while looking for and finding them everywhere else further indicates that they are avoiding seeing what they want to ignore; in other words, they want Dracula to get her. This is not to deny that they also want to save Mina; it is simply to claim that the ambivalence toward the mother is fully realized in the novel.

We can now return to that ambivalence and, I believe, with the understanding of the significance of the mother figure, comprehend the precise perspective of the novel. Several critics have correctly emphasized the regression to both orality and anality[21] in *Dracula*. Certainly, the sexuality is perceived in oral terms. The primal scene already discussed makes abundantly clear that intercourse is perceived in terms of nursing. As C. F. Bentley sees it:

Stoker is describing a symbolic act of enforced fellatio, where blood is again a substitute for semen, and where a chaste female suffers a violation that is essentially sexual. Of particular interest in the . . . passage is the striking image of "a child forcing a kitten's nose into a saucer of milk to compel it to drink," suggesting an element of regressive infantilism in the vampire superstition.[22]

The scene referred to is, in several senses, the climax of the novel; it is the most explicit view of the act of vampirism and is, therefore, all the more significant as an expression of the nature of sexual intercourse as the novel depicts it. In it, the woman is doing the sucking. Bierman comments that "The reader by this point in the novel has become used to Dracula doing the sucking, but not to Dracula being sucked and specifically at the breast."[23] While it is true that the reader may most often think of Dracula as the active partner, the fact is that the scenes of vampire sexuality are described from the male perspective, with the females as the active assailants.[24] Only the acts of phallic aggression, the killings, involve the males in active roles. *Dracula,* then, dramatizes the child's view of intercourse insofar as it is seen as a wounding and a killing. But the primary preoccupation, as attested to by the primal scene, is with the role of the female in the act. Thus, it is not surprising that the central anxiety of the novel is the fear of the devouring woman and, in documenting this, we will find that all the pieces of the novel fall into place, most especially the Jonathan Harker prologue.

As mentioned, Harker's desire and primary anxiety is not with Dracula but with the female vampires. In his initial and aborted seduction by them, he describes his ambivalence. Interestingly, Harker seeks out this episode by violating the Count's (father's) injunction to remain in his room: "let me warn you with all seriousness, that should you leave these rooms you will not by any chance go to sleep in any other part of the castle" (42). This, of course, is what Harker promptly does. When Dracula breaks in and discovers Harker with the vampire women, he acts like both a jealous husband and an irate father: "His eyes were positively blazing. The red light in them was lurid. . . . 'How dare you touch him, any of you?'" (48–49). Jonathan's role as child here is reinforced by the fact that, when Dracula takes him away from the women, he gives them a child as substitute. But most interesting is Jonathan's perspective as he awaits, in a state of erotic arousal, the embraces of the vampire women, especially the fair one: "The other was fair as fair can be, with great wavy masses of golden hair and eyes like pale sapphires. I seemed somehow to know her face and to know it in connection with some dreamy fear, but I could not recollect at the moment how or where" (47). As far as we know, Jonathan never recollects, but we should be able to understand that the face is that of the mother (almost archetypally presented), she whom he desires yet fears, the temptress-seductress, Medusa. Moreover, this golden girl reappears in the early description of Lucy.

At the end of the following chapter, Jonathan exclaims, "I am alone in the castle with those awful women. Faugh! Mina is a woman, and there is nought in common." Clearly, however, there is. Mina at the breast of Count Dracula is identical to the vampire women whose desire is to draw out of the male the fluid necessary for life. That this is viewed as an act of castration is clear from Jonathan's conclusion: "At least God's mercy is better than that of these monsters, and the precipice is steep and high. At its foot a man may sleep—*as a man*. Good-bye, all! Mina!" (4; emphasis mine).

The threatening Oedipal fantasy, the regression to a primary oral obsession, the attraction and destruction of the vampires of *Dracula* are, then, interrelated and interdependent. What they spell out is a fusion of the memory of nursing at the mother's breast with a primal scene fantasy which results in the conviction that the sexually desirable woman will annihilate if she is not first destroyed. The fantasy of incest and matricide evokes the mythic image of the *vagina dentata* evident in so many folk tales[25] in which the mouth and the vagina are identified with one another by the primitive mind and pose the threat of castration to all men until the teeth are extracted by the hero. The conclusion of *Dracula*, the "salvation" of Mina, is equivalent to such an "extraction": Mina will not remain the *vagina dentata* to threaten them all.

Central to the structure and unconscious theme of *Dracula* is, then, primarily the desire to destroy the threatening mother, she who threatens by being desirable. Otto Rank best explains why it is Dracula whom the novel seems to portray as the threat when he says, in a study which is pertinent to ours:

> Through the displacement of anxiety on to the father, the renunciation of the mother, necessary for the sake of life is assured. For this feared father prevents the return to the mother and thereby the releasing of the much more painful primary anxiety, which is related to the mother's genitals as the place of birth and later transferred to objects taking the place of the genitals [such as the mouth].[26]

Finally, the novel has it both ways: Dracula is destroyed[27] and Van Helsing saved; Lucy is destroyed and Mina saved. The novel ends on a rather ironic note, given our understanding here, as Harker concludes with a quote from the good father, Van Helsing:

> "We want no proofs; we ask none to believe us! This boy will some day know what a brave and gallant woman his mother is. Already he knows her sweetness and loving care; later on he will understand how some men so loved her, that they did dare so much for her sake." (416)

Notes

1. Royce MacGillivray, *"Dracula:* Bram Stoker's Spoiled Masterpiece," *Queen's Quarterly,* 79, 518.

2. See Norman N. Holland, *The Dynamics of Literature Response* (New York: W. W. Norton & Co., 1975).

3. Maurice Richardson, "The Psychoanalysis of Ghost Stories," *Twentieth Century,* 166 (December 1959), 427.

4. *Victorian Newsletter,* 42.

5. Bram Stoker, *Dracula* (New York: Dell, 1974), 103–4. All subsequent references will be to this edition and will appear parenthetically.

6. While it is not my concern in this paper to deal biographically with *Dracula,* the Harry Ludlam biography (a book which is admittedly anti-psychological in orientation despite its provocative title, *A Biography of Dracula: The Life Story of Bram Stoker*) includes some suggestive comments about Bram Stoker's relationship with his mother. Ludlam remarks an ambivalence toward women on the part of Charlotte Stoker who, on the one hand, decried the situation of poor Irish girls in the workhouse which was "the very hot-bed of vice" and advocated respectability through emigration for the girls and, on the other, "declared often that she 'did not care tuppence' for her daughters." Too, Charlotte told her son Irish folk tales of banshee horrors and a true story of "the horrors she had suffered as a child in Sligo during the great cholera outbreak that claimed many thousands of victims in Ireland alone, and which provoked the more dreadful cruelties" (New York: The Fireside Press, 1962, p. 14). I cannot help but wonder how old Stoker was when his mother discussed these matters with him. Certainly, they made a vivid impression, for later, Charlotte wrote her story down and Bram based his own "The Invisible Giant" on his mother's tale of the cholera epidemic in Sligo.

7. Richardson, p. 419.

8. C. F. Bentley, "The Monster in the Bedroom: Sexual Symbolism in Bram Stoker's *Dracula,"* *Literature and Psychology,* 22, 1(1972), 29.

9. Joseph S. Bierman, *"Dracula:* Prolonged Childhood Illness and the Oral Triad," *American Imago,* 29, 194.

10. Bebtketmo, 27.

11. See Tsvetan Todorov, *The Fantastic,* translated by Richard Howard (Cleveland: Case Western Reserve, 1973), pp. 136–39.

12. Richardson, p. 427.

13. MacGillivray, p. 522.

14. Richardson, p. 428. The Oedipal fantasy of the destruction of the father is reinforced by a number of additional, and actually gratuitous, paternal deaths in the novel. See also MacGillivray, p. 523.

15. Richardson, p. 428.

16. See, for instance, Richardson, p. 427.

17. Richard Wasson, "The Politics of *Dracula," English Literature in Transition,* 9, pp. 24–27.

18. Freud, *Totem and Taboo*, translated by James Strachey, in *The Standard Edition of the Complete Psychological Works of Sigmund Freud*, 13 (1913–1914) (London: Hogarth Press, 1962), 60–63.

19. Wasson, p. 26.

20. Freud, pp. 37ff.

21. Bentley, pp. 29–30; MacGillivray, p. 522.

22. Bentley, p. 30.

23. Bierman, p. 194. Bierman's analysis is concerned to demonstrate that *"Dracula* mirrors Stoker's early childhood . . . ," and is a highly speculative but fascinating study. The emphasis is on Stoker's rivalry with his brothers but it provides, albeit indirectly, further evidence of hostility toward the rejecting mother.

24. Ludlam cites one of the actors in the original stage production of *Dracula* as indicating that the adaptation was so successful that "Disturbances in the circle or stalls as people felt faint and had to be taken out were not uncommon—and they were perfectly genuine, not a publicity stunt. Strangely enough, they were generally men" (Ludlum, 1. 165).

25. See, for instance, Wolfgang Lederer, M.D., *The Fear of Women* (New York: Harcourt Brace Jovanovich, Inc., 1968), especially the chapter entitled, "A Snapping of Teeth."

26. Otto Rank, *The Trauma of Birth* (New York: Harper & Row, 1973), p. 73.

27. When discussing this paper with a class, two of my students argued that Dracula is not, in fact, destroyed at the novel's conclusion. They maintained that his last look is one of triumph and that his heart is not staked but pierced by a mere bowie knife. Their suggestions that, at least, the men do not follow the elaborate procedures to insure the destruction of Dracula that they religiously observe with regard to that of the women, is certainly of value here, whether one agrees that Dracula still stalks the land. My thanks to Lucinda Donnelly and Barbara Kotacka for these observations.

8

Women and Vampires: *Dracula* as a Victorian Novel

Judith Weissman

The sexually straightforward and insatiable woman, a stock figure in much of English literature, virtually disappears from the novel after Fielding and Richardson—until she is resurrected by Bram Stoker in *Dracula* as a vampire. The vampire, an ancient figure of horror in folk tales, undoubtedly represents in any story some kind of sexual terror, some terror of being weakened and hurt by one's lover, but *Dracula*, a Victorian novel, a novel about marriage, embodies sexual terror in a very particular form. A man's vision of a noble band of men restoring a woman to purity and passivity, saving them from the horrors of vampirism, it is an extreme version of the stereotypically Victorian attitudes toward sexual roles.

Voraciously sexual women are usually presented unsympathetically, but without terror, in literature before the nineteenth century. In Chaucer, Criseyde is indeed as fickle as Troilus fears, and the wife of Bath supports through her actions the contentions of all the anti-feminist satire that she attacks. In Shakespeare, Gertrude is weak and, to Hamlet, disgusting in her sexuality, and women like Juliet's nurse are comic. Only Cleopatra is both sexual and—despite her spitefulness and selfishness—magnificent. The evil of Milton's temptresses is self-evident; the older women who chase young men in Restoration comedy are objects of contempt.

In the eighteeth century, Swift and Pope both treat highly sexual women with anger and disdain, but still take their existence for granted. In the eighteenth century novel, both Fielding and Richardson treat women's sexuality quite explicitly. Few men in English literature treat women with more generosity than Fielding does. In *Tom Jones*, Lady Bellaston, certainly, is an unsavory character, very similar to the women of Restoration comedy, but Fielding dislikes her

This article originally appeared in *Midwest Quarterly* 18 (1977).

for her dishonesty and exploitiveness more than for her sexual appetite. Molly Seagrim and Mrs. Waters are not heroines, but neither are they objects of contempt. They both like sex, and a lot of it, and though Fielding values a woman like Sophia, who can control her sexuality for the sake of her integrity, more than he could value Molly and Mrs. Waters, he treats them not as contemptible or frightening creatures, but simply as less-admirable women. When Mrs. Waters, after sleeping with Tom, discovers that he is in love with someone else, Fielding says, with admirable freedom from rancor:

> She was not nice enough in her amours to be greatly concerned at the discovery. The beauty of Jones highly charmed her eye; but as she could not see his heart, she gave herself no concern about it. She could feast heartily at the table of love, without reflecting that some other already had been, or hereafter might be, feasted with the same repast. A sentiment which, if it deals but little in refinements, deals, however, much in substance; and is less capricious, and perhaps less ill natured and selfish, than the desires of those females who can be contented enough to abstain from the possession of their lovers, provided they are sufficiently satisfied that no one else possesses them. (Book IX, chapter vi)

Fielding values warmth and finds nothing to fear in sexual warmth that transgresses the bounds of modesty and chastity.

Richardson, on the other hand, comes as close to expressing real terror of sexual women as any novelist before Stoker. The licentious women who are the allies of Mr. B. and Lovelace in their efforts to destroy the virtue of Pamela and Clarissa are bestial and disgusting, and to Clarissa, when she is imprisoned, figures of almost supernatural terror. "Thus was I tricked and deluded by blacker hearts of my own sex than I thought there were in the world. I was so senseless, that I dare not aver that the horrible creatures of the house were personally aiding; but some visionary remembrances I have of female figures flitting before my sight, the wretched woman's particularly" (Miss Clarissa Harlowe to Miss Howe, Thursday, July 6, Night). Lovelace, who is not consciously afraid of women (though his behavior suggests that indeed he is, since he treats them as enemies to be conquered) persistently uses the word devil to describe them. There are only two possible kinds of women for Lovelace, and as far as I can tell, for Richardson—devils, sexually active ones; and angels, absolutely chaste ones. The women who are helping him trap Clarissa are devils: "What devils are women, when all tests are got over, and we have completely ruined them" (Mr. Lovelace to John Belford, Esq. Friday Evening [May 26]). And of Clarissa, he says, "Surely, Belford, this is an angel. And yet, had she not been known to be female, they would not from *babyhood* have dressed her such, nor would she, but upon conviction, have continued the dress" (Mr. Lovelace to John Belford, Esq. Sunday, May 21). To be female, in his mind, is to be a potential devil, who needs only sexual initiation. He believes in the sexual theory of *Fanny Hill* and adds demonism to it: in *Fanny Hill* it takes only one sexual experience to make a woman insatiable, and to Lovelace once she is insatiable, she is a devil. Clarissa disproves his mythology by not desiring him after he rapes her: "By my soul, Belford, this dear girl gives the lie to all our rakish maxims. There must be something more than a *name* in virtue! . . . *Once subdued, always subdued*—'tis an egregious falsehood!" (Mr. Lovelace to John Belford, Esq. Monday, June 19). Nevertheless, there is nothing left for Clarissa herself to do but die, since she is not married and no longer a virgin, and can no longer believe in her own sexual myth, that of *Comus*, that chastity can conquer all attempts to defile it. She has proved Lovelace wrong, but she cannot prove that a woman who has been sexually violated can live a human life.

Though the women of the nineteenth century novel are by no means all Pamelas and Clarissas, they are not Molly Seagrims either. Those who bear illegitimate children, as Molly does, like Hetty Sorrell and Tess Durbeyfield, suffer terribly instead of going on to enjoy more sex. The aggressive flirt survives in the novel, for example in Trollope's Madalina Demolines and Thackeray's Becky Sharp, but their aggression is not really sexual. Thackeray does sometimes treat Becky with terror, because she has so much power over men and is so unscrupulous, so selfish, so dishonest. But she is using her sexuality as a source of credit in a capitalist economy and like Moll Flanders is more interested in the money that sex—or, in her case, perhaps only the promise of sex—can get for her, than in sex itself.

The one violently sexual woman in a major Victorian novel is Bertha Rochester, an older woman (after the wedding Rochester learned to his horror that she was several years older than he was) and a Creole, part black. Rochester sees her as a monster and describes her without a hint of compassion:

> What a pigmy intellect she had, and what giant propensities! How fearful were the curses those propensities entailed on me! Bertha Mason, the true daughter of an infamous mother, dragged me through all the hideous and degrading agonies which must attend a man bound to a wife at once intemperate and unchaste . . . a nature the most gross, impure, depraved I ever saw, associated with mine, and called by the law and by society a part of me. And I could not rid myself of it by any legal proceedings: for the doctors now discovered that *my wife* was mad—her excesses had prematurely developed the germs of insanity. (Chapter 27)

Bertha is not she; she is "it." Her sexuality has cost her her humanity in Rochester's eyes. I wish I could believe that Charlotte Brontë disapproved of Rochester's view of his wife, but I see nothing in the novel to indicate that she did not share it. Having learned of Bertha's existence on what was to be her own wedding day, Jane leaves, refusing to live with Rochester—but not out of sympathy for Bertha. She is angry, understandably, that she has been deceived, but she cares about maintaining her own chastity and her own pride rather than about refusing to betray another woman. Her pride is apparently more concerned with the letter of the law than with a new understanding of the defects of

Rochester's character, for she goes back to him as soon as Bertha has been killed by a timely fire and utters not a word of pity for her. In fact, her own vision of Bertha is as extreme as Rochester's.

> Oh, sir, I never saw a face like it! It was a discoloured face—it was a savage face. I wish I could forget the roll of the red eyes and the fearful blackened inflation of the lineaments! . . . The lips were swelled and dark; the brow furrowed; the black eyebrows widely raised over the bloodshot eyes. Shall I tell you of what it reminded me? Of the foul German spectre—the vampire. (Chapter 25)

For Jane too, Bertha is an it, an inhuman demon, a vampire. When she describes Bertha here, she does not know who she is, having seen her only when Bertha came into her bedroom to tear her wedding veil, but even after she knows Bertha's identity, she never retracts these words.

Nor does she ever protest against the language that Rochester uses to describe herself—a bird, an elf, a fairy, a delicate flower—all images which imply frail asexuality. He says that he needs her to cure him from the taint that Bertha has left, the mark of the vampire, in a way. Though there are passages in which Jane speaks of her passionate love for Rochester, and though at the end she says she is bone of his bone, flesh of his flesh, the language of the book suggests that she basically accepts his idea that sexual women are monsters and that good ones are asexual. I would find it impossible to argue that Charlotte Brontë stands apart from Jane Eyre and is using her to expose the power that men's myths have had over women's minds. I think that she shares the sexual myths of men like Richardson and that sexual fear is one of the deepest feelings in Jane Eyre, fear substantiated by the drastic mutilation that Rochester suffers before Jane can come back to him. It would not be hard to control a blind man with one hand.

The vampire is only mentioned in *Jane Eyre,* but Charlotte Brontë clearly understands the psychological connection between sexuality and demonic blood-sucking. Neither the vampire nor the extremely sexual woman is important in the Victorian novel again until *Dracula,* a great horror story and a very extreme version of the myth that there are two types of women, devils and angels. Because it is an epistolary novel it has no narrator whose views might be understood as those of the author, but the band of men who gather to fight vampires are amazingly similar in their thoughts about women, as well as in their actions. Arthur, Quincey Morris, and Dr. Seward all begin as suitors of Lucy; Van Helsing is called in to try to save her, and then all four of them join Jonathan in saving Mina. Their lives are devoted to chivalrous concern for women; they are never jealous of each other, never quarrel, and never argue about how women should behave. They all give Lucy transfusions and apparently agree with Seward's sentiment that "No man knows, till he experiences it, what it is to feel his own lifeblood drawn away into the veins of the woman he loves" (Dr. Seward's Diary, 10 September). Van Helsing, the old-fashioned, courtly man, has most of the big lines on women; perhaps his most striking statement to Mina is, "We are men and are able to bear; but you must be our star and our hope, and we shall act all the more free that you are not in the danger, such as we are" (Mina Harker's Journal, 30 September). He has the last line in the book, about Mina's son: "Already he knows her sweetness and loving care; later on he will understand how some men so loved her, that they did dare much for her sake." It is not easy to find many other books in which women are praised and loved for being passive inspirations to men; Mina sounds like the Virgin Mary of medieval lyrics. Even Pamela and Clarissa have more spirit than Mina as Van Helsing describes her.

The two women (Lucy's mother dies too early in the book to be much of a character) are, at least superficially, perfect objects of such chivalry. Young, beautiful, chaste, coy, they revel in their passivity. Lucy comes under Dracula's evil influence virtually as soon as we meet her and does little but sleep walk and have blood transfusions; when Mina too gets bitten, she learns to resign the active role she had taken in pursing Dracula and becomes passive, helping only by being hypnotized and giving messages while in a trance. She loves being called "little girl" by Quincey Morris, especially because she knows he has called Lucy the same thing. And as she grows weaker and weaker, she says more and more often things like "Oh thank God for good, brave men!" (Johnathan Harker's Journal, 3 October). Knowing that she may become a vampire, she asks her band of men to kill her if they must: "Think, dear, that there have been times when brave men have killed their wives and their womenkind, to keep them from falling into the hands of the enemy. Their hands did not falter any the more because those that they loved implored them to slay them. It is men's duty towards those whom they love, in such time of sore trial" (Dr. Seward's Diary, 11 October). I am not sure what—if any—historical incidents she has in mind; but some women, like Cleopatra and Lucrece, have been capable of killing themselves when faced with what they considered a fate worse than death. Mina, however, relies entirely on the strength of men.

Mina's final proof of her womanhood is acting as an intercessor for Dracula. The men, naturally, approach him with the purest hatred and vindictiveness, but she pleads:

> Jonathan dear, and you all my true, true friends, I want you to bear something in mind through all this dreadful time. I know that you must fight—that you must destroy even as you destroyed the false Lucy so that the true Lucy might live hereafter; but it is not a work of hate. That poor soul who has wrought all this misery is the saddest case of all. Just think what will be his joy when he, too, is destroyed in his worser part that his better part may have spiritual immortality. You must be pitiful to him, too, though it may not hold your hands from his destruction. (Dr. Seward's Diary, 3 October)

As the Virgin Mary intercedes with God for sinners, Mina uses her womanly power of pity to intercede with men even for the worst of criminals, insisting that even he can be redeemed. Her idea of dying to one's worse self so that the better self may live is the traditional Christian idea of dying to the flesh that the spirit may live: vampirism is only an extreme version of the evil of the body against which Christians have been told to fight for almost two thousand years. And Mina is the ideal Christian woman, recalling men to an ideal of charity and love through her holy influence.

Lucy and Mina, however, occasionally say things which reveal —without Stoker's conscious knowledge, I am sure—his anxieties about women's sexuality. Writing to Mina about her three proposals in one day, Lucy says, "Why can't they let a girl marry three men, or as many as want her, and save all this trouble? But this is heresy, and I must not say it" (Letter from Lucy Westenra to Mina Murray, 24 May). The intended meaning is that she would like to be kind to these three fine men who love her; the implicit meaning is that she feels able to handle three men sexually. And her friend Mina, writing ostensibly about the lunch that she and Lucy have eaten, says, "I believe we would have shocked the 'New Woman' with our appetites. Men are more tolerant, bless them!" (Mina Murray's Journal, 10 August, 11 P.M.). Mina of course does not like the "New Woman" and continues: "Some of the 'New Women' writers will some day start an idea that men and women should be allowed to see each other asleep before proposing or accepting. But I suppose the 'New Woman' won't condescend in the future to accept; she will do the proposing herself. And a nice job she will make of it, too!" She wants to defend women from the dangers of feminism, but on the other hand admits that she has an appetite that not even what she imagines nineteenth-century feminism to be would be able to accept.

The only other women in the book are vampires, lost souls controlled by inhuman appetites. Jonathan Harker knows perfectly well that the vampire women in Dracula's castle offer him the temptation of illicit sex:

> I seemed somehow to know her face, and to know it in connection with some dreamy fear, but I could not recollect at the moment how or where. All three had brilliant white teeth that shone like pearls against the ruby of their voluptuous lips. There was something about them that made me uneasy, some longing and at the same time some deadly fear. I felt in my heart a wicked, burning desire that they would kiss me with those red lips. It is not good to note this down; lest some day it should meet Mina's eyes and cause her pain; but it is the truth. (Jonathan Harker's Journal, 15 May)

She seems familiar because he does know, subconsciously, that women are sexual, and terrifying; if they did not represent real women to him, he would have nothing to be ashamed of with respect to Mina. They are the forbidden women, the other women, whose existence is produced by bourgeois marriage. Though he says later, "I am alone in the castle with those awful women. Faugh!

Mina is a woman, and there is nought in common. They are devils of the Pit!" (Jonathan Harker's Diary, 30 June, morning), the whole book reveals the fear that they do indeed have something in common. There is always the possibility that the chaste Victorian wife will become the kind of woman that her husband both desires and fears.

We never know who these women were before Dracula transformed them into vampires, but it is significant that the two women he attacks in the book, Mina and Lucy, are either engaged or newly married. He does not attack single women, preadolescent women, or old women. He attacks women who are desired by other men and who are becoming sexually experienced. We watch Lucy change as she comes more and more under Dracula's influence: during the day she simply becomes weak, sad, absentminded; but at night, even before her death, she becomes very sexual. Seward reports: "In a sort of sleep-waking, vague, unconscious way she opened her eyes, which were now dull and hard at once, and said in a soft, voluptuous voice, such as I had never heard from her lips:—Arthur! Oh, my love I am so glad you have come. Kiss me!" (Dr. Seward's Diary, 20 September). She becomes even more frightening as a vampire: "The sweetness was turned to adamantine, heartless cruelty, and the purity to voluptuous wantonness" (Dr. Seward's Diary, 29 September, Continued). She has again tried to seduce—and therefore, attack—Arthur as a vampire, but she spends most of her time attacking children. The women in the castle are also satisfied with a child when they are denied Jonathan; there is obviously a suggestion that women become child molesters. The one group of people that they never attack is other women.

Mina fights becoming a vampire much harder than Lucy did, and never becomes wantonly sexual. Nevertheless, in the scene where her friends discover Dracula with her, Jonathan has been attacked by a vampire, and is not clear whether she or Dracula was the attacker. Dracula is forcing Mina to drink blood from his chest, while "on the bed beside the window lay Jonathan Harker, his face flushed and breathing heavily as though in a stupor" (Dr. Seward's Diary, 3 October). Van Helsing says that "Jonathan is in a stupor such as we know the Vampire can produce," but he does not say which vampire produced this stupor. Flushed and tired, Jonathan seems to have just had intercourse, and we do not know whether Dracula produced this state in order to have access to Mina, or whether Mina, during what she thought was normal intercourse with her husband, produced the stupor. At any rate, Mina realizes that she must never again have sex with Jonathan, as long as she is a vampire, in order to keep him from becoming one too: "Unclean, unclean! I must touch him or kiss him no more. Oh, that it should be that it is I who am now his worst enemy, and whom he may have most cause to fear." As the women in *Dracula* become vampires, they become too sexual for their husbands or fiancés to endure.

Jonathan, however, seems unaffected the next day by his brush with vampirism. In this book men do not become transformed into sexual demons as women do. Dracula himself is cruel and powerful but not particularly sensual in the same way that the women are. The women at the castle say, "You yourself never loved; you never love" (Jonathan Harker's Journal, The Morning of 16 May), and though he answers, "Yes, I too can love, you yourselves can tell it from the past," the book seems to support what the women say. He seems more interested in power and conquest than in the sensual pleasure of being a vampire, which the women clearly enjoy. His control and brutal power is clear when he forces Mina to drink blood from his chest, a demonic reversal of the Pelican's feeding of its child from its own blood, an image of Christ's sacrifice: "With his left hand he held both Mrs. Harker's hands, keeping them away with her arms at full tension; his right hand gripped her by the back of the neck, forcing her face down on his bosom. . . . The attitude of the two had a terrible resemblance to a child forcing a kitten's nose into a saucer of milk to compel it to drink" (Dr. Seward's Diary, 3 October). Mina does not want to be a vampire—to drink blood—and he is trying to force her to become one. His cold control is also shown by his power over animals, especially wolves, and the zoo-keeper in London reveals the connection between this power and the power that he has over Mina and Lucy when he says, of the wolf which has escaped: "He was a nice well-behaved wolf, that never gave no trouble to talk of. I'm more surprised at 'im for wantin' to get out nor any other animile in the place. But, there, you cannot trust wolves no more nor women" ("The Pall Mall Gazette" 18 September).

✶ ⌈The difference between the sexuality of Dracula and the women vampires is, I think, the key to the psychological meaning of the book. For him, sex is power; for them, it is desire. He is the man whom all other men fear, the man who can, without any loss of freedom or power himself, seduce other men's women and make them sexually insatiable with a sexual performance that the others cannot match.⌋ He is related to Lovelace and to the tradition of noble rakes who ruin middle and lower class women and go scot-free, but the women who are the victims of Lovelace and the young squires of *The Vicar of Wakefield* and *Tom Jones* (the one who preceded Tom in Molly's bed) are not said to be ruined for other men because they are now insatiable. They are, supposedly, simply no longer respectable. And yet I think that *Dracula* reveals one of the reasons *why* they are no longer respectable, why there has been an obsession in western culture with marrying virgins. Our culture is founded on the belief that men are more powerful than women, and perhaps women who are not virgins have not been considered eligible for marriage because they may make invidious sexual comparisons between their husbands and their previous lovers. Fielding, that great man, recognizes this possibility without horror when Shamela Andrews complains that all men are "little" compared with Parson Williams and says that she might have been well enough satisfied, too, on her wedding night, if she had never been acquainted with Parson Williams.

For Fielding, differences in sexual capacity are not a cause for terror; for Stoker, they are. His band of trusty men, loyal and chaste, are not simply trying to destroy Dracula, who has come to England to "create a new and ever-widening circle of semi-demons to batten on the helpless" (Jonathan Harker's Journal, 30 June morning). Their fight to destroy Dracula and to restore Mina to her purity is really a fight for control over women. It is a fight to keep women from knowing what the men and women of the Middle Ages, the Renaissance, the seventeenth and eighteenth centuries knew, and what people of the nineteenth century must also have known, even if they did not want to—that women's sexual appetites are greater than men's.

Bibliographical Note

The sexual imagery in *Dracula* and the varieties of sexual activity implied by vampirism have been discussed by C. F. Bentley in "The Monster in the Bedroom: Sexual Symbolism in Bram Stoker's *Dracula*" (Literature and Psychology 22: 27–34). In "Fictional Conventions and Sexuality in *Dracula*" (Victorian Newsletter 42:20–22) Carrol L. Fry points out that Lucy and Mina are the pure women of Victorian fiction, that Dracula is a rake, and that vampirism is surrogate intercourse; but she does not really pursue Stoker's transformation of the fictional conventions.

9

Dracula: The Gnostic Quest and Victorian Wasteland

Mark M. Hennelly, Jr.

In *Dracula* (1897), when Mina Harker reads her husband's Transylvanian journal and relates it to the recent enigmatic events in London, she discovers that "There seems to be through it all some thread of continuity"[1] and the attentive reader makes an identical discovery in Bram Stoker's long-neglected tale of two cultures. Until now there have been occasional folkloric,[2] psycho-sexual,[3] and even political[4] readings of the novel; but such studies generally see this horror classic as a *sui generis* phenomenon and not as a sign of the times, not as a drama of conflicting epistemologies, which is so much a part of the Victorian tradition and which Dracula presents with brutal candor. Although the "Gothic" tradition is peripheral to this study, it is even more surprising that treatments of the Gothic or Romantic novel have almost totally neglected Stoker's most terrifying example of the genre. For instance, in Robert Kiely's otherwise excellent *The Romantic Novel in England*, the summarial definition seems written precisely for *Dracula:* "the most daring thematic innovations of the romantic novelists—the use of the supernatural and of wild nature, of dreams and madness, of physical violence and perverse sexuality—are played ironically or melodramatically against the conventions which they impugn. In terms of setting, tone, and character grouping, romantic novelists often seem to be writing two books in one." However, on the next and final page, he concludes: "After *Wuthering Heights*, it is difficult to find any work which carries the possibilities of intuition, subjectivity, or lyricism further in the novel without losing the old fashioned outlines of form altogether."[5]

It is the thesis of this study that besides being a masterpiece of Gothicism (which itself is ultimately concerned with the problem of *belief* in the Demiurge), *Dracula* is an allegory of rival epistemologies in quest of a gnosis

This article originally appeared in *English Literature in Transition* 20 (1977).

which will rehabilitate the Victorian wasteland; and as its conclusion dramatizes, this rehabilitation demands a *transfusion*, the metaphor is inevitable, from the blood-knowledge of Dracula. Caught between two worlds, the now anemic nineteenth century all but dead, the twentieth powerless to be born without fertile, ideological conception, fin-de-siècle England desperately needs redemption. As Van Helsing announces: "We go out as the old knights of the Cross to redeem . . . . we are pledged to set the world free" (pp. 354–55).

Symbolizing the battleground between Ancients and Moderns, the Wasteland often provides a psychoscape for Victorian poetry and fiction; and the "waste land" of Tennyson's "Morte d'Arthur," the "ominous tract" of Browning's "Childe Roland," Arnold's "darkling plain" of "Dover Beach," Dickens's Coketown, and Hardy's Egdon Heath are just some examples of its prevalent imagery. In fact, In his study of the subject, Curtis Dahl concludes: "The wastland, often thought to be a modern discovery, had been thoroughly explored by the Victorians before the twentieth century was born."[6] In *Dracula*, Dr. Seward, alter-ego for the Victorian reader, makes clear the relationship between his wasted London, "under brown fog" like T. S. Eliots's, and his own blasted, scientific beliefs: "It was a shock for me to turn from the wonderful smoky beauty of a sunset over London, with its lurid lights and inky shadows and all the marvellous tints that come on foul clouds even as on foul water, and to realize all the grim sternness of my own cold stone building, with its wealth of breathing misery, and my own desolate heart to endure it all" (pp. 127–28). Here the oxymoron suggests that even naturally-wasted London is better than his own artificially-petrified, "desolate heart." However, the most salient passage for the wasteland theme, and one of the more remarkable passages in Victorian literature, locates the "waste of desolation" (p. 418) in London's geographic other-self, Transylvania—even the repeated *desolate* condition serves to link the two cultures. The broken-English here is characteristically Van Helsing's; and this description of Dracula's motivation and kingdom prompts his already mentioned pledge to "set the world free":

I have told them how the measure of leaving his own barren land—barren of peoples—and coming to a new land where life of man teems till they are like the multitude of standing corn, was the work of centuries. Were another of the Un-Dead, like him, to try to do what he has done, perhaps not all the centuries of the world that have been, or that will be, could aid him. With this one, all the forces of nature that are occult and deep and strong must have worked together in some wondrous way. The very place, where he have been alive, Un-Dead for all these centuries, is full of strangeness of the geologic and chemical world. There are deep caverns and fissures that reach none know whither. There have been volcanoes, some of whose openings still send out waters of strange properties, and gases that kill or make to vivify. Doubtless, there is something magnetic or electric in some of these combinations or occult forces which work for physical life in strange way; and in himself were from the first some great qualities. In a hard and warlike time he was celebrate that he have more iron nerve, more subtle brain, more braver heart, than any man. In him some vital principle have in strange way found their utmost; and as his body keep strong and grow and thrive, so his brain grow too. All this without that diabolic aid which is surely to him; for it have to yield to the powers that come from, and are, symbolic of good. (p. 353)

The meaning of this lengthy passage is central to the understanding of *Dracula*. Both nocturnal-lunar Transylvania and diurnal-solar London[7] are "barren land[s]"; and each desperately needs the strength of the other to heal its own sterility. In this sense, not only do the Occidental vampire hunters embark upon a "great quest" (p. 259), "a wild adventure. . . . into unknown places and unknown ways" (p. 395); but Dracula similarly initiates "his quest" (p. 48) for an unknown gnosis. Dracula with his ancient "child-brain" searches for the "man-brain" (pp. 376–77) of modern self-consciousness; while what Van Helsing calls the "man-brains" of the Londoners seek the primitive passion and natural energy of the non-repressed "child-brain" (ibid.) of Transylvania, a condition the British recall subliminally in both memory and desire. In this sense the novel's action concerns the intimate relationships between the two corollary quests and between past and present values. Moreover, the above excerpt reveals that Dracula is a kind of primitive Corn God who "directs the elements" (p. 263), a Fisher King (Stoker's dream of a "vampire king rising from his tomb" precipitated the novel)[8] who has anachronistically as "this man-that-was" (p. 264) lived long past his prime and rests in an unholy Perilous Chapel (p. 265). Now he must be slain and replaced by a viable, young, twentieth century totem—at least he must be slain and his energy reabsorbed if the London wasteland is to be renewed and if Eliot's "hooded hordes swarming" are to be checked. Thus, although once a "vital principle . . . symbolic of good," the Count's energy is now only malign. At the cosmic level of the "geologic and chemical world," these "gases," Dracula's *élan vital,* can either "kill or make to vivify" depending, at the personal level, on whether they are repressed as with Lucy, or honestly accepted as with Mina.

However, we anticipate ourselves. Let us simply conclude by hearing two clarifying but general appraisals of cultural repression, neither of which have *Dracula* in mind. First, Carl Jung describes fiction dealing with the "collective unconscious" in a way particularly relevant to "all the forces of nature that are occult and deep and strong": It "is a strange something that derives its existence from the hinterland of man's mind—that suggests the abyss of time separating us from the pre-human ages, or evokes a super-human world of contrasting light and darkness. It is a primordial experience which surpasses man's understanding, and to which he is in danger of succumbing. The value and the force of the experience are given by its enormity. It arises from timeless depths; it is foreign and cold, many-sided, demonic and grotesque."[9] Secondly, Elliot Gose ends his discussion of the nineteenth century "Irrational" novel (again, *Dracula* is omitted) with an evaluation peculiarly suited to Stoker's archetypal drama and anticipating the symbolism of Dracula's "orderly disorder" (p. 331) in London: "Beneath the ordered society of his time each [novelist of the Irrational] saw an unordered chaos, a world disintegrating, a new order waiting to be established. Each saw a spectacle, perhaps because it was true of Victorian society, but more fundamentally because each had descended within himself and confronted in that heart of darkness not only the death of life but the unborn shape of future life. Their novels embody that life."[10]

As stated earlier, the quest to redeem this wasteland is not a search for a literal grail or treasure, but as Van Helsing understands a search for redemptive knowledge: "We shall go to make our search—if I can call it so, for it is not a search but knowing" (p. 348). Many literary historians have found this gnostic quest to be the central theme of nineteenth-century letters and of the Victorian arts in particular. Morse Peckham, for example, labels the endeavor the "orientative drive" and devotes his entire *Beyond the Tragic Vision*[11] to pursuing the many varieties of this quest. Kristian Smidt, on the other hand, limiting his treatment to "The Intellectual Quest of the Victorian Poets," discovers that "Characteristically the poetry of the Victorian period deals with a search or quest—for knowledge or for something symbolizing knowledge and certainty."[12] And a novel like *Silas Marner*, with its repeated insistence on traditional *faith, belief,* and *trust* in the face of the *mysteries* of life, perfectly exemplifies the orthodox Victorian solution. Thus once-doubting Silas finally discovers the continuity between past and present epistemologies and thereby renews his personal wasteland: "By seeking what was needful for Eppie, by sharing the effect that everything produced on her, he had himself come to appropriate the forms of custom and belief which were the mould of Raveloe life; and as, with reawakening sensibilities, memory also reawakened, he had begun to ponder over the elements of his old faith, and blend them with his new impressions, till he recovered a consciousness of unity between past and present" (chapt. 16).

Dracula, however, explores the unorthodox and alien beliefs demanded by Van Helsing's hypothesis that "There are always mysteries in life" (p. 210). As he repeatedly insists to Seward and the others: "I want you to believe. . . . To believe in things you cannot. Let me illustrate. I heard once of an American who so defined faith: 'that faculty which enables us to believe things we know to be untrue.' For one, I follow that man. He meant that we shall have an open mind . . ." (p. 211). The action of the novel dramatizes the gnostic value of this "open mind" and concurrently tests the epistemological flexibility of various frames of mind: Scepticism (pp. 260, 367–68), Transcendentalism (p. 373), Empiricism and the Philosophy of Crime (p. 377), Superstition (pp. 262–63), and most importantly, Scientific Rationalism: "our scientific, sceptical, matter-of-fact nineteenth-century" (p. 262). As Van Helsing iconoclastically charges: "Ah, it is the fault of our science that it wants to explain all; and if it explains not, then it says there is nothing to explain" (p. 209). And again: "In this enlightened age, when men believe not even what they see, the doubting of wise men would be his [Dracula's] greatest strength" (p. 355). Consequently, the quest for the count is actually a quest for the all-believing "open mind" which, like Silas Marner's, can accommodate both past superstitions and present faith, for as Van Helsing believes: "To superstition we must trust at first; it was man's faith in the early, and it have its root in faith still" (p. 362). And it is past superstitions, particularly the belief in vampires and Dracula's blood-knowledge, from which English orthodox faith so desperately needs a transfusion. As Walter E. Houghton indicates in *The Victorian Frame of Mind*—and this paradox is what makes *Dracula* a tell-tale sign of the times —"The Victorian mind was rigid and dogmatic, but it was criticized [for being so]." However: "It looks as if the open and flexible mind was also Victorian because, unlike the rigid-dogmatic mind with its long history, it was largely indigenous to the nineteenth century."[13]

From the novel's brief Preface (omitted in some editions) to its postscript Note, the epistolary style also argues for the gnostic condition of the "open mind." The Preface maintains that such a collection of personal and public papers "given from the standpoint and within the range of knowledge of those who made them" insures "that a history almost at variance with the possibilities of later-day belief may stand forth as simple fact" (vii). Again, the emphasis here revolves around the questions of "range of knowledge," "latter-day belief," and "simple fact," inherent in earlier-day superstitions, that vampires do exist. Moreover, the epistolary style always insists upon the relativity of knowledge and the problem of absolute certainty. And here, although Stoker "borrowed" his style from contemporary Wilkie Collins,[14] it nevertheless, observing Kiely's criterion of maintaining "old fashioned outlines of form," thematically links Samuel Richardson and the past dawn of English fiction with present practice. Lionel Stevenson's remarks on "The Relativity of Truth in Victorian Fiction" are consequently relevant here: "They [Victorian novelists] stand as transitional figures between the confidence in objective fact that characterizes the age of reason and the unabashed solipsism that came into fiction in the present century through the stream of consciousness technique."[15] In another sense, the disappearance of an omniscient narrator in *Dracula* reflects the atrophy of God and traditional faith so symptomatic of the Victorian wasteland: hence the small, central group of splintered selves is also searching for a new stockpile of communal and personal values. As J. Hillis Miller states the problem: "If Victorian fiction focuses on inter-human relations as the arena of a search for self-fulfillment, this search is governed not only by the apparent absence of God but also by the effacement of any ontological foundation for the self."[16] The last words of the postscript Note echo the diction of the Preface as Harker reports Van Helsing's final thoughts on gnostic credibility: "We want no proofs: we ask none to believe us! This boy [Harker's son] will someday know. . . . Later on

he will understand . . ." (p. 418). Thus, and as we shall later see, it is this final
symbol of the new, twentieth-century man who will ultimately inherit the renewed wasteland and this collective testimonial and legacy of open-minded
belief, the novel itself.

By dramatizing the intimate identity between Transylvania and London,
between vampirism and civilization, the circular structure of *Dracula*, whose
locale shifts from the Carpathians to England and then back to Transylvania,
also reveals the thematic link between the epistemologies of the two wasted
kingdoms. The central point, as Van Helsing understands, is: "For it is not the
least of its terrors that this evil thing is rooted deep in all good" (p. 265). Or in
the cockney accents of Thomas Bilder, the London zoo-keeper: "There's a deal
of the same nature in us as in them theer animiles" (p. 149). For example,
Dracula's castle is a schizoid dwelling with upper, fashionable apartments and
even a Victorian library but also with lower crypts and vaults while, analo-
gously, Dr. Seward's Victorian mansion conceals a lunatic asylum, complete
with fledgling vampire, beneath it. Dracula has three lovers; Lucy has three
suitors. Dracula hypnotizes; Van Helsing hypnotizes. Dracula sucks blood; Van
Helsing transfuses blood; and once, in fact, Seward "suck[ed]" (p. 124) blood
from a gangrenous wound of Van Helsing. Dracula wears Harker's British
clothes to steal babies and later in London even wears a "hat of straw" (p. 350).
Additionally, there is a consistently-stressed analogy between vampirism and
Christianity; and both, given the insights of Frazer, Jessie Weston, and Freud's
Totem and Taboo, seem related to the Oedipal Fisher-King and the wasteland.
Thus vampirism deals with "zoophagy"; Christianity with eating the body and
drinking the blood of Christ—"the Scriptural phrase, 'For the blood is the life!' "
(p. 257). Both employ numerous rituals and complicated liturgy, for example
"the Vampire's baptism of blood" (p. 356). And lastly, both are locked in a
theomachy for control of the world (Crucifix and Host against Demiurge), as
Van Helsing notes: "The devil may work against us for all he's worth, but God
sends us men when we want them" (p. 163). In fact, as Robert Stevens argues
in the "The Exorcism of England's Gothic Demon," the Irish sensibility (like
Stoker's) is most aware of such epistemological problems with religious "certainty": "If that faith in things seen, that affirmative belief that the cosmos
'functions,' can be interpreted as a British and protestant faith, then one should
not be surprised to find a more intense collective anxiety manifest in Catholic
Ireland."[17] At any rate, the holistic and redemptive knowledge which understands this primal identity between "the world . . . of good men [and] . . .
monsters" (p. 246) enables the Victorians to use "various armaments—the spiritual in the left hand, the mortal in the right" (p. 336). Finally, it teaches, in the
words of Van Helsing's favorite metaphor, that the *felix culpa*, or fortunate fall
to belief in vampires, is the only way to save the wasteland: we "must pass

through the bitter waters to reach the sweet" (p. 222, see also pp. 133, 187). Or as Harker learns, each "new pain" is a "means to a good end" (p. 363).

Turning to the allegorical characters, we discover the same Victorian concern with wasteland sterility, open-minded epistemology, and Jekyll-Hyde repression. Renfield, first of all, is a native zoophagist or vampire, one alive and unwell in London before the "foreign" Dracula is ever smuggled ashore. Thus his manic-depressive schizophrenia, that "combination" of "homocidal and religious mania" (p. 111), is emblematic of the latent dualism in the Victorian personality; and his lunacy must be made manifest and resolved for the solar wasteland to be renewed. If so unveiled and openly tamed or domesticated, Renfield's manic but vital energy can certainly prove therapeutic and reveal the inner "method in his madness" (p. 76). He then may truly and wholly become the visionary epistemologist "talking elemental philosophy . . . with the manner of a polished gentleman" (p. 257). And the rich potential of this new gentleman, not bound by the rigidity of caste like Lord Godalming, is most apparent when Renfield self-sacrificially uses his vampire-madness to attempt to trap the Count and save Mina (pp. 360 ff.). Consequently, and much like Harker, Renfield's wish to "not deceive myself" allows him to distinguish between "dream" and "grim reality" (p. 306) and makes this "sanest lunatic" (p. 273) an epistemological model for the other Victorians. As Van Helsing admits, "I may gain more knowledge out of the folly of this madman than I shall from the teaching of the most wise" (p. 281).

Quincey Morris, the Texan and prior suitor of Lucy, is not quite as simple-minded as he seems; or at least his simple-mindedness finally becomes an analogue of open-mindedness. Like Van Helsing and Dracula, he represents a foreign quality which the Victorians need to absorb. Because of his preoccupation with knives and Winchesters, it is easy enough to see Morris, the "dominant spirit" (p. 337), as the symbol of potent, non-paralyzed activity, "always . . . the one to arrange the plan of action" (ibid.). However, the fact that "Quincey's head is level" (p. 294), that "His head is what you call in plane with the horizon' (p. 324), and most importantly that he "accepts all things, and accepts them in the spirit of cool bravery" (p. 230), all suggests that he suffers neither from wasteland duality nor gnostic rigidity. Hence it is most fitting that the new man, the Harkers' child, should be called primarily *Quincey*, besides, as we will see, his other tacit names.

Arthur Holmwood, or *Lord* Godalming, emblemizes class, wealth, and aristocratic values, all instances of decay in the Victorian wasteland. As Renfield, the potential true gentleman, characterizes the gentleman cult: "You . . . who by nationality, by heredity, . . . are fitted to hold your respective" place in society (p. 268). Discussing this epistemological "Problem of Spiritual Authority in the Nineteenth Century," Northrop Frye relevantly observes that "The ascendant class, therefore, and more particularly the aristocracy, comes to represent an ideal authority, expressed in the term 'gentleman,' at the point in history at which its effective temporal authority had begun to decline . . . . The special function of the aristocracy has always included the art of putting on a show, of dramatizing a way of life."[18] However, like King Arthur, this Arthur's way of life is finally ineffectual; his aristocratic code is too divorced from natural values as symbolized by his replacement of the natural *Holmwood* with the divine-right (*God-*) of noblesse oblige pedigree (*-alming*). Thus his bride-to-be is appropriately seduced by Dracula, the demiurge of the natural world; and Arthur's sterile lack of open-minded belief renders him unable "to believe things we know to be untrue.". As he confesses to Van Helsing: "I did not trust you because I did not know you" (p. 243). Consequently, chivalric Arthur "make[s] the only atonement in my power" (p. 243) which, actually, is the provision of funds and influence for the vampire hunt. Thus he loses his Guinevere and wastes his kingdom.

Dr. Seward represents Science but is also the detached alter-ego of the sceptical Victorian reader since his diary consumes so much of the narrative and since what he calls "the dogged argumentativeness of my nature" (p. 217) provokes him repeatedly to question belief in the unknown: "Surely there must be *some* rational explanation of all these mysterious things" (p. 223, italics Stoker's). Thus Van Helsing instructs Seward along with the reader, clue by clue, about the existence of vampires. As the good doctor remarks: "Professor, let me be your pet student again. Tell me the thesis, so that I may apply your knowledge as you go on. At present I am going in my mind from point to point as a mad man, and not a sane one, follows as idea" (p. 211). Moreover, and as this temporary "madness" and his self-identification with Renfield implies (p. 118), Seward himself is corrupted by wasteland duality. As we've heard, he has "sucked" Van Helsing's blood; his mansion embodies a split-personality, and he later betrays a vampirish "savage delight" (p. 232) in contemplating the beheading of his one-time beloved, Lucy. Significantly, his "branch of science" is "brain knowledge"—that "vital aspect—the knowledge of the brain" (p. 78); and very early he confesses that his own personality is guided both by "unconscious celebration" and its "conscious brother" (p. 76). At its best, such Jekyll-Hydeism allows him to see that his homicidal, "unhallowed work" against Dracula ironically comes under the "perils of the law" (p. 219) of the parochial, Victorian penal code. On the other hand, at its most repressive, this dualism renders him a doubting Thomas, willing to convict the "abnormally clever" Van Helsing as the vampire (pp. 223–24). Moreover, his sexual repression is clearly evident when, as "sperm" drops from the candle onto Lucy's coffin, he considers the ghoulish business "as much an affront to the dead as it would have been to have stripped of her clothing in her sleep while living" (p. 217). However, when Seward finally accepts the "dual life" (p. 220) of Lucy, he symbolically (like, hopefully, the Victorian reader) also accepts his own.

If Seward is alter-ego for the reader as detached spectator, Jonathan Harker, who begins the novel on an "unknown night journey" (p. 12), is a "sufficient substitute" (p. 19) for the reader as actively questing knight-errant.[19] In this sense, his name (*Hark!*) flashes a danger-signal or caveat to the Victorian audience lest it too fall victim to the arid beliefs of the wasteland—especially close-minded legalisms since Harker, as London solicitor, allegorically represents the Law. Moreover, his development as scapegoat-questor places him within that favorite nineteenth-century genre, the *Bildungsroman*. He thus is also descendant of the prototypical British slayer of monsters as he arrives in Transylvania on "the eve of St. George's Day" (p. 5). His letter of reference from Mr. Hawkins to the Count provides a fitting prologue to his development since it praises his lifesaving faith but also implies his vulnerable innocence and renders suspect the Victorian definition of "manhood": "He is a young man, full of energy and talent in his own way, and of a very faithful disposition. He is discreet and silent and has grown into manhood in my service" (p. 19).

Thus he becomes Dracula's prisoner in the Perilous Castle "without that protection of the law" (p. 49) which had been his insulation against the realities of natural life. Here Harker's repression, "an agony of delightful anticipation" (p. 42), is most evident when he is nearly seduced by the three succubi in the awful daring of a moment's surrender. In this oneiro-vision, the sexual frustrations of the Victorian groom-to-be serve to prophetically link the blond succubus with his own intended, Mina: "I seemed to know her face, and to know it in connection with some dreamy fear, but I could not recollect at the moment how or where. . . . I felt in my heart a wicked, burning desire that they would kiss me with those red lips. It is not good to note this down; lest some day it should meet Mina's eyes and cause her pain; but it is the truth" (p. 41). Such honesty ultimately saves Harker; and even after he suppresses the Transylvanian experience, he still believes his earlier conviction: "I *must* know the truth" (p. 44, italics Stoker's). Throughout the novel, this Galahad-figure's fate tacitly hinges upon Dracula's, the Fisher King. When he finally returns to the Perilous Castle and with the phallic Kikri knife helps to slay Dracula (p. 416), Harker no longer "felt impotent" (p. 206) but reclaims the sexual prerogatives which Dracula had usurped and produces a new male heir on the very anniversary of the Count's ritualistic beheading and symbolic castration, or "sterilization." Stoker's own honesty here about Victorian sexual repression is reminiscent of Dickens' more fanciful version in *David Copperfield*, for when Uriah Heep (who David says "knew me better than I knew myself") gloats to David: "I love the ground my Agnes walks on," the young hero dreams that he snatches "a red hot . . . poker" from the fire and pierces "him through the body" and is repeatedly "haunted" by this fantasy (chapt. 25). But Harker is more realistic (in both senses) than David; and as questor only he thematically unites cup and lance, or tomb and knife, renews the wasteland, and personally "wake[s] again to the realities of life" (p. 333).

As students are quick to point out, the early correspondence between Lucy and Mina seems to be the only "boring" section of the novel (though the overdrawn and somewhat anti-climactic conclusion is an actual flaw). However, the saccharine melodrama of this brief section creates an appropriate and ironic backdrop for the real horrors about to be visited upon the two girls and hence also serves to explode the life-denying conventions of Victorian sentimentality in whose wasteland, as Eliot implies, symbolic "death had undone so many." The repercussions of this shock further agitate the Victorian reader who has been conditioned to expect no danger for, or ambivalence from, a heroine named *Lucy*, the principle of right light. However, most simply the novel teaches that "There are darknesses in life, and there are lights" (p. 201). When this fiancée of Arthur betrays her "dual life" (p. 220), when "false Lucy" and "true Lucy" (p. 341) begin to merge, and when she becomes through the life-blood of all her various donors a symbolic "polyandrist" and literal "Medusa" (p. 232), her role as Guinevere (etymologically "white" or "fair" lady), scape-goat of an unnatural and wasted courtly-love code, is clear. As Lucy's transformation indicates, the stereotyped Victorian woman, elevated on a pedestal or embowered in an ivory tower like the Lady of Shalott, denies belief in the life-giving forces of carnal nature and produces the wasteland nightmare: "She seemed like a nightmare of Lucy as she lay there; the pointed teeth, the blood-stained, voluptuous mouth—which it made one shudder to see—the whole carnal and unspiritual appearance, seeming like a devilish mockery of Lucy's sweet purity" (pp. 234–35).

However, if the blood of Dracula lethally drowns hitherto one-sided Lucy, it therapeutically baptizes, and provides rebirth for, diminutive *Mina*—Wilhimina, the "resolute protectoress." In this sense, there are also two Minas in the novel. The early Mina, teacher of Victorian "etiquette and decorum" (p. 188), scoffs at the idea of the "New Woman" (p. 98), wishes to "build . . . castles in the air" (p. 59), and feels that her husband holding her arm in public is "improper" (p. 188). However, she grows from this emblem of angelic Victorian morality to the stature of the later Mina who possesses a "man's brain . . . and a woman's heart" (p. 258). Thus as androgynous Teiresias in the wasteland, her open-minded epistemology balances the close-minded gnoses of the vampire hunters: "her tender faith against all our fears and doubting" (p. 340). And of course it is when Mina embraces Dracula in what Seward terms "that terrible and horrid position" (p. 313), that she drinks his baptismal blood and restorative beliefs. This ichor, the "poison that distils itself out of good things" (p. 356), provides an antidote by a kind of homeopathic magic to wasteland sterility. And Mina is able to pass on this old new-life through the veins of her son. As psychopomp, her repeated slogan becomes a liberating epigraph for the theme of the entire novel: "There must be no concealment . . . Alas! we have had too much already" (p. 320).

Finally, Van Helsing and Dracula himself are both quite similar and represent vital, foreign imports which the insular Victorian creed must smuggle in for restoration of domestic tranquility. Like the Count, Van Helsing transfuses blood, has had his blood "sucked" by Seward, is an isolated, enigmatic personality, and is also the same kind of "master amongst men" (p. 353) that Dracula is. Indeed both vie in a psychomachia over Mina's soul; and Van Helsing even boasts of telepathic powers over the Count: "I too, am wily; and I think his mind in a little while" (p. 340). Furthermore, as the Professor peripatetically instructs the others in the ways of vampirism (Hell-Singer?), his constant, thematic imperatives are "trust" and "believe." As Seward suggests:

> He is a seemingly arbitrary man, but this is because he knows what he is talking about better than anyone else. He is a philosopher and metaphysician, and one of the most advanced scientists of his day; and he has, I believe an absolutely open mind. This, with an iron nerve, a temper of ice-brook, an indomitable resolution, self-command, and toleration exalted from virtues to blessings, and the kindliest and truest heart that beats—these form his equipment for the noble work that he is doing for mankind—work both in theory and practice, for his views are as wide as his all embracing sympathy. (p. 123)

However, for all this learning and blessed virtue, Van Helsing, unlike the somewhat similar Mordecai in *Daniel Deronda,* is not an inhuman oracle; rather, as Seward fails to perceive, his personal life too has become a wasteland: "My life is a barren and lonely one, and so full of work that I have not had much time for friendships" (p. 203). Thus, Van Helsing's feet of human clay save him from becoming the type of foreign mentor, like Will Ladislaw in *Middlemarch,* so stereotypically common in Victorian fiction; and he is more like the sympathetic Herr Klesmer in *Daniel Deronda,* though much grander in scale than that music teacher. In fact, he periodically breaks down under the strain of the psychomachia; "the very instinct of man" in him is sorely tempted by the "new emotion" of sex before the "voluptuous" succubi (p. 409); and he "tremble[s]" during his "butchery" (p. 410) of these vampiresses. And even this Merlin-figure was once a non-believer: "I admit that at first I was sceptic. Were it not that through long years I have train myself to keep an open mind, I could not have believe until such time as that fact thunder on my ear" (p. 260). Still armed with his Catholic faith, so foreign to low-church Protestantism, and his "open mind," he is the primary savior of the wasteland. His gospel finally becomes the redeeming deed of the novel: "I may err—I am but man; but I believe in all I do" (p. 181).

And lastly, Dracula. As villain, he transcends the run of the mill malice of such incarnations of Victorian vice as Alex D'Urbeville, Fagin, or George Eliot's Grandcourt although his sometime sneering humor often does echo them. As he taunts his anemic pursuers: "You think to baffle me, you—with your pale faces all in a row, like sheep in a butcher's. You shall be sorry yet, each of you! You think you have left me without a place to rest; but I have more. My revenge is just begun" (pp. 338–39). Still, Dracula's "revenge" brands him as Archetypal Rebel; and his role is much closer to Milton's Satan and his descendants, the nineteenth-century Prometheans—Manfred, Cain, Ahab, Frankenstein's Monster, and Healthcliff. As a matter of fact, as Demiurge or Rival of God, "this terrible and mysterious enemy" (p. 259) is compared to "Judas" (p. 55), but most often to "the Evil one" himself (p. 265); while Renfield's madness is illuminating enough to even call Dracula "God" (p. 296). However, as indicated throughout this essay, the Count is also an anachronistic Fisher King on his own black "quest" (p. 48) of "creeping into knowledge" (p. 334). His "child-brain," the primitive personality or Id, must be re-absorbed by the Victorian "man-brain"; and the Count himself must be "sterilis[ed]" (p. 328) and his literal *sang-froid* replaced with a new warm-blooded King for restoration of the wasteland. His crossing to London on the ship *Demeter* symbolically underscores this need for cyclic rebirth. Moreover, one of Dracula's opening speeches to Victorian Harker heralds his role as redeeming gnostic: "There is reason in all things as they are, and did you see with my eyes and know with my knowledge, you would perhaps better understand" (p. 23).

Finally, we hear that "There have been from the loins of this very one great men and good women" (p. 265); and this anticipates the birth of the Harker child through whose veins run not only the Victorian blood of his parents but also the vitality of the Count whose blood Mina has drunk. And this new, twentieth-century Fisher King, appropriately born on the anniversary of Dracula's death, not only represents the ancient blood-knowledge of his second father; but shoring these fragments against England's ruin, "his bundle of names links all" the allegorical epistemologies of the "little band of men together" (p. 218). The emphasis of the last sentences of the novel on acquired beliefs reveals the polynomial child's inherited, new knowledge: "We want no proofs; we ask none to *believe* us! This boy will some day *know* her sweetness and loving care; later on he will *understand* how some men so loved her that they did dare much for her sake" (p. 418, italics mine). And, we might add, he will *know* how much these Victorian "old knights of the Cross" dared "to redeem" the wasteland and "to set the world free" (pp. 354–55).

Notes

1. Bram Stoker, *Dracula* (New York: Modern Library, 1897), p. 96. All subsequent quotations are from this edition and are incorporated within the text.

2. See Grigore Nandris, "The Historical Dracula: The Theme of His Legend in the Western and in the Eastern Literatures of Europe," *Comparative Literature Studies*, 3:4 (1966), 367–96.

3. See C. F. Bentley, "The Monster in the Bedroom: Sexual Symbolism in Bram Stoker's *Dracula*," *Literature and Psychology*, 22:1 (1972), 27–34; and Joseph S. Bierman, "*Dracula*: Prolonged Childhood Illness, and the Oral Triad," *American Imago*, 29 (Summer 1972), 186–98.

4. See Richard Wasson, "The Politics of *Dracula*," *English Literature in Transition*, 9:1 (1966). 24–27. The interested reader should also consult: Carrol L. Fry, "Fictional Conventions and Sexuality in *Dracula*," *Victorian Newsletter*, No. 42 (Fall 1972), 20–22; Royce MacGillivray, "*Dracula*: Bram Stoker's Spoiled Masterpiece, *Queen's Quarterly*, 79 (Winter 1972), 518–27; and two French studies: Gérard Stein, "*Dracula*, ou la circulation du 'sans,'" *Littérature*, No. 8 (Dec. 1972), 87–99; and Jean Gattegno's essay which generally discusses "belief," "Folie, croyance, et fantastique dans *Dracula*," *Littérature*, No. 8 (Dec. 1972), 72–83. See also the relevant remarks on the quest-romance in Thomas R. Thornburg's "The Questor and the Castle: The Gothic Novel as Myth, with Special Reference to Bram Stoker's *Dracula*," a Ball State University Ph.D. Thesis (1969), seen only in abstract form.

5. (Cambridge: Harvard Univ. Press, 1972), pp. 254–55.

6. "The Victorian Wasteland," in *Victorian Literature: Modern Essays in Criticism*, ed. by Austin Wright (London: Oxford Univ. Press, 1961), p. 40, reprinted from *College English*, 16 (March 1955), 341–47. Other discussions of the wasteland theme are: Robert G. Stange, "The Victorian City and the Frightened Poets," *Victorian Studies*, 11: Supplement (Summer 1968), 627–40; John B. Rosenberg, "Varieties of Infernal Experience," *Hudson Review*, 23 (Autumn 1970), 454–80, especially 465ff.; John R. Reed, "Mixing Memory and Desire in Late Victorian Literature," *English Literature in Transition* 14:1 (1971), 1–15; and especially John Vickery's recent book, *The Literary Impact of the Golden Bough* (Princeton: Princeton Univ. Press, 1973).

7. See p. 128 for a discussion of the "malign influence" of sun and moon at different periods, and p. 264 for a discussion of the limitations of the Count's lunar powers. This "dual life" theme has, of course, become a touchstone for criticism of nineteenth-century literature. For example, John E. Stoll remarks: "Inherited in great part from the 18th century separation of intellect and feeling, judgement and fancy, sense and sensibility, psychological duality is a distinctive characteristic of the 19th century as a whole, affects all forms of literature, and should not be confined to the American *or* British novel alone"; in "Psychological Dissociation in the Victorian Novel," *Literature and Psychology*, 20:2 (1970), 63–64. See also Masao Miyoshi's book-length treatment of the subject, *The Divided Self* (New York: New York Univ. Press, 1969). Miyoshi also fails to mention *Dracula*. Finally see Gattegno's discussion of "madness" in *Dracula*, especially 73–76.

8. See H. Ludlam, *A Biography of Dracula: The Life Story of Bram Stoker* (London: W. Foulsham, 1962), pp. 99–100.

9. *Modern Man in Search of a Soul* (London: Routledge & Kegan Paul, 1933), pp. 180–81.

10. *Imagination Indulged: The Irrational in the Nineteenth Century Novel* (Montreal: McGill-Queen's Univ. Press, 1972), p. 176. Gose also cites the above quotation from Jung, pp. 173–74.

11. (New York: George Braziller, 1962), passim.

12. In *British Victorian Literature: Recent Revaluations*, ed. by Shiv Kamar (New York: New York Univ. Press, 1969), pp. 54–55; from *College English*, 40 (April 1959), 90–102. For other relevant discussions of the gnostic quest in nineteenth-century literature, see L. J. Swingle, "Frankenstein's Monster and Its Romantic Relatives: Problems of Knowledge in English Litera-

ture," *Texas Studies in Literature and Language*, 40 (Spring 1973), 51–66, and my "Oedipus and Orpheus in the Maelström: The Traumatic Rebirth of the Artist," *Poe Studies*, 9 (June 1976), as of this writing, pages not yet assigned.

13. (New Haven: Yale Univ. Press, 1957), p. 176.

14. See Ludlam, p. 101.

15. In *Victorian Essays: A Symposium*, ed. by Warren D. Anderson and Thomas D. Clareson (Oberlin, Ohio: Kent State Univ. Press, 1967), p. 86. See also Stein on *Dracula's* style, *passim*.

16. *The Form of Victorian Fiction* (Notre Dame: Univ. of Notre Dame Press, 1968), p. 45.

17. *Midwest Quarterly*, 14 (Winter 1973), 152. Such anxiety would probably be even more true of Protestant Stoker raised in Clontarf, the arch-Catholic home of a presiding Carmelite monastery, and raised by a quiet, civil-servant father and free-thinking, feminist mother; Ludlam, pp. 11–15.

18. In *Backgrounds to Victorian Literature*, ed. by Richard Levine (San Francisco: Chandler Publishing Co., 1967), p. 126, reprinted from *Literary Views: Critical and Historical Essays*, ed. by Carroll Camden (Chicago: Univ. of Chicago Press, 1964), pp. 145–58.

19. Thornburg makes this same point in his abstract: *Dissertation Abstracts International*, 31 (1969), 4752A (Ball State). For the relevance of the questing-knight of Romance theme to "Romantic" literature, see also my "*Waverley* and Romanticism," *Nineteenth-Century Fiction*, 28 (Sept. 1973), 194–209, especially 194–96, and Harold Bloom, "The Internalization of Quest-Romance," *Yale Review*, 58 (Summer 1969), 526–36, reprinted as Chapter 2 in Bloom's *The Ringers in the Tower* (Chicago: Univ. of Chicago Press, 1971). Finally, see Stein on the "initiation" theme in *Dracula*, especially 96ff.

10

Dracula: The Unseen Face in the Mirror

Carol A. Senf

The fault, dear Brutus, is not in our stars,
But in ourselves, that we are underlings.
                              Julius Caesar, I, ii, 134–35

Published in 1896, *Dracula* is an immensely popular novel which has never
been out of print, has been translated into at least a dozen languages, and has
been the subject of more films than any other novel. Only recently, however,
have students of literature begun to take it seriously, partially because of the
burgeoning interest in popular culture and partially because *Dracula* is a work
which raises a number of troubling questions about ourselves and our society.[1]
Despite this growing interest in Bram Stoker's best-known novel, the majority
of literary critics read *Dracula* as a popular myth about the opposition of Good
and evil without bothering to address more specifically literary matters such as
style, characterization, and method of narration. This article, on the other hand,
focuses on Stoker's narrative technique in general and specifically on his choice
of unreliable narrators. As a result, my reading of *Dracula* is a departure from
most standard interpretations in that it revolves, not around the conquest of Evil
by Good, but on the similarities between the two.

   More familiar with the numerous film interpretations than with Stoker's
novel, most modern readers are likely to be surprised by *Dracula* and its intensely topical themes; and both the setting and the method of narration which
Stoker chose contribute to this sense of immediacy. Instead of taking place in a
remote Transylvanian castle or a timeless and dreamlike "anywhere," most of
the action occurs in nineteenth-century London. Furthermore, Stoker de-empha-

This article originally appeared in *Journal of Narrative Technique* 9 (1979).

sizes the novel's mythic qualities by telling the story through a series of journal extracts, personal letters, and newspaper clippings—the very written record of everyday life. The narrative technique resembles a vast jigsaw puzzle of isolated and frequently trivial facts; and it is only when the novel is more than half over that the central characters piece these fragments together and, having concluded the Dracula is a threat to themselves and their society, band together to destroy him.

On the surface, the novel appears to be a mythic re-enactment of the opposition between Good and Evil because the narrators attribute their pursuit and ultimate defeat of Dracula to a high moral purpose. However, although his method of narration doesn't enable him to comment directly on his characters' failures in judgment or lack of self-knowledge, Stoker provides several clues to their unreliability and encourages the reader to see the frequent discrepancies between their professed beliefs and their actions. The first clue is an anonymous preface (unfortunately omitted in many modern editions) which gives the reader a distinct warning:

> How these papers have been placed in sequence will be made manifest in the reading of them. All needless matters have been eliminated, so that a history almost at variance with the possibilities of later-day belief may stand forth as simple fact. There is throughout no statement of past things wherein memory may err, for all the records chosen are exactly contemporary, *given from the standpoints and within the range of knowledge of those who made them.*[2]

Writers of Victorian popular fiction frequently rely on the convention of the anonymous editor to introduce their tales and to provide additional comments throughout the text; and Stoker uses this convention to stress the subjective nature of the story which his narrators relate. The narrators themselves occasionally question the validity of their perceptions, but Stoker provides numerous additional clues to their unreliability. For example, at the conclusion, Johnathan Harker questions their interpretation of the events:

> We were struck with the fact, that in all the mass of material of which the record is composed, there is hardly one authentic document; nothing but a mass of typewriting, except the later notebooks of Mina and Seward and myself, and Van Helsing's memorandum. We could hardly ask any one, even did we wish to, to accept these as proofs of so wild a story.[3]

The conclusion reinforces the subjective nature of their tale and casts doubts on everything that had preceded; however, because Stoker does not use an obvious framing device like Conrad in *Heart of Darkness* or James in *The Turn of the Screw* or employ an intrusive editor as Haggard does in *She* and because all the narrators come to similar conclusions about the nature of their opponent, the reader is likely to forget that these documents are subjective records, interpretations which are "given within the range of knowledge of those who made them."

While Stoker's choice of narrative technique does not permit him to comment directly on his characters, he suggests that they are particularly ill-equipped to judge the extraordinary events with which they are faced. The three central narrators are perfectly ordinary nineteenth-century Englishmen: the young lawyer Jonathan Harker, his wife Mina, and a youthful psychiatrist Dr. John Seward. Other characters who sometimes function as narrators include Dr. Van Helsing, Seward's former teacher; Quincey Morris, an American adventurer; Arthur Holmwood, a young English nobleman; and Lucy Westenra, Holmwood's fiancée. With the exception of Dr. Van Helsing, all the central characters are youthful and inexperienced—two-dimensional characters whose only distinguishing characteristics are their names and their professions; and by maintaining a constancy of style throughout and emphasizing the beliefs which they hold in common, Stoker further diminishes any individualizing traits.[4] The narrators appear to speak with one voice; and Stoker suggests that their opinions are perfectly acceptable so long as they remain within their limited fields of expertise. The problem, however, is that these perfectly ordinary people are confronted with the extraordinary character of Dracula.

Although Stoker did model Dracula on the historical Vlad V of Wallachia and the East European superstition of the vampire,[5] he adds a number of humanizing touches to make Dracula appear noble and vulnerable as well as demonic and threatening; and it becomes difficult to determine whether he is a hideous bloodsucker whose touch breeds death or a lonely and silent figure who is hunted and persecuted.[6] The difficulty in interpreting Dracula's character is compounded by the narrative technique, for the reader quickly recognizes that Dracula is *never* seen objectively and never permitted to speak for himself while his actions are recorded by people who have determined to destroy him and who, moreover, repeatedly question the sanity of their quest.

The question of sanity, which is so important in *Dracula*, provides another clue to the narrators' unreliability. More than half the novel takes place in or near Dr. Seward's London mental institution; and several of the characters are shown to be emotionally unstable: Renfield, one of Dr. Seward's patients, is an incarcerated madman who believes that he can achieve immortality by drinking the blood of insects and other small creatures; Jonathan Harker suffers a nervous breakdown after he escapes from Dracula's castle; and Lucy Westenra exhibits signs of schizophrenia, being a model of sweetness and conformity while she is awake but becoming sexually aggressive and demanding during her sleepwalking periods. More introspective than most of the other narrators, Dr. Seward occasionally refers to the questionable sanity of their mission, his diary entries mentioning his fears that they will all wake up in straitjackets. Furthermore, his entries on Renfield's condition indicate that he recognizes the narrow margin which separates sanity from insanity: "It is wonderful, however, what intellectual recuperative power lunatics have, for within a few minutes he stood up quite calmly and looked about him" (p. 133).

However, even if the reader chooses to ignore the question of the narrators' sanity, it is important to understand their reasons for wishing to destroy Dracula. They accuse him of murdering the crew of the *Demeter*,[7] of killing Lucy Westenra and transforming her into a vampire, and of trying to do the same thing to Mina Harker. However, the log found on the dead body of the *Demeter*'s captain, which makes only a few ambiguous allusions to a fiend or monster, is hysterical and inconclusive. Recording this "evidence," Mina's journal asserts that the verdict of the inquest was open-ended: "There is no evidence to adduce; and whether or not the man [the ship's captain] committed the murders there is now none to say" (p. 100). Lucy's death might just as easily be attributed to the blood transfusions (still a dangerous procedure at the time Stoker wrote *Dracula*) to which Dr. Van Helsing subjects her; and Mina acknowledges her complicity in the affair with Dracula by admitting that she did not want to prevent his advances. Finally, even if Dracula is responsible for all the Evil of which he is accused, he is tried, convicted, and sentenced by men (including two lawyers) who give him no opportunity to explain his actions and who repeatedly violate the laws which they profess to be defending: they avoid an inquest of Lucy's death, break into her tomb and desecrate her body, break into Dracula's houses, frequently resort to bribery and coercion to avoid legal involvement, and openly admit that they are responsible for the deaths of five alleged vampires. While it can be argued that *Dracula* is a fantasy and therefore not subject to the laws of verisimilitude, Stoker uses the flimsiness of such "evidence" to focus on the contrast between the narrators' rigorous moral arguments and their all-too-pragmatic methods.

In fact, Stoker reveals that what condemns Dracula are the English characters' subjective responses to his character and to the way of life which he represents. The reader is introduced to Dracula by Johnathan Harker's journal. His first realization that Dracula is different from himself occurs when he looks into the mirror and discovers that Dracula casts no reflection:

> This time there could be no error, for the man was close to me, and I could see him over my shoulder. But there was no reflection of him in the mirror! The whole room behind me was displayed; but there was no sign of a man in it, except myself. This was startling, and, coming on the top of so many strange things, was beginning to increase that vague sense of uneasiness which I always have when the Count is near. (p. 34)

The fact that vampires cast no reflection is part of the iconography of the vampire in East European folklore, but Stoker translates the superstitious belief that creatures without souls have no reflection into a metaphor by which he can illustrate his characters' lack of moral vision. Harker's inability to "see" Dracula is a manifestation of moral blindness which reveals his insensitivity to others and (as will become evident later) his inability to perceive certain traits within himself.[8]

Even before Harker begins to suspect that Dracula is a being totally unlike himself, Stoker reveals that he is troubled by everything that Dracula represents. While journeying from London to Transylvania, Harker muses on the quaint customs which he encounters; and he notes in his journal that he must question his host about them. Stoker uses Harker's perplexity to establish his character as a very parochial Englishman whose apparent curiosity is not a desire for understanding, but a need to have his preconceptions confirmed. However, instead of finding someone like himself at the end of his journey, a person who can provide a rational explanation for these examples of non-English behavior, Harker discovers a ruined castle, itself a memento of bygone ages, and a man who, reminding him that Transylvania is not England, prides himself on being an integral part of his nation's heroic past:

> . . . the Szekleys—and the Dracula as their heart's blood, their brains and their swords—can boast a record that mushroom growths like the Hapsburgs and the Romanoffs can never reach. The warlike days are over. Blood is too precious a thing in these days of dishonourable peace; and the glories of the great races are as a tale that is told. (p. 39)

To Harker, Dracula initially appears to be an anachronism—an embodiment of the feudal past—rather than an innately evil being; and his journal entries at the beginning merely reproduce Dracula's pride and rugged individualism:

> Here I am noble; I am *boyar;* the common people know me, and I am master. But a stranger in a strange land, he is no one; men know him not—and to know not is to care not for. . . . I have been so long master that I would be master still—or at least that none other should be master of me. (p. 28)

It is only when Harker realizes that he is assisting to take this anachronism to England that he becomes frightened.

Harker's later response indicates that he fears a kind of reverse imperialism, the threat of the primitive trying to colonize the civilized world, while the reader sees in his response a profound resemblance between Harker and Dracula:

> This was the being I was helping to transfer to London, where perhaps for centuries to come he might . . . satiate his lust for blood, and create a new and ever-widening circle of semi-demons to batten on the helpless. The very thought drove me mad. A terrible desire came upon me to rid the world of such a monster. There was no lethal weapon at hand, but I seized

a shovel which the workmen had been using to fill the cases, and lifting it high, struck, with the edge downward, at the hateful face. (pp. 62–63)

This scene reinforces Harker's earlier inability to see Dracula in the mirror. Taken out of context, it would be difficult to distinguish the man from the monster. Behavior generally attributed to the vampire—the habit of attacking a sleeping victim, violence, and irrational behavior—is revealed to be the behavior of the civilized Englishman also. The sole difference is that Stoker's narrative technique does not permit the reader to enter Dracula's thoughts as he stands over his victims. The reversal of roles here is important because it establishes the subjective nature of the narrators' beliefs, suggests their lack of self-knowledge, and serves to focus on the similarities between the narrators and their opponent. Later in the novel, Mina Harker provides the following analysis of Dracula which ironically also describes the single-mindedness of his pursuers:

> The Count is a criminal and of criminal type . . . and *qua* criminal he is of imperfectly formed mind. Thus, in a difficulty he has to seek resource in habit. . . . Then, as he is criminal he is selfish; and as his intellect is small and his action is based on selfishness, he confines himself to one purpose. (p. 378)

Both Mina and Jonathan can justify their pursuit of Dracula by labeling him a murderer; and Mina adds intellectual frailty to his alleged sins. However, the narrators show themselves to be equally bound by habit and equally incapable of evaluating situations which are beyond their limited spheres of expertise. In fact, Stoker implies that the only difference between Dracula and his opponents is the narrators' ability to state individual desire in terms of what they believe is a common good. For example, the above scene shows that Harker can justify his violent attack on Dracula because he pictures himself as the protector of helpless millions; and the narrators insist on the duty to defend the innocents.

The necessity of protecting the innocent is called into question, however, when Dr. Van Helsing informs the other characters about the vampire's nature. While most of his discussion concerns the vampire's susceptibility to garlic, silver bullets, and religious artifacts, Van Helsing also admits that the vampire cannot enter a dwelling unless he is first invited by one of the inhabitants. In other words, a vampire cannot influence a human being without that person's consent. Dracula's behavior confirms that he is an internal, not an external, threat. Although perfectly capable of using superior strength when he must defend himself, he usually employs seduction, relying on the others' desires to emulate his freedom from external constraints: Renfield's desire for immortality, Lucy's wish to escape the repressive existence of an upper-class woman, and the desires of all the characters to overcome the restraints placed on them by their religion and their law. As the spokesman for civilization, Van Helsing appears to understand that the others might be tempted by their desires to become like Dracula and he warns them against the temptation:

> But to fail here, is not mere life or death. It is that we become as him; that we henceforward become foul things of the night like him—without heart or conscience, preying on the bodies and the souls of those we love best. (p. 265)

Becoming like Dracula, they too would be laws unto themselves—primitive, violent, irrational—with nothing to justify their actions except the force of their desires. No longer would they need to rationalize their "preying on the bodies and souls of their loved ones" by concealing their lust for power under the rubric of religion, their love of violence under the names of imperialism and progress, their sexual desires within an elaborate courtship ritual.

The narrators attribute their hatred of Dracula to a variety of causes. Harker's journal introduces a being whose way of life is antithetical to theirs—a warlord, a representative of the feudal past and the leader of a primitive cult who he fears will attempt to establish a vampire colony in England. Mina Harker views him as a criminal and as the murderer of her best friend; and Van Helsing sees him as a moral threat, a kind of Anti-Christ. Yet, in spite of the narrators' moral and political language, Stoker reveals that Dracula is primarily a sexual threat, a missionary of desire whose only true kingdom will be the human body. Although he flaunts his independence of social restraints and proclaims himself a master over all he sees, Dracula adheres more closely to English law than his opponents in every area except his sexual behavior. (In fact, Dracula admits to Harker that he invited him to Transylvania so he could learn the subtle nuances of English law and business.) Neither a thief, rapist, nor an overtly political threat, Dracula is dangerous because he expresses his contempt for authority in the most individualistic of ways—through his sexuality. In fact, his thirst for blood and the manner in which he satisfies this thirst can be interpreted as sexual desire which fails to observe any of society's attempts to control it—prohibitions against polygamy, promiscuity, and homosexuality.[9] Furthermore, Stoker suggests that it is generally through sexuality that the vampire gains control over human beings. Van Helsing recognizes this temptation when he prevents Arthur from kissing Lucy right before her death; and even the staid and morally upright Harker momentarily succumbs to the sensuality of the three vampire-women in Dracula's castle:

> I felt in my heart a wicked, burning desire that they would kiss me with those red lips. It is not good to note this down, lest some day it should meet Mina's eyes and cause her pain; but it is the truth. (p. 47)

For one brief moment, Harker does appear to recognize the truth about sexual desire; it is totally irrational and has nothing to do with monogamy, love, or even respect for the beloved. It is Dracula, however, who clearly articulates the characters' most intense fears of sexuality: "Your girls that you all love are mine already; and through them you and others shall yet be mine—my creatures, to do my bidding and to be my jackals when I want to feed" (p. 340). Implicit in Dracula's warning is the similarity between vampire and opponents. Despite rare moments of comprehension, however, the narrators generally choose to ignore this similarity; and their lack of self knowledge permits them to hunt down and kill not only Dracula and the three women in his castle, but their friend Lucy Westenra as well.

The scene in which Arthur drives the stake through Lucy's body while the other men watch thoughtfully is filled with a violent sexuality which again connects vampire and opponents:

> But Arthur never faltered. He looked like a figure of Thor as his untrembling arm rose and fell, driving deeper and deeper the mercy-bearing stake, whilst the blood from the pierced heart welled and spurted up around it. His face was set, and high duty seemed to shine through it; the sight of it gave us courage so that our voices seemed to ring through the vault. . . . There in the coffin lay no longer the foul Thing that we had dreaded and grown to hate that the work of her destruction was yielded as a privilege to the one best entitled to it, but Lucy as we had seen her in life, with her face of unequalled sweetness and purity. (p. 241)

Despite Seward's elevated moral language, the scene resembles nothing so much as the combined group rape and murder of an unconscious woman; and this kind of violent attack on a helpless victim is precisely the kind of behavior which condemns Dracula in the narrators' eyes. Moreover, Lucy is not the only woman to be subjected to this violence. At the conclusion, in a scene which is only slightly less explicit, Dr. Van Helsing destroys the three women in Dracula's castle. Again Dr. Van Helsing admits that he is fascinated by the beautiful visages of the "wanton Un-Dead" but he never acknowledges that his violent attack is simply a role reversal or that he becomes the vampire as he stands over their unconscious bodies.

By the conclusion of the novel, all the characters who have been accused of expressing individual desire have been appropriately punished: Dracula, Lucy Westenra, and the three vampire-women have been killed; and even Mina Harker is ostracized for her momentary indiscretion. All that remains after the primitive, the passionate, and the individualistic qualities that were associated with the vampire have been destroyed is a small group of wealthy men who return after a period of one year to the site of their victory over the vampire. The surviving characters remain unchanged by the events in their lives and never come to the realization that their commitment to social values merely masks their violence and their sexuality; and the only significant difference in their condition is the birth of the Harkers' son who is appropriately named for all the men who had participated in the conquest of Dracula. Individual sexual desire has apparently been so absolutely effaced that the narrators see this child as the result of their social union rather than the product of a sexual union between one man and one woman.

The narrators insist that they are agents of God and are able to ignore their similarity to the vampire because their commitment to social values such as monogamy, proper English behavior, and the will of the majority enables them to conceal their violence and their sexual desires from each other and even from themselves. Stoker, however, reveals that these characteristics are merely masked by social convention. Instead of being eliminated, violence and sexuality emerge in particularly perverted forms.

Recently uncovered evidence suggests that Bram Stoker may have had very personal reasons for his preoccupation with repression and sexuality. In his biography of his great-uncle, Daniel Farson explains that, while the cause of Stoker's death is usually given as exhaustion, Stoker actually died of tertiary syphilis, exhaustion being one of the final stages of that disease. Farson also adds that Stoker's problematic relationship with his wife may have been responsible:

> When his wife's frigidity drove him to other women, probably prostitutes among them, Bram's writing showed signs of guilt and sexual frustration. . . . He probably caught syphilis around the turn of the century, possible as early as the year of Dracula, 1896. (It usually takes ten to fifteen years before it kills.) By 1897 it seems that he had been celibate for more than twenty years, as far as Florence [his wife] was concerned.[10]

Poignantly aware from his own experience that the face of the vampire is the hidden side of the human character, Stoker creates unreliable narrators to tell a tale, not of the overcoming of Evil by Good, but of the similarities between the two. *Dracula* reveals the unseen face in the mirror; and Stoker's message is similar to the passage from *Julius Caesar* which prefaces this article and might be paraphrased in the following manner: "The fault, dear reader, is not in our external enemies, but in ourselves."

Notes

1. Recent full-length studies of *Dracula* include the following books: Radu Florescu and Raymond T. McNally, *In Search of Dracula* (New York: New York Graphic Society, 1972); Gabriel Ronay, *The Truth About Dracula* (New York: Stein and Day, 1972); and Leonard Wolf, *A Dream of Dracula: In Search of the Living Dead* (Boston: Little, Brown and Company, 1972).

2. Leonard Wolf, *The Annotated Dracula* (New York: Clarkson N. Potter, Inc., 1975), my italics.

3. Bram Stoker, *Dracula* (1896; rpt. New York: Dell Publishing Company, 1971), p. 416. All future references will be to this edition and will be included in the text.

4. Stephanie Demetrakopoulos addresses another facet of this similarity by showing that male and female sexual roles are frequently reversed in *Dracula*. Her article, "Feminism, Sex Role Exchanges, and Other Subliminal Fantasies in Bram Stoker's *Dracula*," is included in *Frontiers: A Journal of Women Studies*, 2 (1977), pp. 104–13.

5. Stoker could have learned of Vlad from a number of sources. Ronay adds in a footnote that "The Millenary of Honfoglalas, the Hungarian invasion of their present-day territory, was being celebrated with great pomp and circumstance in 1896—the year when Stoker was writing *Dracula*" (p. 56). Another possible source is cited by G. Nandris, "A Philological Analysis of Dracula and Rumanian Placenames and Masculine Personal Names in -a/ea," *Slavonic and East European Review*, 37 (1959), p. 371:

> The Rumanian historian I. Bogdan, who published a monograph in 1896 on the prince of Wallachia, Vlad V, nicknamed Tsepesh (The Impaler), and who edited in it two German and four Russian versions of the Dracula legend . . .

6. Royce MacGillivray explains how Stoker altered the Dracula story:

> In real life Dracula was known for his horrifying cruelty, but Stoker, who wanted a monster that his readers could both shudder at and identify with, omits all mention of the dark side of his reputation and emphasizes his greatness as a warrior chieftain.

"*Dracula*, Bram Stoker's Spoiled Masterpiece," *Queen's Quarterly*, 79 (1972), p. 520.

7. It is significant that Dracula—who is portrayed as a sexual threat—comes to England on a ship named for the Greek goddess of fertility. Furthermore, he returns to his homeland on the *Czarina Catherine;* and Stoker probably expected his readers to know the stories of Catherine's legendary sexual appetite.

8. Wolf comments on this characteristic in the preface to *The Annotated Dracula:*

> Here, then is the figure that Bram Stoker created—a figure who confronts us with primordial mysteries: death, blood, and love, and how they are bound together. Finally, Stoker's achievement is this: he makes us understand in our own experience why the vampire is said to be invisible in the mirror. He is there, but we fail to recognize him since our own faces get in the way.

9. A number of critics have commented on the pervasive sexuality in *Dracula*. C. F. Bentley, "The Monster in the Bedroom," *Literature and Psychology*, 22 (1972), p. 28:

> What is rejected or repressed on a conscious level appears in a covert and perverted form throughout the novel, the apparatus of the vampire superstition described in almost obsessional detail in *Dracula* providing the means for a symbolic presentation of human sexual relationships.

Maurice Richardson, "The Psychoanalysis of Ghost Stories," *The Twentieth Century*, 166 (1959), p. 429 describes Dracula as "a vast polymorph perverse bisexual oral-anal-genital sadomasochistic timeless orgy." In *A Dream of Dracula*, Wolf refers to the sexuality of Dracula:

> His kiss permits all unions: men and women; men and men; women and women; fathers and daughters; mothers and sons. Moreover, his is an easy love that evades the usual failures of the flesh. It is the triumph of passivity, unembarrassing, sensuous, throbbing, violent, and cruel. (p. 303)

Joseph S. Bierman, "Dracula: Prolonged Childhood Illness and the Oral Triad," *American Imago*, 29 (1972), pp. 186–98. Bierman studies Stoker's life and concludes that much of Dracula can be attributed to Stoker's repressed death wishes toward his brothers and toward his employer Henry Irving.

10. Daniel Farson, *The Man Who Wrote Dracula: A Biography of Bram Stoker* (London: Michael Joseph, 1975), p. 234.

Royal Lyceum Theatre.

Sole Lessee and Manager:

HENRY IRVING.

DRACULA

OR

THE UN-DEAD.

FIRST TIME.

Program of a Dramatization of *Dracula*
This was the only one presented in Stoker's lifetime.

11

Dracula: Christian Heretic

Christopher Gist Raible

Hold a mirror up to a vampire, as anyone who has read or seen *Dracula* knows, and there will be no reflection. Perhaps the power of the Dracula story persists— in books, plays and films—because its themes are mirror inversions or perversions of Christian truths.

In the eight decades since Bram Stoker's work was first published, it has never been out of print. Following *Nosferatu* in 1922, at least 40 other films have used the Dracula theme and several more are currently in production. First made into a play in 1927, the drama has been produced many times—two different productions are now running in New York, and others are opening in Chicago and elsewhere. A recent book even unites Dracula with Sherlock Holmes!

Why the endurance of this essentially gothic tale? In combining mythological bloodsucking vampires with a historical bloodthirsty ruler, Bram Stoker created not only the character of Count Dracula, he created also an ominous caricature of Christian theology. The history of the 15th century Transylvanian tyrant, Vlad Tepes or Dracul, has been well documented. Scholars have also noted the almost universal existence of vampire legends (see McNally and Florescu, *In Search of Dracula,* or Ronay, *The Truth About Dracula*). It may be that evil creatures who live by sucking human blood are expressions of the Jungian "collective unconscious" and that alone accounts for the continual recurrence of the idea. But *Dracula*'s popularity derives from a deeper demonic struggle which it represents.

Dracula, is, of course, a morality play. Forces of good and evil, clearly identified, clash until the climax and final destruction of the dread vampire. If the

This article first appeared in *Christian Century* 96 (1979), No. 4 and is reprinted by permission of The Christian Century Foundation.

evil here is more suave and seductive—more intelligent and attractive—than is the devil in medieval morality dramas, that may be simply an expression of modern sophistication. But this morality play, unlike most others, plays on essential elements of Christian faith—constantly twisting basic religious truths.

For example, all through the story the cross is used as a shield which can ward off the forces of evil. A communion wafer has the power to cleanse (as it were, sterilize) boxes of earth so that Dracula can no longer safely sleep in them. But a cross is simply a symbol. The communion host (at least out of the context of the Eucharist) is not in itself holy. Religious objects may direct us toward divinity, but they have no strength of their own. This confusion is common in the history of religion, but it nevertheless results in distortion. The symbol is not the reality it symbolizes ("the map is not the territory"). Symbols may remind us of God, but they are not God. To suggest that objects may themselves radiate divine power is to reduce religion to magic.

There are other such twists in the tale. Garlic offers protection as a sort of perverse frankincense or ritual holy incense. Dracula can take the form of a bat, a flying humanlike figure that is a creature of darkness rather than an angel of light. The vampire moves at night, not in the daytime—his resurrection takes place at sunset rather than at dawn. Dracula is a count (all the earlier English vampire versions also portrayed the central character as a nobleman) rather than a common carpenter.

Dracula lives by blood—the agent of life and the instrument of his eternal life. The symbol of blood as metaphor for the divine essence is thus perverted in the vampire tale: real blood is drunk that he may continue his earthly life. The deaths of many are required so that one may continue to live, whereas Christianity teaches that the death of one occurred that many may live. How is Dracula finally killed? As everyone knows, a vampire dies—is prevented from having eternal life—when a wooden stake is driven through his body. Death by a stake ends an old life, rather than death at the stake beginning new life.

The inversion of Christian truth which portrays Dracula as a heretic is to be seen not merely in the symbols of the story. The heresy is also revealed through the ampire's perverse ethics. Dracula rules by fear and force. His control over others contains no concern for their welfare; his power is that of terror. No wonder the vampire has been used by artists (including Goya and Doré) as a symbol for exploitation, murder and war. To have faith in the power of destruction rather than the power of love is obviously a Christian heresy.

Dracula lives by taking life. He drains his victims of their blood that he may live; they must die to prevent his death. He grabs, clutches, crushes. His existence displays no reciprocity, no mutuality. He is neither giving or forgiving. To live by taking and holding on rather than by letting go constitutes another Christian heresy.

Dracula desires to live forever and has found the secret of eternal life. But what life! He lives only in the darkness, always threatened by possible exposure and death. His one place of rest is a coffin filled with dirt. He is always the same, never changing, never aging. While the world turns and society evolves, Dracula remains as he always was, learning nothing, never growing. To want to live in this world the same way forever is a Christian heresy. On the one hand, such a desire denies any hope of a life after death; on the other, it devalues the meaning of life on earth. Only in accepting the limitations of this life can we learn to appreciate its worth.

Christianity, and other faiths, teach the value of life. Life is limited, but it is lovely. Life is fragile, but filled with great possibilities. We can be hurt, but we can enjoy. We may fall into fault, but we may know truth. We are frail, but we are also strong. The worth of our lives is experienced through sharing, helping, sacrificing. Such is the Christian message that Dracula cannot comprehend: only by giving of ourselves do we gain; only be losing our lives do we find them.

In the original story, Dracula is destroyed through two combined efforts. One is the scientific knowledge of the learned Dr. Van Helsing. His insight and tenacity serve time and again to protect the virtuous from the powers of evil. But reason is not enough; intelligence can fail, and would have failed, were it not for another quality. When the intellectual doctor is going wrong, he is saved by the young woman, Mina, whose native good sense comes to the fore. The clarity of her pure (almost virginal) intuition combines with his scholarship to put down the demonic Dracula forever.

Thus, the triumph of good over evil requires both insight and intuition, knowledge and wisdom. Dracula, in the story, is destroyed. But the dark forces he symbolizes survive; perversions and distortions persist. Greed, tyranny, cruelty, lust in our day wear other than black cloaks. They wear business suits, white coats, military uniforms, academic robes, even clerical vestments. There are Draculas all around us. Their seductive heresies are tempting.

At the close of the original stage play, Dr. Van Helsing speaks as the audience is about to leave the theater. The drama ends with the destruction of Dracula. Then Van Helsing says:

> Just a word of reassurance. When you get home tonight and the lights have been turned out and you are afraid to look behind the curtains and you dread to see a face appear at the window—why, just pull yourself together and remember that after all *there are such things*.

12

The Vampire Myth

James Twitchell

Prior to the Romantic Movement (say before the 1780s), the vampire had been either a subject of ecclesiastical study or a minor concern in folklore—it had no artistic currency.[1] Then quite suddenly in Germany (Ossenfelder, Bürger, Goethe, F. W. A. Hoffman), in France (Nodier, Merimée, Gautier, Baudelaire), and especially in England (Southey, Coleridge, Byron, Shelley, Keats) the vampire had become an eidolon of Romantic consciousness, an apt mythologem for a new view of human interactions.[2] My particular concern has been with adaptations of the vampire used not to shock, but rather to explain how the artist viewed his transactions with others: with his audience, with his friends, and especially with his art. For the Romantic artist, acutely self-conscious, found in this myth an analogy to explain how energy (life, imagination, creativity) was exchanged between the various characters and activities he encountered. Without the vocabulary of transactional analysis, this myth provided a working text, so to speak, to describe human exchanges.

What bothered me in my studies was that I was totally unable to explain the vampire's current popularity. It is one thing to explain why even "modern" writers, such as Henry James, Oscar Wilde or D. H. Lawrence used the analogy of the vampire to describe the inner and outer lives of their characters; it is quite another to explain why there is a vampire puppet on Sesame Street, "Count Count," who teaches numbers to our children, or why vampire comics are one of the most popular genres in that febrile medium, or even why any child would want to eat a "vitamin enriched" breakfast cereal named "Count Chocula." Because the vampire myth is widespread and vibrant in our culture and because so much of our folklore has been influenced by literature, I should like to attempt a psychoanalysis of the vampire from a quasi-literary point of view.

This article originally appeared in *American Imago* 37 (1980).

The culmination of literary interest in the vampire is Bram Stoker's *Dracula*. There is no doubt in my mind that had this novel been published in 1797 instead of 1897, it would be hailed today as a wonderful Romantic novel. Instead, appearing as it did at the height of Realism and Naturalism, *Dracula* is usually cast aside by literary critics as a gothic non sequitur. But in popular culture, this creature Dracula, along with a chronologically Romantic creature, Mary Shelley's Frankenstein monster (1818), has been the most important archetype bequeathed us by our great-grandparents. In fact "Dracula" and "vampire" have become virtually indistinguishable. Since this book has so influenced our folklore (thanks mainly to Hollywood, but also because *Dracula* really is a wonderful *Schauer-roman*) let me first outline the myth as it is currently informed by literature and folklore, and then attempt an analysis.

Any twelve-year-old schoolboy can describe the vampire, and that of course is precisely why it is so important. This story is a cultural scenario learned early and repeated again and again through the pre-teenage years. The vampire, a.k.a. Dracula, the Count, etc., is an older man who both terrorizes and seduces younger women. He is handsome, tall, powerful, rich; has a strange middle European accent (this the influence of Bela Lugosi, for Stoker's Dracula spoke perfect English!) and strange appetites. The first part of the story describes how the vampire sates these horrid appetites. He must have blood, and this blood invariably must be from a young lady. (In Andy Warhol's "Dracula," a cinematic sendup of the myth, much fun is made of the dilemma the modern vampire faces because he cannot find such a young lady or, in the movie's terms, a young virgin; such a species, it is implied, is no longer extant.)

The vampire's actual attack is notable for its total lack of violence. I cannot think of any other monster-molester in our culture who does such terrible things in such a gentlemanly manner. He is always polite and deferential, and his victim is almost always equally decorous in return. In folklore, the female often subtly initiates the affair by granting the demon-lover access to her bedroom, or by helping him across a blessed threshold, or unhasping a window or even looking at him as if she were willing to be his victim. The attack in our contemporary folklore, if it really can be called such, seems boringly pre-scripted. The female victim is most often preparing for bed, dressed in a negligee, usually white and inviting; the vampire mysteriously appears; she somehow encourages the rapprochment; he captivates her (literally "enthralls" her), kisses her, then bites her on her neck and sucks her blood (this is often excised to concentrate on her sensual reaction); and then he leaves her swooning. She soon visibly weakens, he continues to return at night until she seems to die, but is actually transformed into the very type of demon who has "attacked" her. This seems a most intriguing instance of the Doppelgänger motif, as the victim now becomes the vampire seeking new victims.

Here the second part of the story unfolds: this is the "modern" part, influenced by literature and the cinema. The young female, corrupted into sin, now seeks victims of her own. She has become a "lamia" or female vampire. Obviously the story could continue forever into tedium unless the proto-vampire is destroyed, and so of course he must be. In *Dracula,* which is the first story really to emphasize vampire destruction, an older man, Dr. Van Helsing, a wise father figure from across the sea in Belgium, leads the young men (who were all in love with the young victim, appropriately named Lucy) on a spirited chase pursuing Dracula. Much has been made in criticism that Dracula represents the evil father: he is older than the "boys," has his own home in Transylvania, is savvy in the nefarious ways of the world—while Van Helsing is the "good" father, having wisdom and love to offer in place of self-aggrandizement and worldly goods.[3] Hence, the end of the story has the good boys under the tutelage of the wise father chasing the bad patriarch until they capture and destroy him. They kill him, incidentally, not by staking but by decapitation; the female vampires are staked.[4] This chase scene is often played out in our modern renditions with the Van Helsing figure played by a doctor—a hematologist, or in some cases a psychiatrist!

The English anthropologist Maurice Richardson first described the correlation between this chase-to-the-death and Freud's thesis, developed in *Totem and Taboo,* of the primal horde.[5] This interpretation makes considerable sense, for Dracula is indeed the evil father out to control what the boys want (namely women), and so patricide must be committed. The boys may well suffer guilt from this act, but at least they get what they want, and the price seems worth it. Very often in the modern movie versions, Dracula is happy to die, to be freed from his hideous habits, thereby in a sense relieving the boys of unnecessary guilt, but still allowing their sociobiological needs.

The end of the story, Dracula's pursuit and destruction, seems simple enough; as a matter of fact, the primal horde thesis is standard now in both literary criticism and psychology. What is perplexing is the sexual excitement that the first part of the myth seems to arouse. So let us re-examine it, keeping in mind the pubertal nature of the audience, both male and female. The most startling part of the folkloric vampire is that he must first attack members of his own family. The prerequisite has been lost in our modern versions, but it is clear in almost every early story in almost every culture. We may have neglected this because we find it too dull and predictable, but it may also be, as I hope to illustrate, because this familial tie makes all too clear the vampire's sexual function.

We should recall that the only act the vampire commits is sucking.[6] He does not rip bodies apart; he dismembers no one. His only physical deformity is slightly extended incisors, and this aberration does have a rather utilitarian purpose. His sucking, however, produces catastrophic results. I suppose a good case could be make that here the latent, or not-so-latent, oral desires of the pre-adolescent audience are being expressed. Sucking is fun, yes, but you should not do it. Dracula himself is, in a sense, "oral cannibalistic," and that will not do. It is wrong; it violates a prohibition. But if you look at the psychodynamics of the sucking within the myth, you will realize that the woman enjoys it; as a matter of fact, it is highly sexual for both partners.

This scene is still more complex because as the vampire takes blood, he is also inseminating his victim with evil. A rape scene is played out through the gauze of fantasy. There is no mention of this in the mythography, but it is clear when we study the effects. He wants her, she may even want him; yet something is terribly wrong ... something evil is happening. Perhaps this activity is overlapped with a re-creation of the "primal scene." The young male audience especially witnesses the older man defile the virgin (for indeed to this audience the mother is, to them at least, virginal), while at the same time imagining themselves to be that powerful man. Hence the audience response to the vampire is wonderfully oxymoronic: on one hand, the vampire is bad, evil, sucking what he should not be sucking, being sexual where he should not be; yet it is all somehow very alluring. The vampire himself is powerful; he has all the night to himself, all the women he wants, especially this one. This ambivalence is played out in the affective response in which the audience seems to say: "The vampire, if he would play by the rules and not attack (my) woman/mother/sister, is wonderful, but if he mistakes and overreaches his limits, I'll have to fight with him."

Not all is weighted on the vampire's side; he is terrified of the church icons (as the audience itself probably is); he is photophobic; and he has other inexplicable fears: garlic, wolfsbane (here, I suppose, lycanthropic overtones of the myth do make sense), running water, etc. So he is not inaccessible to punishment, although he may posture otherwise and the audience knows it.

The myth is loaded with sexual excitement; yet there is no mention of sexuality. It is sex without genitalia, sex without confusion, sex without responsibility, sex without guilt, sex without love—better yet, sex without mention. The only time sexuality ever surfaces is when the male is victim to the female vampire, the lamia. Here, the pattern of attack is the same but the results are dramatically different. The female vampire is older than her male victim, knowledgeable in the ways of the world, and inducts her novitiate not into evil but into manhood. Whereas the female victim of the male attack is destroyed, the young male victim is strengthened through sex. Ernest Jones, one of the few psychologists who have studied this myth, explains part of it:

> The explanation of these phantasies is surely not hard. A nightly visit from a beautiful or frightful being, who first exhausts the sleeper with passionate embraces and then withdraws

from him a vital fluid: all this can point only to a natural and common process, namely to nocturnal emissions accompanied with dreams of a more or less erotic nature. In the unconscious mind blood is commonly an equivalent for semen. . . ."[7]

When we look in literature, Jones's thesis is reinforced; for instance, when Jonathan Harker, the young protagonist in *Dracula,* is approached by three lamias, the description is full of barely-subliminated sexuality. It is indeed dreamlike:

In the moonlight opposite me were three young women, ladies by their dress and manner. I thought at the time that I must be dreaming when I saw them, for, though the moonlight was behind them, they threw no shadow on the floor. They came close to me, and looked at me for some time, and then whispered together. All three had brilliant white teeth that shone like pearls against the ruby of their voluptuous lips. There was something about them that made me uneasy, some longing and at the same time some deadly fear. I felt in my heart a wicked, burning desire that they would kiss me with those red lips. It is not good to note this down, lest some day it should meet Mina's [Jonathan's wife] eyes and cause her pain; but it is the truth. They whispered together, and then they all three laughed—such a silvery, musical laugh, but as hard as though the sound never could have come through the softness of human lips. The fair girl advanced and bent over me till I could feel the movement of her breath upon me. . . .

I was afraid to raise my eyelids, but looked out and saw perfectly under the lashes. The girl went on her knees, and bent over me, simply gloating. There was a deliberate voluptuousness which was both thrilling and repulsive, and as she arched her neck she actually licked her lips like an animal, till I could see in the moonlight the moisture shining on the scarlet lips and on the red tongue as it lapped the white sharp teeth.[8]

This masturbatory delight is maintained in the cinema: the female seductress takes the young male across puberty into manhood. A price must be paid, of course, but the price is very often that he will destroy her, or at least come to terms with her, while the young female victim will *never* take charge of her male attacker. Clearly, the social stereotypes of male dominance and female passivity are here at an early age being reinforced.

If the myth seems all things to the male adolescent, how can one explain its fascination to the adult audience? Is this the reworking of unresolved sexual tensions, wish-fulfillments, return of the repressed, or could it be as well a recapitulation and condensation of mature sexuality? Why, in short, is the myth sexually exciting to people who should "know better"? Here, I think, a thesis developed by Freud in "On the Universal Tendency to Debasement in the Sphere of Love" may be of some help. Simply put, Freud conjectured that:

Since we must recognize that all the relevant factors known to us—the strong childhood fixation, the incest-barrier and the frustration in the years of development after puberty—are to be found in practically all civilized human beings, we should be justified in expecting psychical impotence to be a universal affliction under civilization and not a disorder confined so some individuals. [The result to the male is that] this is the source of his need for a debased sexual object, a woman who is ethically inferior, to whom he need attribute no aesthetic scruples, who does not know him in his other social relations and cannot judge him in them. It is to such a woman that he prefers to devote his sexual potency, even when the whole of his affection belongs to a woman of a higher kind. [However] in the case of women there is little sign of a need to debase their sexual object. This is no doubt connected with the absence in them as a rule of anything similar to the sexual overvaluation found in men.[9]

Hence, the vampire myth not only reinforces a social paradigm but a psychological one as well. There is considerable sexual hostility in the myth although it is very muted. The male vampire debases the female; he destroys her virginity, makes her an outcast; but the female vampire does not such thing to the male—in fact, she has less interest in him than he has in her.

Then why should the myth appeal to the adolescent female? When she is the aggressor, the *femme fatale*, she does indeed live out a fantasy of power, a fantasy that flows through folklore from Lilith to, I suppose, Theda Bara, the first and most famous of the Hollywood "vamps." Clearly, it is important to be the preserver and destroyer of male power, but why should the female audience respond to the role of victim? Does her passive, even conspiratorial, role support a chauvinist view of rape, in which the raped secretly encourages the raper? Although this Reichean view has been recently debunked by feminists, most notably in Susan Brownmiller's *Against Our Will*, it may indeed be supported by this myth.[10]

A more probable explanation of why the vampire appeals to the pubescent female is offered in another work by Freud in the series "Contributions to the Psychology of Love." Whereas in "The Universal Tendency to Debasement . . .", Freud attempted to explain male impotency, in his next paper, "The Taboo of Virginity," he discusses female frigidity. His thesis simply put is that the adolescent female, denied her primary love object (father/brother), must settle for a husband who can at best mimic her original choice. Adding to this disappointment is the fact that her defloration is an initiation of considerable complexity and of some inevitable disappointment. For sex that is supposed to be pleasurable, the initial act is painful; this act is supposed to be performed by a man who can give ease, yet often awkwardness results. Ideally sex should be with a primary love object, but the taboo of incest is so universally strong that compromise and disillusion result. How to resolve these paradoxes is one of the functions of myth and ritual—often it succeeds. In many "primitive" cultures, the rupturing of the hymen is performed by a surrogate father during a very stylized ceremony. In Freud's words:

The customs of primitive peoples seem to take account of this *motif* of the early sexual wish by handing over the task of defloration to an elder, priest or holy man, that is, to a substitute for the father. There seems to me to be a direct path leading from this custom to the highly vexed questions of the *jus primae noctis* of the medieval lord of the manor.[11]

It is not hard to extend this *droit du seigneur* to not only the mediaeval lord but also to Count Dracula.

Could this not also account for the curious ambivalence of the female in the vampire myth? When the male audience interprets the action, the female represents his own displaced mother, virginal to him, who is being violated by his father, an ironic projection of his own self in the guise of the vampire. But when the adolescent female views the myth, she is the victim, virginal again, but now being swept through her "initiation" by her gentle father—a father who must then disappear into the darkness, leaving her to other men and strange disappointments.

We have few other myths in our culture so supple yet so complete as this. It covers not only the stages of sexual growth, but it does it from both male and female points of view. Little wonder then, that the lead singer with "KISS," a popular singing group whose appeal is primarily to teenagers, is decked out as a vampire; that vampires are almost omnipresent on Saturday morning cartoons; that many vampire movies and television shows have been especially crafted for this audience (*Abbott and Costello meet Dracula, Billy the Kid vs. Dracula,* "The Munsters," "The Groovie Goolies" . . .); that wax teeth complete with incisors are a popular Halloween accoutrement . . . the list goes on and on. I doubt that there is another image of such cultural vitality: Superman, Wonder Woman, Batman (perhaps a mutation of Dracula himself complete with the bat transformation, but this time in the service of goodness, not Prince of Darkness), Mighty Mouse, all pale in comparison. The vampire is the most complete condensation of the problem and the resolutions of pre-adolescence.

Notes

1. My *Living Dead: The Vampire in Romantic Literature* (to be published by Duke University Press, 1980) is almost totally concerned with the "art" version of the myth.

2. Here are the respective titles: the Germans, "The Vampire," "Lenore," "The Bride of Corinth"; the French, *Smarra,* selections from *La Guzla, Clairmonde,* "Metamorphosis of the Vampire," and for the English, *Thalaba the Destroyer,* "Christabel," *The Giaour, The Cenci,* "Lamia." This is only a brief catalogue; see "Introduction" to Christopher Frayling's *The Vampyre: A Bedside Companion.*

3. A number of critics have claimed that Dracula is a "father-figure": Maurice Richardson, "The Psychoanalysis of Ghost Stories," *Twentieth Century,* 166 (1959), 427; Royce MacGillivray; "*Dracula:* Bram Stoker's Spoiled Masterpiece," *Queens Quarterly,* 79 (Winter 1972), 522; and Leonard Wolf, *A Dream of Dracula: In Search of the Living Dead,* Chapter 6.

4. This point (along with all of its sexual connotations) as well as many others is made in an excellent study, C. F. Bentley's "The Monster in the Bedroom: Sexual Symbolism in Bram Stoker's *Dracula*," *Literature and Psychology*, 22 (1972), 27–34. On various other aspects of the book's sublimated sexuality, see Joseph S. Bierman, *"Dracula:* Prolonged Childhood Illness, and the Oral Triad," *American Imago*, 29 (Summer 1972), 186–98; Phyllis R. Roth, "Suddenly Sexual Women in Bram Stoker's *Dracula*," *Literature and Psychology*, 27 (1977), 113–21; and Carrol L. Fry, "Fictional Conventions and Sexuality in *Dracula*," *Victorian Newsletter*, 42 (Fall 1972), 20–22.

5. Richardson, "The Psychoanalysis of Ghost Stories," p. 430.

6. I have wondered if the "hickey," the crimson badge placed by teenagers on the necks of their current loves, is a vestige of displaced sucking.

7. Ernest Jones: *On the Nightmare* (1931; rpt. New York: Liveright Publication Corp., 1971), p. 119.

8. Bram Stoker: *Dracula* (1897; rpt. New York: Dell Paperbacks, 1973), 47, 48.

9. Sigmund Freud, "On the Universal Tendency to Debasement in the Sphere of Love," St. Ed. XI, 184, 185, 186.

10. It is probably best to keep in mind that there is a considerable body of psychological thought, also from the female point of view, that would contradict Brownmiller. See for instance, Helene Deutsch, *The Psychology of Women* (New York: Grune & Stratton, 1944, 1945) Vol. I, Chap. 6, "Feminine Passivity"; Chap. 7, "Feminine Masochism," pp. 219–78; Vol. II, Chap. 4, "The Psychology of the Sexual Act," pp. 77–105 and Karen Horney, "The Problem of Feminine Masochism" (1935), *Feminine Psychology* (New York: Norton, 1967) pp. 214–33; *The Neurotic Personality of Our Time* (New York: Norton, 1937) p. 280; *New Ways in Psychoanalysis* (New York: Norton, 1939) pp. 113–17. For Horney on young girls "instinctive" rape dreams see "The Denial of the Vagina" (1933), *Feminine Psychology*, pp. 154–55.

11. Sigmund Freud, "The Taboo of Virginity," St. Ed., XI, 204.

13

The Return of the Repressed/Oppressed in Bram Stoker's *Dracula*

Burton Hatlen

Marxist criticism has until recently generally assumed that only "realistic" literary works are worthy of serious critical analysis. As a result, Marxist critics have only occasionally concerned themselves with the literary mode that is today generally called "romance." The writings of Georg Lukács offer us perhaps our clearest example of the preoccupation with "realism" which has generally been characteristic of Marxist criticism. As G. H. R. Parkinson has noted, to Lukács "realism is the artistic basis of every authentic creation. . . . In other words, for Lukács the words 'work of art' (used in their evaluative sense) and 'realistic work of art' have the same reference."[1] Lukács's literary theory thus simply rules out *ipso facto* any serious analysis of works in the romantic mode. In the process, Lukács relegates to limbo much of our literary heritage. Marxist criticism cannot, I submit, simply ignore the romances of Chrétien and Malory, Ariosto and Spenser, the Brontës and William Morris. Furthermore, works in the romance mode seem more deeply rooted in popular culture than are works in the realistic mode. As Mikhail Bakhtin has demonstrated in his brilliant study of Rabelais, the popular imagination is far more likely to give birth to flamboyantly unrealistic characters like Pantagruel than to "typical" human beings like Emma Bovary.[2] If Marxist criticism takes seriously the idea that the people as a whole rather than this or that elite are the ultimate source of all that is vital in human culture, then a literary theory which cannot offer a plausible account of the role of the romance mode in literature seems decidedly inadequate. Fortunately, however, conditions now seem propitious for the development of a Marxist theory of romance. Such a theory can, as Frederic Jameson has argued,

---

This article originally appeared in *Minnesota Review* 15 (1980).

Henry Irving, 1876
Irving has been suggested as one of Stoker's models for *Dracula*.

build upon the important work of Northrop Frye in this area, while simultaneously subjecting Frye's critical categories to an explicitly Marxist critique.[3] Frye's principal virtue as a critic is his insistence that all texts, even those which orthodox academic criticism has dismissed as merely "commercial" or "popular," are equally worth the critic's attention; and Frye has been especially interested in charting the position of romance, a form once respectable but in our century generally dismissed as trivial, amid the galaxy of literary forms. Frye sees romance as bordered on the one side by comedy (with which romance shares a confidence in the ability of human energy to triumph over all obstacles) and on the other side by myth (with which romance shares a conception of life as a struggle between divine and demonic powers). Romance itself is, says Frye, "nearest of all literary forms to the wish-fulfillment dream," in that the romance hero (unlike the comic hero) confronts genuine Evil, and always triumphs.[4] Frye's critical categories are static and ahistorical. Therefore his treatment of romance can only be a starting point for the development of a Marxist theory on this subject. Yet as Jameson has demonstrated, Frye's categories can be used to good effect by the critic who, rather than simply classifying a work as a romance, instead looks both at the "generic affiliations" of the work and its "systematic deviations" from the conventions of the genre. The critic who looks at both similarities *and differences* (rather than, like Frye, at similarities alone) will, says Jameson, find "clues which lead us back to the concrete historical situation of the individual text itself, and allow us to read its structure as ideology, as a socially symbolic act, as a protopolitical response to a historical dilemma" (Jameson, p. 157). Jameson's brilliant redaction of Frye's theory of romance can, I believe, show us how to move beyond Lukács's sterile preoccupation with "realism," and how to move toward a Marxist theory of romance. And my hope here is to further, in however small a way, the emergence of such a theory.

In this essay, I shall attempt to bring to bear upon one particular example of the romance mode some methods of analysis that derive primarily from Frye and Jameson. The work I shall examine is Bram Stoker's *Dracula*.[5] *Dracula* is an interesting work for my purposes, first, because it is assertively "unrealistic," insofar as it asks us to believe (or to suspend our disbelief in) the existence of vampires. Stoker's novel has also been enormously popular throughout our century, and Count Dracula himself has moved out of Stoker's novel and into folklore—or at least into that artificial substitute for folklore which the electronic media represent. Despite the popularity and the influence of *Dracula*, however, literary critics have until recently almost wholly ignored the work. Only in the last decade has the increasing willingness of critics to take romance seriously, a willingness resulting in large measure from Frye's influence, issued in some useful critical work on Stoker's vampire fantasy. But most commentaries on *Dracula* to date have been primarily concerned with the psychological implications of the novel—understandably so, since psychoanalytic criticism offers a plausible way of explaining works of fantasy, especially such obviously sexual fantasies as *Dracula*.[6] Marxist critics too, however, should learn to look closely at such cultural phenomena as the myth and cult of Count Dracula; for an analysis of *Dracula* can, I believe, tell us a good deal about the temper of our epoch, and I also believe that such an analysis can help us to understand the social functions of romance. *Dracula*, like many romances, describes a struggle between the forces of light and the forces of darkness, and I take from Frederic Jameson my principal categories for describing the form that this struggle assumes in Stoker's novel. In romance, Jameson suggests, "the most important . . . organizational [category] is the conceptual opposition between good and evil, under which all the other types of attributes and images (light and darkness, high and low, etc.) are clearly subsumed." But as Jameson emphasizes, concepts of "good" and "evil" are not, to a Marxist, metaphysical categories. Rather they are "as little natural, as historical and as humanly 'constructed' as, say, the totemic systems of certain primitive tribes. . . ." And today, Jameson further proposes,

> It is becoming increasingly clear that the concept of evil is at one with the category of Otherness itself: evil characterizes whatever is radically different from me, whatever by virtue of precisely that difference seems to constitute a very real and urgent threat to my existence. So from earliest times, the stranger from another tribe, the "barbarian" who speaks an incomprehensive language and follows "outlandish" customs, or, in our own day, the avenger of cumulated resentments from some oppressed class, or else that alien being—Jew of Communist— behind whose apparently human features an intelligence of a malignant and preternatural superiority is thought to lurk—these are some of the figures in which the fundamental identify of the representative of Evil and the Other are [sic] visible. The point, however, is not that in such figures the Other is feared because he is evil; rather he is evil *because* he is Other, alien, different, strange, unclean, and unfamiliar. (Jameson, p. 140)

In the figure of Count Dracula, Stoker created an image of "otherness" which entered and quickly disseminated itself throughout American and European popular culture. Count Dracula represents the physically "other": the "dark" unconscious, the sexuality that Victorian England denied, more specifically a sado-masochistic sexuality that recognizes no limits and that no structured social order can accept. He is also culturally "other": a *revenant* from the ages of superstition when people believed that the communion wafer *was* the flesh of Christ. But more significantly of all he is the socially other: the embodiment of all the social forces that lurked just beyond the frontiers of Victorian middle class consciousness. Count Dracula represents, then, the repressed and the oppressed: the psychically repressed and the socially oppressed. It is for this reason that our response to him is so ambivalent. When the repressed/oppressed returns, we shudder with horror, *and* with hunger. And it is the various kinds of horrors and hungers which hover about the figure of Count Dracula that I propose to explore here.

If Dracula is the embodiment of "otherness," what is he other *than?* To answer this question, we must look briefly at the "good" characters in Stoker's novel. Some of these characters (Quincey Morris, Arthur Godalming, Lucy Westenra and Mina Harker) are independently wealthy; others (Jonathan Harker, Dr. Seward, Prof. Van Helsing) are engaged in such eminently respectable professions as law or medicine, which they seem to pursue less to earn a living than to do good for humanity. We are here dealing, it is clear, with members of the ruling class. The core members of this group are English: one member of the aristocracy (Lord Godalming), two representatives of the professional classes (Seward and Harker), and two delicately bred young ladies who lead lives of (apparently) total leisure (Lucy and Mina). From my point of view, Lord Arthur Godalming is particularly interesting. His first name, evoking as it does the memory of King Arthur, suggests that he embodies England's heritage; and his last name, which seems to conceal at least one pun ("God almighty"— and possibly "God damning" as well) suggests that he enjoys both divine sanction for his aristocratic status and divine protection in his daily life. Yet he is a humble fellow, and he seems to prefer the society of Harker and Seward to that of his fellow peers, even though his title prevents him from pursuing a useful profession. Even more significantly, he loves and intends to marry a commoner, Lucy Westenra. All in all, Godalming represents, I would propose, the "safe" aristocrat, the "tamed" aristocrat, indeed the "bourgeois aristocrat." (Victoria, we might remember, was occasionally described as a "bourgeois monarch.") He poses no threat to the *haut bourgeois* ethos of the other English characters; indeed he asks only to join the *haute bourgeoisie*, by marrying into it. If Godalming represents English tradition, Harker and Seward represent the groups which, to their own eyes at least, keep English society functioning. As a lawyer, Harker represents the state, the juridicial and political system. Seward is a doctor, specifically an "alienist," dedicated to exploring the causes of unreason and extirpating them. In general, he represents science and technology—the science and technology that have, Stoker implies, made England a powerful nation. The key decisions in Victorian society were made by people like Godalming, Harker, Seward; and if asked to justify their power and privilege, male members of this ruling elite would point immediately to women like Lucy Westenra and Mina Harker. They are pure sweetness and light. They are immune from such human feelings as lust, envy, anger, and (until Count Dracula appears, at least) fear. The *function* of English society is, we are asked to believe, to produce such delicate blooms as these young ladies, which can grow only in the most sheltered of locations; and any society which *can* produce such angels must be, we are also asked to believe, *ipso facto* good. The other two "good " characters are not English, but they are as dedicated to protecting the purity of English maidenhood as are Godalming, Harker, and Seward. One of these foreigners is Quincey Morris, a rich young Texan. Morris has sought Lucy's hand, and has been rejected. Her rejection of him (and his peculiar accent as well) mark him as "inferior" to the English characters. But after Lucy rejects him he dedicates himself to serving her, and the purity of his devotion seems to make him at least an honorary Englishman. As a reward, he receives the privilege of dying to protect England from Dracula; and if we feel it is ironic that the only person to die in the struggle to save England from Count Dracula is an American, there is no evidence that Stoker ever imagined that an American would see such a fate as anything but glorious. The other "outsider" is the Dutch doctor Van Helsing, who is undoubtedly the most memorable of the "good" male characters. Like Quincey's American accent, Van Helsing's peculiar speech marks him as "different"; and again like Quincey, he demonstrates his virtue by wholeheartedly dedicating himself to protecting the purity of English womanhood. But there the similarities end, for Van Helsing differs from the other "good" characters in one important respect: when we first meet him he is already a fallen creature, for he "knows" evil as well as good, whereas the English characters are all unfallen, immaculately innocent. Van Helsing's knowledge of evil gives him a unique role. It is his task to instruct the English characters and their American ally about the evil that lurks beyond the English Channel—it is significant that he comes from a country *just* across the channel. And because he already knows the ways of evil, it is also Van Helsing's task to lead the forces of light in their struggle against the forces of darkness.

Dracula threatens the tight, tidy world of upper middle class England because he is, first of all, sexually "other." The "good" characters in the novel, especially the women, seem wholly free of sexual desire; but the sexuality they have denied returns with a vengeance in the person of Count Dracula. No modern reader can fail to recognize the sexual implications of *Dracula*. Indeed, in Stoker's novel vampirism often seems to be a metaphor for sexuality—in particular, the female sexuality which so terrified the Victorians. In life Lucy Westenra is immaculately, implacably virginal. But as she begins her metamorphosis into a vampire she displays flashes of overt sexuality:

> Arthur took her hand and knelt beside her, and she looked her best, with all the soft lines matching the angelic beauty of her eyes. Then gradually her eyes closed, and she sank to sleep. For a little bit her breast heaved softly, and her breath came and went like a tired child's.
>
> And then insensibly there came the strange change which I had noticed in the night. Her breathing grew stertorous, the mouth opened, and the pale gums, drawn back, made the teeth look longer and sharper than ever. In a sort of sleep-waking, vague, unconscious way she opened her eyes, which were now dull and hard at once, and said in a soft voluptuous voice, such as I had never heard from her lips:—
>
> "Arthur! Oh, my love. I am so glad you have come! Kiss me!" (Stoker, pp 180–81).

And when Dr. Seward and his fellow vampire-hunters encounter her in the graveyard after her "death," she has become a rapaciously sexual creature:

> As she looked, her eyes blazed with unholy light, and the face became wreathed with a voluptuous smile. Oh, God, how it made me shudder to see it! . . . when she advanced to [Arthur] with outstretched arms and a wanton smile he fell back and hid his face in his hands.
>   She still advanced, however, and with a languorous, voluptuous grace, said:—
>   "Come to me, Arthur. Leave these others and come to me. My arms are hungry for you. Come, and we can rest together. Come, my husband, come!" (Stoker, p. 286)

If vampirism is here a metaphor for sexuality, it is not surprising that the *fons et origo* of vampirism, Count Dracula himself, should emanate a powerful sexual aura. As Carrol Fry has argued, Dracula is in some respects a lineal descendant of the "rakes" of 18th-century fiction. These rakes felt an overwhelming need to seduce "pure women," who then became "fallen women." In *Dracula*, Fry proposes, Dracula seduces (vampirizes) Lucy, who then becomes a fallen woman (a vampire).[7] Pursuing a somewhat similar argument, Judith Weissman has suggested that Stoker's novel dramatizes the male fear of the sexually voracious woman, a fear which is here displaced onto Count Dracula:

> [Dracula] is the man whom all other men fear, the man who can, without any loss of freedom or power himself, seduce other men's women and make them sexually insatiable with a sexual performance that the others cannot match.[8]

Weissman contends that the sexual anxiety evoked by *Dracula* is directed principally toward female sexuality, and on this point I believe she is right. In his descriptions of the impossibly pure Lucy, Stoker reveals the degree to which he shares in his society's obsession with "purity" in women. But to Stoker's credit it should be pointed out that he also reveals an awareness that the sexuality which this society has denied will, in some form, return. Lucy, we learn early in the novel, has been a sleepwalker since childhood. Clearly there was, even before Dracula entered her life, a hunger within her that her *haut bourgeois* world could not satisfy. And as soon as Count Dracula does arrive in England, she walks out in her sleep to meet him. Mina Harker too confesses that at some level she hungers for the vampire's kisses:

> ". . . With a mocking smile, he placed one hand upon my shoulder and, holding me tight, bared my throat with the other, saying as he did so, "First, a little refreshment to reward my exertions. You may as well be quiet; it is not the first time, or the second, that your veins have appeased my thirst!' I was bewildered, and, strangely enough, I did not want to hinder him. I suppose it is a part of the horrible curse that such is, when his touch is on his victim."
> (Stoker, p. 318)

Denied by Victorian society an opportunity to express their sexuality openly, Lucy and Mina find in Count Dracula an "objective correlative" of their lost sexuality; and blindly, unconsciously they give themselves to their demon lover.

The relationship of Lucy and Mina to Count Dracula is receptive but passive. As the common expression has it, they "give themselves" to the Count. Nothing is asked of them but "surrender"; he will do the rest. The role they assume vis-à-vis the Count is close enough to Western stereotypes of female sexuality that their behavior may seem to us understandable, perhaps even "normal." But we should note that their passivity is *total*, and that the end result of their sexual encounters with the Count is death. In these respects the response of Lucy and Mina to the Count is deeply masochistic. Indeed, I would contend that *all* the sexuality in *Dracula* is sado-masochistic, as we can see when we turn from Lucy and Mina to their male companions. There are only two moments in the novel in which male characters manifest sexual excitement. The first of these is the scene in which Jonathan Harker finds himself facing three female vampires and discovers that he feels a deep attraction to them:

> I lay quiet, looking out under my eyelashes in an agony of delightful anticipation. The fair girl advanced and bent over me till I could feel the movement of her breath upon me. Sweet it was in one sense, honey-sweet, and sent the same tingling through the nerves as her voice, but with a bitter underlying the sweet, a bitter offensiveness, as one smells in blood. (Stoker, pp. 47–48)

What seems to me most striking about Harker's behavior here is his passivity. He wants to "give himself" to the kisses of the vampire woman; he wants them to penetrate him with their phallic teeth; he wants to lie back and wait as *they* do the work. In these respects the sexual feelings that Harker here experiences are identical with (and no less masochistic than) the feelings of Lucy and Mina toward Count Dracula. In one other episode, we see a male character break out of his passivity and perform a sexual *act*. But, significantly, the act in question seems profoundly, grotesquely sadistic. I am referring to the scene in which Arthur drives a stake through Lucy's heart:

> Arthur took the stake and the hammer, and when once his mind was set on action his hands never trembled nor even quivered. . . . Arthur placed the point over the heart, and as I looked I could see its dint in the white flesh. Then he struck with all his might.
> The thing in the coffin writhed; and a hideous, bloodcurdling screech came from the opened red lips. The body shook and quivered and twisted in wild contortions; the sharp white teeth clamped together till the lips were cut, and the mouth was smeared with a crimson foam. But Arthur never faltered. He looked like a figure of Thor as his untrembling arm rose and fell, driving deeper and deeper the mercy-bearing stake, whilst the blood from the pierced heart welled and spurted up around it. (Stoker, pp. 240–41)

As C. F. Bentley has noted, "Lucy's reactions" in this scene "are described in terms reminiscent of sexual intercourse and orgasm, and especially the painful deflowering of a virgin, which Lucy still is" (Bentley, p. 31). But it also seems clear that sexual intercourse is here seen as an act of brutal aggression which results in death. Stoker's male characters, it seems, have a few more options than his female characters: they can choose between (or alternate between) sadism and masochism, whereas his female characters are condemned to masochism. But neither his male nor his female characters can experience a loving, non-destructive relationship with the other sex. In practice, then, the book not only equates vampirism with sexuality, but it also equates sexuality with sadomasochism. The consequence of this equation is that Count Dracula becomes the incarnation of sexuality itself. There is in the book no "clean" sexuality which can constitute an alternative to the "unclean" sexuality of the Count. In him, our sexuality confronts us as irreducibly alien, irreducibly "other." We can re-possess this sexuality only violently, by ecstatically surrendering ourselves to the dark hunger for death, or by standing above the beloved and driving a stake into her heart. That is to say, we *cannot* recover our lost sexuality, for in the very act of recovering it, it turns into something else. Nevertheless, insofar as Count Dracula incarnates our lost sexuality, he becomes the shape not only of our most terrible fears but also of our deepest desires. He is the other that we cannot escape, because he is part of us. He is the other that we loathe *and* love.

But if Count Dracula represents the sexually "other," he also (and no less powerfully) represents the culturally "other." The Victorian society which Stoker describes for us is firmly committed to the values of technology, rationality, and progress. The "good characters" show a naïve delight in machinery for its own sake: Dr. Seward dictates his diary into a phonograph rather than writing it, Mina Harker diligently transcribes everyone's diaries on her typewriter, and Quincey Morris is identified for us as an American partly by his fondness for "Kodaks" and "Winchesters." They are also sweetly reasonable people. Their minds are free of superstition, and their hearts are free of fear. When they are troubled or ill, they summon, not a priest, but a doctor. While vacationing at Whitby, Lucy and Mina meet a superstitious old mariner named Mr. Swales, and they find him quaint and amusing but a little foolish. Lucy, Mina, and their male admirers are vaguely aware that surrounding the island of light that is England there is a vast darkness; but they, like Conrad's Kurtz, are confident that the light will gradually penetrate the darkness. As he travels east toward Castle Dracula, however, Jonathan Harker discovers, again like Kurtz, how deep this darkness is, and he himself is very nearly swallowed up by it. Dracula's castle—in the middle of "one of the wildest and least known portions of Europe," a region, says Harker, of which "there are no maps . . . as yet to compare with our own Ordnance Survey maps" (Stoker, p. 8)—is a true heart of darkness.

As he approaches Castle Dracula, Harker must leave behind him one by one all the symbols of civilization: trains, comfortable hotels, the English language. And he find himself entering a world of barbaric foods and tongues, and of primitive superstitions. At first he tries to comport himself as a tourist—that is, he tries to see the inhabitants of this world as actors in a quaint spectacle staged for his delight: "the Slovaks . . . are very picturesque, but do not look prepossessing. On the stage they would be set down at once as some old Oriental band of brigands" (Stoker, p. 9). But when he finds these people giving him "the sign of the cross and the guard against the evil eye" (Stoker, p. 16), he discovers that he cannot remain a detached spectator of this primitive world. There is in Harker himself, as he soon learns, a "darkness" which makes him vulnerable to the Count. (Perhaps the clearest instance of this darkness within Harker is his decision, in violation of an express warning from Dracula, to sleep in the room where the three vampire women find him.) And eventually, with the unwitting assistance of Harker, the darkness invades the "heart of light," England itself. Count Dracula himself incarnates the darkness not only by virtue of his country of origin but also in at least four other ways. First, we learn that he was born and grew up in a mysteriously distant past. He is apparently about four hundred years old, and thus he is a *revenant* from a pre-enlightenment world. In him, the "dark ages" have literally returned to life. Second, we also learn that he must carry with him everywhere he goes coffins of earth from his place of birth. He is thus, even while he is traveling to England, rooted in the soil in a way that the enlightened characters in the novel are not. Third, Van Helsing tells us that he became a vampire, not through the bite of an older vampire, but rather through the study of magic. Fourth and last, Dracula represents a dark, primitive strata of civilization because he is, paradoxically, religious in a way that the other characters, Van Helsing perhaps excepted, are not. Dracula has a hunger for the infinite. He demands *eternal* life, whereas people like Mina and Jonathan Harker are content with their brief years on this earth. Dracula's hunger for the infinite makes him both more terrible and more magnificent than any other character in the novel. Dracula is also "religious" in the means by which he aspires to achieve eternal life. He is a kind of Christian literalist. If the communion wine *is* the blood of Jesus, then to drink blood would seem to be the simplest way of achieving at/one/ment, of uniting oneself with the source of all Being. Dracula, in his pride, rejects the blood of Jesus. But he is ferociously dedicated to the proposition that—as his one true disciple, Renfield, puts it—"the blood is the life" (Stoker, p. 159). Because Dracula emerges out of a dark, primordial world, he can be fought only by equally primordial means. Thus we have the astonishing spectacle of good scientists like Seward holding up crucifixes to ward off the Prince of Darkness, and good members of the Church of England helping Van Helsing to purify Dracula's boxes of earth with holy wafers— blessed, presumably, by a *Catholic* priest. We may find such scenes ridiculous.

But they also suggest how profoundly the "dark," magical, primordial ambience of Dracula challenges the complacent rationality of the Victorian bourgeoisie.

However, it is not Dracula himself but rather Stoker's most memorable minor character, the madman Henry Renfield, who most powerfully dramatizes the nature and effects of the culturally "other." I would define insanity itself as nothing more than a condition of absolute cultural "otherness." The madman displays patterns of thinking that the dominant culture defines as unacceptable. What constitutes madness therefore varies from one culture to another; and the particular mode of madness characteristic of a culture illuminates, by contrast, the distinctive qualities of that culture itself. The association of madness with "otherness" is suggested repeatedly in *Dracula* by the temporary madness which many of the characters feel when they are in the presence of Dracula. Harker, for example, suffers from a "violent brain fever" (Stoker, p. 114) for six weeks after his escape from Dracula's castle. But the only true madman in the novel is Renfield, a patient in Dr. Seward's asylum; and the particular form of madness he displays is of considerable thematic importance. Renfield, we learn, will eat any living thing, from flies on up the food chain. He is particularly interested in eating living beings that have consumed other living beings, for he seems to think of "lives" as atomistic "things" which remain "in" any animal that has eaten other living beings. Seward at one point describes as follows the behavior that results from Renfield's delusion:

> My homicidal maniac is of a peculiar kind. I shall have to invent a new classification for him, and call him a zoöphagous (life-eating) maniac; what he desires is to absorb as many lives as he can, and he has laid himself out to achieve it in a cumulative way. He gave many flies to the spider and many spiders to one bird, and then wanted a cat to eat the many birds. (Stoker, p. 83)

Seward is fascinated by Renfield, and with good reason. For Seward is a scientist, and there is something grotesquely "scientific" about Renfield's view of things. Renfield represents a mechanistic materialism gone mad—a materialism that would treat life, not as a process which results from certain functional relationships among the parts of an organism, but rather as one part of that organism. This kind of mechanistic materialism was not uncommon in 19th-century science, and Renfield's logic seems, to Seward, at least half plausible. "How well the man reasoned" (Stoker, p. 84), Seward notes in his diary. And immediately after the description of Renfield quoted above, Seward toys for a moment with the idea of completing Renfield's experiment, just to see what would happen:

> Men sneered at vivisection, and yet look at its results to-day! Why not advance science in its most difficult and vital aspect—the knowledge of the brain? Had I even the secret of one such mind—did I hold the key to the fancy of even one lunatic—I might advance my own branch

of science to a pitch compared with which Burdon-Sanderson's physiology or Ferrier's brain-knowledge would be as nothing. If only there were a sufficient cause! I must not think too much of this, or I may be tempted; a good cause might turn the scale with me, for may not I too be of an exceptional brain, congenitally? (Stoker, pp. 83–84)

Seward's fear of the consequences of such an experiment suggests that both he and his creator recognized the dangers of a mode of thought that would reify everything, including human beings. The passage quoted above also suggests an awareness on Stoker's part of how easily 19th-century rationalism could degenerate into such a reifying materialism. Significantly, it is Renfield's mad materialism that makes him vulnerable to Dracula. Apparently Renfield and Dracula have been in some sort of psychic contact even before the Count arrives in England. Dracula has promised Renfield an infinite supply of "lives," and Renfield in turn has agreed to assist Dracula in the latter's attempt to establish for himself a new base of operations in England. If I am correct in seeing Renfield as a mad materialist, then his willingness to help Dracula suggests that the scientific rationalism to which England is committed not only makes the country vulnerable to Dracula's assault but also in some fashion *longs* for that assault. The ethereal purity of Lucy Westenra longs for its "other," a degraded sexuality. Similarly, the scientific rationalism of England longs for its "other": a "dark," primordial superstition. And in the person of the mad Henry Renfield, we can see the scientific and technological cast of mind reaching out toward its "other."[10]

Furthermore, and in my judgement most significantly of all, Dracula also represents the socially "other." That Stoker's fable might have social and political implications has been suggested by one previous critic, Richard Wasson. Unfortunately, Wasson seeks to turn the book into a piece of cold-war propaganda, with Dracula representing "those forces in Eastern Europe which seek to overthrow, through violence and subversion, the more progressive democratic civilization of the West."[11] Wasson's interpretation of Dracula is clearly jingoistic and anachronistic, but I think he is correct in seeing the East/West opposition as crucially important to the novel. Dracula represents a character type that we encounter fairly frequently in Western literature: the centurion of the empire who, despairing of the possibility that he will ever receive due recognition from the home office, has "gone native" and now threatens to sack the heartland of the empire. Historically, Julius Caesar may be the prototype of the vengeful centurion; in our literature, Conrad's Kurtz is perhaps our clearest example. It is Dracula's historical mission which establishes him as a centurion of Christian Europe. He first won his fame, Van Helsing tells us, by guarding the Carpathian mountain passes against the Turks; and Dracula himself suggests to Mina that his raid on England is motivated in part by the desire for vengeance against an ungrateful Europe. "[I] intrigued for them, and fought for them hundreds of years before they were born ... ," he tells her (Stoker, p. 319). Apparently, Dracula has spent so much time guarding the frontier against the dark, barbaric outsider that he has become such an outsider: a metaphoric Turk. (From this point of view, Quincey Morris seems to represent the "good centurion." He too has been guarding one of the frontiers: Texas. But his loyalty to English values remains unshakeable.) Insofar as Dracula has become a Turk, his invasion of England represents an assault by a racial outsider, who threatens the purity of the English blood flowing in the veins of Lucy and Mina. Dracula's status as a racial outsider is suggested not only by his less-than-total mastery of English (a problem he shares with Van Helsing) and his peculiar sexual tastes (no Englishman would do something like *that*) but also by the sexual ambience that surrounds him. The belief, deeply ingrained in Western civilization and fully elucidated a few years ago in Cleaver's *Soul on Ice*, that dark men (the darker the better) are sexually more vigorous than fair men seems to have partially shaped Stoker's treatment of Dracula.[12] Dracula's skin is, of course, pale; but his black clothes and cape, his affinity with the night, and his penchant for entering bedrooms at midnight through windows combine to make him an archetype of the dreaded black rapist. Dracula's status as a symbol of the racial outsider is also suggested by his smell, a subject to which Stoker and his narrators, especially Harker, repeatedly refer:

> As the Count leaned over me and his hands touched me, I could not repress a shudder. It may have been that his breath was rank, but a horrible feeling of nausea came over me, which, do what I would, I could not conceal. . . . (Stoker, p. 26)
>
> There was an earthy smell, as of some dry miasma, which came through the fouler air. But as the odour itself, how shall I describe it? It was not alone that it was composed of all the ills of mortality and with the pungent, acrid smell of blood, but it seemed as though corruption had become itself corrupt. Faugh! it sickens me to think of it. Every breath exhaled by that monster seemed to have clung to the place and intensified its loathsomeness. (Stoker, p. 279)

The notion that "they" (those who are racially "other") smell "different" from us is a recurrent theme of racist rhetoric. Furthermore, the supposed smell of these "other" races ("we," of course, don't smell) is clearly associated with their presumed hyper-sexuality. As Freud argued, there seems to be an inescapable connection between sex and smell. The fear that the racial outsider will creep out of the stinking sewer to rape our women (and then, probably, slit our throats too) has been endemic in our century; and in the figure of Count Dracula we find a nightmarish embodiment of these fears.

The pattern of attributes (an odd accent, a "dark" aura, an irresistible sexual potency, a powerful smell) which Westerners generally ascribe to the races that threaten "our" purity are also, at least by the English, often ascribed to the socio-economic groups whose labors make possible the comfort and leisure of the ruling classes. In *Women in Love*, D. H. Lawrence describes a visit by

Gudrun and Ursula to a working-class area of town. The cerebral Gudrun, whose ancestral ties to the working class have long been severed, feels a powerful sexual attraction to this working-class world:

> Miners already cleaned were sitting on their heels, with their backs near the walls, talking and silent in pure physical well-being, tired, and taking physical rest. Their voices sounded out with strong intonation, and the broad dialect was curiously caressing to the blood. It seemed to envelop Gudrun in a labourer's caress, there was in the whole atmosphere, a resonance of physical men, a glamorous thickness of labour and maleness, surcharged in the air. But it was universal in the district, and therefore unnoticed by the inhabitants.
>
> To Gudrun, however, it was potent and half-repulsive. . . . [T]his was the world of powerful, underworld men who spend most of their time in the darkness. In their voices she could hear the voluptuous resonance of darkness, the strong, dangerous underworld, mindless, inhuman.[13]

On the subject of middle-class English beliefs concerning the smell of the working class, George Orwell offers some illuminating evidence:

> . . . [T]he real secret of class distinctions in the West—the real reason why a European of bourgeois upbringing, even when he calls himself a Communist, cannot without a hard effort think of a working man as his equal— . . . is summed up in four frightful words which people nowadays are chary of uttering, but which were bandied about quite freely in my childhood. The words were: *The lower classes smell.*[14]

The various signs of Dracula's "otherness"—his accent, his "dark" sexuality, his foul smell—thus make him a representative not only of all dark, foreign (i.e., non-English) races but also all "dark," foreign (i.e., non-bourgeois) classes. Like the coal miner, Dracula comes up out of the lower depths; like the peasant, his life is rooted in the soil. The labors of the workers and the peasant made possible the comfortable, leisurely lives of people like Mina and Lucy, Godalming and Seward. The knowledge that people of such elegant tastes and refined sensibilities are living off the labor of workers and peasants is firmly excluded from the consciousness of the *haute bourgeoisie*. However, as the dark outsider Dracula attempts to invade the closed world of the Victorian *haute bourgeoisie*, a knowledge of the relationship of oppressor to oppressed and a sense of the smoldering anger of the oppressed toward their oppressors also threatens to break through into consciousness. The hatred that Dracula arouses among Van Helsing's band of vampire fighters derives some of its intensity from the fear that "they" want "our" women. But this fear masks, I think, an even deeper fear—that once "they" get "our" women "they" will want everything else too. In driving Dracula back to his lair, the English characters and their allies thus seem to be defending themselves not only against a sexual and a cultural threat but also against a social threat, the threat of a revolutionary assault by the dark, foul-smelling, lustful lower classes upon the citadels of privilege. At the same time, Count Dracula also represents, paradoxically, another kind of threat to the *haute bourgeoisie*, the threat posed by an aristocracy which, although moribund, might suddenly revive. Count Dracula's status as an aristocrat is suggested by his title, his crumbling castle, and his suave manners. The 18th-century rake, we might also remember, was always an aristocrat, and the object of his attentions was always a good bourgeois girl. Behind the figure of the rake, C. F. Bentley has suggested, lurks a medieval lord demanding the *droit du seigneur*, and Bentley argues that in vampirizing Lucy Count Dracula is merely acting like a medieval nobleman:

> [Dracula's] nocturnal visits to Lucy, pre-empting the claims of her fiancé, have a distinct echo of the medieval *jus primae noctis*, the more so as Dracula, who is several centuries old, once was a feudal lord, and certainly retains the outlook and behavior of one. (Bentley, p. 32)

Bentley's comments might remind us that, in the eyes of the bourgeoisie, both the lower and upper classes enjoyed a sexual license denied the bourgeoisie themselves. In this respect Dracula seems to have the best of both the proletarian and the aristocratic worlds. Dracula's hard egoism and his insolent contempt for ordinary human beings also seem "aristocratic"; and the hatred he evokes in people like Harker and Seward derives part of its strength from a lingering bourgeois resentment of the aristocrat. (Just as Morris represents the "good centurion," Arthur Godalming represents the "good aristocrat"—the aristocrat who not only accepts but welcomes the hegemony of the bourgeoisie.) My suggestion that Dracula represents both the repressed masses of workers and a decaying aristocracy may seem contradictory. But if we see Dracula as representing everything that is "other" to the Victorian bourgeoisie—the "dark" captive races over whom this social class ruled, the equally "dark" masses of workers and peasants, and the "dark," exotic aristocracy—then this problem disappears. It is "otherness" itself, not some particular social group, that Dracula represents; and, for the bourgeoisie, the modes of otherness are infinite.

Count Dracula evokes—in the other characters of Stoker's novel, and in us as we read—a complex response, compounded equally of fear and fascination. The reason for the fear is clear enough: he threatens to destroy all existing forms of order, whether in the ego or in the social order. The reason for the fascination may be less clear but is no less important: he represents all that bourgeois society has repudiated, and as these rejected areas of experience emerge into consciousness the ghost of desires past also re-emerge. We hate and fear Count Dracula, but we also long to give ourselves up to him. Conversely, even while we applaud the efforts of Van Helsing and his band of vampire fighters, we are secretly a little contemptuous of these pallid, prissy, asexual people. I will not argue that the ambiguity at the heart of *Dracula* is intentional.

Indeed, I suspect that Stoker's conscious intention was to portray *haut bourgeois* English society as absolutely good, and Dracula as absolutely evil. I have no evidence to support this statement except the text of *Dracula* itself. But I would contend that, for example, the sudden "sexualization" of Lucy is artistically powerful because it seems to erupt into the book like a force emerging out of the unconscious; and I believe that Stoker is no less surprised by her transformation that we are. If Stoker had begun with the conscious conviction that there is a sexually voracious animal buried within every virtuous maiden, a tinge of irony would certainly have crept into his numerous scenes of "girl-talk" between Lucy and Mina. Yet I can detect no trace of irony in these scenes. As far as I can tell, Stoker *really believes* (or really *thinks* he believes) in the Victorian "good girl," and he shares our shock when one of his good girls suddenly becomes ravenously sexual. As Stoker's dark fable unfolded, something other than conscious intention apparently took control. The psychoanalytic critic might be tempted to see this controlling power as Stoker's personal sexual neurosis. But I find it more plausible to see the book as an "acting out" of a social situation which Stoker himself felt very acutely, even though he perhaps had little conscious understanding of this situation. Stoker was himself, like several of his characters, an outsider in Victorian England. He was the son of an Irishman who worked for several decades as a dedicated but ill-paid civil servant in Dublin. The elder Stoker was thus himself a centurion of an empire which often treated its most faithful servants with some neglect, especially if these servants belonged to alien races like the Irish. Bram Stoker himself spent several years as a Dublin civil servant; but he longed for the glamour of London, and he soon escaped from Ireland by attaching himself to the actor Sir Henry Irving, whom he served as secretary for several decades. In his capacity as Irving's factotum, Stoker had occasion to spend a good deal of time with members of the English ruling class, and his admiration for these elegant people was clearly very strong. Yet he also retained throughout his life a strong sense of his Irish identity. He wrote a pamphlet advocating Home Rule for Ireland, and we were told that he was disappointed at his failure to persuade Irving to espouse this cause. As an Irishman and as a paid dependent of Irving, it seems probable that Stoker occasionally felt like something of an outsider among Irving's wealthy and aristocratic friends. He apparently comported himself as a kind of stage Irishman in these circles, but it seems likely that his external geniality concealed a certain resentment against the supercilious English ladies and gentlemen whom he so entertained. There are no Irish characters in *Dracula*. But there are three outsiders in the book and the various concrete forms that "Irishness" took in Stoker's world are displaced onto these three characters: the eager, good-hearted, but somewhat bumbling Quincey Morris, the wise and powerful (powerful primarily because he has access to certain magical substances available only to *Catholics*) Van Helsing, and the erotic, demonic, vengeful Count Dracula. And Stoker, I

think, identified himself with all three of these characters—that is, I think that
he saw himself as a genial clown, *and* as a representative of an older, wiser race
that retained access to magical powers, *and* as a dark avenger determined to
punish the English for their insults against himself and his people. Again, I am
not suggesting that these identifications were conscious on Stoker's part. But I
am arguing that in this book Stoker has given symbolic expression to certain
concrete truths concerning his life situation, and that the energy of the book
derives principally from this fact.[15]

To give expression to his own ambivalence toward his English masters,
Stoker created a set of powerful symbols which also encode certain truths about
our life situation—and this, I think, is the principal reason why the book still
fascinates us. The real subject of *Dracula* is not sexual or psychic repression;
if this were the theme, then the sexual permissiveness of our century would
have made the book merely a quaint anachronism. Nor is the subject racial and
social oppression, for the book tells us nothing very useful about why or how
ruling elites preserve their power. Rather the real subject of the book is, I
submit, the *relationship between* psychosexual repression and social oppression.
In other words, the book is not about the repressed masochistic desires of Stoker
or his characters; nor is it about the way bourgeois society excludes the dark,
racial outsider or the smelly worker. Rather it is about our desire (by "our" I
mean middle-class whites) to "submit" ourselves (I am here using the word
"submit" in the explicitly masochistic sense that it has acquired in pornographic
literature) to—i.e., to be sexually violated by—the "dark," "foul smelling"
outsider. The point at which sexuality and politics meet—this is the point at
which Stoker's book locates itself. Modern feminists have become acutely sensi-
tive to the nuances of sexual politics, and so it is not surprising that some of the
most useful recent commentaries on *Dracula* have come from feminist critics.
However, I think these critics sometimes oversimplify the book by treating it
as nothing more than an expression of Stoker's sexist attitudes.[16] As I have here
attempted to show, the view of women encoded in the book is inextricably
bound up with certain attitudes toward the culturally, racially, and socially
"other." Women like Lucy and Mina are certainly oppressed, but the sort of
oppression they suffer is quite different from the oppression experienced by
women who are *not* members of the ruling elite. As the example of Lucy and
Mina suggests, female members of the ruling class were desexualized by Victorian English society; but women born outside the magic circle of the ruling elite
(the only concrete examples in *Dracula* are perhaps the three vampire women
at Castle Dracula) were instead generally *hyper*sexualized by this same society.
We cannot, then, understand the role of women in Victorian society unless we
also understand the various ways in which racial and class differences manifested themselves in this society. In a society divided between rulers and ruled,
sexual relations are *inevitably* infected by the patterns of dominance and sub-

mission, violence given and violence endured, which operate throughout the society as a whole. But at the same time, power relations in such a society are *inevitably* sexualized, simply because we are inherently sexual beings and therefore experience all our interpersonal relationships in sexual terms. So it is that the slave hates his master—and gives his own children the master's name. So it is too that the master flogs his slave—and then begs the slave's mother to nurse him, and the slave's daughter to love him. At the beginning of the 19th century, Hegel memorably analyzed the master/slave dialectic; at the end of the century, Stoker demonstrated that this dialectic still determined the structure of English society; and we today, as we watch the latest son of Count Dracula mesmerize the most recent child of Lucy, testify by our rapt attention that the master/slave dialectic is still working itself out in our own lives. The force of Stoker's book lies in its capacity to mobilize the feelings that surround the master/slave relationship. We can, of course, simply surrender ourselves to these feelings, as Lucy and Mina surrender themselves to Count Dracula. But unlike Lucy and Mina, we have a choice. We can ask ourselves *why* Stoker's symbols affect us so powerfully. We can make his novel an object of reflection. In this way, *Dracula* can help us to understand why we are compelled to create the "other" as the object of our hatred and our hunger. Thus rather than offering us an escape from the "real" world, Stoker's flamboyantly "unrealistic" novel can, if we will let it, finally return us to the world of history and responsibility, with a new awareness that in this "real" world all forms of good and evil, the positive and the negative, are contingent and must, if we are ever to become fully human, finally dissolve in that "negation of the negation" which will mark an end to "otherness" itself.

Notes

1. G. H. R. Parkinson, "Lukács on the Central Category of Aesthetics," in *Georg Lukács: The Man, His Work, and His Ideas*, ed. G. A. R. Parkinson (New York: Vintage, 1970), p. 132.

2. Mikhail Bakhtin, *Rabelais and His World*, trans. Helene Iswolsky (Cambridge: M.I.T. Press, 1968).

3. Frederic Jameson, "Magical Narratives: Romance as Genre," *New Literary History*, 7 (1975), 135–63.

4. Northrop Frye, *Anatomy of Criticism* (Princeton: Princeton University Press, 1957), p. 186 and ff.

5. Bram Stoker, *Dracula* (New York: Dell, 1973). There is no standard scholarly edition of Stoker's novel, and the Dell edition will do as well as any other. All references to Stoker's novel will be to this edition and will be incorporated into the text.

6. See for example, C. F. Bentley, "The Monster in the Bedroom: Sexual Symbolism in Bram Stoker's *Dracula*," *Literature and Psychology*, 22 (1972), 27–34; and Phyllis A. Roth, "Suddenly Sexual Women in Bram Stoker's *Dracula*," *Literature and Psychology*, 27 (1977), 113–21.

Only one previously published interpretive essay on *Dracula* verges on a Marxist reading of the novel: Gérard Stein, *"Dracula,* on la circulation du 'sans'," *Literature,* 8 (1972), 84–99. Stein, however, is more interested in the linguistic than in the socio-political implications of Stoker's novel. He raises a cluster of questions about the role of racist and imperialist motifs in the novel (Stein, p. 98), but he makes no serious effort to answer these questions. Instead most of his essay is devoted to a Derridesque meditation on the silence of Count Dracula.

7. Carrol L. Fry, "Fictional Conventions and Sexuality in *Dracula," The Victorian Newsletter,* 42 (1972), 20–22.

8. Judith Weissman, "Women and Vampires: *Dracula* as a Victorian Novel," *The Midwestern Quarterly,* 18 (1977), 404 and *passim.*

9. One previous critic, Phyllis Roth, mentions the sado-masochistic implications of *Dracula.* Stoker's novel, she says, "dramatizes the child's view of intercourse . . . as a wounding and a killing" (Roth, p. 119). I should add that the sado-masochistic sexuality of the novel affects the male and female characters somewhat differently. Some of the male characters, Van Helsing for example, are able to liberate themselves entirely from sexual feeling. In contrast the female characters are clearly unable to do so. Something in them calls out to Dracula across the seas; and he knows what they are thinking and feeling even when he is far away from them. The result is that women, generically, become in effect Count Dracula's "fifth column" within bourgeois English society. In its suggestion that men can liberate themselves from their sexuality while women cannot, *Dracula* is undoubtedly a sexist book. Yet more significant than Stoker's patronizing conception of women as the slaves of their sexuality, I believe, is his equation of sexuality itself with brutal domination and with "ecstatic" submission.

10. For a full and lucid discussion of Renfield's role in the novel, see Jean Gattegno, "Folie, croyance et fantastique dans *Dracula," Littérature,* 8 (1972), 72–83.

11. Richard Wasson, "The Politics of *Dracula," English Literature in Transition,* 9 (1966), 24.

12. Eldridge Cleaver, *Soul on Ice* (New York: Dell, 1968), pp. 155–90.

13. D. H. Lawrence, *Women in Love* (New York: Viking, 1971), p. 108.

14. George Orwell, *The Road to Wigan Pier* (New York: Harcourt Brace, 1961), p. 127.

15. My information about Stoker's life comes primarily from Harry Ludlam, *A Biography of Dracula: The Life Story of Bram Stoker* (London: Fireside Press, 1962).

16. A tendency to treat *Dracula* as primarily a manifestation of Stoker's sexist attitudes is apparent in Weissman's essay and in Stephanie Demetrakopoulos, "Feminism, Sex Role Exchanges, and Other Subliminal Fantasies in Bram Stoker's *Dracula," Frontiers,* 2 (1977), 104–13.

14

"Your Girls That You All Love Are Mine": *Dracula* and the Victorian Male Sexual Imagination

Gail B. Griffin

The Dracula myth, like its namesake, lives forever, feeding on all of us. Like all myths, it draws from the deepest reserves of human psychology and culture, upon ancient fears and desires, symbols and taboos. And like most of our well-known myths, it is essentially male, but its particular maleness is usually misunderstood. The common view of the Dracula story today is that it portrays threatening male sexuality and passive female innocence, and to an extent this interpretation is borne out by Bram Stoker's 1897 novel. But the reader schooled in modern versions of the myth may find the novel a very different animal, in which the horror of Dracula is rooted in another kind of sexual threat, one which, to the male Victorian imagination, was far worse.

The first surprise is the near-absence of Dracula from the novel, after Jonathan Harker's sojourn at Castle Dracula in chapters 1–4. Thereafter, his appearances are few, momentary, often ambiguous and mostly silent. He appears as a wolf or a bat; he surfaces in second-hand accounts—that is, reports from other than the five chief narrators; he appears occasionally in the journals of these five, but fleetingly and silently. In England he has precisely two speaking appearances in the accounts of the primary narrators: in Mina's description of his attack upon her, and in his confrontation with the five heroes in London.

There are two points to be made about Dracula's relative invisibility in the novel named for him. The first is, of course, that it is crucial to Stoker's purposes that Dracula be a pervasive presence, a force, rather than a "charac-ter." He is more dangerous when incorporeal than when visible. The second

This article originally appeared in *International Journal of Women's Studies* 3 (1980), No. 5.

point is that active vampirism, with its dimension of sexuality, is dissociated from Dracula and associated instead with the four female vampires seeking male victims. The Count himself is caught in the act only once, when Mina sees him bending over Lucy, but only dimly, from a distance, at night. His scene with Mina is much more detailed and openly sexual, but it is Mina who is doing the drinking. In addition, the Count's physical appearance, when he makes one, comes as a surprise to readers expecting Frank Langella or even Bela Lugosi: Dracula is tall, bony, hook-nosed, emaciated unless recently fed, and usually quite elderly, though this last is subject to change without notice. He does not seem designed as a sexual entity; only once is he described as "sensual,"[1] a word which in any case had not exclusively sexual connotations in the nineteenth century.

In striking contrast are the female vampires: Lucy Westenra in her posthumous appearance to her mourners near the middle of the novel, and the trio at Castle Dracula near the beginning and end of the novel. These latter, when Harker· first meets them, begin to illuminate Stoker's use of the vampire myth, which will become fully clear later in his descriptions of Lucy in her Undead state.

In the first four chapters of the novel, Stoker carefully lays the groundwork for the collision of the stodgy priggishness and determined rationalism of Victorian England with primeval irrational forces, a conflict upon which the rest of the novel will depend. Jonathan Harker stands, dazed, before the portal of Castle Dracula and muses, "Was this a customary incident in the life of a solicitor's clerk?" (p. 22). In his coach trip through the Borgo Pass, Harker has slowly lost his hold on England and the world of daylight and rationality; he is steadily submerging in what he will later call "a whole world of dark and dreadful things" (p. 394). When he wanders into the chambers Dracula has forbidden to him and meets the three vampires, he is still English enough to make the crucial distinction between women and ladies; this trio belongs to the latter category "by their dress and manner," making them all the more perversely exciting, as Stephanie Demetrakopoulos reminds us, since only lower-class women were supposed to have sexual desires.[2] But we know how dangerously he has responded to Dracula's world when he immediately recognizes the blonde vampire "in connection with some dreamy fear." This is a fairly significant line, as it is virtually the only one in the novel which acknowledges the link between the female vampires and some part of the heroes' psychology. The roots of this most horrific of Harker's experiences in the castle are, of course, in himself: uneasiness and fear mingle with "longing"; the "dark and dreadful things" are in his own "wicked, burning desire." He discovers reserves of sexuality within himself and explores his own sexual masochism in his "agony of delightful anticipation" of the vampire's kiss (p. 47). In Harker's mind the trio is immediately contrasted with Mina, the good girl back home, an opposition which will be very important in the second half of the novel.

The blonde's assault on Jonathan is described in singular detail and luridly sensual language:

> I was afraid to raise my eyelids, but looked out and saw perfectly under the lashes. The girl went on her knees, and bent over me, simply gloating. There was a deliberate voluptuousness, which was both thrilling and repulsive, and as she arched her neck she actually licked her lips like an animal, till I could see in the moonlight the moisture shining on the scarlet lips and on the red tongue as it lapped the sharp teeth. Lower and lower went her head as the lips went below the range of my mouth and chin and seemed to fasten on my throat. Then she paused, and I could hear the churning sound of her tongue as it licked her teeth and lips, and I could feel the hot breath on my neck. Then the skin of my throat began to tingle as one's flesh does when the hand that is to tickle it approaches nearer—nearer. I could feel the soft, shivering touch of the lips on the super-sensitive skin of my throat, and the hard dents of the two sharp teeth, just touching and pausing there. I closed my eyes in languorous ecstasy and waited— waited with beating heart. (p. 48)

Compared to this, Dracula himself is quite tame. In fact, although he suggests that he is saving Harker for himself, nothing comes of it. The Count remains a veiled threat; the palpable reality is this female trio.

The scene introduces several ideas and images of later importance as the significance of Stoker's vampire women unfolds. First and foremost is the word "voluptuous," which occurs twice in this episode, representing a sexuality, as Harker puts it, "both thrilling and repulsive," just as the vampire's voice is "honey-sweet . . . but with . . . a bitter offensiveness" (p. 48). For the first time vampirism is linked with stifled, obsessive sexuality, all the more urgent because forbidden; and this sexuality is represented as female. Second, the animalism of the vampires will have important thematic ramifications. Third, the color red—in their lips, their cheeks, the tongue of the blonde, the eyes of the other two and by implication, of course, their nourishment—is perhaps the central symbol of the novel, often juxtaposed, as here, with white. Fourth is the presence of moonlight. And finally, the trio are left to devour the blood of a living child, an act which particularly appalls Harker and which will recur later.

Back in England, land of reason and science, typewriters and recording machines, where they build asylums for apprentice vampires like Renfield, Dracula emerges only gradually, with the help of Stoker's array of narrators. He is a scattering of puzzle pieces that slowly come together, a dark shadow that eventually solidifies. But it is extremely important that his reality explodes upon the other characters not in his own person but in Lucy's.

His attack on the sleepwalking Lucy, as described earlier, is veiled, indistinct, as Mina records it. As Lucy begins to waste away, the important alignments in the novel start to clarify themselves: four of the heroes, Van Helsing, Seward, Morris, and Lucy's fiancé Arthur Holmwood, form an ever-tightening circle around her. A brotherhood is born when three of them propose to her on the same day. The two rejects swear eternal fealty and friendship to her, and Lucy asks Mina, "Why can't they let a girl marry three men, or as many as want her ...?" (p. 71). She would "give herself" to all of them in sheer gratitude, one presumes. The trio of lovers gathers to cement their friendship and drown their rivalry. But four months later the three of them, plus Van Helsing, whom we suspect of harboring a crush on Lucy as well, are called upon to donate blood to their mysteriously fading beloved. Like a sexual conqueror Seward reflects on his contribution: "It was with a feeling of personal pride that I could see a faint tinge of color steal back into the pallid cheeks and lips. No man knows, till he experiences it, what it is to feel his own lifeblood drawn away into the veins of the woman he loves" (p. 145). Likewise, Van Helsing assures Quincey Morris, when it is his turn, that "A brave man's blood is the best thing on this earth when a woman is in trouble" (p. 168). The sexual symbolism of the transfusions enhances the suggestion of some mystical, ritualistic undertone to this scientific procedure, a suggestion substantiated when Arthur describes the transfusion as a marriage (p. 195) and Van Helsing refers to Lucy as a polyandrist (p. 197): in fact, Lucy has her wish and marries all of them. The quartet becomes a kind of knighthood, bound to Lucy literally by blood, as well as by the previous oaths of friendship and love. She, like countless women in literature, is the common ideal to which they pledge themselves.

The transfusions which symbolize this relation are at once ritualistic and comical: Lucy is actually nothing more than a pipeline from one set of veins to another. She is Dracula's victim but also his tool for acquiring other victims. She is already a vampire, for she drains men's blood, as women are traditionally said to weaken men sexually; but she is a passive one at this point, unlike her sisters at Castle Dracula. By the time she dies, however, a change is occurring which only Van Helsing perceives, a change hinting broadly at the future:

> Her breathing grew stertorous, the mouth opened, and the pale gums, drawn back, made the teeth look longer and sharper than ever. In a sort of sleep-waking, vague, unconscious way she opened her eyes, which were now dull and hard at once, and said, in a soft, voluptuous voice, such as I had never heard from her lips:—
> "Arthur! Oh my love, I am so glad you have come! Kiss me!" (p. 181)

Lucy recovers from her voluptuousness just long enough to elicit from Van Helsing another oath—to protect Arthur and, in effect, to destroy the other self that has just spoken.

It is this other self, released to its full expression, that manifests the real horror of Dracula to our heroes. The scene of confrontation outside the tomb is certainly the climax of the novel, structurally and emotionally. As Dracula is Antichrist, sharing eternal life through a communion/baptism of blood, this scene is a mock-Resurrection, where Lucy's apostles find an empty tomb and meet with their risen beloved, as the moon emerges from the clouds:

> Lucy Westenra, but yet how changed. The sweetness was turned to adamantine, heartless cruelty, and the purity to voluptuous wantonness. . . . Van Helsing raised his lantern and drew the slide; by the concentrated light that fell on Lucy's face we could see that the lips were crimson with fresh blood, and that the stream had trickled over her chin and stained the purity of her lawn death-robe.
>
> When Lucy—I call the thing that was before us Lucy because it bore her shape—saw us she drew back with an angry snarl such as a cat gives when taken unawares; then her eyes ranged over us. Lucy's eyes in form and colour, but Lucy's eyes unclean and full of hell-fire, instead of the pure, gentle orbs we knew . At that moment the remnant of my love passed into hate and loathing; had she then to be killed, I could have done it with savage delight. As she looked, her eyes blazed with unholy light, and the face became wreathed with a voluptuous smile. Oh, God, how it made me shudder to see it! With a careless motion, she flung to the ground, callous as a devil, the child that up to now she had clutched strenuously to her breast, growling over it as a dog growls over a bone. The child gave a sharp cry, and lay there moaning. There was a cold-bloodedness in the act which wrung a groan from Arthur; when she advanced to him with outstretched arms and a wanton smile he fell back and hid his face in his hands.
>
> She still advanced, however, and with a langorous, voluptuous grace, said:—
>
> "Come to me, Arthur. Leave these others and come to me. My arms are hungry for you. Come, and we can rest together. Come, my husband, come!"
>
> There was something diabolically sweet in her tones—something of the tinkling of glass when struck. . . . (pp. 235–36)

That sound should be familiar to us from the laughter of the vampires at Castle Dracula, described identically. Likewise "voluptuous," occurring here three times within a short space, along with "wantonness" and "wanton." Again, as on her deathbed, Lucy approaches Arthur and nearly seduces him into her arms. The trait that most obviously ties Lucy and her Transylvanian sisters is sexual aggressiveness, the first hint to Van Helsing that Lucy was becoming a vampire. Herein lies the ultimate horror of Dracula for the male consciousness represented by Van Helsing, Morris, Seward, and Arthur, as well as for Stoker and his audience: he turns their women into sexual predators. For this reason are the truly horrific scenes in the novel consistently related to female sexuality.

In this context the blood motif acquires a new richness. The blood from Lucy's mouth "had trickled over her chin and stained the purity of her lawn death-robe." The opposition of the white and the red, the purity and the obviously impure blood, suggests that the horror Lucy embodies is an ancient one, as old as the menstrual taboo and the concept of the unclean woman. The shedding of female blood is traditionally associated with two events in a woman's life: the loss of virginity and the menarche, both involving sexuality and concepts of defilement, impurity. Simone de Beauvoir writes, ". . . [O]n the day she can reproduce, a woman becomes impure. . . ."[3] Since woman is historically defined in sexual terms, these critical points in her life represent an alteration of identity as well. Menstruation carries a particular cultural load; the menstruating woman is a figure of enormous power, evil and good. We do well to keep in mind that in 1878, less than twenty years before *Dracula* appeared, the *British Medical Journal* asserted as an "undoubted fact" that the touch of a menstruating woman could spoil meat.[4] Menstruation indicates fertility, the height of female power, "the essence of femininity," in de Beauvoir's words,[5] and therefore it has catalyzed both hatred and fear of womanhood on the part of men.

Most critics interested in the sexuality in *Dracula* have seen the blood as a semen substitute, since female vampirism is portrayed in terms suggestive of fellatio.[6] Inasmuch as the vampire women represent, to the male imagination in the novel, the man-eating, castrating woman, depleting male strength, this interpretation is a good one. But the connection with menstrual blood is more obvious and direct, and its broader implications are more central to Stoker's handling of the myth. The prominence of the moon and moonlight in the scenes of female vampirism seems to support this connection, as the moon probably grew into a symbol for woman from its relation to the menstrual cycle. Nineteenth-century doctors believed that the menstruating woman was prone to temporary insanity and fits of violence,[7] doubtless in part because of this mystical synchronism with the moon, from which *lunacy* takes its name. Lucy is a horrible caricature of the "moody woman," ruled by the inconstant moon, victim of her own biology and subject to sudden, violent personality changes. In *Dracula* the moon unites the "mysteries" of female physiology and power with other supernatural mysteries it traditionally suggests. Under the light of the moon this raging, hungry female force is released.

Stoker may subconsciously have been drawing upon the common confusion of menstruation and estrus, especially since Lucy and the Transylvanian women are described as bestial—as animals in heat. The idea of woman as a subhuman, wholly sexual, animalistic creature is part of a larger association of vampirism with animalism in *Dracula*. All the vampires are described as animals at some point; Dracula, of course, takes animal form, and Renfield creates a sort of ecological chain of predation, with himself at the top. Vampirism expresses the fear of the animal within, and as such, as Judith Weissman has noted, "is only an extreme version of the evil of the body against which Christians have been told to fight for almost 2000 years."[8] For the Victorian mind the threat of the beast within was particularly great, because of the immense tension surrounding sexuality, because of a larger fear of the irrational and instinctual, and because Darwin had sensitized the whole of society to the proximity of simian ancestors. This is the anxiety of Tennyson's *In Memoriam*, a poem which struggles at length to reclaim humanity as the crown of creation, to find some alternative to a nature red in tooth and claw—a world of vampires.

It has always been easy for a male-dominated culture to project the beast within upon the woman without, violently repressing her sexuality while just as violently encouraging it. "In all civilizations and still in our day," writes de Beauvoir, "woman inspires man with horror; it is the horror of his own carnal contingence, which he projects upon her."[9] The gothic horror of Dracula, then, is an ancient terror surfacing in particularly intense form in the Victorian age. The vampire women in *Dracula* represent the worst nightmare and dearest fantasy of the Victorian male: the pure girl turned sexually ravenous beast.

Lucy and her three sisters are linked by another force which violates the norm of Victorian womanhood: anger, almost as repellent to the male observers as sexual aggressiveness. When Dracula drags the blonde head away from Harker's neck, Jonathan sees "the blue eyes transformed with fury, the white teeth champing with rage, and the fair cheeks blazing red with passion" (p. 77). Lucy's transformation is even more radical: "The beautiful color became livid, the eyes seemed to throw out sparks of hell-fire, the brows were wrinkled as though the folds of the flesh were the coils of Medusa's snakes, and the lovely, blood-stained mouth grew to an open square, as in the passion masks of the Greeks and Japanese. If ever a face meant death—if looks could kill—we saw it at that moment" (p. 236). It is a truly appalling description. The horror is that Lucy, who would formerly have married three men to avoid hurting their feelings, who fulfilled completely the Victorian ideal of the placid, compliant, proto-wife, whose mother rejoices that she will "have someone to protect her" (p. 110), is capable of this archetypal rage, this absolute hatred. The word "passion" occurs in both descriptions, and passion—either sexual or emotional— was forbidden fruit for the Victorians, particularly for the women. So the worst that Dracula can do is transform Lucy into a creature of pure passion, an abstract of passion itself, "as in the passion masks of the Greeks and Japanese."

Lucy outrages the Victorian ideal in one more important way. The scene at the tomb makes clear that she is indeed the mysterious "bloofer lady" who has been luring children away and draining their blood. She has become a demonic mother-parody, taking nourishment from children instead of giving it, as do the three women at the Castle. When Lucy dashes her small victim to the ground, Stoker's point is clear: Dracula has so completely polluted her femininity that she has lost all maternal feeling.[10] God's designated protector of children has become their predator. The transformation from woman to monster is complete.

We have seen Lucy in two roles in the novel, eliciting two male responses: she is either pitied as a victim or despised as a predator. These are not unfamiliar roles for women, in literature or in life. Part of the fascination of *Dracula* is the way in which Stoker uses these two traditional attitudes as elements in a story of metamorphosis and horror.

"She seemed like a nightmare of Lucy" (p. 239), Seward laments when the knightly brethren return to the tomb to do the final deed; and he is right: she is their collective nightmare of Lucy, the Victorian nightmare of womanhood befouled. The nightmare has a "bloodstained, voluptuous mouth" again, and a "carnal and unspirited appearance" (p. 239). The essence of the nightmare is in those last words: a body "unspirited" is merely a body, "carnal," bestial. The unspirited woman was an especially monstrous development, for Victorian culture nourished the dichotomy of the angel and the whore: if a woman was not pure spirit, she was pure body. To this Lucy has come, and there is only one punishment for the carnal woman. The aptly named Arthur, the nobleman, is designated to perform this ritual execution, which is, significantly, termed an "ordeal" by Van Helsing, enhancing the medieval spirit that increasingly informs the group's actions in quest of an ancient evil. The body is killed and the spirit reappears in "unequalled sweetness and purity" (p. 241). Here Seward drops a telling remark: he mentions that the signs of her illness and mental strain were visible upon the repurified Lucy, but that they "were dear to us, for they marked her truth to what we knew" (p. 242). The real terror of this "ordeal" was confronting a Lucy who was not "what we knew," who violated their conceptions of her. Arthur, keeper of the flame, reasserts this communal ideal in destroying the body of Lucy.

If the Lucy who is "what we knew" is a projection of a male ideal of femininity, it is not surprising that she is transformed into a vampire, for within the traditional dichotomized view of woman, the angel and the whore are not opposite poles but yin and yang, totally interdependent. Phyllis Roth has noted that when Lucy appears as a vampire, her formerly "sunny" hair has turned dark, underscoring the coexistence within her of the two female archetypes.[11] Idealization of femininity coexists with—in fact, nurtures—the most venomous misogyny; they are sides of the same coin. In *Dracula*, the idealization of womanhood is sustained by a streak of antifemale sentiment running the length of the tale. To give it credence, much of it is put into the mouths of Lucy and Mina, who define their gender as unfair, cowardly, unworthy of noble men. In the leading male characters, "amazingly similar in their thoughts about women,"[12] chivalric glorification of womanhood commingles with disparagement and suspicion. In particular, the alleged weakness of woman is a constant theme. But this is the point at which angel and whore touch: weakness makes woman lovable, innocent, protectable, while at the same time it is the quality which permits evils such as Satan—or Dracula—to attack mankind. If woman's capacity for virtue contains her capacity for vice, she is always suspect, dangerous. Weissman suggests that Lucy's desire for three husbands and Mina's remark about having appetites that would shock the New Woman are actually hints of submerged sexual capacity beyond the respectable norm[13]—indications of latent vampirism, in fact, threatening to men. Thomas Bilder, the London Zoo wolfkeeper, probably captures the attitude of the men in the novel and the man behind it when he remarks that "you can't trust wolves no more nor women" (p. 155). And this is a novel about wolflike women.

What happens when the virtuous woman turns wolf? What is left to strive for when the dream-Lucy becomes a "nightmare of Lucy"? There is Mina, of course. Her credentials as Lucy's successor are carefully established from the first, when Jonathan sets her in opposition to the tempting trio at Castle Dracula: "I am alone in the castle with those awful women. Faugh! Mina is a woman, and there is nought in common" (p. 64). In the following chapters, Mina presents herself as an excellent example of "advanced" Victorian womanhood: accomplished, but only so that she can be a "useful wife"; disparaging of the New Woman and her tampering with sex roles; obsessed with her "duty" as a wife. That Victorian byword occurs frequently in *Dracula,* but no more frequently than in the journals of Mina, who uses it no less than four times in her account of her wedding. She is bright and talented enough to be an acceptable heroine for the 1890s and to distinguish herself from Lucy as the woman of the future,[14] but conventional enough to replace Lucy in the men's imaginations. She is a praiseworthy but rather ordinary female character for the first half of the novel, but after Lucy's second death, Mina rapidly assumes monumental mythic proportions.

The transformation is initiated by Van Helsing, who barely knows her yet begs to serve her—an echo of the oaths to Lucy—and then erupts in passionate paeans to her womanly virtue: "Oh, Madam Mina, good women tell all their lives, and by day and by hour and by minute, such things that angels can read; and we men who wish to know have in us something of angel's eyes." Even Mina is taken aback: "But, doctor, you praise me too much, and—you do not know me" (p. 206). But Van Helsing, intent on mythologizing Mina, continues to define her as exceptional, implicitly contrasting her with the fallen Lucy: "You have given me hope . . . that there are good women still left to make life happy—good women, whose lives and whose truths may make good lesson for the children that are to be" (p. 207). The next day he tells Jonathan exactly what he has married: "She is one of God's women, fashioned by his own hand to show us men and other women that there is a heaven where we can enter, and that its light can be here on earth. So true, so sweet, so noble, so little an egoist—and that, let me tell you, is much in this age, so sceptical and selfish" (p. 211). Clearly, Mina is no longer merely a housewife-stenographer. She is the "pearl among women" (p. 244), and later, in Seward's words, "that sweet, sweet, good, good woman" (p. 341).

As the archetypal Good Woman, Mina must now bear all the symbolic weight Lucy has abandoned. Following Van Helsing's lead, the rest of the brotherhood, one by one, take their places around this new center as the group gathers at Seward's asylum. Alone with the weeping Arthur, Mina muses about the "mother-spirit" evoked by male tears. Arthur then asks her to permit him to "be like a brother . . . for all our lives—for dear Lucy's sake" (p. 257). Mina thus assumes two of the roles which comprise the Good Woman: Mother and Sister, asexual and nurturant. Arthur now swears fealty, in his turn. No sooner has Mina left him than she meets Quincy Morris and extends her motherhood to him. He proceeds to assign her a third role by calling her "little girl": the Good Woman must also be eternal Child, pre-sexual and dependent. Significantly, "little girl" was Morris's pet name for Lucy: the transfer of symbolic identity is accomplished.

Mina now plays an interesting dual role as both the *bel ideal* of the brotherhood—as Van Helsing puts it, "our star and our hope" (p. 270)—and its secretary. As the former, she can have no active role in the proceedings; ironically, she is attacked by Dracula on the very night the men reach this decision and leave her behind on a trip to Carfax. Even Mina finds "their chivalrous care of [her] to be a bitter pill . . . to swallow" (p. 270), but her role is, for the moment, beyond her control.

The second climactic scene in *Dracula* is the discovery of Dracula forcing Mina to drink his blood; again the "white night dress . . . smeared with blood" (p. 313), an image repeated soon after when Mina's lips leave a red stain on Jonathan's white nightshirt. Mina's own purity is befouled now that she has crossed the border into sexuality, and by association, her husband's is tainted as well. Her reaction in this scene is that of the guilty adultress, "as if [Jonathan] were the injured one" (p. 319). "Unclean, unclean!" she cries (p. 315), and she will repeat this word like a ritual incantation until Dracula's death. When the sacred wafer scars her forehead—again leaving the red stain on the white field— she cries, "Unclean! Unclean!" (p. 329). And later:

> I caught sight in the mirror of the red mark upon my forehead; and I knew that I was still unclean. (p.356)
> Alas! I am unclean to His eyes. . . . (p. 399)

The Undead Lucy's eyes were likewise described as "unclean," but the images of Mina's stained gown and forehead connect the word explicitly with the menstrual blood of the unclean woman, pariah, unfit to touch a good man. The scar, often referred to as a stain, of course duplicates Dracula's, but it is actually closer kin to Hester Prynne's red "A."

This outward token of impurity in the Good Woman has immediate effect on the bretheren, who "knelt down together, and, all holding hands, swore to be true to each other. We men pledged ourselves to raise the veil of sorrow from the head of her who, each in his own way, we all loved . . ." (p. 330). But Dracula's threat to them will become even clearer. In the third climactic moment in the novel, the brotherhood confronts Dracula at his Piccadilly townhouse and elicits from him the speech which holds the key to the novel. He rags of his invincibility, his alliance with time itself, and then issues his ultimate boast: "Your girls that you all love are mine already; and through them you and others shall yet be mine . . ." (p. 340). The threat is twofold: As a Victorian Satan, he attacks, like his Edenic forefather, at the weakest spot, womanhood, in order to infect the whole. But his most immediate threat lies in the first part of his statement. He can destroy this collective male unconscious symbolically, by transforming its ideal Good Women into sexual wolves. He is both a sexual competitor gloating over his superior prowess[15] and a subliminal voice within our heroes, whispering that at heart, the girls they all love are potential vampires, that their angels are, in fact, whores.

The ultimate gauntlet has been thrown. The brethren leave for Transylvania "as the old knights of the Cross to redeem more [souls]" (p. 355), and Mina is their "lady," the incarnation of the ideal. In fact, as Weissman notes, Mina's mythic dimension includes the Virgin Mary, whom she imitates in interceding for Dracula, exhorting pity and sympathy for his lost soul.[16] At her behest, the knights take a final oath: to kill her rather than allow her to become like Lucy. She analogizes her case to that of woman in wartime, killed as an ultimate act of love rather than forfeited to the enemy. She sees herself as ground for which opposing forces struggle; like Lucy she enters a period wherein she is a passive vehicle—this time for hypnotic suggestion rather than blood transfusions. In this phase Van Helsing becomes a sort of counter-Dracula; Seward remarks, "He seems to have power at these particular moments to simply will, and her thoughts obey him" (p. 368), a description befitting Dracula himself. The two emblems of paternal authority[17] battle for control of her mind as a source of information about each other. At this stage the Good Woman is tainted to the extent that she does not readily comply with the will of her "good" father-figure, Van Helsing.

Before Mina can move from the passive stage to the beginnings of aggressive voluptuousness, Dracula meets his fate. But his death seems almost anticlimactic, and the reason is that once more the female vampires steal the show. Dracula does not appear through the extended final chase, but his three ladies-in-waiting materialize from the snow before the eyes of Mina and Van Helsing: again the "voluptuous lips," the emphasis on redness ("ruddy color") and white teeth. Van Helsing mentions their "bright hard eyes," and we may recall that Lucy's eyes became hard when she attacked Jonathan on her deathbed, and that the change in Mina first manifests itself when Van Helsing notices that "her eyes are more hard" and her teeth slightly sharper (p. 357). Hardness is a quality unknown to the Good Woman. In Van Helsing's account of his destruction of the three women, "voluptuous" appears three times, and Van Helsing, like Jonathan, feels their appeal to something within him. The three deaths, like Lucy's earlier, are depicted in graphic and sexual terms: the "screeching," the stake "driving home," the "plunging of writhing form," the bloody lips (p. 409). By comparison, Dracula dies very quietly indeed, and without benefit of driving stake.

The final sentences of the novel are devoted to the now "stainless" Mina, the ideal whom "some men so loved . . . , that they did dare much for her sake." This ideal and its underlying misogyny are the real heart of *Dracula*. Though it draws on ancient myths of femininity, Stoker's gothic is quintessentially Victorian: the worst horror it can imagine is not Dracula at all but the released, transforming sexuality of the Good Woman.

Notes

1. Bram Stoker, *Dracula* (New York: Dell, 1971), p. 193. All references will be to this edition and will appear parenthetically.

2. Stephanie Demetrakopoulos, "Feminism, Sex Role Exchanges, and Other Subliminal Fantasies in Bram Stoker's Dracula," *Frontiers*, 11 (1977), 106–7).

3. *The Second Sex* (New York: Vintage, 1974), p. 167.

4. Quoted by de Beauvoir, p. 168.

5. Ibid, p. 168.

6. Ernest Jones equates the blood taken by the vampire with semen in *On the Nightmare* (London, 1931), p. 98. For the suggestions of fellatio in Stoker's vampire women, see C.F. Bentley, "The Monster in the Bedroom: Sexual Symbolism in *Dracula*," *Literature and Psychology*, 22 (1972), 30. Bentley sees the blood as menstrual once (pp. 30–31), in the scene of Mina's forced vampirism, when blood trickles from a "thin open wound," but he does not generalize from this incident.

7. Carroll Smith-Rosenberg, "Puberty to Menopause: The Cycle of Femininity in Nineteenth-Century America," *Feminist Studies*, 1 (1973), 25.

8. Judith Weissman, "Women and Vampires: *Dracula* as a Victorian Novel," *Midwest Quarterly*, 18 (1977), 400.

9. de Beauvoir, p. 167.

10. Demetrakopoulos also discusses this idea, p. 107.

11. Phyllis A. Roth, "Suddenly Sexual Women in Bram Stoker's *Dracula*, " *Literature and Psychology*, 27 (1977), 117.

12. Weissman, 397.

13. Ibid, 400.

14. Demetrakopoulos, 108–9.

15. Weissman, 404.

16. Ibid, 399.

17. Roth, 115.

Good Men and Monsters: The Defenses of *Dracula*

Thomas B. Byers

One of the most memorable and often-interpreted scenes in Bram Stoker's *Dracula* is that in which Jonathan Harker, during his imprisonment in Castle Dracula, is assaulted by three female vampires. This scene, as presented to us in Harker's account, provides the first (and some of the most obvious) evidence that vampirism is a sexual activity. It also gives the first expression of that "fear of the devouring woman" which Phyllis A. Roth claims is "the central anxiety of the novel."[1] Yet despite the importance generally attributed to the episode, relatively little has been said about its resolution. What happens is this: just as the women—who are obviously former victims/brides of Dracula—are about to sink their teeth into the young solicitor, Dracula himself appears and drives them away from their prey. However, he promises them that they shall have Harker later, and for the present he gives them a substitute—a baby. They immediately take it and disappear.[2]

This resolution is remarkable for more than its overt horror and grotesquerie. It provides a striking reminder of an aspect of the vampire's nature which has generally been slighted by the critics. On a symbolic level, these vampire brides are not only frighteningly sexual, but frighteningly dependent as well.[3] Dracula offers them the child not because it will fulfill (in any direct way) their sexual needs, but because it can fulfill their dependency needs. This Dracula himself cannot do, any more than the brides can continue to satisfy him, for both male and female vampires require living victims. So he gives them a baby, whose life they can drain for their nourishment, and who will then presumably become a vampire itself. It does not take much in the way of critical gymnastics to read this material as an allegory of a common family situation, in which a woman, having given up her former life to the fulfillment of a man and having received

---

This article originally appeared in *Literature and Psychology* 31 (1981), No. 4.

little in return, invests herself emotionally in her children. This investment enables her to displace her sexual and emotional needs, but at the expense of transmitting a neurotic dependency to the children. In such family situations, the terms of Maurice Richardson's description of the vampiric relationships in *Dracula* may be painfully applicable: "Frightful cruelty, aggression and greed is [sic] accompanied by a madly possessive kind of love."[4]

However, to hold the woman to blame for such family problems is to overlook their origins, and to emphasize the horror of the female vampires is to divert attention from the ultimate source of the horror—Dracula himself. The Don Juan of the horror genre, he has seduced these women, has attained their submission and gotten what he needed from them for as long as they could feed him, and has now gone on to other victims. They experience the parasitic needs which make them prey upon children because Dracula has transmitted these needs to them. The text also suggests the psychological sources of his needs. If the Don Juan figure is seeking a mother, this objective is even more apparent in Dracula's case, for as Joseph Bierman has pointed out, his form of sexual assault has as much to do with nursing as with intercourse.[5] Further, Van Helsing suggests that one of the Count's last hopes when he is being pursued is "that he might hide in the tomb [read 'womb'] that he think poor Miss Lucy, being as he thought like him, keep open to him" (p. 320).

Interestingly, however, neither the text nor the critical literature makes much of this. While the weakness and dependency which necessitate blood-sucking may be freely admitted in the case of the females, the text constantly tempers or even represses these needs in the case of the male. Further, to the degree that his story does recognize these traits in a male figure, it attempts to confine them to Dracula alone. Phyllis Roth and Judith Weissman to the contrary, the issue in *Dracula* is not only men's fear of women and their sexuality; it is men's fear of themselves and their vulnerability. Ultimately the text may be seen as a complex system of psychological and political defenses, all working to deny and/or disguise male dependency needs. These defenses include the compensations of Dracula himself, the isolation and neutralization which result from his status as myth and from the treatment of other characters, and the diversions and deceptions provided by the text's overt themes.

Though all the vampires are inherently dependent, this vulnerability is much less evident in Dracula than in the others, for he has tremendous power and potency by way of compensation. Indeed, his physical strength and endurance, supplemented by his supernatural powers, make him more formidable than any human character. And his sexual attractiveness and prowess make him superior to the female vampires. Not only is he their lord and master, but he is both more sexually secure and more successful than they. While they are capable only of the most overt assault, and hence seem frightening and repulsive (though at the same time enticing) to the men, Dracula himself is more able to woo his victims, and to persuade them to come to him and submit to his will. Moreover, in at least some cases his victims' submission is irrevocable, and they are lost to him. On the other hand, with the exception of the one baby who disappears when the brides carry it off, all the victims of the females are saved.

As various critics have indicated, these differences are in part a consequence of the fact that the book is a male fantasy, in which men are to take some pleasure in identification with the villain's immorality and sadistic prowess, more in the dream of passivity and sex without responsibility with the sexually aggressive "fallen women," and still more in the self-serving, self-assertive act of destroying these momentarily exciting but ultimately threatening evil creatures.[6] This line of interpretation is one reason for the general assent to Maurice Richardson's characterization of Dracula as "a father-figure of huge potency."[7] But this assent also suggests the effectiveness of the compensation which is the book's first line of defense against the weakness at the heart of the character.

Nonetheless, the disguise is neither complete, nor completely effective. The mechanism itself suggests that not all is well—that there is something for which compensation is required. So Dracula's potency serves to conceal his vulnerability and his needs, but not fully to neutralize them. Other, even more complex mechanisms are necessary as well. Hence the story as a whole, and the character of Dracula in particular, also enact a strategy of disguise by *mythification*. In his famous study of the nightmare, Ernest Jones indicates that "the two chief metaphorical connotations of the word [vampire] are: 1) a social or political tyrant who sucks the life from his people . . . [and] 2) an irresistible lover who sucks away energy, ambition, or even life for selfish reasons."[8] Both of these connotations concern actual fields of conflict—in the former case class structure, in the latter sexual relationships—as they exist within history. And both of these types of "vampirism" clearly suggest political issues arising within a particular set of political arrangements. However, by creating such a character as Dracula, the text attempts to remove the problem of dependency from its historical and political context, and thereby to neutralize the vampire as a trope by emptying out the trope's meaning. This emptying out is essential, for otherwise the vampire could be taken as a more traditional, straightforward symbol, with a more direct application to history outside the story. Following this line of interpretation, one would see Dracula as simply a way of recognizing and dramatizing the horror of extreme male dependency, and of expressing how difficult it is to overcome that destructive tendency. But Stoker's handling of plot and character does not invite this general symbolic application; rather, it attempts to *isolate* the qualities of the vampire. His qualities are not seen as generalizable, but as unique, freakish, and unnatural. His isolation is accomplished in part by the presentation of Van Helsing and the other men in the book as foils and antagonists to the title character, about which more later. But it is also enforced by the presentation of Dracula himself.

As a supernatural creature, Dracula is not portrayed as part of "nature" or the "normal" world of men, but as apart from it. Not only in his essence but in his origins, his habits, even his nationality, he is an alien creature, exotic to the point of being unique. Indeed, he is threatening to the normal, and his destruction is not only justifiable, but morally incumbent upon "normal," "decent" men. In destroying him they destroy also that parasitic weakness which makes him prey upon females. And they destroy it completely, so far as we are told. Given Dracula's life history, and the relatively short time it takes him to use up Lucy and go on to Mina, it would be reasonable to expect the existence of whole hordes of vampires. Yet as far as the text indicates, no further steps are necessary once Dracula and his four women have been eliminated. By laying these five misfits to rest, the men end the threat and restore the "natural" order in which the good woman can be assured that "some men so love . . . her that they [will] dare much for her sake" (see the novel's ending, p. 382), and that "a brave man's blood is the best thing on this earth when a woman is in trouble" (p. 157).[9]

The process of removing the problem from history, then, is to make Dracula the sole repository of it and to make it clear that he is a unique violation of nature. This is precisely the converse of the mythic process described by Roland Barthes in his essay on "Myth Today." Barthes points out that *"myth* is depoliticized speech," and that it "deprives the object of which it speaks of all History. In it, history evaporates,"[10] just as happens in *Dracula* when the problem of male dependency is "solved" for good and all by the destruction of the title character. Barthes claims that myth generally accomplishes this deprivation by *naturalizing* the object:

> What the world supplies to myth is an historical reality . . . and what myth gives in return is a natural image of this reality. . . . A conjuring trick has taken place; it has turned reality inside out, it has emptied it of history and has filled it with nature, it has removed from things their human meaning so as to make them signify a human insignificance. The function of myth is to empty reality. (*M.*, p. 143; see also p. 129)

Barthes' chief example of this process is a *Paris-Match* cover photo of a young black soldier in a French uniform, saluting with his eyes uplifted:

> I see very well what it signifies to me: that France is a great Empire, that all her sons, without any colour discrimination, faithfully serve under her flag, and that there is no better answer to her detractors of an alleged colonialism than the zeal shown by this Negro in serving his so-called oppressors. (*M.*, p. 116)

This, Barthes explains, is an attempt to alienate the image from its meaning, by depriving it of its history and making it seem simply natural: *"(The French Empire? It's just a fact: look at this good Negro who salutes like one of our own boys)" (M.,* p. 124). Here the dominant culture de-historicizes and disguises its identity as oppressor by naturalizing and domesticating an image of the (alien) *victim*—by bringing him into the "natural" order. In *Dracula,* on the other hand, the male weakness at the heart of the oppression of the women is de-historicized and disguised by the supernaturalization and alienation of an image of the *oppressor*—by his expulsion from that same ahistorical "natural" order. Just as in Barthes' example, the world supplies the myth with a historical reality—in this case, the oppression of women for the satisfaction of male dependency needs—but the "conjuring trick" in *Dracula* is the myth's presentation of a *super*natural image of this reality.

The end is the same in both cases: "to immobilize the world" *(M.,* p. 155) for the sake of the status quo, and to protect the political arrangements which normalize and thereby conceal oppression. It is for the sake of such protection that the text takes the risk of creating a male character who, despite his compensatory powers, inevitably calls attention to male dependency. If in Barthes' analysis myth today serves the interests of bourgeois ideology, so as Mary Daly puts it, "patriarchy perpetuates its deception through myth."[11]

At the heart of the deception, as Judith Weissman indicates, is "the belief that men are more powerful than women."[12] If the mythic character of Dracula is this text's main line of defense, it is reinforced by the treatment of the other characters and their relationships. Weissman and Phyllis Roth are both right when they point out that the book's covert misogyny (Roth) and the value it places on female passivity (Weissman) help to protect the men from open female sexuality. But other aspects of power are also at stake in these attitudes and values. Female passivity and dependency are valued in part because the men can more easily believe in their own superior strength of character if the women play the role of "weaker vessels." And the hostility toward women results not only from fear of women's sexual powers and demands, but (as suggested earlier) from fear that in their relationships with women, the men may be unable to deny or disguise their emotional vulnerability. In personal relationships as in strictly economic ones, it is generally in the oppressor's interest to deny what he gets from his victims, and to emphasize what he gives them (think of the stereotypical slave-owner complaining about his "ungrateful" slaves). This denial not only assuages the oppressor's conscience and superficially ameliorates his moral appearance, but also affirms his (illusory) strength and freedom by denying the very existence of the needs which his victims meet for him.

Such affirmations are typical of the view of the male characters, and indeed of men in general, in *Dracula*—a view which in a sense provides the obverse of Dracula's exoticism and further compensates for his dependency. Almost without lapse or exception, the male characters are high-minded and altruistic, strong and courageous, and endowed with an unsullied virtue. Mina Harker herself is one of the witnesses called to testify to all this goodness: "The world seems full of good men," she writes in her journal, "—even if there *are* monsters in it" (p. 230),[13] and later, "How can women help loving men when they are so earnest, and so true, and so brave!" (p. 360). Indeed, the men are reason for a prayer of thanksgiving; as she embraces her (surprisingly ineffectual) husband, Mina exclaims, "Oh, thank God for good brave men!" (p. 316). And lest there be any petty suspicion that the men are motivated by self-interest, Van Helsing explicitly contrasts them with Dracula in this regard: the vampire's "child-brain that grow not yet to our stature" can "do only work selfish and therefore small," whereas "we, however, are not selfish, and we believe that God is with us through all this blackness" (pp. 345, 347). The men act "for the good of mankind [which is ironically true, so long as we do not allow ourselves to be taken in by the pretense that 'man' is generic], and for the honour and glory of God" (p. 326).

All the talk of God is no accident, of course. If Dracula's power is "diabolic" (p. 325), that of the men is granted and certified by the highest patriarch of all—God the Father. It is He on whom the men claim to depend: "In the end we shall win," says Van Helsing, "so sure as that God sits on high to watch over His children" (p. 321). Consequently, the obedience which Van Helsing demands of Lucy (see, for instance, his "we must obey . . . " etc., p. 139) is implicitly justified by a hierarchy in which even the venerable doctor himself, whose "personal dominance" has "made him so long a master among men" (p. 324), submits himself to a higher Father. Given the rigidities of the order of dominance and submission assumed by Van Helsing, there is a remarkable (if unintentional) appropriateness to the detail that his own wife has gone completely mad (see p. 182).

If the characterizations serve to isolate male dependency in the character of Dracula and to reaffirm the patriarchal hierarchy, the book's overt themes subtly reinforce these functions. As is often the case in works whose origins and significance seem largely unconscious, the ostensible themes of *Dracula* are not particularly integral to the action. Rather, they seem superimposed upon it, and hence they have generally been of little critical interest. Still, they too have a place in the system of defenses. The first of these is the theme of belief, as presented in terms of Van Helsing's constant battle against the doubts of the others, which he says "would be [the vampire's] greatest strength" (p. 326). He tells Seward, who is naturally skeptical about the monster's existence, "you are too prejudiced. You do not let your eyes see nor your ears hear, and that which is outside your daily life is not of account to you" (p. 196). He presents many examples of strange phenomena which he claims are real despite their improbable and inexplicable nature, in an effort to get the young doctor "to believe in things that you cannot" (p. 198; see also pp. 196–98 passim). In overcoming these doubts, the heroic father-figure establishes not only Dracula's actuality, but his own credibility.

All of this seems innocent enough; Stoker is, after all, writing a story of the fantastic in an increasingly skeptical age, and one of his problems is how to enforce the necessary suspension of disbelief. Moreover, even if it is in many details inaccurate, Van Helsing's critique of the blindness of narrow science seems to place him on the humanistic side of the "two cultures" debate. Though the theme is neither particularly new nor particularly convincing in this manifestation, it at least seems respectable as a kind of stock item in fiction of this sort. Perhaps such stock respectability should always be suspect where ideas are concerned. In this instance, the theme not only promotes the authority of the patriarchs (Van Helsing and his supernatural God), but also disguises the text's real (if covert) mission. This mission is not to propound the existence of literal vampires, but to conceal the existence of figurative ones. The emphasis on belief in the mythic reification helps to divert our attention from the frightening realities which may be signified by the vampire interpreted as a trope.

In the latter parts of the book, once Dracula's existence has been established, the issue of belief is superseded by the book's second overt theme—the need for trust. This theme is most explicitly related to the erroneous (and later reversed) decision to exclude Mina from the men's councils (see pp. 328, 331, 354–55). It has, if anything, received even less attention than the other issue, no doubt because it has even more spurious and less integral connection to the book's overall action. But it is also an even more insidious diversion than the belief theme. If the value placed on trust, and even (wonder of wonders) on trust of women, is psychologically a reaction-formation against the work's misogyny, it is politically a kind of liberal windowdressing for the corrupt power structure behind it. In the first place, it subtly reinforces the patriarchal hierarchy, for the most trust is to be placed in the heroic male figures, and especially in their God. And beyond this is the ultimate (even if unconscious) duplicity of proclaiming trust as a value in a book whose overriding motive is the articulation of a myth which denies or disguises everything that is really at issue in it.

Nevertheless, these matters of theme, like the portrayal of the "good" characters, are adjunct to the central defense mechanism, which is the mythification of male dependency in the character of Dracula. This characterization is the most lively (most un-dead?) aspect of the book, and the one which has captured the popular imagination. Its function as a male myth operates by a process similar to what Barthes calls "inoculation" (see *M.*, pp. 150–51), whereby a small dose of the exotic is admitted to the body politic so that it can be used to manufacture an immunity to larger doses of the same threat. Thus the book covertly points to male dependency and the manipulation of women so as to isolate them and produce a greater resistance to their admission. But inoculation is a tricky business; if the process is not carefully controlled it can result in the very "infection" it is designed to prevent. Read as myth, *Dracula* is finally profoundly historical; it leads us to recognize precisely those historical and political actualities which it strives to conceal. Seen in this light, the text ultimately gives lie to the claim Van Helsing makes for himself and those he represents, when he declares (p. 326), "But we are pledged to set the world free."

Notes

1. Phyllis A. Roth, "Suddenly Sexual Women in Bram Stoker's *Dracula*," *Literature and Psychology*, 27 (1977), 119. See also Judith Weissman, "Women and Vampires: *Dracula* as a Victorian Novel," *Midwest Quarterly*, 18 (1976–77), pp. 404, 405. While I have a few quarrels with both of these articles, they are both exceptionally enlightening and useful. For the scene itself, see Bram Stoker, *Dracula* (1897; rpt. New York: Signet Classics, 1965), pp. 44–48. All future references to *Dracula* are to this edition; hereafter, page numbers will be included in parentheses within my text.

2. Weissman, p. 402, does consider this resolution, as does Stephanie Demetrakopoulos, "Feminism, Sex Role Exchanges, and Other Subliminal Fantasies in Bram Stoker's *Dracula*," *Frontiers*, 2, No. 3 (1977), 107, Weissman reads the scene as "obviously a suggestion that women become child molesters"; Demetrakopoulos sees it as a rejection of motherhood. My disagreement with both will become apparent in a moment.
   The implications of the scene's ending are made more explicit in a recent PBS Television production of *Dracula*, starring Louis Jourdan. In this version, we actually see the baby lying on the floor. Then we see the brides bend down to it (out of the picture frame); when they reappear, their faces are smeared with blood and twisted into hideous leers.

3. Royce MacGillivray, "*Dracula*: Bram Stoker's Spoiled Masterpiece," *Queen's Quarterly*, 79 (1972), pp. 523–24 does suggest this issue in one extremely relevant sentence: "It is hard not to suggest that vampire stories, including *Dracula*, reflect, in a sensationalized but recognizable form, the truth that the close association of any two persons is almost certain to involve, however faintly, some 'vampirish' exploitation, be it economic, intellectual, or emotional, of one of them by the other." Unfortunately MacGillivray does not pursue this insight: the article's major intention seems to be a formalistic defense of the novel, and it goes so far as to claim (p. 526) that "*Dracula* is a thoroughly unpolitical novel." Other recognitions of the vampire's dependent nature (though not in the context of commentary on *Dracula*) may be found in contemporary feminist writing; see, for example, Mary Daly, *Gyn/Ecology: The Metaethics of Radical Feminism* (Boston: Beacon Press, 1978), pp. 30–31, 81, 375.

4. Maurice Richardson, "The Psychoanalysis of Ghost Stories," *The Twentieth Century*, 166 (1959), 426. Lucy Westenra repeats this pattern of displacement later in the novel when, having become a vampire, she preys on children as the "bloofer lady."

5. Joseph S. Bierman, "*Dracula*: Prolonged Childhood Illness and the Oral Triad," *American Imago*, 29 (1972), 195 states that "*Dracula* concerns itself with . . . primal scenes expressed in nursing terms." See also Roth, p. 119. While I am indebted to Bierman on this point, I cannot accept his rigidly Freudian argument that sibling rivalry and perhaps the interruption of his sleep by his parents' lovemaking drove Stoker to write *Dracula*.

6. See, respectively, Roth, p. 117; Demetrakopoulos, p. 106; Weissman, pp. 392, 399, 404 and passim.

7. Richardson, p. 427. See also Weissman, pp. 403, 404; Roth, pp. 116, 117.

8. Ernest Jones, M.D., *On the Nightmare*, Vol. 20 of *The International Psycho-Analytical Library*, ed. Ernest Jones (1931; new edition New York: Liveright, 1951), pp. 124–25.

9. This ludicrous line becomes more than a little sinister in light of Ernest Jones' remark that "In the unconscious mind blood is commonly an equivalent for semen" (Jones, p. 119).

10. Roland Barthes, "Myth Today," in his *Mythologies*, tr. Annette Lavers (New York: Hill and Wang, 1972), pp. 143–51. Further page references are generally included in parentheses within my text, preceded by *M*.

11. See Barthes, pp. 131–45 and passim; Daly, p. 44. Daly uses a narrower definition of myth as "stories that express intuitive insights and relate the activities of gods" (ibid.) But the principles of myth as a tool of deception are the same for these myths as for those included under Barthes' broader definition.

    It is also worth noting that this particular myth protects not only the patriarchy but capitalism as well, by virtue of the fact that Dracula is a feudal lord. See Jones, pp. 124–25 (quoted above) on the vampire as a metaphor for "a social or political tyrant," and Richardson's suggestion of "A Marxist interpretation of the Vampire myth" which "might, with justice, make more of this [economic] aspect, viewing it as a perverted extension of the feudal *droit du seigneur*, based on a solid foundation of exploitation: he starves us and sucks our children's blood" (Richardson, p. 430). The book confines this tyranny to the feudal count, thereby excluding the possibility of capitalist exploitation. His feudalism is merely another example of Dracula's exoticism, which has no place in the "natural" world of Victorian bourgeois capitalism.

12. Weissman, p. 404.

13. Roth, p. 114, points out the "remarkable contrast!" between this view of men in general, and Van Helsing's hope "that there are good women still left to make life happy" (p. 191).

Van deme quaden thyrāne
Dracole wyda·

Vlad the Impaler, the Historical Dracula
Woodcut, from a 15th-century German pamphlet.

16

Lombroso's Criminal Man and Stoker's *Dracula*

Ernest Fontana

Studies of Bram Stoker's *Dracula* (1897) have not given sufficient emphasis to the precise Lombrosian pseudoscientific conception of the criminal personality that underlies not only the conception of Dracula himself, but also of Renfield, and even Dracula's female victims, Lucy Westenra and and Mina Harker.[1] Lombroso and his German disciple, Max Nordau, are specifically cited by the precocious Mina, after Dr. Van Helsing's Lombrosian disquisition on Dracula as a born criminal "predestinate to crime." Mina replies that "The Count is a criminal and of a criminal type. Nordau and Lombroso would so classify him and *quâ* criminal he is of imperfectly formed mind."[2]

Cesare Lombroso's *Uomo Delinquente* (1876) was available to Stoker in a two volume French translation *L'homme criminel* (1895). An English reduction and translation of *Uomo Delinquente* by Lombroso's daughter, Gina Lombroso-Ferrero, was not available until 1911. An English translation of Max Nordau's *Degeneration* was published in 1895.[3] Nordau's book, which is dedicated to Lombroso as "Dear and Honoured Master," extends Lombroso's ideas to the realm of culture, demonstrating that degenerates are not always criminals, anarchists, and lunatics, but "often authors and artists."[4]

For Lombroso the criminal was a reversion to past races of mankind; "The criminal is an atavistic being, a relic of a vanished race,"[5] Dracula, who has survived for almost half a millenium as an "Undead," presents himself to Jonathan Harker as a relic of the Szekelys, the descendents of the Huns, "whose warlike fury had swept the earth like a living flame" (30). Stoker's Dracula (unlike the historical Wallachian Vlad, the Impaler)[6] claims to be a survivor of a conquering race that was once the scourge of Europe. "What devil or what witch was ever so great as Attila whose blood is in these veins" (30)? Dracula is a survivor from

This article originally appeared in *Victorian Newsletter* 66 (1984).

an earlier warlike period when his race's bloodthirsty behavior on the battlefield was functional and even necessary; "The warlike days are over. Blood is too precious a thing in these days of dishonourable peace; and the glories of the great races are as a tale that is told" (31). In the late nineteenth century, his practice of vampirism and his journey to England are attempts to enact the conquests of his ancestors and of himself in the more evolved and "pacific" modern world. In Stoker's plot, Dracula's "criminality" is not presented as a reversion back to an earlier, atavistic state, but as a sublime and fabulous survival from an earlier historical period of humanity. Dracula's practice of vampirism is a defiance of the evolutionary cycle. By resisting his personal death, and by infecting others into the condition of the "nosferatu," Dracula threatens to conquer not merely the civilized world, as his ancestor Attila, but the entire race of evolved and evolving humanity. His final triumph, according to Dr. Van Helsing, quoting his friend Dr. Arminius of Buda-Pesth, would be to father "a new order of beings, whose road must lead through Death, not Life" (320.)[7]

Dracula is a powerful image of cultural and social otherness, as Burton Hatlen has shown,[8] because his character is conceived in terms of the Lombrosian criminal as "an atavistic being, a relic of a vanished race." Secondly, since "He may not enter anywhere, at the first unless there be some one of the household who bid him to come" (253), Dracula selects as his victims those persons among the more evolved races who are, unknown to themselves, kindred to him: that is, who contain the innate biological and psychological potential of savage reversion. Dracula is a threat to societies of predominantly morally and socially evolved humanity, because there survives within these societies, even in England, a minority of potentially "diseased" individuals who are driven, subconsciously, to a reversion back to the atavistic, pre-civilized world from which Dracula survives, and who, subconsciously, "bid him to come," and who become, for Dracula, "flesh of my flesh, blood of my blood, kin of my kin" (304). Such are, as I shall show, Renfield, Lucy and Mina.

In *Uomo Delinquente*, Lombroso presents with amazing confidence the physical and psychological traits of the born criminal or atavistic being. He also asserts that "the born criminal is an epileptic"; and that "the anatomical and psychological characteristics of the criminal and the epileptic are identical" (72). Leonard Wolf has shown that some of Dracula's physical characteristics are derived from Lombroso's concept of criminal man, but he has not extended the Lombrosian conception to Dracula's motivation, nor to the other characters in the book.[9] Dracula's "aquiline nose," "massive" eyebrows, and "pointed" ears (18) correspond to characteristics identified by Lombroso: "the nose is often aquiline like the beak of a bird of prey" (15); "the eyebrows are generally bushy in murderers and violators of women" (236) and "tend to meet across the nose"

(18); and there is "a protuberance on the upper part of the posterior margin" of the ear, "a relic of the pointed ear characteristic of apes" (14–15).

There are other characteristics, not noted by Wolf, that Dracula shares with Lombroso's criminal type. His "peculiarly sharp white teeth" that protrude over his lips (18) correspond to Lombroso's observation that a criminal often has "supernumerary teeth, amounting to a double row" (235) and often "strongly developed" canines (17). Dracula's "rank breath" (19) may be related to the "premature caries" (17) (although "premature" is hardly an appropriate word for Dracula) that Lombroso notes is common to the criminal type. Except for a white mustache Dracula's face is "clean-shaven" (16); Lombroso observes "that the beard is scanty in born criminals and altogether absent in epileptics" (233), and he quotes an Italian proverb: "There is nothing worse under Heaven than a scanty beard and coulourless face" (50). Although Dracula is clean-shaven, there are ape-like hairs in the center of his palms and his fingers are "broad and squat" (20).[10] Lombroso notes that those who commit crimes against persons have "short, clumsy fingers" and that the principal lines of their palms "are reduced to one or two of horizontal or transverse direction as in apes" (20).

Dracula's extraordinary agility, his bat-like ability to crawl down a sheer castle wall that overlooks a dreadful abyss "face down with his cloak spreading out around like wings" relates to the extraordinary agility Lombroso notes in criminals, even those of advanced age. Vilella, a celebrated thief whom Lombroso examined, was able to spring "like a goat up the steep rocks of his native Calabria," "and when quite an old man, escaped from his captors by leaping from a high rampart at Pavia" (27). Lombroso also notes that criminals have great mobility in their toes and, often, great strength in their large toe, giving them a "prehensile foot" which is used in grasping (20–21). This may be the source of Stoker's vivid image of Dracula crawling downward like a bat.

Dracula's obsession with drinking from the throats of his victims and leaving there a mark can be related to the Lombrosian criminal's obsession with tatooing his women on their faces. "Of atavistic origin, also, is the practice, common to members of the *camorra*, of branding their sweethearts on the face, not from motives of revenge, but as a sign of proprietorship, like the chiefs of savage tribes, who mark their wives and other belongings" (48). Indeed, Mina, after drinking blood from Dracula's breast, after becoming through this rite both his symbolic child and wife, is tatooed or seared when Van Helsing places the Sacred Wafer on her forehead. This "tatoo" is not removed until Dracula's death in the Borgo Pass when his "proprietorship" over her ceases.

The characterization of Renfield, an inmate in Dr. Seward's asylum, is also derived from Lombroso. His excitability, his susceptibility to paroxysms, and, more specifically, his consumption of live animals all are symptoms of what Lombroso identifies as the epileptic-criminal type. "The criminal is only a diseased person, an epileptic, in whom the cerebral malady, begun in some cases during prenatal existence or later, in consequences of some infection or cerebral poisoning, produces, together with certain signs of physical degeneration in the skull, face, teeth and brain, a return to the early brutal egotism natural to primitive races" (72–73).

Whereas atavistic man has survived for over four centuries in Dracula through vampirism, Renfield is a reversion or throwback to the atavistic type. Neither his education, nor his acquired sentiments, which he manifests when he attempts to warn Dr. Seward of the approaching menace to Mina, are strong enough to overcome his innate criminality, which is, in Lombrosian terms, an incurable disease. In fact for Lombroso the disease is epilepsy. According to Lombroso, the epileptic in his seizures manifests "paroxysms of rage or ferocious and brutal impulse (devouring animals alive), which if consciously committed, would be considered criminal" (58–59). Dr. Seward identifies Renfield as "a zoöphagus (life-eating) maniac" (75), and his description of Renfield's consumption of animals is an imaginative elaboration of Lombroso. "He disgusted me much while with him, for when a horrid blowfly, bloated with some carrion food, buzzed into the room, he caught it, held it exultantly for a few moments between his finger and thumb, and, before I knew what he was going to do, put it in his mouth and ate it" (73). As Leslie Fielder has observed, Renfield seems "the prototype of the side-show Geek,"[11] but unlike the Geek he is not made by other men exploiting his need, but born to his condition. The contrast between Renfield's zoöphagus and raging paroxysms on the one hand and, on the other hand, his scientific and philosophical sophistication, which he shows in Chapter 18, is, for Lombroso, also characteristic of the epileptic-criminal. "In epileptics, this divergence is sometimes manifested in one and the same person in the space of twenty-four hours. An individual at one time afflicted with loss of willpower and amnesia, and incapable of formulating the simplest notion, will shortly afterwards give expression to original ideas and reason logically" (61).

If Renfield is obviously a Lombrosian criminal type, who comes under Dracula's power because of their biological and psychological kinship, Lucy Westenra is less obviously so. What links her to the epileptic-criminal is her somnambulism, which, according to Lombroso, is a frequent characteristic of epileptics.[12] Lucy is assaulted by Dracula, for the first time, after having sleepwalked to the churchyard at Whitby the day after Dracula's arrival on the *Demeter*. As the *Demeter* approaches Whitby, Lucy, as observed by Mina, becomes restless and her sleepwalking increases. Since it is Lucy's somnambulistic nature that links her to Dracula as a criminal reversion, she is drawn to him as he approaches and, subconsciously, she seeks him out, bidding him to come to her the night after his disembarcation. In the moonlit graveyard of St. Mary's

Church at Whitby, Stoker brings together the ancient atavistic survivor and the vulnerable Lucy, an epileptic atavistic reversion. Mina writes:

> . . . there on our favourite seat, the silver light of the moon struck a half-reclining figure, snowy white. The coming of the cloud was too quick for me to see much, for shadow shut down on light almost immediately; but it seemed to me as though something dark stood behind the seat where the white figure shone, and bent over it. What it was, whether man or beast, I could not tell. (96)

Lucy's latent criminal nature "bids" Dracula to come to her, despite her acquired morality and her betrothal to Arthur. Dracula's power over her derives from their biological and psychological kinship. Later, when she describes to Mina the intense eroticism of her first nocturnal encounter with Dracula, she presents the experience as if it were a dream: " . . . and something very sweet and very bitter all around me at once; and then I seemed sinking into deep green water, and there was a singing in my ears, as I have heard there is to drowning men; and then everything seemed passing away from me; my soul seemed to go out from my body and float about the air" (104). The vertigo that informs Lucy's dream is, according to Lombroso, a frequent experience of epileptics during their seizures,[13] which, Lombroso asserts, resemble the reproductive act, both being characterized by "the tonic tension of the muscles, loss of consciousness, and mydriasis [dilation of the pupil]" (63). After this experience, which evokes both orgasm and epileptic seizure, Lucy's will is helpless; she is drawn to Dracula, despite her conscious, acquired, civilized resolutions. Neither Van Helsing's transfusions nor her own "best" sentiments can arrest the inevitable progress of her disease towards the Medusa-like horror Dr. Seward beholds in the graveyard in London. For Stoker, the condition of being a vampire is a metaphor for the posthumous survival and full realization of Lombroso's concept of innate criminal epilepsy.

Lucy's epilepsy is incurable. Mina's disease is not. After being assaulted by Dracula, Mina manifests the symptoms of "hysteria," which, as Thomas Szaz has shown, is an invention or fiction of early modern psychiatry.[14] For Lombroso, "Hysteria is a disease allied to epilepsy of which it appears to be a milder form. One characteristic of the hysteric is her susceptibility to suggestion" (95). Through his hypnotism of Mina, Dr. Van Helsing uses Mina's hysteria as a way of tracking Dracula, with whom she is in telepathic contact, on his return journey to Transylvania. Like Renfield and Lucy, Mina is linked on an innate, subconscious level to Dracula. She too is a diseased reversion. But because her disease is milder than that of the others, it can be a source of insight in the final pursuit of Dracula.

Stoker departs finally from Lombroso in his portrayal of Mina. Here, the science of Van Helsing and the love of Harker are strong enough to reverse the innate, degenerative tendencies of her nature. In fact, these atavistic traits that Mina carries and that, symbolically, enter her body when she is forced to drink blood from Dracula's bosom, in a parody of the mother-child relation, serve to resolve the conflict between the evolved and atavistic that is the organizing principle of the text. The world of Victorian modernity, enervated like Well's Eloi, in the *Time Machine* (1896), by virtue of its moral and social evolution, is vivified, as Mark Hennelly has argued, through a "transfusion . . . from the blood knowledge of Dracula."[15] The hysterical Mina by feeding upon the blood of him who feeds upon the blood of others is empowered to bear the man-child whose birth is celebrated in the coda of the book.[16] Caught between the poles of civilization and Lombrosian criminal atavism, Mina is shocked into becoming a vessel of evolution rather than a victim of reversion. She comes to bear the child "in whose veins run not only the Victorian blood of his parents but also the vitality of the Count whose blood Mina had drunk."[17]

Although the underlying schema of Stoker's *Dracula* is Lombrosian, the book finally goes beyond the pseudo-science of Lombroso. Atavistic man for Lombroso is diseased, an incurable epileptic among the healthy who must protect themselves through rational forms of incarceration from the contamination of the alien menace. But Stoker's *Dracula* shows that the infected carrier of the infection of degeneration contains within his blood mysterious sources of renewal and regeneration. Although Dracula's body "crumbled into dust and passed from our sight" (398) in the Borgo Pass, traces of Draculian atavistic blood survive commingled in the blood of future life.

Notes

1. Charles Blinderman, in "Vampurella, Darwin, and Count Dracula," *Massachusetts Review* 21 (1980), 411–28, argues that Dracula is a degenerate, but he links, without internal evidence, Stoker's notion of degeneracy to E. Ray Lankester's *Degeneration: A Chapter in Darwinism* (1889). My argument attempts to show that Lombroso's well-known theories were the primary "scientific" schemes in which Stoker worked. The immediate literary sources of *Dracula* have been cited by many: e.g., Le Fanu's *Carmilla* and Emily Gerard's *Land Beyond the Forest*. See Raymond T. McNally's and Radu Florescu's *In Search of Dracula* (New York: Graphic Society, 1972), pp. 171–81.

2. Bram Stoker, *Dracula* (New York: Bantam Books, 1981), pp. 360–61. Hereafter cited in the text.

3. Stoker began *Dracula* in August of 1895; see Daniel Farson, *The Man Who Wrote Dracula* (New York: St. Martin's, 1975), p. 175.

4. Max Nordau, *Degeneration* (New York: D. Appleton and Co., 1895), p. vii. Donald Pizer shows the influence of Lombroso on Frank Norris in his portrayal of McTeague. *The Novels of Frank Norris* (Bloomington: Indiana Univ. Press, 1966), pp. 57–63.

5. Gina Lombroso-Ferrero, *Criminal Man* (Montclair, N.J.: Paterson Smith, 1972), p. 135. This is a reprint of the 1911 edition, published by G. P. Putnam's Sons. Hereafter cited in the text.

6. The Historical Dracula was a Wallachian, not a Szekely. For clarification, see Grigore Nandris, "The Historical Dracula: The Theme of His Legend in the Western and in the Eastern Literatures of Europe." *Comparative Literature Studies*, 3 (1966), 367–96.

7. Carrol L. Fry notes "the contagious nature of vampirism." Vampires like fictional rakes "pass on their conditions . . . to their victims." *Victorian Newsletter*, No. 42 (1972), 21.

8. Burton Hatlen, "The Return of the Repressed/Oppressed in Bram Stoker's *Dracula*," *Minnesota Review* 15 (1980), 80–97.

9. Leonard Wolf, *The Annotated Dracula by Bram Stoker* (New York: Clarkson N. Potter, 1975), p. 300.

10. Wolf links Dracula's hairy palms to "the standard nineteenth-century image of the masturbator," p. 22.

11. Leslie Fiedler, *Freaks* (New York: Simon and Schuster, 1978), p. 343.

12. Lombroso-Ferrero, p. 63.

13. Lombroso-Ferrero, p. 58.

14. On this point see Szasz's *The Myth of Mental Illness* (New York: Harper & Row, 1974).

15. Mark M. Hennelly, Jr., "*Dracula:* The Gnostic Quest and Victorian Wasteland," *English Literature in Transition.* 20 (1977), p. 13.

16. The conflict between moral evolution and degeneration also informs Tennyson's *In Memoriam*, whose coda ends not with the birth of a child but, in #CXXI, with the imagined conception of the child who will be "a closer link/betwixt us and the crowning race." The conclusion of *Dracula* appears to be a structural and thematic echoing of the conclusion of Tennyson's poem.

17. Hennelly, p. 23.

"Kiss Me with Those Red Lips": Gender and Inversion in Bram Stoker's *Dracula*

Christopher Craft

When Joseph Sheridan Le Fanu observed in *Carmilla* (1872) that "the vampire is prone to be fascinated with an engrossing vehemence resembling the passion of love" and that vampire pleasure is heightened "by the gradual approaches of an artful courtship," he identified clearly the analogy between monstrosity and sexual desire that would prove, under a subsequent Freudian stimulus, paradigmatic for future readings of vampirism.[1] Modern critical accounts of *Dracula*, for instance, almost universally agree that vampirism both expresses and distorts an originally sexual energy. That distortion, the representation of desire under the defensive mask of monstrosity, betrays the fundamental psychological ambivalence identified by Franco Moretti when he writes that "vampirism is an excellent example of the identity of desire and fear."[2] This interfusion of sexual desire and the fear that the moment of erotic fulfillment may occasion the erasure of the conventional and integral self informs both the central action in *Dracula* and the surcharged emotion of the characters about to be kissed by "those red lips."[3] So powerful an ambivalence, generating both errant erotic impulses and compensatory anxieties, demands a strict, indeed an almost schematic formal management of narrative material. In *Dracula* Stoker borrows from Mary Shelley's *Frankenstein* and Robert Louis Stevenson's *Dr. Jekyll and Mr. Hyde* a narrative strategy characterized by a predictable, if variable, triple rhythm. Each of these texts first invites or admits a monster, then entertains and is entertained by monstrosity for some extended duration, until in its closing pages it expels or repudiates the monster and all the disruption that he/she/it brings.[4]

This article originally appeared in *Representations* 8 (1984).

Obviously enough, the first element in this triple rhythm corresponds formally to the text's beginning or generative moment, to its need to produce the monster, while the third element corresponds to the text's terminal moment, to its need both to destroy the monster it has previously admitted and to end the narrative that houses the monster. Interposed between these antithetical gestures of admission and expulsion is the gothic novel's prolonged middle,[5] during which the text affords its ambivalence a degree of play intended to produce a pleasurable, indeed a thrilling anxiety. Within its extended middle, the gothic novel entertains its resident demon—is, indeed, entertained by it—and the monster, now ascendent in its strength, seems for a time potent enough to invert the "natural" order and overwhelm the comforting closure of the text. That threat, of course, is contained and finally nullified by the narrative requirement that the monster be repudiated and the world of normal relations restored; thus, the gesture of expulsion, compensating for the original irruption of the monstrous, brings the play of monstrosity to its predictable close. This narrative rhythm, whose tripartite cycle of admission-entertainment-expulsion enacts sequentially an essentially simultaneous psychological equivocation, provides aesthetic management of the fundamental ambivalence that motivates these texts and our reading of them.

While such isomorphism of narrative method obviously implies affinities and similarities among these different texts, it does not argue identity of meaning. However similar *Frankenstein, Dr. Jekyll and Mr. Hyde,* and *Dracula* may be, differences nevertheless obtain, and these differences bear the impress of authorial, historical, and institutional pressures. This essay therefore offers not a reading of monstrosity in general, but rather an account of Bram Stoker's particular articulation of the vampire metaphor in *Dracula,* a book whose fundamental anxiety, an equivocation about the relationship between desire and gender, repeats, with a monstrous difference, a pivotal anxiety of late Victorian culture. Jonathan Harker, whose diary opens the novel, provides *Dracula's* most precise articulation of this anxiety. About to be kissed by the "weird sisters" (64), the incestuous vampiric daughters who share Castle Dracula with the Count, a supine Harker thrills to a double passion:

> All three had brilliant white teeth, that shone like pearls against the ruby of their voluptuous lips. There was something about them that made me uneasy, *some longing and at the same time some deadly fear.* I felt in my heart a wicked, burning desire that they would kiss me with those red lips. (51; emphasis added)

Immobilized by the competing imperatives of "wicked desire" and "deadly fear," Harker awaits an erotic fulfillment that entails both the dissolution of the boundaries of the self and the thorough subversion of conventional Victorian gender codes, which constrained the mobility of sexual desire and varieties of genital behavior according to the more active male the right and responsibility of vigorous appetite, while requiring the more passive female to "suffer and be still." John Ruskin, concisely formulating Victorian conventions of sexual difference, provides us with a useful synopsis: "The man's power is active, progressive, defensive. He is eminently the doer, the creator, the discoverer, the defender. His intellect is for speculation and invention; his energy for adventure, for war, and for conquest. . . ." Woman, predictably enough, bears a different burden: "She must be enduringly, incorruptibly, good; instinctively, infallibly wise—wise, not for self-development, but for self-renunciation . . . wise, not with the narrowness of insolent and loveless pride, but with the passionate gentleness of an infintely variable, because infinitely applicable, modesty of service—the true changefulness of woman."[6] Stoker, whose vampiric women exercise a far more dangerous "changefulness" than Ruskin imagines, anxiously inverts this conventional pattern, as virile Jonathan Harker enjoys a "feminine" passivity and awaits a delicious penetration from a woman whose demonism is figured as the power to penetrate. A swooning desire for an overwhelming penetration and an intense aversion to the demonic potency empowered to gratify that desire compose the fundamental motivating action and emotion in *Dracula.*

This ambivalence, always excited by the imminence of the vampiric kiss, finds its most sensational representation in the image of the Vampire Mouth, the central and recurring image of the novel: "There was a deliberate voluptuousness which was both thrilling and repulsive. . . . I could see in the moonlight the moisture shining on the red tongue as it lapped the white sharp teeth" (52). That is Harker describing one of the three vampire women at Castle Dracula. Here is Dr. Seward's description of the Count: "His eyes flamed red with devilish passion; the great nostils of the white acquiline nose opened wide and quivered at the edges; and the white sharp teeth, behind the full lips of the blood-dripping mouth, champed together like those of a wild beast" (336). As the primary site of erotic experience in *Dracula,* this mouth equivocates, giving the lie to the easy separation of the masculine and the feminine. Luring at first with an inviting orifice, a promise of red softness, but delivering instead a piercing bone, the vampire mouth fuses and confuses what Dracula's civilized nemesis, Van Helsing and his Crew of Light,[7] works so hard to separate—the gender-based categories of the penetrating and the receptive, or, to use Van Helsing's language, the complementary categories of "brave men" and "good women." With its soft flesh barred by hard bone, its red crossed by white, this mouth compels opposites and contrasts into a frightening unity, and it asks some disturbing questions. Are we male or are we female? Do we have penetrators or orifices? And if both, what does that mean? And what about our bodily fluids, the red and the white? What are the relations between blood and semen, milk and blood? Furthermore, this mouth, bespeaking the subversion of the stable and lucid distinctions of gender, is the mouth of all vampires, male and female.

Yet we must remember that the vampire mouth is first of all Dracula's mouth, and that all subsequent versions of it (in *Dracula* all vampires other than the Count are female)[8] merely repeat as diminished simulacra the desire of the Great Original, that "father or furtherer of a new order of beings" (360). Dracula himself, calling his children "my jackals to do my bidding when I want to feed," identifies the systematic creation of female surrogates who enact his will and desire (365). This should remind us that the novel's opening anxiety, its first articulation of the vampiric threat, derives from Dracula's hovering interest in Jonathan Harker; the sexual threat this novel first evokes, manipulates, sustains, but never finally represents is that Dracula will seduce, penetrate, drain another male. The suspense and power of *Dracula's* opening section, of that phase of the narrative which we have called the invitation to monstrosity, proceeds precisely from this unfulfilled sexual ambition. Dracula's desire to fuse with a male, most explicitly evoked when Harker cuts himself shaving, subtly and dangerously suffuses this text. Always postponed and never directly enacted, this desire finds evasive fulfillment in an important series of heterosexual displacements.

Dracula's ungratified desire to vamp Harker is fulfilled instead by his three vampiric daughters, whose anatomical femininity permits, because it masks, the silently inderdicted homoerotic embrace between Harker and the Count. Here, in a displacement typical both of this text and the gender-anxious culture from which it arose, an implicitly homoerotic desire achieves representation as a monstrous heterosexuality, as a demonic inversion of normal gender relations. Dracula's daughters offer Harker a feminine form but a masculine penetration:

> Lower and lower went her head as the lips went below the range of my mouth and chin and seemed to fasten on my throat. . . . I could feel the soft, shivering touch of the lips on the supersensitive skin of my throat, and the hard dents of the two sharp teeth, just touching and pausing there. I closed my eyes in a langorous ecstasy and waited—waited with a beating heart. (52)

This moment, constituting the text's most direct and explicit representation of a male's desire to be penetrated, is governed by a double deflection: first, the agent of penetration is nominally and anatomically (from the mouth down, anyway) female; and second, this dangerous moment, fusing the maximum of desire and the maximum of anxiety, is poised precisely at the brink of penetration. Here the "two sharp teeth," just "touching" and "pausing" there, stop short of the transgression which would unsex Harker and toward which this text constantly aspires and then retreats: the actual penetration of the male.

This moment is interrupted, this penetration denied. Harker's pause at the end of the paragraph ("waited—waited with a beating heart"), which seems to anticipate an imminent piercing, in fact anticipates not the completion but the interruption of the scene of penetration. Dracula himself breaks into the room, drives the women away from Harker, and admonishes them: "How dare you touch him, any of you? How dare you cast eyes on him when I had forbidden it? Back, I tell you all! This man belongs to me" (53). Dracula's intercession here has two obvious effects: by interrupting the scene of penetration, it suspends and disperses throughout the text the desire maximized at the brink of penetration, and it repeats the threat of a more direct libidinous embrace between Dracula and Harker. Dracula's taunt, "This man belongs to me," is suggestive enough, but at no point subsequent to this moment does Dracula kiss Harker, preferring instead to pump him for his knowledge of English law, custom, and language. Dracula, soon departing for England, leaves Harker to the weird sisters, whose final penetration of him, implied but never represented, occurs in the dark interspace to which Harker's journal gives no access.

Hereafter *Dracula* will never represent so directly a male's desire to be penetrated; once in England Dracula, observing a decorous heterosexuality, vamps only women, in particular Lucy Westenra and Mina Harker. The novel, nonetheless, does not dismiss homoerotic desire and threat; rather it simply continues to diffuse and displace it. Late in the text, the Count himself announces a deflected homeroticism when he admonishes the Crew of Light thus: "My revenge is just begun! I spread it over the centuries, and time is on my side. Your girls that you all love are mine already; and *through them you and others shall yet be mine . . .*" (365; italics added). Here Dracula specifies the process of substitution by which "the girls that you all love" mediate and displace a more direct communion among males. Van Helsing, who provides for Lucy transfusions designed to counteract the dangerous influence of the Count, confirms Dracula's declaration of surrogation; he knows that once the transfusions begin, Dracula drains from Lucy's veins not her blood, but rather blood transferred from the veins of the Crew of Light: "even we four who gave our strength to Lucy it also is all to him [*sic*]" (244). Here, emphatically, is another instance of the heterosexual displacement of a desire mobile enough to elude the boundaries of gender. Everywhere in this text such desire seeks a strangely deflected heterosexual distribution; only through women may men touch.

The representation of sexuality in *Dracula*, then, registers a powerful ambivalence in its identification of desire and fear. The text releases a sexuality so mobile and polymorphic that Dracula may be best represented as bat or wolf or floating dust; yet this effort to elude the restrictions upon desire encoded in traditional conception of gender then constrains that desire through a series of heterosexual displacements. Desire's excursive mobility is always filtered in *Dracula* through the mask of a monstrous or demonic heterosexuality. Indeed,

Dracula's mission in England is the creation of a race of monstrous women, feminine demons equipped with masculine devices. This monstrous heterosexuality is apotropaic for two reasons: first, because it masks and deflects the anxiety consequent to a more direct representation of same sex eroticism; and second, because in imagining a sexually aggressive woman as a demonic penetrator, as a ursurper of a prerogative belonging "naturally" to the other gender, it justifies, as we shall see later, a violent expulsion of this deformed femininity.

In its particular formulation of erotic ambivalence, in its contrary need both to liberate and constrain a desire indifferent to the prescriptions of gender by figuring such desire as monstrous heterosexuality, *Dracula* may seem at first idiosyncratic, anomalous, merely neurotic. This is not the case. *Dracula* presents a characteristic, if hyperbolic, instance of Victorian anxiety over the potential fluidity of gender roles,[9] and this text's defensiveness toward the mobile sexuality it nonetheless wants to evoke parallels remarkably other late Victorian accounts of same sex eroticism, of desire in which the "sexual instincts" were said to be, in the words of John Addington Symonds, "improperly correlated to [the] sexual organs."[10] During the last decades of the nineteenth century and the first of the twentieth, English writers produced their first sustained discourse about the variability of sexual desire, with a special emphasis upon male homoerotic love, which had already received indirect and evasive endorsement from Tennyson in "In Memoriam" and from Whitman in the "Calamus" poems. The preferred taxonomic label under which these writers categorized and examined such sexual desire was not, as we might anticipate, "homosexuality" but rather "sexual inversion," a classificatory term involving a complex negotiation between socially encoded gender norms and a sexual mobility that would seem at first unconstrained by those norms. Central polemical texts contributing to this discourse include Symonds's *A Problem in Greek Ethics* (1883), and his *A Problem in Modern Ethics* (1891); Havelock Ellis's *Sexual Inversion*, originally written in collaboration with Symonds, published and suppressed in England in 1897, and later to be included as volume 2 of Ellis's *Studies in the Psychology of Sex* (1901); and Edward Carpenter's *Homogenic Love* (1894) and his *The intermediate Sex* (1908). Admittedly polemical and apologetic, these texts argued, with considerable circumspection, for the cultural acceptance of desire and behavior hitherto categorized as sin, explained under the imprecise religious term "sodomy,"[11] and repudiated as "the crime *inter Christianos non nominandum.*"[12] Such texts, urbanely arguing an extremist position, represent a culture's first attempt to admit the inadmissible, to give the unnamable a local habitation and a name, and as Michael Foucalt has argued, to put sex into discourse.[13]

"Those who read these lines will hardly doubt what passion it is that I am hinting at," wrote Symonds in the introduction to *A Problem in Modern Ethics*, a book whose subtitle—*An Inquiry into the Phenomenon of Sexual Inversion*,

Addressed Especially to Medical Psychologists and Jurists—provides the *OED Supplement* with its earliest citation (1896) for "inversion" in the sexual sense. Symonds's coy gesture, his hint half-guessed, has the force of a necessary circumlocution. Symonds, Ellis, and Carpenter struggled to devise, and then to revise, a descriptive language untarnished by the anal implications, by suggestions of that "circle of extensive corruption,"[14] that so terrified and fascinated late Victorian culture. Symonds "can hardly find a name that will not seem to soil" his text "because the accomplished languages of Europe in the nineteenth century provide no term for this persistant feature of human psychology without importing some implication of disgust, disgrace, vituperation." This need to supply a new term, to invent an adequate taxonomic language, produced more obscurity than clarity. A terminological muddle ensued, the new names of the unnameable were legion: "homosexuality," "sexual inversion," "intermediate sex," "homogenic love," and "uranism" all coexisted and competed for terminological priority. Until the second or third decade of this century, when the word "homosexuality," probably because of its medical heritage, took the terminological crown, "sexual inversion"—as word, metaphor, taxonomic category— provided the basic tool with which late Victorians investigated, and constituted, their problematic desire. Symonds, more responsible than any other writer for the establishment of "inversion" as Victorian England's preferred term for same sex eroticism, considered it a "convenient phrase" "which does not prejudice the matter under consideration." Going further, he naively claimed that "inversion" provided a "neutral nomenclature" with which "the investigator has good reason to be satisfied."[15]

Symonds's claim of terminological neutrality ignores the way in which conventional beliefs and assumptions about gender inhabit both the label "inversion" and the metaphor behind it. The exact history of the word remains obscure (the *OED Supplement* defines sexual inversion tautologically as "the inversion of the sex instincts" and provides two perfunctory citations) but it seems to have been employed first in English in an anonymous medical review of 1871; Symonds later adopted it to translate the account of homoerotic desire offered by Karl Ulrichs, an "inverted" Hanoverian legal official who wrote in the 1860s in Germany "a series of polemical, analytical, theoretical, and apologetic pamphlets" endorsing same sex eroticism.[16] As Ellis explains it, Ulrichs "regarded uranism, or homosexual love, as a congenital abnormality by which a female soul had become united with a female's body—*anima muliebris in corpore virili inclusa*."[17] The explanation for this improper correlation of anatomy and desire is, according to Symonds's synopsis of Ulrichs in *Modern Ethics*, "to be found in physiology, in that obscure department of natural science which deals with the evolution of sex."[18] Nature's attempt to differentiate "the indeterminate ground-stuff" of the foetus—to produce, that is, not merely the "male and female organs of procreation" but also the "corresponding male and female appetites"—falls short of complete success: "Nature fails to complete her work regularly and in every instance. Having succeeded in differentiating a male with full-formed sexual organs from the undecided foetus, she does not always effect the proper differentiation of that portion of the psychical being in which resides the sexual appetite. There remains a female soul in a male body." Since it holds nature responsible for the "imperfection in the process of development," this explanation of homoerotic desire has obvious polemical utility; in relieving the individual of moral responsibility for his or her anomalous development, it argues first for the decriminalization and then for the medicalization of inversion. According to this account, same sex eroticism, although statistically deviant or abnormal, cannot then be called unnatural. Inverts or urnings or homosexuals are therefore "abnormal, but natural, beings"; they constitute the class of "the naturally abnormal." Symonds, writing to Carpenter, makes his point succinctly: "The first thing is to force people to see that the passions in question have their justification in nature."[19]

As an extended psychosexual analogy to the more palpable reality of physical hermaphroditism, Ulrichs's explanation of homoerotic desire provided the English polemicists with the basic components for their metaphor of inversion, which never relinquished the idea of a misalignment between inside and outside, between desire and the body, between the hidden truth of sex and the false sign of anatomical gender. ("Inversion," derived from the Latin Verb *vertere*, "to turn," means literally to turn in, and the *OED* cites the following meaning from pathology: "to turn outside in or inside out.") This argument's intrinsic doubleness—its insistence of the simultaneous inscription within the individual of two genders, one anatomical and one not, one visible and one not—represents an accommodation between contrary impulses of liberation and constraint, as conventional gender norms are subtilized and manipulated but never fully escaped. What this account of same sex eroticism cannot imagine is that sexual attraction between members of the same gender may be a reasonable and natural articulation of a desire whose excursiveness is simply indifferent to the distinctions of gender that desire may not be gendered intrinsically as the body is, and that desire seeks its objects according to a complicated set of conventions that are culturally and institutionally determined. So radical a reconstitution of notions of desire would probably have been intolerable even to an advanced reading public because it would threaten the moral priority of the heterosexual norm, as the following sentence from Ellis suggests: "It must also be pointed out that the argument for acquired or suggested inversion logically involves the assertion that normal sexuality is also acquired or suggested."[20] Unable or unwilling to deconstruct the heterosexual norm, English accounts of sexual inversion instead repeat it; desire remains, despite appearances, essentially and irrevocably heterosexual. A male's desire for another male, for instance, is from the beginning assumed to be a feminine desire referable not to the gender of the body (*corpore virili*) but rather to another invisible sexual self composed of the opposite gender (*anima muliebris*). Desire, according to this explanation, is always already constituted under the regime of gender—to want a male cannot not be a female desire, and vice versa—and the body, having become an unreliable signifier, ceases to represent adequately the invisible truth of desire, which itself never deviates from respectable heterosexuality. Thus the confusion that threatens conventional definitions of gender when confronted by same sex eroticism becomes merely illusory. The body, quite simply, is mistaken.

Significantly, this displaced repetition of heterosexual gender norms contains within it the undeveloped germ of a radical redefinition of Victorian conventions of female desire. The interposition of a feminine soul between erotically associated males inevitably entails a certain feminization of desire, since the very site and source of desire for males is assumed to be feminine (*anima muliebris*). Implicit in this argument is the submerged acknowledgment of the sexually independent woman, whose erotic empowerment refutes the conventional assumption of feminine passivity. Nonetheless, this nascent redefinition of notions of feminine desire remain largely unfulfilled. Symonds and Ellis did not escape their culture's phallocentrism, and their texts predictably reflect this bias. Symonds, whose sexual and aesthetic interests pivoted around the "pure & noble faculty of understanding & expressing manly perfection,"[21] seems to have been largely unconcerned with feminine sexuality; his seventy-page *A Problem in Greek Ethics,* for instance, offers only a two-page "parenthetical investigation" of lesbianism. Ellis, like Freud, certainly acknowledged sexual desire in women, but nevertheless accorded to masculine heterosexual desire an ontological and practical priority: "The female responds to the stimulation of the male at the right moment just as the tree responds to the stimulation of the warmest days in spring."[22] (Neither did English law want to recognize the sexually self-motivated woman. The Labouchère Amendment to the Criminal Law Amendment Act of 1885, the statute under which Oscar Wilde was convicted of "gross indecency," simply ignored the possibility of erotic behavior between women.) In all of this we may see an anxious defense against recognition of an independent and active feminine sexuality. A submerged fear of the feminization of desire precluded these polemicists from fully developing their own argumentative assumption of an already sexualized feminine soul.

Sexual inversion, then, understands homerotic desire as misplaced heterosexuality and configures its understanding of such desire according to what George Chauncey has called "the heterosexual paradigm," an analytical model requiring that all love repeat the dyadic structure (masculine/feminine, husband/wife, active/passive) embodied in the heterosexual norm.[23] Desire between anatomical males requires the interposition of an invisible femininity, just as desire between anatomical females requires the mediation of a hidden masculinity. This insistent ideology of heterosexual mediation and its corollary anxiety about independent feminine sexuality returns us to *Dracula,* where all desire, however, mobile, is fixed within a heterosexual mask, where a mobile and hungering woman is represented as a monstrous usurper of masculine function, and where, as we shall see in detail, all erotic contacts between males, whether directly libidinal or thoroughly sublimated, are fulfilled through a mediating female, through the surrogation of the other, "correct," gender. Sexual inversion and Stoker's account of vampirism, then, are symmetrical metaphors sharing a fundamental ambivalence. Both discourses, aroused by a desire that wants to elude or flaunt the conventional prescriptions of gender, constrain that desire by constituting it according to the heterosexual paradigm that leaves conventional gender codes intact. The difference between the two discourses lies in the particular articulation of that paradigm. Sexual inversion, especially as argued by Symonds and Ellis, represents an urbane and civilized accommodation of the contrary impulses of liberation and constraint. Stoker's vampirism, altogether more hysterical and hyperbolic, imagines mobile desire as monstrosity and then devises a violent correction of that desire; in *Dracula* the vampiric abrogation of gender codes inspires a defensive reinscription of the stabilizing distinctions of gender. The site of that ambivalent interplay of desire and its correction, of mobility and fixity, is the text's prolonged middle, to which we now turn.

Engendering Gender

> *Our strong game will be to play with our masculine against her feminine.*
>
> Stoker, *The Lair of the White Worm*

The portion of the gothic novel that I have called the prolonged middle, during which the text allows the monster a certain dangerous play, corresponds in *Dracula* to the duration beginning with the Count's arrival in England and ending with his flight back home; this extended middle constitutes the novel's prolonged moment of equivocation, as it entertains, elaborates, and explores the very anxieties it must later expel in the formulaic resolution of the plot. The action within this section of *Dracula* consists, simply enough, in an extended battle between two evidently masculine forces, one identifiably good and the other identifiably evil, for the allegiance of a woman (two women actually— Lucy Westenra and Mina Harker nee Murray).[24] This competition between alternative potencies has the apparent simplicity of a black and white opposition. Dracula ravages and impoverishes these women. Van Helsing's Crew of Light restores and "saves" them. As Dracula conducts his serial assaults upon Lucy, Van Helsing, in a pretty counterpoint of penetration, responds with a series of defensive transfusions; the blood that Dracula takes out Van Helsing then puts back. Dracula, isolated and disdainful of community, works alone; Van Helsing enters this little English community, immediately assumes authority, and then works through surrogates to cement communal bonds. As critics have noted, this pattern of opposition distills readily into a competition between antithetical fathers. "The vampire Count, centuries old," Maurice Richardson wrote twenty-five years ago, "is a father figure of huge potency" who competes with Van Helsing, "the good father figure."[25] The theme of alternate paternities is, in short, simple, evident, unavoidable.

This oscillation between vampiric transgression and medical correction exercises the text's ambivalence toward those fundamental dualisms—life and death, spirit and flesh, male and female—which have served traditionally to constrain and delimit the excursions of desire. As doctor, lawyer, and sometimes priest ("The Host. I brought it from Amsterdam. I have an indulgence."), Van Helsing stands as the protector of the patriarchal institutions he so emphatically represents and as the guarantor of the traditional dualisms his religion and profession promote and authorize.[26] His largest purpose is to reinscribe the dualities that Dracula would muddle and confuse. Dualities require demarcations, inexorable and ineradicable lines of separation, but Dracula, as a border being who abrogates demarcations, makes such distinctions impossible. He is *nosferatu,* neither dead nor alive but somehow both, mobile frequenter of the grave and boudoir, easeful communicant of exclusive realms, and as such he toys with the separation of the living and the dead, a distinction critical to physician, lawyer, and priest alike. His mobility and metaphoric power deride the distinction between spirit and flesh, another of Van Helsing's sanctified dualisms. Potent enough to ignore death's terminus, Dracula has a spirit's freedom and mobility, but that mobility is chained to the most mechanical of appetites: he and his children rise and fall for a drink and for nothing else, for nothing else matters. This con- or inter-fusion of spirit and appetite, of eternity and sequence, produces a madness of activity and a mania of unceasing desire. Dracula lives an eternity of sexual repetition, a lurid wedding of desire and satisfaction that parodies both.

But the traditional dualism most vigorously defended by Van Helsing and most subtly subverted by Dracula is, of course, sexual: the division of being into gender, either male or female. Indeed, as we have seen, the vampiric kiss excites a sexuality so mobile, so insistent, that it threatens to overwhelm the distinctions of gender, and the exuberant energy with which Van Helsing and the Crew of Light counter Dracula's influence represents the text's anxious defense against the very desire it also seeks to liberate. In counterposing Dracula and Van Helsing, Stoker's text simultaneously threatens and protects the line of demarcation that insures the intelligible division of being into gender. This ambivalent need to invite the vampiric kiss and then to repudiate it defines exactly the dynamic of the battle that constitutes the prolonged middle of this text. The field of this battle, of this equivocal competition for the right to define the possible relations between desire and gender, is the infinitely penetrable body of a somnolent woman. This interposition of a woman between Dracula and Van Helsing should not surprise us; in England, as in Castle Dracula, a violent wrestle between males is mediated through a feminine form.

The Crew of Light's conscious conception of women is, predictably enough, idealized—the stuff of dreams. Van Helsing's concise description of Mina may serve as a representative example: "She is one of God's women fashioned by His own hand to show us men and other women that there is a heaven we can enter, and that its light can be here on earth" (226). The impossible idealism of this conception of women deflects attention from the complex and complicitous interaction within this sentence of gender, authority, and representation. Here Van Helsing's exegesis of God's natural text reifies Mina into a stable sign or symbol ("one of God's women") performing a fixed and comfortable function within a masculine sign system. Having received from Van Helsing's exegesis her divine impress, Mina signifies both a masculine artistic intention ("fashioned by His own hand") and a definite didactic purpose ("to show us men and other women" how to enter heaven), each of which constitutes an enormous constraint upon the significative possibilities of the sign or symbol that Mina here becomes. Van Helsing's reading of Mina, like a dozen other instances in which his interpretation of the sacred determines and delimits the range of activity permitted to women, encodes woman with a "natural" meaning composed according to the textual imperatives of anxious males. Precisely this complicity between masculine anxiety, divine textual authority, and a fixed conception of femininity—which may seem benign enough in the passage above— will soon be used to justify the destruction of Lucy Westenra, who, having been successfully vamped by Dracula, requires a corrective penetration. To Arthur's anxious importunity "Tell me what I am to do," Van Helsing answers: "Take this stake in your left hand, ready to place the point over the heart, and the hammer in your right. Then when we begin our prayer for the dead—I shall read him; I have here the book, and the others shall follow—strike in God's name . . . " (259). Here four males (Van Helsing, Seward, Holmwood, and Quincey Morris) communally read a masculine text (Van Helsing's mangled English even permits Stoker the unidiomatic pronominalization of the genderless text: "I shall read him"),[27] in order to justify the fatal correction of Lucy's dangerous wandering, her insolent disregard for the sexual and semiotic constraint encoded in Van Helsing's exegesis of "God's women."

The process by which women are construed as signs determined by the interpretive imperatives of authorizing males had been brilliantly identified some fifty years before the publication of *Dracula* by John Stuart Mill in *The Subjection of Women*. "What is now called the nature of women," Mill writes, "is an extremely artificial thing—the result of forced repression in some directions, unnatural stimulation in others."[28] Mill's sentence, deftly identifying "the nature of women" as an "artificial" construct formed (and deformed) by "repression" and "unnatural stimulation," quietly unties the lacings that bind something called "woman" to something else called "nature." Mill further suggests that a correct reading of gender becomes almost impossible, since the natural difference between male and female is subject to cultural interpretation: " . . . I deny that anyone knows, or can know, the nature of the two sexes, as long as they have only been seen in their present relation to one another." Mill's agnosticism regarding "the nature of the sexes" suggests the societal and institutional quality of all definitions of the natural, definitions which ultimately conspire to produce "the imaginary and conventional character of women."[29] This last phrase, like the whole of Mill's essay, understands and criticizes the authoritarian nexus that arises when a deflected or transformed desire ("imaginary"), empowered by a gender-biased societal agreement ("conventional"), imposes itself upon a person in order to create a "character." "Character" of course functions in at least three senses: who and what one "is," the role one plays in society's supervening script, and the sign or letter that is intelligible only within the constraints of a larger sign system. Van Helsing's exegesis of "God's women" creates just such an imaginary and conventional character. Mina's body/character may indeed be feminine, but the signification it bears is written and interpreted solely by males. As Susan Hardy Aiken has written, such a symbolic system takes "for granted the role of women as passive objects or signs to be manipulated in the grammar of privileged male interchanges."[30]

Yet exactly the passivity of this object and the ease of this manipulation are at question in *Dracula*. Dracula, after all, kisses these women out of their passivity and so endangers the stability of Van Helsing's symbolic system. Both the prescriptive intention of Van Helsing's exegesis and the emphatic methodology (hypodermic needle, stake, surgeon's blade) he employs to insure the durability of his interpretation of gender suggest the potential unreliability of Mina as sign, an instability that provokes an anxiety we may call fear of the mediatrix. If, as Van Helsing admits, God's women provide the essential mediation ("the light can be here on earth") between the divine but distant patriarch and his earthly sons, then God's intention may be distorted by its potentially changeable vehicle. If woman-as-signifier wanders, then Van Helsing's whole cosmology, with its founding dualisms and supporting texts, collapses. In short, Van Helsing's interpretation of Mina, because endangered by the proleptic fear that his mediatrix might destabilize and wander, necessarily imposes an *a priori* constraint upon the significative possibilities of the sign "Mina." Such an authorial gesture, intended to forestall the semiotic wandering that Dracula inspires, indirectly acknowledges woman's dangerous potential. Late in the text, while Dracula is vamping Mina, Van Helsing will admit, very uneasily, that "Madam Mina,

our poor, dear Madam Mina is changing" (384). The potential for such a change
demonstrates what Nina Auerbach has called this woman's "mysterious amal-
gam of imprisonment and power."[31]

Dracula's authorizing kiss, like that of a demonic Prince Charming, trig-
gers the release of this latent power and excites in these women a sexuality so
mobile, so aggressive, that it thoroughly disrupts Van Helsing's compartmental
conception of gender. Kissed into a sudden sexuality,[32] Lucy grows "voluptuous" (a word used to describe her only during the vampiric process), her lips
redden, and she kisses with a new interest. This sexualization of Lucy, meta-
morphosing woman's "sweetness" to "adamantine, heartless cruelty, and [her]
purity to voluptuous wantonness" (252), terrifies her suitors because it entails a
reversal or inversion of sexual identity; Lucy, now toothed like the Count,
usurps the function of penetration that Van Helsing's moralized taxonomy of
gender reserves for males. *Dracula*, in thus figuring the sexualization of woman
as deformation, parallels exactly some of the more extreme medical uses of the
idea of inversion. Late Victorian accounts of lesbianism, for instance, super-
scribed conventional gender norms upon sexual relationships to which those
norms were anatomically irrelevant. Again the heterosexual norm proved paradigmatic. The female "husband" in such a relationship was understood to be
dominant, appetitive, masculine, and "congenitally inverted"; the female "wife"
was understood to be quiescent, passive, only "latently" homosexual, and, as
Havelock Ellis argued, unmotivated by genital desire.[33] Extreme deployment
of the heterosexual paradigm approached the ridiculous, as George Chauncey
explains:

> The early medical case histories of lesbians thus predictably paid enormous attention to their
> menstrual flow and the size of their sexual organs. Several doctors emphasized that their
> lesbian patients stopped menstruating at an early age, if they began at all, or had unusually
> difficult and irregular periods. They also inspected the woman's sexual organs, often claiming
> that inverts had unusually large clitorises, which they said the inverts used in sexual intercourse
> as a man would his penis.[34]

This rather pathetic hunt for the penis-in-absentia denotes a double anxiety: first,
that the penis shall not be erased, and if it is erased, that it shall be reinscribed
in a perverse simulacrum; and second, that all desire repeat, under the duress
of deformity, the heterosexual norm that the metaphor of inversion always
assumes. Medical professionals had in fact no need to pursue this fantasized
amazon of the clitoris, this "unnatural" penetrator, so vigorously, since Stoker,
whose imagination was at least deft enough to displace that dangerous simulacrum to an isomorphic orifice, had by the 1890s already invented her. His
sexualized women are men too.

Stoker emphasizes the monstrosity implicit in such abrogation of gender codes by inverting a favorite Victorian maternal function. His New Lady Vampires feed at first only on small children, working their way up, one assumes, a demonic pleasure thermometer until they may feed at last on full-blooded males. Lucy's dietary indiscretions evoke the deepest disgust from the Crew of Light:

> With a careless motion, she flung to the ground, callous as a devil, the child that up to now she had clutched strenuously to her breast, growling over it as a dog growls over a bone. The child gave a sharp cry, and lay there moaning. There was a cold-bloodedness in the act which wrung a groan from Arthur; when she advanced to him with outstretched arms and a wanton smile, he fell back and hid his face in his hands.
>
> She still advanced, however, and with a langorous, voluptuous grace, said:
> "Come to me Arthur. Leave those others and come to me. My arms are hungry for you. Come, and we can rest together. Come, my husband, come!" (253–54)

Stoker here gives us a *tableau mordant* of gender inversion: the child Lucy clutches "strenuously to her breast" is not being fed but is being fed upon. Furthermore, by requiring that the child be discarded that the husband may be embraced, Stoker provides a little emblem of this novel's anxious protestation that appetite in a woman "(My arms are hungry for you") is a diabolic ("callous as a devil") inversion of natural order, and of the novel's fantastic but futile hope that maternity and sexuality be divorced.

The aggressive mobility with which Lucy flaunts the encasements of gender norms generates in the Crew of Light a terrific defensive activity, as these men race to reinscribe, with a series of pointed instruments, the line of demarcation which enables the definition of gender. To save Lucy from the mobilization of desire, Van Helsing and the Crew of Light counteract Dracula's subversive series of penetrations with a more conventional series of their own, that sequence of transfusions intended to provide Lucy with the "brave man's blood" which "is the best thing on earth when a woman is in trouble" (180). There are in fact four transfusions, which begin with Arthur, who as Lucy's accepted suitor has the right of first infusion, and include Lucy's other two suitors (Dr. Seward, Quincey Morris) and Van Helsing himself. One of the established observations of *Dracula* criticism is that these therapeutic penetrations represent displaced marital (and martial) penetrations; indeed, the text is emphatic about this substitution of medical for sexual penetration. After the first transfusion, Arthur feels as if he and Lucy "had been really married and that she was his wife in the sight of God" (209); and Van Helsing, after his donation, calls himself a "bigamist" and Lucy "this so sweet maid . . . a polyandrist" (211–12). These transfusions, in short, are sexual (blood substitutes for semen here)[35] and constitute, in Nina Auerbach's superb phrase, "the most convincing epithalamiums in the novel."[36]

These transfusions represent the text's first anxious reassertion of the conventionally masculine prerogative of penetration; as Van Helsing tells Arthur

before the first transfusion, "You are a man and it is a man we want" (148).
Countering the dangerous mobility excited by Dracula's kiss, Van Helsing's
penetrations restore to Lucy both the stillness appropriate to his sense of her
gender and "the regular breathing of healthy sleep," a necessary correction of
the loud "stertorous" breathing, the animal snorting, that the Count inspires.
This repetitive contest (penetration, withdrawal; penetration, infusion), itself
an image of *Dracula's* ambivalent need to evoke and then to repudiate the fluid
pleasures of vampiric appetite, continues to be waged upon Lucy's infinitely
penetrable body until Van Helsing exhausts his store of "brave men," whose
generous gifts of blood, however efficacious, fail finally to save Lucy from the
mobilization of desire.

But even the loss of this much blood does not finally enervate a masculine
energy as indefatigable as the Crew of Light's, especially when it stands in the
service of a tradition of "good women whose lives and whose truths may make
good lesson [*sic*] for the children that are to be" (222). In the name of those
good women and future children (very much the same children whose throats
Lucy is now penetrating), Van Helsing will repeat, with an added emphasis, his
assertion that penetration is a masculine prerogative. His logic of corrective
penetration demands an escalation, as the failure of the hypodermic needle
necessitates the stake. A woman is better still than mobile, better dead than
sexual:

> Arthur took the stake and the hammer, and when once his mind was set on action his hands
> never trembled nor even quivered. Van Helsing opened his missal and began to read, and
> Quincey and I followed as well as we could. Arthur placed the point over the heart, and as I
> looked I could see its dint in the white flesh. Then he struck with all his might.
>
> The Thing in the coffin writhed; and a hideous, blood-curdling screech came from the
> opened red lips. The body shook and quivered and twisted in wild contortions; the sharp white
> teeth champed together till the lips were cut and the mouth was smeared with a crimson foam.
> But Arthur never faltered. He looked like the figure of Thor as his untrembling arm rose and
> fell, driving deeper and deeper the mercy-bearing stake, whilst the blood from the pierced
> heart welled and spurted up around it. His face was set, and high duty seemed to shine through
> it; the sight of it gave us courage, so that our voices seemed to ring through the little vault.
>
> And then the writhing and quivering of the body became less, and the teeth ceased to champ,
> and the face to quiver. Finally it lay still. The terrible task was over. (258–59)

Here is the novel's real—and the woman's only—climax, its most violent and
misogynistic moment, displaced roughly to the middle of the book, so that the
sexual threat may be repeated but its ultimate success denied: Dracula will not
win Mina, second in his series of English seductions. The murderous phallicism
of this passage clearly punishes Lucy for her transgression of Van Helsing's
gender code, as she finally receives a penetration adequate to insure her future
quiescence. Violence against the sexual woman here is intense, sensually imagined, ferocious in its detail. Note, for instance, the terrible dimple, the "dint in

the white flesh," that recalls Jonathan Harker's swoon at Castle Dracula ("I could feel . . . the hard dents of the two sharp teeth, just touching and pausing there") and anticipates the technicolor consummation of the next paragraph. That paragraph, masking murder as "high duty," completes Van Helsing's penetrative therapy by "driving deeper and deeper the mercy-bearing stake." One might question a mercy this destructive, this fatal, but Van Helsing's actions, always sanctified by the patriarchal textual tradition signified by "his missal," manage to "restore Lucy to us as a holy and not an unholy memory" (258). This enthusiastic correction of Lucy's monstrosity provides the Crew of Light with a double reassurance: it effectively exorcises the threat of a mobile and hungering feminine sexuality, and it counters the homoeroticism latent in the vampiric threat by reinscribing (upon Lucy's chest) the line dividing the male who penetrates and the woman who receives. By disciplining Lucy and restoring each gender to its "proper" function, Van Helsing's pacification program compensates for the threat of gender indefinition implicit in the vampiric kiss.

The vigor and enormity of this penetration (Arthur driving the "round wooden stake," which is "some two and a half or three inches thick and about three feet long," resembles "the figure of Thor") do not bespeak merely Stoker's personal idiosyncratic anxiety but suggest as well a whole culture's uncertainty about the fluidity of gender roles. Consider, for instance, the following passage from Ellis's contemporaneous *Studies in the Psychology of Sex*. Ellis, writing on "The Mechanism of Detumescence" (i.e., ejaculation), employs a figure that Stoker would have recognized as his own:

> Detumescence is normally linked to tumescence. Tumescence is the piling on of the fuel; detumescence is the leaping out of the devouring flame whence is lighted the torch of life to be handed on from generation to generation. The whole process is double yet single; it is exactly analogous to that by which a pile is driven into the earth by the raising and the letting go of a heavy weight which falls on the head of the pile. In tumescence the organism is slowly wound up and force accumulated; in the act of detumescence the accumulated force is let go and by its liberation the sperm-bearing instrument is driven home.[37]

Both Stoker and Ellis need to imagine so homely an occurrence as penile penetration as an event of mythic, or at least seismographic, proportions. Ellis's pile driver, representing the powerful "sperm-bearing instrument," may dwarf even Stoker's already outsized member, but both serve a similar function: they channel and finally "liberate" a tremendous "accumulated force" that itself represents a trans- or supra-natural intention. Ellis, employing a Darwinian principle of interpretation to explain that intention, reads woman's body (much as we have seen Van Helsing do) as a natural sign—or, perhaps better, as a sign of nature's overriding reproductive intention:

> There can be little doubt that, as one or two writers have already suggested, the hymen owes its development to the fact that its influence is on the side of effective fertilization. It is an obstacle to the impregnation of the young female by immature, aged, or feeble males. *The hymen is thus an anatomical expression of that admiration of force which marks the female in her choice of mate.* So regarded, it is an interesting example of the intimate matter in which sexual selection is really based on natural selection.[38] (italics added)

Here, as evolutionary teleology supplants divine etiology and as Darwin's texts assume the primacy Van Helsing would reserve for God's, natural selection, not God's original intention, becomes the interpretive principle governing nature's text. As a sign or "anatomical expression" within that text, the hymen signifies a woman's presumably natural "admiration of force" and her invitation to "the sperm-bearing instrument." Woman's body, structurally hostile to "immature, aged, or feeble males," simply begs for "effective fertilization." Lucy's body, too, reassures the Crew of Light with an anatomical expression of her admiration of force. Once fatally staked, Lucy is restored to "the so sweet that was." Dr. Seward describes the change:

> There in the coffin lay no longer the foul Thing that we had so dreaded and grown to hate that the work of her destruction was yielded to the one best entitled to it, but Lucy as we had seen her in her life with her face of unequalled sweetness and purity. . . . One and all we felt that the holy calm that lay like sunshine over the wasted face and form was only an earthly token and symbol of the calm that was to reign for ever. (259)

This post-penetrative peace[39] denotes not merely the final immobilization of Lucy's body, but also the corresponding stabilization of the dangerous signifier whose wandering had so threatened Van Helsing's gender code. Here a masculine interpretive community ("One and all we felt") reasserts the semiotic fixity that allows Lucy to function as the "earthly token and symbol" of eternal beatitude, of the heaven we can enter. We may say that this last penetration is doubly efficacious; in a single stoke both the sexual and the textual needs of the Crew of Light find a sufficient satisfaction.

Despite its placement in the middle of the text, this scene, which successfully pacifies Lucy and demonstrates so emphatically the efficacy of the technology Van Helsing employs to correct vampirism, corresponds formally to the scene of expulsion, which usually signals the end of the gothic narrative. Here, of course, this scene signals not the end of the story but the continuation of it, since Dracula will now repeat his assault on another woman. Such displacement of the scene of expulsion requires explanation. Obviously this displacement subserves the text's anxiety about the direct representation of eroticism between males; Stoker simply could not represent so explicitly a violent phallic interchange between the Crew of Light and Dracula. In a by now familiar heterosexual mediation, Lucy receives the phallic correction that Dracula deserves. Indeed, the actual expulsion of the Count at novel's end is a disappointing anticlimax. Two rather perfunctory knife strokes suffice to dispatch him, as *Dracula* simply forgets the elaborate ritual of correction that vampirism previously required. And the displacement of this scene performs at least two other functions; first, by establishing early the ultimate efficacy of Van Helsing's corrective technology, it reassures everyone—Stoker, his characters, the reader—that vampirism may indeed be vanquished, that its sexual threat, however powerful and intriguing, may be expelled; and second, in doing so, in establishing this reassurance, it permits the text to prolong and repeat its flirtation with vampirism, its ambivalent petition of that sexual threat. In short, the displacement of the scene of expulsion provides a heterosexual locale for Van Helsing's demonstration of compensatory phallicism, while it also extends the duration of the text's ambivalent play.

This extension of the text's flirtation with monstrosity, during which Mina is threatened by but not fully seduced into vampirism, includes the novel's only explicit scene of vampiric seduction. Important enough to be twice presented, first by Seward as spectator and then by Mina as participant, the scene occurs in the Harker bedroom, where Dracula seduces Mina while "on the bed lay Jonathan Harker, his face flushed and breathing heavily as if in a stupor." The Crew of Light bursts into the room; the voice is Dr. Seward's:

> With his left hand he held both Mrs. Harker's hands, keeping them away with her arms at full tension; his right hand gripped her by the back of the neck, forcing her face down on his bosom. Her white nightdress was smeared with blood, and a thin stream trickled down the man's bare breast, which was shown by his torn-open dress. The attitude of the two had a terrible resemblance to a child forcing a kitten's nose into a saucer of milk to compel it to drink. (336)

In this initiation scene Dracula compels Mina into the pleasure of vampiric appetite and introduces her to a world where gender distinctions collapse, where male and female bodily fluids intermingle terribly. For Mina's drinking is double here, both a "symbolic act of enforced fellation"[40] and a lurid nursing. That this is a scene of enforced fellation is made even clearer by Mina's own description of the scene a few pages later; she adds the graphic detail of the "spurt":

> With that he pulled open his shirt, and with his long sharp nails opened a vein in his breast. When the blood began to spurt out, he took my hands in one of his, holding them tight, and with the other seized my neck and pressed my mouth to the wound, so that I must either suffocate or swallow some of the—Oh, my God, my God! What have I done? (343)

That "Oh, my God, My God!" is deftly placed; Mina's verbal ejaculation supplants the Count's liquid one, leaving the fluid unnamed and encouraging us to voice the substitution that the text implies—this blood is semen too. But this scene of fellation is thoroughly displaced. We are at the Count's breast, encouraged once again to substitute white for red, as blood becomes milk: "the attitude of the two had a terrible resemblance to a child forcing a kitten's nose into a saucer of milk." Such fluidity of substitution and displacement entails a confusion of Dracula's sexual identity, or an interfusion of masculine and feminine functions, as Dracula here becomes a lurid mother offering not a breast but an open and bleeding wound. But if the Count's sexuality is double, then the open would may be yet another displacement (the reader of *Dracula* must be as mobile as the Count himself). We are back in the genital region, this time a woman's, and we have the suggestion of a bleeding vagina. The image of red and voluptuous lips, with their slow trickle of blood, has, of course, always harbored this potential.

We may read this scene, in which anatomical displacements and the confluence of blood, milk, and semen forcefully erase the demarcation separating the masculine and the feminine, as *Dracula's* most explicit representation of the anxieties excited by the vampiric kiss. Here *Dracula* defines most clearly vampirism's threat of gender indefinition. Significantly, this scene is postponed until late in the text. Indeed, this is Dracula's last great moment, his final demonstration of dangerous potency; after this, he will vamp no one. The novel, having presented most explicitly its deepest anxiety, its fear of gender dissolution, now moves mechanically to repudiate that fear. After a hundred rather tedious pages of pursuits and flight, *Dracula* perfunctorily expels the Count. The world of "natural" gender relations is happily restored, or at least seems to be.

A Final Dissolution

If my last sentence ends with an equivocation, it is because *Dracula* does so as well; the reader should leave this novel with a troubled sense of the difference between the forces of darkness and the forces of light. Of course the plot of *Dracula*, by granting ultimate victory to Van Helsing and a dusty death to the Count, emphatically ratifies the simplistic opposition of competing conceptions of force and desire, but even a brief reflection upon the details of the war of penetrations complicates this comforting schema. A perverse mirroring occurs, as puncture for puncture the Doctor equals the Count. Van Helsing's doubled penetrations, first the morphine injection that immobilizes the woman and then the infusion of masculine fluid, repeat Dracula's spatially doubled penetrations of Lucy's neck. And that morphine injection, which subdues the woman and improves her receptivity, curiously imitates the Count's strange hypnotic power; both men prefer to immobilize a woman before risking a penetration.[41] Moreover, each penetration announces through its displacement this same sense of danger. Dracula enters at the neck, Van Helsing at the limb; each evades available orifices and refuses to submit to the dangers of vaginal contact. The shared displacement is telling: to make your own holes is an ultimate arrogance, an assertion of penetrative prowess that nonetheless acknowledges, in the flight of its evasion, the threatening power imagined to inhabit woman's available openings. Woman's body readily accommodates masculine fear and desire, whether directly libidinal or culturally refined. We may say that Van Helsing and his tradition have polished teeth into hypodermic needles, a cultural refinement that masks violation as healing. Van Helsing himself, calling his medical instruments "the ghastly paraphernalia of our beneficial trade," employs an adjectival oxymoron (ghastly/beneficial) that itself glosses the troubled relationship between paternalism and violence (146). The medical profession licenses the power to penetrate, devises a delicate instrumentation, and defines canons of procedure, while the religious tradition, with its insistent idealization of women, encodes a restriction on the mobility of desire (who penetrates whom) and then licenses a tremendous punishment for the violation of the code.

But it is all penetrative energy, whether re-fanged or refined, and it is all libidinal; the two strategies of penetration are but different articulations of the same primitive force. *Dracula* certainly problematizes, if it does not quite erase, the line of separation signifying a meaningful difference between Van Helsing and the Count. In other words, the text itself, in its imagistic identification of Dracula and the Crew of Light, in its ambivalent propensity to subvert its own fundamental differences, sympathizes with and finally domesticates vampiric desire; the uncanny, as Freud brilliantly observed, always comes home. Such textual irony, composed of simultaneous but contrary impulses to establish and subvert the fundamental differences between violence and culture, between desire and its sublimations, recalls Freud's late speculations on the troubled relationship between the id and the superego (or ego ideal). In the two brief passages below, taken from his late work *The Ego and the Id,* Freud complicates the differentiation between the id and its unexpected effluent, the superego:

> There are two paths by which the contents of the id can penetrate into the ego. The one is direct, the other leads by way of the ego ideal.

And:

> From the point of view of instinctual control, of morality, it may be said of the id that it is totally non-moral, of the ego that it strives to be moral, and of the super-ego that it can be supermoral and then become as cruel as only the id can be.[42]

It is so easy to remember the id as a rising energy and the superego as a suppressive one, that we forget Freud's subtler argument. These passages, eschewing as too facile the simple opposition of the id and superego, suggest instead that the id and the superego are variant articulations of the same primitive energy. We are already familiar with the "two paths by which the contents of the id penetrate the ego." "The one is direct," as Dracula's penetrations are direct and unembarrassed, and the other, leading "by way of the ego ideal," recalls Van Helsing's way of repression and sublimation. In providing an indirect path for the "contents of the id" and in being "as cruel as only the id can be," the superego may be said to be, in the words of Leo Bersani, "the id which has become its own mirror."[43] This mutual reflectivity of the id and superego, of course, constitutes one of vampirism's most disturbing features, as Jonathan Harker, standing before his shaving glass, learns early in the novel: "This time there could be no error, for the man was close to me, and I could see him over my shoulder. But there was no reflection of him in the mirror! The whole room behind me was displayed; but there was no sign of a man in it, except myself" (37). The meaning of this little visual allegory should be clear enough: Dracula need cast no reflection because his presence, already established in Harker's image, would be simply redundant; the monster, indeed, is no one "except myself." A dangerous sameness waits behind difference; tooth, stake, and hypodermic needle, it would seem, all share a point.

This blending or interfusion of fundamental differences would seem, in one respect at least, to contradict the progress of my argument. We have, after all, established that the Crew of Light's penetrative strategy, subserving Van Helsing's ideology of gender and his heterosexual account of desire, counters just such interfusions with emphatic inscriptions of sexual difference. Nonetheless, this penetrative strategy, despite its purposive heterosexuality, quietly erases its own fundamental differences, its own explicit assumptions of gender and desire. It would seem at first that desire for connection among males is both expressed in and constrained by a traditional articulation of such fraternal affection, as represented in this text's blaring theme of heroic or chivalric male bonding. The obvious male bonding in *Dracula* is precipitated by action—a good fight, a proud ethic, a great victory. Dedicated to a falsely exalted conception of woman, men combine fraternally to fulfill the collective "high duty" that motivates their "great quest" (261). Van Helsing, always the ungrammatical exegete, provides the apt analogy: "Thus we are ministers of God's own wish. . . . He have allowed us to redeem one soul already, and we go out as the old knights of the Cross to redeem more" (381). Van Helsing's chivalric analogy establishes this fraternity within an impeccable lineage signifying both moral rectitude and adherence to the limitation upon desire that this tradition encodes and enforces.

Yet beneath this screen or mask of authorized fraternity a more libidinal bonding occurs as male fluids find a protected pooling place in the body of a woman. We return, for a last time, to those serial transfusions which, while they pretend to serve and protect "good women," actually enable the otherwise inconceivable interfusion of the blood that is semen too. Here displacement (a woman's body) and sublimation (these are medical penetrations) permit the unpermitted, just as in gang rape men share their semen in a location displaced sufficiently to divert the anxiety excited by a more direct union. Repeating its subversive suggestion that the refined moral conceptions of Van Helsing's Crew of Light express obliquely an excursive libidinal energy, an energy much like the Count's, *Dracula* again employs an apparently rigorous heterosexuality to represent anxious desire for a less conventional communion. The parallel here to Dracula's taunt ("Your girls that you all love are mine already; and through them you . . . shall be mine") is inescapable; in each case Lucy, the woman in the middle, connects libidinous males. Here, as in the Victorian metaphor of sexual inversion, an interposed difference—an image of manipulable femininity— mediates and deflects an otherwise unacceptable appetite for sameness. Men touching women touch each other, and desire discovers itself to be more fluid than the Crew of Light would consciously allow.

Indeed, so insistent is this text to establish this pattern of heterosexual mediation that it repeats the pattern on its final page. Jonathan Harker, writing in a postscript that compensates clearly for his assumption at Castle Dracula of a "feminine" passivity, announces the text's last efficacious penetration:

> Seven years ago we all went through the flames; and the happiness of some of us since then is, we think, well worth the pain we endured. It is an added joy to Mina and to me that our boy's birthday is the same day as that on which Quincey Morris died. His mother holds, I know, the secret belief that some of our brave friend's spirit has passed into him. His bundle of names links all our little band of men together; but we call him Quincey. (449)

As offspring of Jonathan and Mina Harker, Little Quincey, whose introduction so late in the narrative insures his emblematic function, seemingly represents the restoration of "natural" order and especially the rectification of conventional gender roles. His official genesis, is obviously enough, heterosexual, but Stoker's prose quietly suggests an alternative paternity: "His bundle of names links all our little band of men together." This is the fantasy child of those sexualized transfusions, son of an illicit and nearly invisible homosexual union. This suggestion, reinforced by the preceding pun of "spirit," constitutes this text's last and subtlest articulation of its "secret belief" that "a brave man's blood" may metamorphose into "our brave friend's spirit." But the real curiosity here is the novel's last-minute displacement, its substitution of Mina, who ultimately refused sexualization by Dracula, for Lucy, who was sexualized, vigorously penetrated, and consequently destroyed. We may say that Little Quincey was luridly conceived in the veins of Lucy Westenra and then deftly relocated to the purer body of Mina Harker. Here, in the last of its many displacements, *Dracula* insists, first, that successful filiation implies the expulsion of all "monstrous" desire in women and, second, that all desire, however mobile and omnivorous it may secretly be, must subject itself to the heterosexual configuration that alone defined the Victorian sense of the normal. In this regard, Stoker's fable, however hyperbolic its anxieties, represents his age. As we have seen, even polemicists of same sex eroticism like Symonds and Ellis could not imagine such desire without repeating within their metaphor of sexual inversion the basic structure of the heterosexual paradigm. Victorian culture's anxiety about desire's potential indifference to the prescriptions of gender produces everywhere a predictable repetition and a predictable displacement; the heterosexual norm repeats itself in a mediating image of femininity—the Count's vampiric daughters, Ulrichs's and Symonds's *anima muliebris*, Lucy Westenra's penetrable body—that displaces a more direct communion among males. Desire, despite its propensity to wander, stays home and retains an essentially heterosexual and familial definition. The result in *Dracula* is a child whose conception is curiously immaculate, yet disturbingly lurid: child of his father's violations. Little Quincey, fulfilling Van Helsing's prophecy of "the children that are to be," may be the text's emblem of a restored natural order, but his paternity has its unofficial aspect too. He is the unacknowledged son of the Crew of Light's displaced homoerotic union, and his name, linking the "little band of men together," quietly remembers that secret genesis.

Notes

1. Joseph Sheridan Le Fanu, *Carmilla*, in *The Best Ghost Stories of J. S. Le Fanu* (New York, 1964), p. 337; this novella of lesbian vampirism, which appeared first in Le Fanu's *In A Glass Darkly* (1872), predates *Dracula* by twenty-five years.

2. Franco Moretti, *Signs Taken for Wonders* (Thetford, 1983), p. 100.

3. Bram Stoker, *Dracula* (New York, 1979), p. 51. All further references to *Dracula* appear within the essay in parentheses.

4. The paradigmatic instance of this triple rhythm is Mary Shelley's *Frankenstein*, a text that creates—bit by bit, and stitch by stitch—its resident demon, then equips that demon with a powerful Miltonic voice with which to petition both its creator and the novel's readers, and finally drives its monster to polar isolation and suicide. Stevenson's *Dr. Jekyll and Mr. Hyde* repeats the pattern: Henry Jekyll's chemical invitation to Hyde corresponds to the gesture of admission; the serial alternation of contrary personalities constitutes the ambivalent play of the prolonged middle; and Jekyll's suicide, which expels both the monster and himself, corresponds to the gesture of expulsion.

5. Readers of Tzvetan Todorov's *The Fantastic* (Ithaca, 1975) will recognize that my argument about the gothic text's extended middle derives in part from his idea that the essential condition of fantastic fiction is a duration characterized by readerly suspension of certainty.

6. John Ruskin, *Sesame and Lilies* (New York, 1974), pp. 59–60.

7. This group of crusaders includes Van Helsing himself, Dr. John Seward, Arthur Holmwood, Quincey Morris, and later Jonathan Harker; the title Crew of Light is mine, but I have taken my cue from Stoker: Lucy, *lux*, light.

8. Renfield, whose "zoophagy" precedes Dracula's arrival in England and who is never vamped by Dracula, is no exception to this rule.

9. The complication of gender roles in *Dracula* has of course been recognized in the criticism. See, for instance, Stephanie Demetrakopoulos, "Feminism, Sex Role Exchanges, and Other Subliminal Fantasies in Bram Stoker's *Dracula*," *Frontiers*, 2 (1977), pp. 104–13. Demetrakopoulos writes: "These two figures I have traced so far—the male as passive rape victim and also as violator-brutalizer—reflect the polarized sex roles and the excessive needs this polarizing engendered in Victorian culture. Goldfarb recounts the brothels that catered to masochists, sadists, and homosexuals. The latter aspect of sexuality obviously did not interest Stoker. . . . " I agree with the first sentence here and, as this essay should make clear, emphatically disagree with the last.

10. John Addington Symonds, *A Problem in Modern Ethics* (London, 1906), p. 74.

11. The semantic imprecision of the word "sodomy" is best explained by John Boswell, *Christianity, Social Tolerance, and Homosexuality* (Chicago, 1980), pp. 91–116. "Sodomy," notes Boswell, "has connoted in various times and various places everything from ordinary heterosexual intercourse in an atypical position to oral sexual contact with animals" (93).

12. This is the traditional Christian circumlocution by which sodomy was both named and unnamed, both specified in speech and specified as unspeakable. It is the phrase, according to Jeffrey Weeks, "with which Sir Robert Peel forbore to mention sodomy in Parliament," quoted in Weeks, *Coming Out* (London, 1977), p. 14.

13. Michel Foucault, *The History of Sexuality* (New York, 1980). My argument agrees with Foucault's assertion that "the techniques of power exercised over sex have not obeyed a principle of rigorous selection, but rather one of dissemination and implantation of polymorphous sexualities" (12). Presumably members of the same gender have been copulating together for uncounted centuries, but the invert and homosexual were not invented until the nineteenth century.

14. I cite this phrase, spoken by Mr. Justice Wills to Oscar Wilde immediately after the latter's conviction under the Labouchère Amendment to the Criminal Law Amendment Act of 1885, as an oblique reference to the orifice that so threatened the homophobic Victorian imagination; that Wilde was never accused of anal intercourse (only oral copulation and mutual masturbation were charged against him) seems to me to confirm, rather than to undermine this interpretation of the phrase. Wills's entire sentence reads: "And that you, Wilde, have been the centre of a circle of extensive corruption of the most hideous kind among young men, it is equally impossible to doubt"; quoted in H. Montgomery Hyde, *The Trials of Oscar Wilde* (New York, 1962), p. 272. The Labouchère Amendment, sometimes called the blackmailer's charter, punished "any act of gross indecency" between males, whether in public or private, with two years imprisonment and hard labor. Symonds, Ellis, and Carpenter argued strenuously for the repeal of this law.

15. Symonds, *A Problem in Modern Ethics*, p. 3.

16. Ibid., p. 84. To my knowledge, the earliest English instance of "inversion" in this specific sense is the phrase "Inverted Sexual Proclivity" from *The Journal of Mental Science* (October, 1871), where it is used anonymously to translate Carl Westphal's neologism *die conträre Sexualempfindung*, the term that would dominate German discourse on same gender eroticism. I have not yet been able to date precisely Symonds's first use of "inversion."

17. Havelock Ellis, *Sexual Inversion*, volume 2 of *Studies in the Psychology of Sex* (Philadelphia, 1906), p. 1.

18. This and the two subsequent quotations are from Symonds's *Modern Ethics,* pp. 86, 90, and 85 respectively.

19. Symonds's letter to Carpenter, December 29, 1893, in *The Letters of John Addington Symonds,* volume 3, eds. H. M. Shueller and R. L. Peters (Detroit, 1969), p. 799; also quoted in Weeks, p. 54.

20. Ellis, *Sexual Inversion,* p. 182.

21. Symonds in *Letters,* volume 2, p. 169.

22. Ellis, quoted in Weeks, p. 92.

23. George Chauncey, Jr., "From Sexual Inversion to Homosexuality: Medicine and the Changing Conceptualization of Female Deviance," *Salamagundi,* 58–59 (1982), pp. 114–46.

24. This bifurcation of women is one of the text's most evident features, as critics of *Dracula* have been quick to notice. See Phyllis Roth, "Suddenly Sexual Women in Bram Stoker's *Dracula,*" *Literature and Psychology,* 27 (1977), p. 117, and her full-length study *Bram Stoker* (Boston, 1982). Roth, in an argument that emphasizes the pre-Oedipal element in *Dracula,* makes a similar point: " . . . one recognizes that Lucy and Mina are essentially the same figure: the Mother. Dracula is, in fact, the same story told twice with different outcomes." Perhaps the most extensive thematic analysis of this split in Stoker's representation of women is Carol A. Senf's *"Dracula:* Stoker's Response to the New Woman," *Victorian Studies,* 26 (1982), pp. 33–39, which sees this split as Stoker's "ambivalent reaction to a topical phenomenon—the New Woman."

25. Maurice Richardson, "The Psychoanalysis of Ghost Stories," *The Twentieth Century,* 166 (1959), p. 427–28.

26. On this point see Demetrakopoulos, p. 104.

27. In this instance at least Van Helsing has an excuse for his ungrammatical usage; in Dutch, Van Helsing's native tongue, the noun *bijbel* (Bible) is masculine.

28. John Stuart Mill, *The Subjection of Women* in *Essays on Sex Equality,* ed. Alice Rossi (Chicago, 1970), p. 148.

29. Ibid., p. 187.

30. Susan Hardy Aiken, "Scripture and Poetic Discourse in *The Subjection of Women,*" *PMLA,* 98 (1983), p. 354.

31. Nina Auerbach, *Woman and the Demon* (Cambridge, 1982), p. 11.

32. Roth, "Suddenly Sexual Women," p. 116.

33. An adequate analysis of the ideological and political implications of the terminological shift from "inversion" to "homosexuality" is simply beyond the scope of this essay, and the problem is further complicated by a certain imprecision or fluidity in the employment by these writers of an already unstable terminology. Ellis used the word "homosexuality" under protest and Carpenter, citing the evident bastardy of any term compounded of one Greek and one Latin root, preferred the word "homogenic." However, a provisional if oversimplified discrimination between "inversion" and "homosexuality" may be useful: "true" sexual inversion, Ellis argued, consists in "sexual instinct turned by *inborn constitutional abnormality* toward persons of the same sex" (*Sexual Inversion,* p. 1; italics added), whereas homosexuality may refer to same sex eroticism generated by spurious, circumstantial (*faute de mieux*), or intentionally perverse cau-

sality. The pivotal issue here is will or choice: the "true" invert, whose "abnormality" is biologically determined and therefore "natural," does not choose his/her desire but is instead chosen by it; the latent or spurious homosexual, on the other hand, does indeed choose a sexual object of the same gender. Such a taxonomic distinction (or, perhaps better, confusion) represents a polemical and political compromise that allows, potentially at least, for the medicalization of congenital inversion and the criminalization of willful homosexuality. I repeat the caution that my description here entails a necessary oversimplification of a terminological muddle. For a more complete and particular analysis see Chauncey, pp. 114–46; for the applicability of such a taxonomy to lesbian relationships see Ellis, *Sexual Inversion*, pp. 131–41.

34. Chauncey, p. 132.

35. The symbolic interchangeability of blood and semen in vampirism was identified as early as 1931 by Ernest Jones in *On The Nightmare* (London, 1931), p. 119: "in the unconscious mind blood is commonly an equivalent for semen. . . . "

36. Auerbach, p. 22.

37. Havelock Ellis, *Erotic Symbolism*, volume 5 of *Studies in the Psychology of Sex* (Philadelphia, 1906), p. 142.

38. Ibid., 140.

39. Roth correctly reads Lucy's countenance at this moment as "a thank you note" for the corrective penetration: "Suddenly Sexual Women," p. 116.

40. C. F. Bentley, "The Monster in the Bedroom: Sexual Symbolism in Bram Stoker's *Dracula*," *Literature and Psychology*, 22 (1972), p. 30.

41. Stoker's configuration of hypnotism and anaesthesia is not idiosyncratic. Ellis, for instance, writing at exactly this time, conjoins hypnosis and anaesthesia as almost identical phenomena and subsumes them under a single taxonomic category: "We may use the term 'hypnotic phenomena' as a convenient expression to include not merely the condition of artificially-produced sleep, or hypnotism in the narrow sense of the term, but all those groups of psychic phenomena which are characterized by a decreased control of the higher nervous centres, and increased activity of the lower centres." The quality that determines membership in this "convenient" taxonomy is, to put matters baldly, a pelvis pumped up by the "increased activity of the lower centres." Ellis, in an earlier footnote, explains the antithetical relationship between the "higher" and "lower" centres: "The persons best adapted to propagate the race are those with the large pelves, and as the pelvis is the seat of the great centres of sexual emotion the development of the pelvis and its nervous and vascular supply involves the greater heightening of the sexual emotions. At the same time the greater activity of the cerebral centres enables them to subordinate and utilise to their own ends the increasingly active sexual emotions, so that reproduction is checked and the balance to some extent restored." The pelvic superiority of women, necessitated by an evolutionary imperative (better babies with bigger heads require broader pelves), implies a corresponding danger—an engorged and hypersensitive sexuality that must be actively "checked" by the "activity of the cerebral centres" so that "balance" may be "to some extent restored." Hypnotism and anaesthesia threaten exactly this delicate balance, and especially so in women because "the lower centres in women are more rebellious to control than those of men, and more readily brought into action." Anesthesiology, it would seem, is not without its attendant dangers: "Thus chloroform, ether, nitrous oxide, cocaine, and possibly other anaesthetics, possess the property of exciting the sexual emotions. Women are especially liable to these erotic hallucinations during anaesthesia, and it has sometimes been almost impossible to convince them that their subjective sensations have had no objective cause. Those who have to

administer anaesthetics are well aware of the risks they may thus incur." Ellis's besieged physician, like Stoker's master monster, and his monster master, stands here as a male whose empowerment anxiously reflects a prior endangerment. What if this woman's lower centers should take the opportunity—to use another of Ellis's phrases—"of indulging in an orgy"? Dracula's kiss, Van Helsing's needle and stake, and Ellis's "higher centres" all seek to modify, constrain, and control the articulation of feminine desire. (But, it might be counter-argued, Dracula comes precisely to excite such an orgy, not to constrain one. Yes, but with an important qualification: Dracula's kiss, because it authorizes only repetitions of itself, clearly articulates the destiny of feminine desire; Lucy will only do what Dracula has done before.) Havelock Ellis, *Man and Woman* (New York, 1904), pp. 299, 73, 316, and 313 respectively. I have used the fourth edition; the first edition appeared in England in 1895.

42. Sigmund Freud, *The Ego and the Id* (New York, 1960), pp. 44–45.

43. Leo Bersani, *Baudelaire and Freud* (Berkeley, 1977), p. 92.

18

The Narrative Method of *Dracula*

David Seed

When Bram Stoker's *Dracula* first appeared in 1897, it was greeted with a chorus of acclaim for its power from the reviewers. One dissenting voice was that of the *Athenaeum*, which charged the novel with structural weakness:

> *Dracula* is highly sensational, but it is wanting in the constructive art as well as in the higher literary sense. It reads at times like a mere series of grotesquely incredible events; but there are better moments that show more power.[1]

This aloof dismissal seems to have established a consensus attitude toward the novel that has met with an almost complete critical silence. Only of recent years have critics begun to examine its methods, and even now all too little attention is paid to its formal complexities.

The main emphasis in *Dracula* criticism has been on its sexual themes. Stephanie Demetrakopoulos declares confidently: "It is obvious that the very attraction of the novel was that all this sexuality was masked and symbolic; it can be enjoyed surreptitiously and hence denied even to oneself."[2] And C. F. Bentley has given a thorough, Freudian account of this area of the novel, proposing incest, rape (the "killing" of Lucy), and repulsion at menstruation (Mina's stained nightgown) as subjects that receive this oblique treatment.[3] His argument demonstrates conclusively that the novel introduces issues that the English characters treat as taboo and that can be understood only by probing beneath the text's surface. Thus when a wolf leaps at Lucy's bedroom window and literally frightens her mother to death, it can be interpreted as an emblematic representation of the incursion of the animal and the death of the maternal in Lucy. Hence her haunting of Hampstead Heath inverts motherhood into callousness when she

Copyright 1985 by the Regents of The University of California. Reprinted with permission from *Nineteenth-Century Fiction* 40 (1985), No. 1.

seizes children for prey.[4] Or again, Dracula's assault on Mina is presented as a literal defilement of the marriage bed. Her husband (Jonathan Harker) lies in a drugged stupor as Dracula forces Mina to drink his blood. This quasi-sexual tableau is followed by some heavily underlined symbolism. The blood from her mouth stains her husband's white nightrobe and a piece of the host brands her forehead with a mark of Cain, which can only be purged by Dracula's death.

An alternative tack is taken by Franco Moretti and Burton Hatlen. In the course of Marxist readings of the novel, Moretti sees Dracula as a personification of capital, while Hatlen takes him to represent "the threat of a revolutionary assault by the dark, foul-smelling, lustful lower classes upon the citadels of privilege."[5] The one argument depends on crude transposition, the other on an astonishing distortion of Dracula's true nature. He represents a reversion to a feudal aristocracy that imperiously claims allegiance independently of legal checks and balances. As David Punter rightly notes, "the vampire in English culture, in Polidori, in Bram Stoker and elsewhere, is a fundamentally anti-bourgeois figure. He is elegant, well dressed, a master of seduction, a cynic, a person exempt from prevailing socio-moral codes."[6] In short, he is a combination of Gothic villain, Regency rake, and monster.

While both if these approaches shed useful light on certain areas of the novel—particularly its repeated mating of sexuality with death and defilement, and its terminology of battle—neither pays adequate attention to the rigorous narrative method that Stoker uses. Unlike *The Lady of the Shroud* (1909) in which vampirism turns too easily into romance, Stoker followed out the logic of this chosen method in *Dracula* quite consistently.[7] The recent discovery of Stoker's notes for the novel in the Rosenbach Foundation library of Philadelphia has now made it possible to see how he planned the structure of the novel. It was to consist of four books, each containing seven chapters, and to be entitled "To London," "Tragedy," "Discovery," and "Punishment," respectively.[8] Book One was to start with the letters between Dracula and lawyer Hawkins of Exeter, whereas the final novel actually begins during these negotiations. A surviving fragment from the original draft of the novel, which Stoker's widow published under the title "Dracula's Guest," and his notes indicate that he had originally intended to set the novel in Styria as a tribute to J. Sheridan Le Fanu's "Carmilla."[9] Eventually this plan was dropped.

While Book One corresponds more or less to the opening section of the novel (chapters 1–5), Book Two received considerable changes. The Whitby sections were contracted from three to two chapters, and the rest of the section was enlarged as Stoker developed Lucy's role. Chapters 6–16 of the novel describe Lucy's "illness," the fight for her life, her death, and the subsequent opening of her tomb. The ceremonial vow to pursue Dracula to the end is retained as a conclusion to that section. Stoker originally planned to have Quincey Morris go to Transylvania in the middle of Book Three; this would have awkwardly complicated the novel's use of setting and perhaps for that reason was dropped. Book Three corresponds to chapters 17–21, and Book Four to chapters 22–27 of the novel. Stoker seems to have seen his four books as representing a narrative preamble, the working out of Dracula's intentions, their discovery, and the final pursuit. Although he altered the relative lengths of the sections, he retained these broad distinctions.

The first section of the novel dramatizes the gradual breakdown of rational explanation before mystery. Jonathan Harker, though a "business-like" lawyer, is denied the privileged prominence of Wilkie Collins's first narrator in *The Woman in White*, Walter Hartright. Rather, the fact of his professional status makes his subsequent breakdown all the more ominous. Harker constantly tries to normalize the strange into the discourse of the nineteenth-century travelogue. As a defensive reaction to his voyaging into an unmapped area beyond the reach of train timetables, he first tries to rationalize his experiences in terms of local color, and then, failing that, through muffled unease. When a peasant woman begs him on her knees not to go to Castle Dracula, he comments: "It was all very ridiculous, but I did not feel comfortable."[10] In practice this ostensible rejection of the strange becomes more and more difficult to maintain. Harker's entry into the East, which he notes starts at Budapest, is signaled by the narrating pronoun shifting from "we" to "I" and is further confirmed by Harker's total loss of direction in his journey to the castle.

The four chapters of Harker's journal all end on a point of crisis: the attack by the wolves, his realization that he is a prisoner, his near seduction, and his vision of Dracula in his box. The progression of events is remorselessly toward confronting Dracula's own vampirism, confronting the very thing that Harker's rationalism is unwilling to accept. There is therefore a constant backwards pull in Harker's journal, an attempt to retard or even suspend the flow of events so that he can organize them into some kind of explanation. Thus on the morning after his encounter with the "young women," he notes: "If it be that I had not dreamt, the Count must have carried me here. I tried to satisfy myself on the subject, but could not arrive at any unquestionable result" (p. 40). The language of proof and evidence breaks down before the gaps and ambiguities in Harker's experiences. Franco Moretti has rightly pointed out that the first-person narratives in this novel represent characters' efforts to preserve their individual identities against the threat posed by Dracula, but without indicating how precarious they are.[11] In common with Seward and Mina, Harker decides to record events in as much detail as possible in the anxious hope the circumstantiality can counter strangeness. Keeping his journal thus becomes a therapeutic act of self-preservation, apparently all the more secure from Dracula's scrutiny because it is written in shorthand. In spite of this defense, Harker's journal breaks off at the point where he has resigned himself to meeting death at Dracula's hands, and we subsequently learn that Harker has gone through a complete mental and physical collapse.

His journal gives the reader a "memory," a store of images that enables him to interpret the fragmentary signs that fill characters' later accounts. Their very incapacity to analyze their accounts—in this respect as in others, Harker sets the pattern—compels them to be as accurate as they can. One of the crucial events in the novel's opening sections is Harker's vision of Dracula shortly after one of his feasts. He is described thus:

> There lay the Count, but looking as if his youth had been half-renewed, for the white hair and moustache were changed to dark iron-grey; the cheeks were fuller, and the white skin seemed ruby-red underneath; the mouth was redder than ever, for on the lips were gouts of fresh blood, which trickled from the corners of the mouth and ran over the chin and neck. Even the deep, burning eyes seemed set amongst swollen flesh, for the lids and pouches underneath were bloated. It seemed as if the whole awful creature were simply gorged with blood. (p. 51)

An exclusively sexual interpretation of this passage would not do justice to its multiple suggestiveness. Blood here brings rejuvenation as well as repletion from sex and from the consumption of food. Blood is extended metaphorically in the novel to include feeling (Arthur Godalming's heart as well as body bleeds for Lucy), sexuality, and the vital principle itself. The lunatic Renfield's repetition of the biblical phrase "the blood is the life!" (p. 141) draws explicit attention to this line of symbolism, which is introduced by Dracula's view of his blood as inheritance.[12] His assaults are thus dictated as much by ancestral pride as by magical necessity. The redness of his eyes visually extends the blood-symbolism to the color of the setting sun, which brings the vampires to life. Similarly Stoker plays on the double meaning of "sanguine," which defines Renfield's temperament and hints at his susceptibility to Dracula. The main point, however, about the description is that, whatever meaning it may carry, visually it is completely unambiguous. Considering the treatment of the supernatural in nineteenth-century literature, Andrew Lang suggests that the writer is caught between the Scylla of vagueness and the Charybdis of being absurdly explicit: "If you paint your ghost with too heavy a hand, you raise laughter, not fear. If you touch him too lightly, you raise unsatisfied curiosity, not fear."[13] Stoker contains these rather stagy revelations within a journal that tries to avoid recognizing their disturbing implications. Nevertheless, Harker's journal conveys the overwhelming physical force of Dracula, on which later chapters can capitalize, and sensitizes the reader to the significance of dogs or wolves, bats, the sunset (which characters naively insist on treating as merely "beautiful"), and other details. The reader is thus invited to make a series of recognitions, to spot resemblances between later events and those in the opening four chapters.

The excursion to Whitby, for example, repeats Harker's travelogue; Mina thinks she sees Dracula's eyes glowing in the night but dismisses it as an optical illusion, exactly the kind of rationalizing reflex that Harker makes; and Dr. Seward thinks, again like Harker, that he is going mad. In all these cases a principle of delay is involved. Until the third section of the novel, only the reader has access to all the journals and letters, and he is therefore in a position more favorable to making these recognitions.

A rhetoric of resemblances is implied at many points in the novel, in chapter 5, for instance. There is no greater jolt in *Dracula* than this abrupt transition from horror to domestic happiness in Lucy's letters from Mina. It is as if the novel has changed mode without sacrificing immediacy. Richardson, after all, insisted that *Clarissa* would contain "*instantaneous* Descriptions and Reflections."[14] In his discussion of the epistolary novel, Ian Watt has stressed its historical connections both with suburban privacy and with revealing the individual self,[15] but Stoker's use of the letter form stresses its *social* significance as an act of communication from sender to recipient. Harker can only rhetorically address his journal to Mina in its closing lines because he has no confidence that anyone else will see it, whereas in chapter 5 we suddenly find ourselves within a set of social relationships. It is only here that the characters who will be Dracula's opponents begin to define themselves. The stylistic gap between these letters and Harker's journal implies a moral gap between two worlds that cannot have contact, and yet details like the Bradshaw in Dracula's library have already indicated that the remote and exotic can join, albeit grotesquely, with the facts of contemporary life. Lucy's triple proposals parallel in inverted and sexually reversed form Harker's near seduction by the female vampires. This rhetorical parallelism looks forward to further similarities (between Lucy and Renfield particularly), defines Lucy's role as prize, and forces together two spheres that the characters' culture and very assumptions about reality lead them to keep separate. Such a parallel thus forms a rhetorical anticipation of the sequence of events that begin with Dracula's arrival in England. The second phase of the novel is introduced appropriately by a guidebook description of Whitby that repeats the rhetorical pattern of Harker's journal. In both cases local lore and jargon of the picturesque give way to sublime terminology and the reluctant admission of mystery.

At this point we need to recognize a crucial difference between the respective structures of *The Woman in White* and *Dracula*. Walter M. Kendrick has argued convincingly that "the reader of a sensation novel engages in the discovery of an artificial pattern, and the enterprise need not teach him anything."[16] In spite of Hartright's editorial role as an arranger of texts, Kendrick shows that the promised continuity emerges only at the very end of the novel. This is not the case with *Dracula*. In spite of the complexity of its second section, Stoker never uses so peripheral narrators as does Collins, and he allows the pattern of events to emerge well before the end of the novel. We shall see in a moment how this process takes place, but it is also important to note that in the second section Stoker presents two sequences of action (that of Dracula and that of his opponents), one explicit and one implicit. His principle of narration is that only Dracula's opponents are granted narrative voices and they can only record what in each case they have plausibly experienced.[17] One of Wilkie Collins's characters obligingly summarizes his author's principles in this way:

> The plan he has adopted for presenting the story to others, in the most truthful and most vivid manner, requires that it should be told, at each successive stage in the march of events, by the persons who were directly concerned in those events at the time of their occurrence.[18]

No such summary could be provided in *Dracula* because the narrative means varies according to the four stages of the novel.

Vincent Gilmore's explanation only approximately fits the practice of Section Two, the section in which Dracula reaches England and corrupts Lucy. The proliferation of letters, journals, telegrams, and newspaper articles fragments this section far more than any other. Stoker is here creating a narrative in which the gaps between the narrating documents become as important as the sections of narrative proper. Pierre Macherey has drawn attention to the silence out of which a book grows, "a matter which it endows with form, a ground on which it traces a figure."[19] Stoker's novel increasingly exploits its own silences in such a way that Dracula himself in Section Two becomes paradoxically a personification of absence. Since his actions now take place "offstage," we only apprehend them through tantalizing glimpses or through the parallel pathologies of Lucy and Renfield. Stoker simultaneously emphasizes the modern means of recording and transmitting information (telegram, portable typewriter, phonograph, etc.) and their inadequacy to cope with Dracula's protean threat. Dracula's opponents are drawn together by misfortune and also by the socially cohesive means that they use to communicate with each other. This is why the letters take on importance as summons or requests for help and why they repeatedly give way to the urgency of telegrams. The transmission of these letters not only reassures the correspondents as to their mutual dependability but also agonizingly reminds them of how much may be taking place in the gaps between those letters.

This textual complexity in the second section must surely be related to Stoker's treatment of the Gothic mode. The first four chapters seem to present a miniature pastiche-Gothic novel. In place of the Apennines, as in Ann Radcliffe's *The Mysteries of Udolpho*, we now have the mountains of Transylvania. Although Dracula claims that his descendants stretch back to Attila the Hun, his literary pedigree is rather more obvious. Like Montoni and Heathcliff, he is defined by his strength, pride, and recurring association with darkness. Transylvania clearly supplied Stoker with a revamped Gothic setting, which he then filled out by drawing on contemporary anthropological accounts.[20] After chapter 4, however, he had the problem of introducing fantastic and feudal materials into a familiar contemporary country. Here again we should turn to Wilkie Collins. Reviewing M. E. Braddon's *Aurora Floyd* in 1865, Henry James praised Collins for introducing "the mysteries which are at our own doors" into fiction and for getting rid of hackneyed Gothic props. He continues: "Instead of the terrors of 'Udolpho,' we were treated to the terrors of the cheerful countryhouse and the busy London lodgings. And there is no doubt that these were infinitely the more terrible."[21] The historical shift that James sees taking place in fiction of mystery happens within *Dracula*. Stoker exploits the reader's memory of Section One, an intensely literary memory, by keeping Dracula well below the surface of the text once the novel has shifted the setting to England. By so doing he avoids a head-on collision between modern and ancient materials.

Literary allusion performs a very specific function in nineteenth-century accounts of mysteries or the supernatural. A dismissive reference to earlier Gothic fiction usually increases the authenticity of the narrative and paves the way for a fresh evocation of the mysterious. Thus the narrator of Le Fanu's *Uncle Silas* rejects Ann Radcliffe's laborious descriptions, or the governess in *The Turn of the Screw* denies that her house was a Udolpho or that it possessed a confined lunatic. The one allusion precedes a violent murder, the other notoriously ambiguous apparitions. In the same way, Stoker introduces references to the fantastic in order to challenge the reader's secure distinction between literature and reality. A fellow passenger of Harker's quotes Gottfried Bürger's "Lenore" when Dracula's coachman arrives, as if to confirm that the dead can walk. As his skepticism decreases Harker himself compares his journal to the *Arabian Nights*. Even more important for complicating the relation of fantastic texts to reality are the allusions to "The Ancient Mariner" in the Whitby chapters. Mina's own mariner, Mr. Swales, actually reverses Coleridge's character in arguing against the lies and exaggerated claims inscribed on the tombstones of dead sailors in Whitby graveyard. But then a newspaper account of the arrival of Dracula's ship quotes Coleridge's poem to better convey the mystery of the event. This transposition of one kind of text to another reflects what is happening at this point in the novel. As if to put the minimum strain on the reader's credulity, Stoker presents Dracula's voyage to England through a medium at several removes from direct narrative. The ship's log is translated by the Russian consul, transcribed by a local journalist, and finally pasted by Mina into her journal.

Section Two then begins with a proliferation of narrative details that cannot immediately be understood. Stoker's exploitation of literary allusion and the journal form both increases the reader's uncertainty and fragments the narrative. It is true, initially at least, that the journals' style reflect character, Harker's being rather ceremonious, Lucy's more girlish and verbose, Seward's business-like, and so on. But the characters of all the protagonists except Mina are superficial and easy to grasp. When Lucy states, "I must imitate Mina, and keep writing things down" (p. 108), she is echoing the compulsion felt by the main journal writers to record experience in as much detail as possible. Each partial and individual account is based on the general principle that the recorder's capacity to analyze lags well behind the circumstantial detail recorded. And this is where Van Helsing comes in.

Abraham Van Helsing combines the roles of detective, psychic investigator, philosopher, and scientist. He seems to have been based partly on Max Müller (a friend of Stoker's) and partly on Le Fanu's Dr. Hesselius.[22] Whatever his origins, his narrative role is clear. He is called into the novel to cure Lucy, who becomes the rallying point for Dracula's opponents. It is Van Helsing who counteracts the fragmenting effects of the narrative documents in Section Two. His injunction at the end of chapter 12 ("wait and see") is as much a comment to the reader as to Dr. Seward, since Van Helsing is gradually leading characters and reader alike out of their bewilderment. He articulates the confidence that an explanation exists for the partial and diverse phenomena that fill the narrative and accelerates the process of coming together that takes place in the second half of Section Two. That section's concluding chapter (16) is startlingly homogeneous after the interruptions of letters, telegrams, and newspaper articles. It consists not only of one single journal entry but of a group action (the second killing of Lucy), whose solidarity is confirmed by the final vow of resolution.

Van Helsing not only confronts the irrational but explains it. At two key points in the novel (in chapters 14 and 24) he expounds vampire lore to his skeptical companions by locating vampirism within a broad context of Nature's mysteries. Even the caves inhabited by Dracula are "full of strangeness of the geologic and chemical world." The caves become a Shelleyan metaphor of man's ignorance: "There are deep caverns and fissures that reach none know whither" (p. 319). In the article quoted earlier Andrew Lang expresses astonishment at the survival of the supernatural in an era of scientific progress: "Why, as science becomes more cocksure, have men and women become more and more fond of old follies, and more pleased with the stirring of ancient dread within their veins?"[23] Lang finds a partial answer in evident dissatisfaction with positivism, and Van Helsing similarly criticizes Seward for being too literal-minded. The former then embodies an authoritative intellectual evolutionism that acknowledges the persistence of the primitive and that leads toward a Manichaean account of the clash between good and evil. Van Helsing's standpoint in this respect anticipates Stoker's own in a 1908 article entitled "The Censorship of Fiction." Here, as in *Dracula,* Stoker suggests a battle that is both internal as well as external:

The force of evil, anti-ethical evil, is the more dangerous as it is a natural force. It is as natural for man to sin as to live and to take a part in the necessary strife of living. But if progress be a good and is to be aimed at in the organization of national forces, the powers of evil, natural as well as arbitrary, must be combated all along the line. it is not sufficient to make a stand, however great, here and there; the whole frontier must be protected.[24]

Dracula comes from a frontier area and in a sense emerges from the mysteries of nature herself. Van Helsing's rallying of the troops parallels the masculine rhetoric of steeling one's self to duty.[25] The possibility of demonic depths to the self must be suppressed so that Dracula can be disposed of through external action.

Both Van Helsing and Stoker in his article insist that opposition to evil must be a collaborative, even national, enterprise; and Hatlen has rightly pointed out that Dracula's opponents represent key areas of the Victorian establishment: Seward and Harker are members of the medical and legal professions; Lord Arthur Godalming is the liberal aristocrat; Quincey Morris (in effect a courtesy Englishman) is a man of action and a protector of frontiers.[26] Their collective action thus represents society, even civilization itself, turning to the defensive, and the first signs of this process are textual. When Lucy dies, Van Helsing seizes the opportunity to read her diary and correspondence. This is the first in a series of instances in which characters read each other's records. This act of information gathering fills Section Three of the novel, although it begins earlier in chapter 14, for instance, where Mina reads her husband's journal. We are given no description of their wedding ceremony, but a ritual transmission of texts takes place. Mina wraps Harker's journal in white paper and seals it as "an outward and visible sign for us all our lives that we trusted each other" (p. 105). Mina does not act on this textual sacrament until sixty pages later when she reads it, transcribes it, and then calls on Van Helsing to validate it. This he does and thereby releases Harker from his agonizing uncertainty about the truth of his record. In chapter 17 Mina strikes a bargain with Seward, exchanging Harker's journal with the doctor's phonograph cylinders, partly so that they can get to know each other better.

This collaboration makes explicit the social dimension to recording characters' experiences. Stoker's surprisingly modern emphasis on the means and transmission of information brings society's self-defense into the very narrative process of the novel. Since understanding Dracula is a necessary precondition to defeating him, the exchange and accumulation of information literally is resistance to him. Characters become proportionately less vulnerable the more they act together, and the more they act together the more conscious they become of recording. Mina, for instance, recognizes the crucial role Harker's journal had to play in predisposing her to accept Lucy's fate ("If I had not read Jonathan's journal first, I should never have accepted even a possibility"; p.

181). And Van Helsing urges Seward, as he gives him Lucy's diary, "Read all, I pray you, with the open mind" (p. 219). At this stage the novel draws repeated attention to its own processes. Thus on 30 September Seward notes: "Harker has gone back, and is again collating his material. He says that by dinner-time they will be able to show a whole connected narrative" (p. 225). Whereas *The Woman in White* moves toward an end point where all the pieces will fall into place, *Dracula* narrates its own textual assembly. The reader participates in this formation of continuity. He becomes a reader among other readers.

As this collaboration takes place the surface of the text changes radically. In chapter 17, the first of Section Three, Seward's diary breaks off at the point where Mina is entering his study. Her journal takes over immediately from that point. There is, in other words, no gap between their accounts, only a shift in perspective. This is crucial. As the gaps between individual accounts close, so Dracula becomes better known, better defined, and therefore the easier to resist. This explains why Dracula simultaneously assaults Mina and tries to destroy the journals (luckily, there is another copy). Their very existence poses a threat to him and enables the initiative to action to swing round to Van Helsing. The less Dracula is formulated, the more of a threat he represents. Once the different accounts have been put together, Dracula begins to diminish in stature. He turns out to be subject to Nature's laws (though only some of them) and to be a disappointingly conventional embodiment of Nordau's and Lombroso's criminal type. In spite of the rather whipped-up excitement of the chase back to Transylvania, Dracula's actual death comes as rather an anticlimax, partly because he has been progressively scaled down in the preceding chapters.

The concluding section of the novel (chapters 22–27) revolves around the formulation of a plan of pursuit and the pursuit itself. It contains the resolving action that the assembling of information facilitates, and, as Moretti has pointed out, is narrated collectively.[27] It is no longer relevant for Stoker to maintain stylistic idiosyncrasies, so these attenuate themselves more or less out of existence. Although the narrative is still refracted through three journals (those of Harker, Seward, and Mina), nothing stands in the way of the narrative's linear impetus. On the contrary, Stoker exploits the brevity of entries in chapter 26 to accelerate the flow of events toward their predictable conclusion.

The note that precedes the text of *Dracula* makes it clear that Stoker was anticipating skeptical resistance to his subject from the reader. He therefore builds the skepticism into his characters and into the very organization of the narrative. The two central sections fragment and distance the true nature of events and then lead the reader toward acceptance through an arduous process of comparison and assembly. The existence and nature of Dracula is confirmed by the plausibility of the text, by our predisposition toward evidence, proof, and verification. All the non-Transylvanian characters keep records (even Renfield has a notebook to tot up his finds) or contribute to the record; the porters, sailors, and lawyers on the periphery of the action primarily serve to supply information. And Mina even goes to the lengths of converting herself into a text to be studied when she examines the transcript of her hypnotic trances. It is the authenticity of this assembled text that Stoker tries to shake in his post-script to the novel, as if to demand through Van Helsing an act of faith in the reading. In fact, *Dracula* demands no such leap and demonstrates a considerable agility in manipulating the reader's imagination.

Notes

1. Review of *Dracula*, in *Athenaeum*, 26 June 1897, p. 835; also quoted by Harry Ludlam, *A Biography of Dracula: The Life Story of Bram Stoker* (London: W. Foulsham, 1962), p. 108.

2. "Feminism, Sex Role Exchanges, and Other Subliminal Fantasies in Bram Stoker's *Dracula*," *Frontiers*, 2, No. 3 (1977), 105–6.

3. "The Monster in the Bedroom: Sexual Symbolism in Bram Stoker's *Dracula*," *Literature and Psychology*, 22 (1972), 27–34.

4. Demetrakopoulos, "Feminism, Sex Role Exchanges, and Other Subliminal Fantasies," p.107.

5. Moretti, "The Dialectic of Fear," *New Left Review*, No. 136 (1982), p. 73; Hatlen, "The Return of the Repressed/Oppressed in Bram Stoker's *Dracula*," *Minnesota Review*, N.S., No. 15 (1980), p. 92.

6. *The Literature of Terror: A History of Gothic Fictions from 1765 to the Present Day* (London: Longman, 1980), p. 119.

7. In *The Lady of the Shroud* the protagonist Rupert St. Leger inherits a castle in the Balkans, where he is visited at night by a woman dressed in grave-cloths. The hints that she is a vampire evaporate when it is revealed that she is actually a princess hiding from the Turks. The two marry and live happily ever after.

8. Raymond McNally and Radu Florescu print these chapter headings in *The Essential Dracula* (New York: Mayflower Books, 1979), p. 27.

9. McNally and Florescu, *The Essential Dracula*, p. 40; Bram Stoker, *Dracula's Guest and Other Weird Stories* (London: G. Routledge, 1914), p. 9.

10. *Dracula*, ed. A. N. Wilson, World's Classics (Oxford: Oxford Univ. Press, 1983), p. 5. Subsequent page references are incorporated into the text.

11. "The Dialectic of Fear," p. 77.

12. Punter discusses some aspects of the novel's blood symbolism in *The Literature of Terror*, pp. 256–58.

13. "The Supernatural in Fiction," in his *Adventures Among Books* (London: Longmans, Green, 1905), p. 277.

14. Samuel Richardson, *Clarissa*, abridged and ed. George Sherburn (Boston: Houghton Mifflin, 1962), p. xx.

15. *The Rise of the Novel* (London: Chatto and Windus, 1957), ch. 6.

16. "The Sensationalism of *The Woman in White*," *Nineteenth-Century Fiction*, 32 (1977), 21.

17. The one apparent exception to this plan is the lawyer's letters relating to the transportation of Dracula's boxes from Whitby to London. Harker reads them approximately a hundred pages after they appear in the text. This probably reflects a concession to narrative clarity on Stoker's part.

18. William Wilkie Collins, *The Woman in White*, ed. Harvey Peter Sucksmith, Oxford English Novels (London: Oxford Univ. Press, 1975), p. 112.

19. *A Theory of Literary Production*, trans. Geoffrey Wall (London: Routledge and Kegan Paul, 1978), p. 85.

20. For these sources, see McNally and Florescu, *The Essential Dracula*, p. 23.

21. *Notes and Reviews*, ed. Pierre de Chaignon la Rose (1921; rpt. Freeport, N.Y.: Books for Libraries Press, 1968), p. 110.

22. See McNally and Florescu, *The Essential Dracula*, pp. 26, 117.

23. "The Supernatural in Fiction," p. 279.

24. "The Censorship of Fiction," *The Nineteenth Century and After*, 64 (1908), 481–82.

25. The various connections between narration and gender have been admirably explored by Geoffrey Wall in his "'Different from Writing': *Dracula* in 1897," *Literature and History*, 10 (1984), 15–23.

26. "The Return of the Repressed/Oppressed in Bram Stoker's *Dracula*," pp.82–83.

27. "The Dialectic of Fear," pp. 77–78.

19

Dracula's Voyage: From Pontus to Hellespontus

Devendra P. Varma

> Like to the Pontic Sea,
> Whose icy current and compulsive course
> Nev'r keeps returning ebb, but keeps due on
> To the Propontic and the Hellespont,
> Even so my bloody thoughts, with violent pace,
> Shall nev'r look back, nev'r ebb to humble love,
> Till that a capable and wide revenge
> Swallow them up.
>
> *(Othello, III. iii. 450–57)*

> And now there came both mist and snow
> And it grew wonderous cold
>
> God save thee, ancient Mariner!
> From the Fiends, that plague thee thus!—
>
> With throats unslaked, with black lips baked . . .
> I bit my arm, I sucked the blood,
> And cried, A sail! a sail!
>
> *(Rime of the Ancient Mariner)*

The environs of the Black Sea, since legendary times, have been famed for their rare verdant plants, wildest flora, strange blossoms and herbal vegetation. The magical properties of its herbs like the wolf-bane, ash-wood, rose-bush and garlic have been hinted at by Shakespeare. It was on the shores of the Black Sea, where under the moon's eclipse:

This article was given as an address to the Eighteenth Annual Convention, American Association of Slavic Studies, 1986.

Medea gather'd the enchanted herbs
That did renew old Aeson.

(*Merchant of Venice*, V. i. 12–14)

These strange flora of swampy dandelions, blue phacelia, in the stream washes, seeps and springs present a full kaleidoscope of flowering plants. The solitude, beauty and serenity of its hidden trails evoke the ghosts of an earlier era, in the crisp Slavic moonshine enriched by the dramas of nature in such a mystic terrain.

The geography of Greek mythology centres both in Thessaly and about the Black Sea. Dracula's boat begins its voyage upon the same waters and retraces the same route ventured by Jason and the Argonauts in search of the Golden Fleece. Only the direction is reversed. In Greek mythology, the Argonauts who sailed in the ship *Argo* with Jason departed from Iolcos and headed for Colchis on the Black Sea via Hellespont, Dardanelles, Bosphorus, Propontis and the Black Sea.

Aeêtés, King of Colchis, consented to surrender the fleece, which possessed valuable magical properties, if Jason could sow a dragon's teeth from which armed men would arise. With the help of the magic arts of Medea, the King's daughter who had fallen in love with Jason, the task was successfully accomplished, and Jason and Medea and the other Argonauts returned to Iolcos with the Golden Fleece.

In their flight from Colchis, Medea murdered and cut in pieces her younger brother Absyrtus and scattered the fragments on sea waves, so that the father seeking them would be delayed in his chase. And at Iolcos, Medea restored Aeson, Jason's father, to youth by boiling him in a cauldron with magic herbs.

Demeter was the mother of Persephone who was ravished from the face of the earth by Hades, the ruler of the underworld. Persephone was permitted to return to her mother one third of each year when the earth bloomed with fragrant flowers of spring. Demeter also represents the Goddess of Fertility in classical mythology, the Mother-earth figure, who controls the progress of crops and fertility of women. In *Dracula, Demeter* is a coherent choice for the name of the schooner that brings the vampire count from the Black Sea to the shores of England because of the goddess Demeter's connection, by her daughter's marriage, with the King of the Underworld.

A ship named *Demetra* had sailed out of the Norwegian port of Christiania throughout the 1890s. Her skipper in 1896 and 1897 was E. Jorgensen. Although Leonard Wolf[1] has asserted that there is no record of any sailing ship named *Demeter* ever registered with Lloyd's, Professors McNally and Florescu's[2] researches of Stoker's notes reveal the truth of a Russian schooner named *Demeter* carrying sand from the Danube delta, which wrecked near Whitby.

Stoker had carefully studied the coastguard records and scribbled copious notes about this wreck.

The log of *Demeter* records the strange happenings during the various stages of the voyage. It set sail on July 6 from Varna on the Black Sea with crew, five hands, two mates and the Captain. It carried silver sand, a small amount of cargo, and a number of large wooden crates. In one of the fifty boxes in the hold invoiced as "clay" rested the body of Dracula, in whose veins flowed the blood of ferocious and lion-hearted races, who had inherited the fighting spirit of the Ugric tribes and of Thor and Wodin, the blood of Attila and the warlike fury of Huns who swept the earth like a living flame; in whose veins ran the blood of ancient witches expelled from Scythia who had mated with desert devils; one of the conquering race, who drove back the Magyar, the Lombard, the Bulgar and the Turk from his frontiers; the Voivode who crossed the Danube and had beaten the Turk on his own ground!

What a scene it must have been in Varna! It recalls *The Ancient Mariner:*

> The ship was cheered, the harbour cleared,
> Merrily did we drop
> Below the kirk, below the hill,
> Below the lighthouse top.

The Pontic Sea or Black Sea, famous for its strong and constant current, flows through Bosphorus into the Mediterranean, where the water level is lower. Bosphorus is an 18-mile long strait between the Black Sea and the Sea of Marmara, famed in Turkish history as the spot where the Turkish emperors disposed of their garroted wives, lovers, or political adversaries. The swollen current and impetuous course of the Pontic Sea (Black Sea) merges in the Propontic or Sea of Marmara and Hellespont or the Dardanelles, a 40-mile strait connecting the Sea of Marmara with the Aegean Sea.

> The ship drove fast, loud roard the blast
> And southward aye we fled.

The ship passed into Archipelago at dusk on July 12,

> Now, by yond marble heaven . . .
> Witness you ever-burning lights above,
> You elements that clip us round about.

And on the 13th of July the boat veered round Cape Matapan, the most southerly point of Morea Peninsula in Greece,

> While all the night, through fog-smoke white
> Glimmered the white moon-shine.

Exactly after one week of the voyage, it is at this point, on July 13, that we sense the first *uneasiness* amongst the crew. They *seem scared,* but they *say nothing.*

> And every tongue . . .
> Was withered at the root
> We would not speak, no more than if
> We had been choked with soot.

On the 16th of July one of the crew, Petrofsky, disappears. This causes the remaining crew to say *something* was aboard; *now they begin to speak.* It is the realisation of the immediate presence of the UNKNOWN. The first mate denies any possibility of there being any *unknown,* and dismisses the idea of search (July 17).

The ship passes Gibraltar on the 24th of July and enters the Bay of Biscay. Another man disappears. They face terrific seas and winds:

> And now the Storm-blast came and he
> Was tyrannous and strong.

On July 30, both the man of watch and steersman are missing; only the Captain, the mate and two hands are left to man the ship. They are nearing England. On August 1 a thick fog descends upon the English Channel, and *the schooner now begins to take life of its own.* The four who survive are becoming robots, automatons, becoming less than human, stolid. By now the *Visible Nature turns Human,* and the Human becomes *Visible Nature.*

August 2 is disturbed by a midnight scream and a rush on the deck. There is one more gone. In the dense fog, perhaps the boat has passed the Straits of Dover and is heading off in the North Sea. On the 3rd of August the helmsman is gone, and only the Captain and the first mate are remainders of the "ghastly crew." Rushing up the deck, wild-eyed and haggard, he whispers to the Captain: "*It* is here. I know it, now. . . . Last night I saw *It,* like a man tall and thin, and ghastly pale. . . . *I gave it my knife;* but the knife went through *It,* empty as the air." The mate had tried to stab the figure. One who refuted earlier, now realizes the *Reality* of the *Unknown:* "It is here; I know it, now." By bequeathing his knife, he has given life to Dracula; he cannot kill Dracula. It is "Life-in-Death" of Coleridge. It is Hamlet, it is Macbeth in this dramatic scene!

Now he goes into the hold with his tool chest and a lantern to unscrew and examine the boxes invoiced as "clay." He returns up the hatchway with a sudden, startled scream: "Save me! Save me!" peering through a blanket of fog.

> We listened and looked sideways up!
> Fear at my heart, as at a cup
> My life-blood seemed to sip!
> The stars were dim, and thick the night,
> The steerman's face by his lamp gleamed white;
> From the sails the dew did drip—

"He is there. I know the secret now. the sea will save me from him," and he springs from the bulwark and jumps into the turbulent waves. "Save me!" Surely, the only way to salvation is death; otherwise he would have turned into a vampire! And in this state of mind, Life and Death have been reversed.

On August 4, the Captain is now alone:

> Alone, alone, all all alone
> Alone on a wide, wide sea
> And never a saint took pity on
> My soul in agony.

He says: "I shall baffle this *fiend* or *monster*." The Captain ties his hands to the wheel, and then becomes a part of the ship. And what a picture! The ship being steered into the port by a dead man, tied to the wheel with a crucifix and beads!

> The loud wind never reached the ship,
> Yet now the ship moved on!

On basis of the log of *Demeter* we find that it turned from a *fully manned* ship into a *fully un-manned* ship; from full crew to no crew; from Dracula being *Unknown*, to Dracula *Known* without any crew. This is a reversal.

In its voyage from Varna to Whitby, the *Material Ship* turns into a *Phantom Ship*. During its course through Propontic and the Hellespont, she is controlled by a full crew, and also aboard is Dracula the "Unknown and *Unrecognized*." By the time it touches Whitby, there is no crew, the ship is apparently uncontrolled, Dracula is still unknown but *recognized*. It has become a phantom ship.

Stoker is playing with the "unknown"; this "unknown" is transformed into "Reality." Fantasy and psychic dread shape into corporeal flesh and blood.

The stormy evening of August in Whitby is the preparation for what is going to happen. Nature becomes convulsed. "Visible Nature" is being seen as "human." Stoker's figures of speech are carefully designed. The images are most significant: nature is *convulsed;* waves rise in growing fury, each overlapping its *fellow;* the glassy sea is like a roaring and devouring *monster;* peals of thunder reverberate in the sky overhead trembling under the shock of the *footsteps* of the storm. The fog drifting inland, wet clouds sweeping in ghostly fashion, so dank and cold, are like spirits of those lost at sea, touching their living brethren with *clammy hands of death*. This manifestation of visible nature is human; it is the human configuration in nature.

Thus the Storm becomes a *living thing*, a human being. The strange schooner has a life of its own. The crew have disappeared; they are non-existent. Only a corpse is on the helm. It is sailing on its own. The *Ship* is moving the *Man*.

The searchlight had discovered some distance away a schooner with all sails set, *apparently* the same vessel which had been noticed earlier in the evening. "*Apparently* the same schooner." Is it? It is ambiguous. Or is it a phantom ship? What were the contents of the boxes? All invoiced as "clay." We are all clay!

If it is a phantom ship, "apparently" then it is identical with the phantom ship of *Rime of the Ancient Mariner*. The terms in which either phantom ship is preceived are identical. The states of mind depicted in these two works are the same.

In the *Ancient Mariner* the crew and ship become static, unmoving. Two things are noticeable: they are apparently "static," and apparently "dead." It is a highly ambiguous situation, with elements of both "living" and "dead," that gives rise to the spectre-ship, which embodies death in motion, carrying on board the figures of Death and Life-in-Death, who are gambling for the Mariner's existence.

> Her lips were red, her looks were free,
> Her locks were yellow as gold:
> Her skin was as white as leprosy
> The Nightmare Life-in-Death was she,
> Who thicks man's blood with cold.

The sighting of the foreign schooner is in a direct quotation from Coleridge:

> As idle as a painted ship
> Upon a painted ocean.

The coastguard with his spy-glass spots "a strange ship," a foreign schooner with all sails set. "I can't make her out," he says, "she's a Russian, by the look of her. . . . Knocking about in the queerest way, steering strangely." When signalled to reduce sail in face of her danger, she is seen with sails idly flapping.

Stoker creates an effective atmosphere by subtle details: the oppressive air, distant bark of a dog, a strange sound from over the sea, a faint hollow booming; another rush of sea-fog, mass of white foam, dank mist, roar of tempest, crash of thunder. We are reminded of Coleridge:

At first it seemed a little speck,
And then it seemed a mist
It moved and moved, and took at last
A certain shape, I wist.

A speck, a mist, a shape, I wist!
And still it neared and neared:
As if it dodged a water-sprite,
It plunged and tacked and veered.

And leaping from wave to wave the strange schooner rushed at headlong speed to gain the safety of the harbour:

With far-head whisper, o'er the sea,
Off shot the spectre bark.

The searchlight followed her, and a shudder ran through all who saw her, for lashed to the helm was a corpse, with drooping head, which swung to and fro at each motion of the ship. No other form could be seen on deck at all. A great awe came on all as they realized that the ship, as if by a miracle, had found the harbour, unsteered save by the hand of a dead man!

His hands were tied one over the other to a spoke of the wheel. Between the inner hand and the wood was a crucifix, the set of beads on which it was fastened being around both wrists and wheel, all kept fast by the binding cords. The man had been dead for quite two days. In his pocket was a bottle, carefully corked, empty save for a little roll of paper, the addendum to the log.

And an immense dog with savage eyes and bristling hairs sprang up on deck, jumped from the bow onto the sand, and disappeared into the darkness.

The stage had ever fascinated Bram Stoker's mind. He had a strong feeling for drama and dramatic situations. And there is such poetic vision in the force of his creation Count Dracula, that each successive generation of readers senses in him a living presence. Where is he buried, in what unhallowed ground lies the dead Count of the un-dead? The answer is in the reader's own imagination. For just as Stoker embroidered on the myth, so his readers perpetuate it and make for themselves a grave or a tomb of their own imaginings.

And this is what all art is about. The log-book of *Demeter*, contained in the seventh chapter of the novel, recalls the powerful imagination of a Coleridge, and touches the sublime heights of situations and scenes in Shakespeare.

Notes

1. Wolf, Leonard, ed. *The Annotated Dracula*. New York: Clarkson N. Potter, 1975.

2. McNally, Raymond T., and Radu Florescu. *Dracula: A Biography of Vlad the Impaler*. New York: Hawthorn Books, 1973.

20

Sauron and Dracula

Gwenyth Hood

Superficial similarities between the Sauron of Tolkien's *The Lord of the Rings* and the Dracula of Bram Stoker's *Dracula* will strike anyone who reads both works. But the relationship between the two chief antagonists goes far beyond the superficial. Sauron and Dracula are tyrant-monsters of similar motives and powers. Both are counter-creators of a mode of existence associated with the powers of darkness which is parasitical on the natural life of creation and at active war with it, called not "living" but "Un-Dead" (spelled "undead" in Tolkien, III, 116) in both. Both seek to draw others into this "undeath" and hold them there by establishing a bond of intimate psychological domination over them. Both tyrants use hypnotic eyes in order to feed their visions into the minds of their victims, and control their actions once it is there. In both works, domination by the tyrant represents high spiritual terror because it is a kind of damnation-on-earth which cuts off its victims from the possibility of release by a natural death. Finally, both raise troubling questions about people's moral responsibility for the content of their unconscious. But intriguing as all these similarities are, the divergences in their work are still more striking, because they show a darkening in the concept of evil, and a heightened consciousness on Tolkien's part of his protagonists' struggle to maintain their own good vision of the world despite the power of the Eye of the tyrant, in whose vision hope is unreal.

Dracula

Taken by himself, Dracula is ghastly enough. A Vampire, he governs Vampire-slaves from his grave, consuming, enslaving, and ruthlessly killing men and

This article originally appeared in *Mythlore* 52 (1987).

women and children when it suits his fancy. In his desire to spread his unliving empire, he uses two tactics: enticement, in which he inflames the irrational desires of his would-be converts for those corrupt but intoxicating powers and pleasures to which he has access; and terrorization, by which he batters and torments his victims' minds and emotions, trying to break their grip on their own visions so that they will be unable to perceive anything better than his. For of course the lure of a corrupt vision is much more powerful to one who does not have true vision.

Dracula and his followers still possess much of the allure which attaches to all vivid human personalities. Dracula himself is a tall, powerful and striking person (though not conventionally handsome); and also witty, energetic and passionate. As for his followers, all the Vampire ladies in his service are beautiful. The bond between Dracula and his followers comprises both love and hate and is apparently held in permanent tension by a sexual ecstasy which Stoker repeatedly suggests without explaining outright.

All these qualities might lure self-centered, unreflecting sensualists into the Vampire existence, but Stoker's main characters are altruistic, self-critical and chaste. For them the Vampires clearly possess repulsive qualities so inextricably linked with the alluring ones as to make Vampires altogether sinister. That the Vampires have bound themselves into this limited bodily existence beyond its appointed time and selfishly absorbed the life-blood of others to maintain it shows in their most prominent features and in their manner and gesture. Hence the main characters describe the Vampire allure in a way which undercuts it. Dracula is first described as having "a hard-looking mouth, with very red lips and sharp-looking teeth as white as ivory" (17). Bright red lips and ivory teeth are attractive features in most catalogues of beauty, but the former do not go well with a hard mouth and the latter do not require sharpness. Those elements suggest what is later made explicit, that the sharp teeth are used to bite the jugular vein and the lips are red from sucking blood.

That description of Dracula is relatively objective, however, as the observer, Jonathan Harker, is not subject to his sexual allure. On the other hand, Jonathan's description of the Vampire ladies, his designated tempters, is all a-tremble with a desire and fear, attraction and repulsion. He writes,

"In the moonlight opposite me were three young women, *ladies* by their dress and manner. . . . Two were dark, and had . . . great dark, *piercing eyes,* that seemed to be almost *red* when contrasted with the pale yellow moon. . . . The other was fair . . . with great wavy masses of golden hair and *eyes like pale sapphires.* . . . All three had *brilliant white teeth* that shone like pearls against the *ruby* of their *voluptuous lips.* There was something about them that made my uneasy, *some longing, and at the same time some deadly fear.* I felt in my heart a *wicked desire* that they would kess me with those *red lips.* . . . They whispered together, and then all three laughed—such a *silvery, musical laugh,* but as *hard* as though the sound never could have come through the *softness of human lips*. It was like the *intolerable, tingling sweetness* of water glasses when played on by a *cunning* hand. (47; italics mine)

Hardness and an attractiveness that is intense at the same time it is perceived to be ruthless and calculated is a characteristic of all Stoker's vampires. Yet Dracula's tyrannical domination is not all cunning. Even he is sometimes overwhelmed by passion, as appears in the passage that succeeds the one above. Just as the blonde lady is about to "kiss" Jonathan Harker, who lies half-hypnotized, in "an agony of delightful anticipation," Dracula sweeps in upon the scene. As Jonathan describes it:

> As my eyes opened involuntarily I saw his [Dracula's] strong hands grasp the slender neck of the fair woman and with giant power draw it back. . . . Never did I imagine such wrath and fury, even to [sic] the demons of the pit. His eyes were positively blazing. . . . With a fierce sweep of his arm, he hurled the woman from him. . . . In a voice which, though low . . . seemed to cut through the air . . . he said, "How dare you touch him, any of you? . . . This man belongs to me." (49)

At such terrible wrath, Dracula's slaves might well grovel and whine for mercy, but instead the blonde lady responds with a "laugh of ribald coquetry" and talks back to him. "You yourself never loved; you never love," she accuses. The other Vampire ladies punctuate her remark with "such a mirthless, hard, soulless laughter . . . ; it seemed like the pleasure of fiends" (49). But pleasure it is, and moved by this criticism, Dracula denies the charge, declaring, "Yes, I too can love; you yourselves can tell it from the past." He assures them that they may consume Jonathan after he has served his purposes. Then he permits them to take away the whimpering child he has carried into the castle in a sack. Jonathan faints (49).

Thus Dracula and his fiendish followers cannot quite do without some fossilized affection for one another. Nevertheless the residue of allure and affection which they possess would hardly, by itself, make their mode of existence appealing to most normal, healthy human beings, let alone altruistic, reflective and chaste ones. Therefore, in drawing converts, Dracula cannot rely on allure alone. He must also terrorize his victims and destroy their own visions. To a victim who sees himself teetering on the brink of annihilation, Dracula can indeed appear as a saviour in default of anything better. We see this combination of seduction and terrorization at work on many victims throughout Stoker's book.

The first individual upon whom we see Dracula work is Jonathan Harker, the young solicitor whom Count Dracula has brought from London for legal purposes. Because Jonathan first sees Dracula in his waking state, we are able to study the work of the vision upon him more clearly than with the other victims, who first meet him unconsciously in a trance-state. Sitting in the carriage with Dracula as a driver and watching his recent traveling companions ride away from them down over the hill in the public coach, Jonathan feels "a strange chill," and "a lonely feeling." Some unconscious, intuitive sense tells him that he is all alone with death. But Dracula reassures Jonathan by precise and detailed attention to his comfort, throwing a cloak across his shoulders and a rug across his knees and offering him plum brandy (17–18). Once again at the castle, on shaking hands with the Count, Jonathan feels a chill, and notes that the Count's hand is "more like the hand of a dead than a living man" (23). But provided with a fire and a good supper and the Count's fascinating company, he lets these feelings go. Allurement and terrorization have both begun already, on a subtle level. Dracula is already inducing him to suppress those intuitions which perceive the Vampire's evil. Indeed, Jonathan is already induced to discount the evidence of his senses. He explains away the supernatural things he has witnessed as nightmares brought on by his sleepy and half-hypnotized state (20).

This strategy, of inducing Jonathan to overlook his offenses by behaving charmingly to him sometimes, works well for a few days, but gradually the anomalies pile up until even the tolerant, good-natured Jonathan can no longer regard Dracula as a normal, decent person, even making allowances for foreignness and eccentricity. A turning point is the shaving incident. Dracula comes in when Jonathan is shaving and does not register in his mirror; when Jonathan notices him, he starts and cuts himself. Inflamed by the sight of blood, Dracula leaps at him, but is quelled by the sign of the crucifix. Dracula then smashes Jonathan's mirror and exits with soft-spoken but cryptic lines about how dangerous it is to cut oneself in Transylvania (34). Suspicious, Jonathan explores the castle and finds out that all the doors are locked and he is a prisoner (35). Jonathan's options are to confront the Count, or to play along with him, pretending not to have taken offense, thereby forestalling sterner measures to control him, or more clever ones to deceive him while he seeks means to escape. He chooses the latter. What he does not realize is that this is the strategy Dracula expects him to adopt, and the only one he will tolerate. He writes the following night of his attempts to draw Dracula into conversation, and reports his success in his journal:

> [Dracula] warmed up to the subject wonderfully. . . . He grew excited as he spoke, and walked about the room pulling his great white moustache and grasping anything on which he laid his hands as though he would crush it by main strength. (37)

The impression is created that Dracula genuinely enjoys this chance to discuss his country with an intelligent and admiring foreigner. But his apparent spontaneity in this scene is also an act, for he knows that Jonathan is upset about the mirror scene. By rewarding Jonathan's compliant behavior with his own "charming host" behavior, he is subtly encouraging Jonathan to continue compliance. In order to do so successfully, Jonathan must develop in his own mind an image or vision of Dracula and Dracula's world as Dracula wishes it to be seen, so that he will not inadvertently step outside it and trigger some other behavior. When more of Jonathan's energy has been channeled into inventing this Vision and making it vivid, than into resisting it and developing his own vision, Jonathan will gradually perceive Dracula's vision as more real than his own.

Jonathan never reaches this state, but Dracula does develop some power to control his actions and perceptions with his eyes. The psychological explanation may be that in the course of their interaction, Jonathan has learned to look to the Count's eyes for directions about what he may or may not do. Unconsciously he has resigned control of his moods and intentions from his own will to Dracula's, expressed in his eyes. Hence, when with great daring, Jonathan gains access to the Count's room and finds Dracula's encoffined body, a "look of hate" from the dead and unconscious eyes has the power to prevent him from searching him for keys (59). The power is not absolute, and when Jonathan returns later, more desperate, he manages to search the body, but finds no key. Then noticing that the Count is bloated with new blood (of a child Jonathan had heard whimpering in the night), he seizes a shovel with righteous anger and attempts to strike him.

> But as I did so the head turned, and the eyes fell upon me, with all their blaze of basilisk horror. The sight seemed to paralyze me, and the shovel turned in my hand and glanced from the face, merely making a deep gash above the forehead. (63)

The battle of wills between the two is thus dramatized: Jonathan can begin but not end the action forbidden by Dracula's eyes.

Jonathan in fact resists quite vigorously and intelligently but still falls below Dracula in their trials. In one crucial scene, Jonathan tests the limits to which he can exploit Dracula's public pose as courteous host. Challenging Dracula's decree that he shall leave the next day (knowing indeed that the Vampire Ladies will claim him then), Jonathan insists that he will leave that very night and walk to the Pass if the carriage is not available. He perceives in his own vision that Dracula must permit him to go or use open force to keep him, but Dracula quickly alters that perception. He outwardly consents and begins opening the doors, but simultaneously uses his mind-powers to summon wolves. As Jonathan stands watching, the wolves surge against the opening door and only Dracula's body is between him and them. Seeing that Dracula will cheerfully feed him to the wolves unless he capitulates, Jonathan delays until the last possible moment, and then cries out, "Shut the door! I shall wait until morning!" He weeps openly at his defeat. But Dracula acts the part of a saviour within his own distorted vision, and leads him courteously away, with "a red light of triumph in his eyes, and with a smile that Judas in Hell might be proud of" (61).

Jonathan's open weeping might easily be mistaken as a sign that his vision is yet independent, but in fact it demonstrates precisely the opposite—that Jonathan has temporarily fallen into Dracula's vision. He does act precisely along the lines which Dracula's Eye prescribes, and does not seem to perceive other options. Dracula wanted Jonathan to give up the idea of leaving that night, *because* he perceived that Dracula would allow the wolves to eat him, but *without admitting that he perceived it*. In other words, he wanted his victim to perceive compulsion and freedom at the same time. Since that vision is self-contradictory and destructive to the human mind, no human could accept it without pain. Hence Jonathan's tears. It could be argued that in his submission, Jonathan is reverting to rational play-acting in order to gain time. However, Jonathan does not play-act very well when he weeps. A truly rational bit of play-acting would have been to invent *some other reason* apart from the wolves, not to leave that night. Jonathan might have said, "On second thought, Count, I need my baggage after all." This would have impelled Dracula back into his courteous-host role while ironically signaling Jonathan's independence. But distracted by fear of death, Jonathan sees his options with Dracula's eyes at this moment, and weeps.

The condition does not last, however, and Jonathan risks death the next day to escape Dracula's castle. He winds up in a sanitorium in Budapest, with brain fever, utterly confused about the reality or unreality of his experience (114–15). Meanwhile, the help he gave Dracula during his compliance has made it easier for Dracula to reach England and ensnare other victims.

These victims, both female, are approached first in trance states, so we cannot trace the beginnings of the Vampire influence on them. We can, however, assume that the influence he exercises over them is like his influence over Jonathan, except for being stronger, since for the women the Vampire temptations of terror and sexual allure are concentrated into the figure of Dracula, while for Jonathan they were distributed among Dracula and his Ladies. Like Jonathan, both women respond to Dracula's red eyes as if they compelled obedience. The stealthy origin of the bond makes it possible to hide Dracula's unconscious control of his victims much more completely. Gentle Lucy Westenra, whom her friend Mina fears "is of too super-sensitive a nature to get through the world without trouble" (101–2), goes down without even knowing what hit her. Dracula gets her under his hypnotic control during a sleeping-walking episode, and soon she is suffering from a mysterious illness. She makes no connection between it and her first encounter with Dracula, which she does not recognize the approach of a tyrant anyway. All she can tell Mina about it is:

I had a vague memory of something long and dark with *red eyes . . . and something very sweet and very bitter around me all at once; then I seemed to be sinking into deep green water . . . my soul seemed to go out of my body and float in the air.* (112; italics mine)

Some part of her, however, does remember meeting a man, and this causes her to say, in a disjointed way "*his* red eyes" (109) at sunset one day.

But though Lucy's concerned fiancé finally brings in Dr. Abraham Van Helsing with his knowledge of Vampires, the measures they take to save her fall short of Dracula's to subdue her. The turning point in her decline, annulling all their efforts, is an episode not of allure but of terrorization. Dracula uses his mind-powers to drive a wolf to break the garlic-protected window which Van Helsing has placed there to keep him out (162). Lucy is in bed with her ailing mother; the sight of the wolf gives the latter a heart attack, and she dies. Lucy calls out for Dr. Seward, whom she expects to be in the next room, but he is not. Terror-stricken, "alone with the dead" (162) as she puts it, Lucy faces Dracula's attack once more. The inexorable return of the tyrant into a scene from which everything good is departed, finally breaks her will and destroys her resistance to the vampire vision. The next day she does not rally at Van Helsing's ministrations as she had before. She dies shortly, and while doing so, she fluctuates between a Vampire-consciousness and an ordinary Lucy-conscious-ness. Waking, she clutches to her throat the garlic flowers which repel Vam-pires; sleeping, she thrusts them away. Waking, she composes a detailed letter explaining everything she can remember about her illness, in order to exonerate her friends of any blame in her death; sleeping, she tries to tear it up. Waking, she thanks Van Helsing for protecting her fiancé Arthur (181) from the "volup-tuous" Vampire kiss she offers him in her trance state, a kiss that would have drawn him after her into Vampirization (181, 239). Dead, she becomes one of Dracula's Vampire-slaves, and her fiancé must, at Van Helsing's directions, ritually mutilate her body to set her free.

The victim in whose mind the battle is most thoroughly fought and won is Wilhelmina or Mina Harker, now Jonathan's wife. She combines Lucy's sweet-ness with Jonathan's resilience. She is quite self-aware, an inveterate journal-writer (124–25). Due to these analytical tendencies, she has less trouble than Lucy in recapturing the dream-state in waking life. Though like Lucy, Mina is first approached in her sleep, and she does not at first recognize the encounters for what they are, she recalls from the first dream "a livid white face bending over me from out of the mist" (288), not just "something" as Lucy had done. When Dracula resorts to the violent Vampire baptism, in which she is forced to drink some of his blood (313), she manages to give a full account of the scene to her husband and the company, braving their periodic exclamations of revul-sion and horror. She is even able to declare that when the Count was holding her, "I did not want to hinder him. I suppose it is part of the horrible curse that

such is, when his touch is on his victim" (318). Her own admission of susceptibility to Vampire allure is a key to the success of her resistance.

Mina still is subject to Dracula's control of her trance-state, and as the story
advances, she cannot by her own will prevent her own Vampirization in small
ways. Van Helsing is the first to notice subtle changes: "Her teeth are some
sharper, and at times her eyes are more hard" (357). She sleeps more and more
during the day (371, 372, 402, 405) and stays awake at night, in imitation of
the Vampire manner (400, 402, 403). During these Vampire states, she ceases
writing in her journal (400). The consecrated host, which Van Helsing touches
to her forehead to protect her, burns her and gives her a red scar, as it would a
Vampire (329).

But Mina also takes the lead in the resistance to Dracula in his vision. She
demands that the others agree to kill her when they believe that she is irrevers-
ibly Vampirized. She requires them to read the burial service to give them
resolve and remind them that death can be friendly, not a horror as in Dracula's
eyes (367). She also instructs the company not to tell her their plans because
Dracula can get them from her by their hypnotic bond (358), and not to leave
her behind, because Dracula will find some way to use her against them (362).
This admission of her weakness prompts Van Helsing to exclaim, "Oh, but her
soul is true. It is to her an agony to tell us so much as she has done" (362).
With her help—and in knowing when they can and cannot trust her—they are
able to hunt down and destroy Dracula just a moment before he regains the
refuge of his castle. As soon as he is dead, the red scar made by the Host on
Mina's forehead completely disappears (416). She and Jonathan live happily for
at least seven years afterwards.

Thus the successful strategy against Dracula demands not only that the
characters understand and reject his perverted vision, but also that they recognize their susceptibility to it, and in effect outwit themselves in the process of
destroying it. The same is true of the conflict against evil in *The Lord of the
Rings*.

Sauron

Compared to Sauron, however, Dracula is a warm and likable character. It is
in their uses of their Eyes and Vision, in which the two of them are so similar,
that the differences between them become the most pronounced. As demonstrated above, because Dracula's use of his eyes is so important in dominating
his victims, it is his eyes they remember best, and frequently, when he materializes from the mist, his eyes appear first. Once he materializes first as a single
red eye which later separates into two eyes (288).

But Sauron appears as a single Red Eye not once but always. For him the
Eye is not merely a source of power, it is himself. All the psychic energies

which used to animate his body have gone into his Eye. Sauron is first introduced as "the eye of the dark power which rules the ring" (I, 56). The Ring, his
invention, is a conduit for the Eye's powers and is early felt by Bilbo as an eye
watching him (I, 43). Sauron's mind is revealed as an Eye in Galadriel's mirror
(I, 379), where Frodo sees it looking for him, and later on Amon Hen where it
almost finds him. The Eye is constantly alluded to throughout the trilogy as a
symbol for Sauron, accompanied by many epithets, including "Lidless Eye"
(III, 96), "Red Eye" (II, 18, 54), "Great Eye" (II, 49, 55), "Eye of Barad-dur"
(II, 194), and "Evil Eye" (III, 165). That his single abstract Eye, out of facial
context, remains consistently Sauron's chief and most characteristic signature,
reveals that his will has immolated all other physical and mental capacities for
the sake of this power of seeing into others' minds and imposing vision on them.
Unlike Dracula, he has completely lost his body "in the wreck of Numenor,"
surviving only as "a spirit of hatred borne on a dark wind" (III, 317). Unable
to take "a form that seemed fair to men" (III, 317), he can now only terrorize.
Dracula's ability to embody himself in human and animal form beyond the
appearance of his Eye correlates with his ability to use sensation and instinct to
weaken the will so that he can dominate. Sauron's bodilessness correlates with
a greatly lessened ability to seduce by instinct, and a greater need to weaken
pleasure in order to destroy the will.

Dracula was, for Van Helsing and his company, motivated by "selfishness"
(379), willing to absorb the lives of others and dominate them in order to
maintain an existence which he found pleasurable but to which he no longer had
a right. His attitude was offensive to the moral nature of man, but perfectly
compatible with the instinctual nature of animals. As Van Helsing says of
Dracula, "he is brute and more than brute" (264). Hence Dracula can use nature
on his side against Van Helsing's party. He can control "the elements: the storm,
the fog, the thunder" and also animal life: "the rat, the owl, and the bat—the
moth and the fox, and the wolf" (265).

But Sauron's evil destroys even ordinary selfishness. His Wraiths do not
cling to their physical existence through wicked pleasure, but "until every last
minute is a weariness" (I, 56). Their brand of evil is perversely self-contradict-
ing, hating what it desires and rejecting what it wants. Tolkien conveys this
vividly in a number of passages. The Nazgul's cries are "evil and lonely" (I,
100). One of their few remaining senses is the power to smell the blood within
the veins of living creatures, which they "desire" and "hate" (I, 202). The
Barrow-wight, an "evil spirit" or wraith associated with the chief Ringwraith
(III, 321), gives a cry in which "The night was railing against the morning of
which it was bereaved, and the cold was cursing the warmth for which it
hungered" (I, 151).

Being so weak in instinct, Sauron and his wraiths cannot stir up the elements or lower animals in their support merely because they are irrational. On

the contrary, it is the Elves who can stimulate and inspire nature on their side, insofar as it is still natural; Elrond causes a flood, for example. Insofar as nature is personified in the Ents, it has motives of its own and chooses to fight against Sauron's Vision (II, 64–90).

Sauron must weaken nature before it will serve him. He has no elements for allies except the ones he artificially tampers with, such as the smoggy wind which puts Minas Tirith and Mordor into darkness during the crisis of war, only to be blown aside at significant moments by the true elemental wind (III, 45, 103). He has for allies not the "meaner" animals, but only the "evil" ones, perhaps (though not clearly) those bred in his programs. Frodo says, "All other animals are terrified when [the Ringwraiths] draw near . . . . The dogs howl and the geese scream at them" (234). A good deal of nature must die in this "taming" process, even when Sauron does not destroy deliberately. Mordor is choked with what resembles industrial pollution, a "desolation . . . diseased beyond all healing" (II, 239). The parts through which the protagonists travel are so strikingly bare of life that Samwise is astonished to find even thorns growing there. "Bless me, Mr. Frodo, but I didn't know as anything grew in Mordor!" he cries (III, 194).

Having lost natural instincts, Sauron and his wraiths cannot form bonds with one another not directly related to domination and submission. Control cannot be forgotten even for an instant in animal pleasure. Thus the wraiths lack the residual affection which Dracula and his slaves have for one another. Nazgul exist only to express Sauron's "will and his malice" which is "filled with evil and horror" (III, 97), and when the Sauron is destroyed, they apparently disappear altogether with the other evil beings who "run hither and thither mindless" (III, 227).

Since he lacks ordinary selfishness, what was for Dracula at least partly a means to pleasure, has become an end in itself to Sauron. His one remaining instinct or goal is to destroy the natural, individual vision of his victims, imposing his own corrupted vision upon them and holding them, tormented, within it. It becomes a passion for him. At least once he yields to it in a manner that damages his cause, in fact destroying his only chance at a quick and easy victory. This is when Pippin steals the Palantir. Gandalf explains how narrowly the quest has been saved.

> If he had questioned you, then and there, almost certainly you would have told all that you know, to the ruin of us all. But he was too eager. He did not want information only: he wanted *you* quickly, so that he could deal with you in the Dark Tower, slowly. (II, 199)

Sauron was not always this alienated, nor was his brand of evil always this clearly perverse and self-contradictory. In fact the indication is that he was once more like Dracula. The Ring survives from the time when he had more power to allure. Without it, he cannot regain control of Middle-earth. The Ring adds a further refinement to Tolkien's treatment of evil.

The Ring, in fact, tempts to "selfishness," though not always Dracula's kind of selfishness. It does not always tempt with instinctual pleasure. It does tempt each character to use its powers of compulsion to gain whatever end is most important to that character at the moment, at the expense of everyone else's concern and right to be persuaded. Gandalf fears it will appeal to him through "pity, pity for weakness and the desire of strength to do good" (I, 71). Samwise, the gardener, is tempted at the prospect of making all Mordor into a garden (III, 177), while Gollum sees himself as a well fed petty tyrant honored by those around him: "Lord Smeagol? Gollum the Great? *The* Gollum! Eat fish every day, three times a day, fresh from the Sea" (II, 241). At the beginning, each character sees his desires as good, but in assenting to use force, he somewhat destroys his own perceptiveness and his power to recognize and honor the good done by others. The more insensitive he becomes, the more he must resort to compulsion, until like Sauron he lacks the capacity to understand anything else. We see this process of degeneration in Saruman. Talking to Gandalf, Saruman claims to have good motives, seeing the Ring as a shortcut for doing good when "the Elves and dying Numenor" cannot succeed. "We must have power, power to order all things as we will, for the good only the Wise can see" (I, 272) he says. He implies that he shares the Vision of the Wise about what is to be done, but in fact, of the five members of the Council of the Wise, Saruman has just called one "simple" (Radagast), stated there is no help in two (Elrond and Galadriel) and threatened to torture the fourth (Gandalf) if he will not immediately join his side. By wisdom, he now means his own vision. He wishes to impose it on others with the Ring. Being, like Dracula, younger in evil, Saruman has more powers of seduction than Sauron, in his case centered in his Voice. But powers of persuasion atrophy in the Vision of Domination, and Saruman's powers of Voice become weaker as the story progresses. As Gandalf points out, "He cannot be both tyrant and counselor" (II, 190). Ultimately Saruman turns the Shire into something Frodo describes as "Mordor" (III, 297), and dies while trying to use raw compulsion on the wretched Wormtongue.

The Ring, thus, does not act directly to subject its possessor to Sauron's vision. It tempts its victims, in fact, to rivalry with him. But it can be useful to him all the same. In accepting a vision involving domination, the tempted characters move themselves onto ground where Sauron is preeminent. Sauron has every skill to manipulate those visions and draw them subtly into conformity with his own, and then dominate them within it because he is strongest there. Yet a stronger and wiser character might develop a Vision of Domination yet more comprehensive than Sauron's and dominate *him* within it. Gandalf, Elrond and Galadriel suppose themselves capable of this, but fear it as much as a victory by Sauron and therefore refuse to take the Ring.

Thus the inner-struggle in the characters who resist Sauron is different from that in those who resist Dracula. The former were fighting a one-front war against Dracula's Vision, but the latter, at the same time they are fighting off Sauron's Vision, must fight to keep their own true Visions without the Ring's subtle corruption in it. It is the struggle against the personal Ring-generated vision which proves most treacherous.

Many characters are tempted by the Ring and the Eye in *The Lord of the Rings*, but Frodo's conflict is treated in the most detail. When the story begins, the Ring has already gained control of some parts of Frodo's mind. When Gandalf tells him its tremendous peril, he wishes to destroy it, but is unable even to act out the intention (I, 70). Still, in the early chapters of the trilogy the Ring's main role is to open Frodo's mind to Sauron's barren and cruel Vision, an action which is accelerated when the Ring arranges his stabbing by the Morgul blade on Weathertop (I, 208). With difficulty he resists the encroaching vision, in the which the natural world becomes "pale and empty" (I, 244) and only the threatening Ringwraiths are "dark and solid" (I, 225). Part of his resistance involves invoking beautiful names outside Sauron's Vision: Elbereth and Luthien the Fair (I, 226). Somehow this helps delay the Eye's progress long enough for Elrond's flood to rescue him.

Frodo emerges from Elrond's healing strengthened. His true insight and Vision have actually increased because of the exercise he has had in resisting evil. But at the same time conceptions planted in his mind by the Sauronic Vision assert themselves and influence his behavior. We first see this when Bilbo asks Frodo to show him the Ring again.

> Slowly [Frodo] drew [the Ring] out. . . . To his distress and amazement he found that he was no longer looking at Bilbo; a shadow seemed to have fallen between them, and through it he found himself eyeing a little wrinkled creature with a hungry face and bony groping hands. He felt a desire to strike him. (I, 244)

Images from this Sauronic Vision are difficult to root out because they are not wholly false, only distorted. Bilbo really has taken on some of Gollum's irresistible lust for the Ring, and even starts calling the Ring "my precious" (I, 42). What is temporarily blocked from Frodo's perception is Bilbo's effective resistance to the Ring.

Another element enters here. The desire to strike Bilbo is a Sauronic response, not one belonging to Frodo's usually fair and compassionate personality. It is called up by the corrupted vision, which tends to produce a set of reactions all its own, belonging to an embryonic Dark Lord personality which struggles with the personality Frodo has consciously chosen, for control of Frodo. The struggle between the Ring-generated and the "free" personality parallels the struggle in Lucy and Mina between the true personality and the

Vampire personality. In Smeagol-Gollum, the two personalities become separate enough to argue out loud with one another. In Frodo this never happens; the embryonic Dark Lord personality shares many memories, responses and affections with the "free" personality, but is always trying to corrupt them and draw them toward a Vision of Domination.

The closer they draw to Mordor, the less energy Frodo has left to develop his vision, and the more Sauron's Vision increases in his mind, thus aiding Frodo's Dark Lord personality. The development of Frodo's Dark Lord personality is also accelerated by the appearance of Gollum. Gollum could bring out the Dark Lord in almost anyone. His "free" personality is too weak to be trusted. Since he is already dominated by the Ring, using the Ring to control him is an obvious expedient, one which Smeagol himself proposes, demanding to swear his loyalty on "the Precious" (II, 225). But once Frodo undertakes to enforce this oath, he becomes a Dark Lord to Gollum, and Sam begins to perceive elements of the Dark Lord in him without quite understanding what he is seeing. In one case, he describes a scene:

> For a moment it appeared to Sam that his master had grown and Gollum had shrunk: a tall stern shadow, a mighty lord who hid his brightness in grey cloud, and at his feet a little whining dog. (II, 225)

It is in Sauron's vision, not in that of the Fellowship, that the holder of power is a great lord hiding his power, and the subject commanded is dehumanized. The aura of brightness about the scene suggests the purity which still adheres to Frodo's character even in the midst of attack, but it should be noted that all characters see their causes as pure in the early stages of temptation.

Though as they continue, Frodo treats Smeagol-Gollum with almost heroic courtesy and benevolence, he is forced to resort to the Ring twice more to control him. Once he grimly declares that he has the power to put on the Ring and command Smeagol to leap from a cliff, and he would obey because "the Precious mastered you long ago" (II, 248).

On another occasion, Frodo threatens to use the Ring to induce Gollum to choke on fishbones.

> "Smeagol!" said Frodo desperately. "Precious will be angry. I shall take Precious, and I shall say: make him swallow the bones and choke. Never taste fish again. Come, Precious is waiting." (II, 296)

At a later stage, the Dark Lord personality also infects Frodo's relationship with Sam, who is transmogrified in vision when he tries to help Frodo by offering to continue to carry the Ring for a while.

> "No, no!" cried Frodo, snatching the Ring and chain from Sam's hands. "No you won't, you thief!" He panted, staring at Sam with eyes wide with fear and enmity.

Though repentance immediately succeeds, Frodo has now, as never before, acted on a Sauronic Vision instead of merely seeing it. He further explains that the Eye has got him almost where it wants him, stripped of all his natural perceptions apart from what the Eye and Ring give him:

> No taste of food, no feel of water, no sound of wind, no memory of tree or grass or flower, no image of moon or star are left to me. I am naked in the dark, Sam, and there is no veil between me and the wheel of fire. I begin to see it even with my waking eyes, and all else fades. (III, 215)

This parallels the time when Lucy was "alone with the dead." Frodo has temporarily lost use of the creative powers of his imagination to beat off Sauron's vision. Because his own Dark Lord vision is weaker than Sauron's, yielding to it makes him more susceptible to Sauron's Eye. As a foreshadowing of his final failure on Mount Doom, Frodo even loses his ability to control the movement of his hand toward the Ring when he meets the Eye. His hand moves toward the Ring, and he cries, "Help me, Sam! Help me, Sam! Hold my hand! I can't stop it." (III, 220)

Frodo defeats Sauron finally by a means far more subtle and intricate than Mina used. As he is making the final ascent to Mount Doom, he is attacked by Gollum, and repelling him with the use of the Ring, once more stands to him as a Dark Lord. There he cries out a doom to him:

> "Down, down!" he gasped, clutching his hand to his breast, so that beneath the cover of his leather shirt he clasped the Ring. "Down, you creeping thing, and out of my path!"
>
> "Begone, and trouble me no more! If you touch me ever again, you shall be cast yourself into the Fire of Doom." (III, 221)

Here his Dark Lord *persona* is still acting with much input from the true personality. Frodo could, had he wished, have destroyed Gollum then and there, commanding him to jump off a precipice (there were plenty around), as he had previously threatened. But the compassion of the true personality restrains that tyrannical impulse and makes Gollum's death contingent on his continued evil behavior. The uneasy compromise struck between Frodo's two struggling personalities is also shown in the words with which Frodo departs on the final stretch to Mount Doom: "On Mount Doom, doom shall fall."

Though grandiose, and thus appropriate to the Dark Lord personality, these words are quite ambiguous. What doom will fall? The doom of the Ring? But as the story's opening showed, not even the true personality of Frodo can easily resolve to destroy the Ring. The doom of the quest? But his long hesitation at the Crack of Doom shows that Frodo did not go there intending to claim the Ring; in fact if he had intended to claim it earlier, he should have gone somewhere else. No, clearly there was inner struggle in Frodo up until that very moment when he announced that the Ring was his. Up until that point Frodo's "good" personality was able to keep Frodo walking toward the Crack of Doom, no matter what else he did, but at the cost of concealing from himself exactly what he was supposed to do there. He was only able to express the intention of throwing the Ring into the fire by setting it upon Gollum, in the words implied but not spoken in his doom: "You shall *yourself* [in addition to what? to the Ring of course] be cast into the Fire of Doom." So obsessed was the Dark Lord personality by its sadistic desire to impose its will upon Gollum that it did not notice these implications. At the Crack of Doom, when the decision to destroy the Ring or not can no longer be put off, the will of the good personality at last falls before the Sauronic one, but this earlier oblique stroke wins. For then Gollum and his conditional doom take over. Having seized the Ring, Gollum is "cast" into the fire by those parts of his mind which are subjected to it, much as Jonathon's hand had been turned by the parts of his mind which had put themselves at the command of Dracula's Eye. The effect may perhaps be something like post-hypnotic suggestion; Frodo's earlier threat to make Gollum choke on fishbones shows that he understood the Ring's power to cause accidents as well as compel conscious obedience. Once the Ring is destroyed, Frodo's original personality regains control.

Like Mina, he is never blamed for his partial absorption into evil, only honored for his valiant part in the quest. Unlike Mina, however, he is not completely free. He is no longer in danger from Sauron's Eye, but his Dark Lord personality remains and torments him. He is found at times mourning the loss of the Ring: "it is gone forever . . . and now all is dark and empty" (III, 304). He cries "I am wounded . . . wounded; it will never really heal" (III, 305). He must seek insight beyond Middle-earth to bring his perceptions of evil back into balance with his perceptions of good, and so he goes to the Blessed Realm for healing. Samwise, far less drawn into the evil vision than Frodo though not wholly unaffected by it, is the one who can return happily to ordinary life, his insight and gusto both increased by what he has gone through, and his happiness a foreshadowing of the hope there is for Middle-earth.

Conclusion

There is a haunting similarity between these tyrants, Sauron and Dracula, and an ominous difference. Both Sauron and Dracula present visions of Hell and a kind of damnation on earth. They put characters in danger not merely of their lives, but their souls, and no quick and easy way out of the conflict is offered. Mina thinks of suicide, but is warned that this would precipitate rather than prevent her Vampirization (323). Frodo would like to throw away the Ring, but is told that keeping it and guarding it from Sauron is a morally more responsible tactic, despite its spiritual dangers for him. Both, thus, present a vision in which the struggle for salvation is presented in earthly terms, is made emotionally significant, and in which the consequences of its failure are all but unbearable to contemplate. Also, for victory, innocence is not enough; the characters must struggle both bravely and cleverly, outwitting the evil parts of themselves and strategically exploiting not only their strengths but their weaknesses as well. So far the works are similar, and both seem to reflect increasingly sophisticated questioning of the relationship between perception and moral responsibility. But in the later work, though the power of personal resistance is emphasized more, the evil is crueler, darker, more ambitious, harder to eradicate, and not less tempting to the characters for all that. Alas, the later work seems to have more plausibility on its side; between the two books lies the dark chasm of the two world wars and the present threat of nuclear annihilation. It is amusing but also somewhat shocking to perceive that Stoker in 1897 just did not imagine that evil could be so evil, or that so many souls as Tolkien envisions could sell themselves into a state so negative and self-contradictory. Indeed, the nightmare of modern civilization has deepened.

On the brighter side, the sweet dream is sweeter, since Lorien and Valinor are more idyllic and grander than the domestic happiness achieved by Mina and Jonathan, pleasant though that was. The very desperation also adds a note of hope, since just as the acts of Frodo's true personality continued to affect the outcome of the quest even after it had capitulated to the Dark Lord personality, so could ours. Entanglement in evil does not prevent a character's good acts from intertwining with a Providential pattern to produce a good result. So, no matter how deep the nightmare gets, we all still have our motives to keep on our journey through Middle-earth, with Elbereth and Luthien the Fair firmly in mind, and a friend nearby to hold our hands when we reach convulsively for that Ring.

Bibliography

Stoker, Bram. *Dracula*. 1897; New York: Dell, 1965.
Tolkien, J. R. R. *The Lord of the Rings*. Collector's Edition. Boston: Houghton Mifflin, 1965.

21

Bent and Broken Necks:
Signs of Design in Stoker's *Dracula*

Alan Johnson

One of the striking characteristics of the considerable number of critical essays written about Bram Stoker's *Dracula* (1897) in the past thirty years is that, more often than not, they deny that Stoker really knew what he was doing as he wrote it. The book and its author certainly seem to invite such a conclusion. The novel's central figure, Dracula, has been transformed by Stoker from an incredibly cruel but historical, fifteenth-century tyrant into a fictional vampire with rich folkloric associations. Knowing readers quickly reach for their copies of Ernest Jones's *On the Nightmare* (1931), with its chapter on the psychological symbolism of vampires in dreams. The novel is framed and punctuated with episodes which glow with sexual symbolism that seems lurid even in a horror story: the temptation of the young, supine solicitor, Jonathan Harker, by female vampires at Dracula's Transylvanian castle at the beginning; the staking of Lucy Westenra, Dracula's first victim, by her fiancé Arthur Holmwood under the direction of the old wise man, Dr. Van Helsing, to release her from her vampirism; the scene in which Dracula forces his second victim, Jonathan's wife Mina, to drink from a wound Dracula has opened in his own chest; and the shearing of Dracula's throat by Jonathan in the final episode. Freudian readings are virtually irresistible, and along with them the assumption that the story comes straight from Stoker's repressed drives and fantasies.

This assumption of virtually unconscious authorship seems to be supported by the pedestrian, sometimes ludicrous quality of Stoker's other fiction and by the life of the man himself. Stoker published a number of short stories for popular consumption in periodicals such as *The Illustrated Sporting and Dra-*

This article originally appeared in *Victorian Newsletter* 72 (1987).

matic News and *Pall Mall Magazine* beginning in the 1870s, while he was a young legal clerk in Dublin, a book of fairy tales for his son in 1881, and eleven romance and adventure novels in the period 1890 to 1911, but only a few of the stories—particularly "The Squaw," which is preserved in *Dracula's Guest and Other Weird Stories* (1914)—seem to have drawn enduring critical praise, and Stoker's final novel, *The Lair of the White Worm* (1911), is frequently singled out for critical astonishment at its bizarre representation of an evil woman who is really a great white worm living in a well beneath her mansion.[1] While this fiction does not seem to elicit critical confidence in Stoker's subtlety and literary skill, his life invites the speculation that it was divided into public success and private frustration in a typically "Victorian" way. The public Stoker was the affable, capable business manager of the famous Henry Irving's Lyceum Theatre company from 1878 to its liquidation in 1903 and was married to a noted beauty who had been courted by Oscar Wilde and sketched by Burne-Jones. Privately Stoker may have both idealized and envied his "chief," Irving, and may have had a sexless marriage which led him to extra-marital sources of satisfaction. It is indisputable that his death certificate identifies the cause of his death as locomotor ataxia (syphilis) in 1912.[2]

Maurice Richardson's witty essay, "The Psychoanalysis of Ghost Stories," in 1959 established *Dracula* as an unpremeditated revelation of Stoker's psychic depths for several successive generations of critics. In a felicitous figure, Richardson begins with the premise that "some ghost stories . . . can be compared to little volcanoes that go straight down into the primitive strata of the mind. . . . The phantasy material that erupts . . . has been expressed and disguised by symbolism but . . . has not been transformed out of all recognition. . . . The author . . . is quite likely to be completely unconscious of its inner meaning" (421). To Richardson, only "from a Freudian standpoint—and from no other—does [*Dracula*] really make any sense": it is a "blatant demonstration of the Oedipal complex"(427), and Richardson "doubt[s] whether Stoker had any inkling of the erotic content of the vampire superstition" from which he drew his stand-in for the enviable but hated "father" (429).

Indeed the novel does make sense as an Oedipal contest, and successive critics have embellished Richardson's explanation and repeated his caveat about Stoker's conscious ignorance of the essence and eroticism of his novel. In 1972 C. F. Bentley, for example, acutely studied its sexual symbolism and concluded, "Nothing in Stoker's other writing or in what is known of his life suggests that he would consciously write quasipornography, and it must be assumed that he was largely unaware of the sexual content of his book" (72).

Also in 1972 Leonard Wolf, borrowing his terminology from Jung, described *Dracula* as a "visionary novel"—that is, one which presents material from "the hinterland of man's mind . . . primordial experience which surpasses man's understanding" and eludes the shaping powers of the novelist (206). In

Wolf's view Stoker was a "part-time hack" (205), and the "work that Stoker made," consciously, is an epic struggle between good and evil, personified in Van Helsing and Dracula, with a "Christian message" (180, cf. 206). This message, however, is "entangled" with implications of homosexuality among the novel's good men (210), the potential deadliness of erotic beauty such as is embodied in the Transylvanian vampire women, Lucy, and even Mina (213, 217), the sexual hunger and power discovered in and by Jonathan (211, 213–14), and the human potential for self-gratification embodied especially in Dracula (223). These implications are "probably unconscious on Stoker's part" (181), and he "evades what he guesses—while he decks it out in the safer Christian truths that he repeats" (206, cf. 222).[3]

Stoker's most knowledgeable biographer, Daniel Farson, expresses the same view although it was Farson who recently discovered and published the evidence that Stoker died of syphilis. To that evidence, Mr. Farson adds the hearsay evidence from Stoker's granddaughter that the Stoker marriage was celibate after the birth of a child in 1879, and the totally unsupported assertion that Stoker was known as a "womaniser" and probably turned to prostitutes in London or Paris.[4] Farson concludes that the sexually symbolic materials in *Dracula* are the product of Stoker's "sexual frustration" and subsequent "sense of guilt" for his alternative satisfactions (213–14, 234). Farson introduces his discussion by quoting from, and agreeing with, Richardson on the applicability of "a Freudian standpoint" to *Dracula* and on Stoker's ignorance of the novel's "erotic content." "I am sure," Farson adds, "that my great-uncle [Stoker] would have been aghast" to learn that his novel is (and here Farson returns to Richardson's words) a "sado-masochistic orgy"(211).

In the past ten years or so, feminist criticism has brought psychological analysis to bear on *Dracula* and has often reiterated the description of Stoker as an author unconscious of the essential nature of his novel. In 1977, for example, Stephanie Demetrakopoulos stated that "Stoker's conscious authorial intentions" were to demonstrate the vulnerability of the traditionally Victorian "Womanly Woman," personified in Lucy, and the strength of the more modern, rational, but nevertheless sexually temperate Mina (109), but Demetrakopoulos drew also upon Bentley's analysis of "the novel's covert treatment of perverted sexuality" (105) to argue that the male phallicism of Dracula and the vampire hunters and the aggressive sexuality of the female vampires reveal "Stoker's backlash against Victorian sexual mores," a theme that is "probably unconscious, rising out of his own dream reservoir" (109). Other feminist criticism provocatively finds beneath the novel's surface an unconscious fear, in Phyllis Roth's fine phrase, of "suddenly sexual women." She argues that "central to the structure and unconscious theme of *Dracula* is ... primarily the desire to destroy the threatening mother," the "*vagina dentata*" of folklore, personified by Lucy and Mina in their vampirism.[5] A similar analysis is offered by Judith

Weissman, who observes that "Lucy and Mina . . . say things [such as Lucy's wish to marry three men at once] which reveal—without Stoker's conscious knowledge, I am sure—his anxieties about women's sexuality" (400).[6] Thomas Byers agrees with Roth and Weissman that *Dracula* shows "covert misogyny" (in fact "covert" goes back to Bentley, p. 28), particularly the fear that men may be unable to conceal their "emotional dependence" on, and "vulnerability" to, women. The male dependence is symbolized by Dracula's need for blood. Byers argues that since the novel represents the dependence by means of a mere "myth," to be dismissed ultimately as unreal by the reader, the novel's "real (if covert) mission . . . is not to propound the existence of literal vampires, but to conceal the existence of figurative ones" (29).

Not all recent *Dracula* criticism by any means stipulates a "covert" theme or motif which rose volcanically from Stoker's psychic depths without his conscious knowledge. Particularly useful criticism has set the novel in its cultural context: Richard Wasson's examination of *Dracula's* political connotations in relation to late nineteenth-century imperialism; Mark Hennelly's interpretation of the novel as a "gnostic quest" by its young men in the context of an intellectual continuum from the "wasteland" of Victorian rationalism through turn-of-the-century vitalism (embodied in the novel by Dracula) which Hennelly associates with Henri Bergson (15) and especially with the anthropology of Frazer's *Golden Bough* and Jessie Weston's *From Ritual to Romance*; the provocative development of Leonard Wolf's characterization of the novel as a Christian epic with Dracula as a Satanic "hero of despair" by Brian Murphy, who places *Dracula* between post-Enlightenment disillusionment with the theory of the natural goodness of man and the twentieth-century religious revival typified by G. K. Chesterton, C. S. Lewis, and W. H. Auden; and Carol Senf's extension of Stephanie Demetrakopoulos's observation that the novel is a conscious response to the "New Woman" of the 1890s.[7]

None of the analyses of *Dracula* in its cultural context rests necessarily upon the assumption that its author must consciously understand or even deliberately use the cultural terms to be found in his text, and most of the culturally based analyses do not address the question of authorial intention. However, two of them comment on the denial of conscious authorial understanding to Stoker by previous, psychological analyses of the novel. Noting that Phyllis Roth describes both Lucy and Mina as predatory "mother" figures (with the implication that both are signs of Stoker's unadmitted fear of "sexual women"), Carol Senf comments, "It is just possible, however, to assume that Stoker is consciously contrasting the sexually liberated New Woman [the vampire Lucy] with the more traditional woman," Mina (46), and Senf then concludes that Stoker has formed the novel for a conscious purpose: "he tries to show that modern women can combine the best of the traditional and the new when he creates . . . Mina," with her practical intelligence and her ultimate choice of old-fashioned loyalty to civilized society over indulgence in individualistic self-gratification (49). In response to Wolf's claim that, although Stoker reveals psychic depths in *Dracula*, "he tries to avoid knowing what they mean," Brian Murphy (whose essay is written as an open letter to Stoker) virtually cries out in protest:

> What I find baffling is that anyone who has read your novel would conclude that you were unaware of the sexual implications of the story. (10)

Apparently no letters or similar documents by Stoker or persons close to him have come to light to reveal what he himself thought he was doing in the writing of his novel.[8] His notebooks for the novel survive in the Rosenbach Foundation Library but show only that he worked on it for seven years and devoted considerable study to such subjects as vampirism, Transylvania, and the Whitby area.[9] The practical question raised by recent criticism, however, is not what Stoker's conscious intentions were, or whether unconscious concerns emerge in the novel. The question of conscious or unconscious intention will probably never receive a settled answer. As Jeffrey Spear observes with regard to attempts to find links between John Ruskin's eventually unmistakable insanity and his social commentary, the attempts "reveal more about the critic and his age than about Ruskin. What seems mad to one generation of critics may be prescient to the next" (13, cf. 252n.96). Readers of *Dracula* who seek authorial intention look for design, but at present there seems to be considerable prejudice against the likelihood of finding design of a sort that supports the hypothesis of subtle, skillful authorship, together with a corresponding predisposition to find materials in the novel which are "volcanic," "visionary," and sexually "Victorian." The practical question is simply the configuration of the text. Although this design will inevitably depend somewhat on readers' presuppositions, I suggest that the language of the novel in fact has far more, and other, design than most of its recent readers' preconceptions have allowed them to see. It repays close reading, or, in the current substitute for that New Critical phrase, it provides not only the pleasures of psychoanalysis and polemical indignation but also the pleasures of a text. Its language resonates with interconnections which create and amplify a theme of desperate, post-Romantic egoism—particularly in the form of rebellious feminism—which the combined analyses by Murphy and Senf have suggested.

One source of the novel's resonance is its structure as a vehicle for psychological allegory. *Dracula* is a novel in the tradition of the novels of Dickens, Charlotte Brontë, and Hawthorne. Carl Keppler has aptly called such works "literature of the second self." Julian Moynahan has pointed out in a classic essay on *Great Expectations* that when the adolescent Pip asks for a half-holiday to pursue his dreams of upper-class love and wealth by visiting Miss Havisham, into the novel suddenly pops the Cainlike journeyman Orlick, who sulkily asks for his own half-holiday and remains in the novel to personify Pip's aggressive selfishness until Pip finally attains his moral education. Helene Moglen and others[10] have noted that when Jane Eyre is fresh from the celibate discipline of Lowood School and has just stood on the leads of Mr. Rochester's Thornfield Hall and yearned for passionate life, she hears the low laughter of the maniac in the attic, Bertha Rochester, who remains in the novel as a personification of Jane's own passionate potentiality and its dangers. Keppler usefully notes that the second-self character—the Orlick or Bertha—not only personifies some quality or motivation in the first self—the Pip or Jane—but also, and crucially, the second-self character enters the narrative at just that point when the central character is, or can be supposed to be, feeling or thinking what the second character personifies (12, 196). Readers of Dickens will recall scenes such as the lime-kiln scene near the end of *Great Expectations* or the figurative "explosion" of Uriah Heep by Traddles and Micawber in *David Copperfield,* in which the central character—Pip or David—is vacuously passive while the embattled secondary characters, who represent the separate elements of his inner, mental strife, act out that strife projectively in their own, external confrontation like characters in a medieval morality drama.

Stoker does not seem to have drawn obviously upon Dickens or Brontë but upon Wilkie Collins and Sheridan Le Fanu. Along with Collins's conception of a novel as a compendium of first-hand documents, Stoker may well have noted, in *The Woman in White,* a model for Dracula's relationship to Lucy and Mina in Count Fosco's relationship to Laura Fairlie and Marian Halcombe. Stoker's original but cancelled first chapter, which was posthumously published as "Dracula's Guest," makes it certain that he drew upon Le Fanu's Laura and the vampire Carmilla, who embodies Laura's longings in the story "Carmilla" (Ludlam 123, 128). Stoker, however, would have had no need to go to literary precedents for fictions which are based on psychological dissociation and use the method of the literary double or second-self characterization to dramatize it. As the business manager for Henry Irving's Lyceum Theatre company from 1878 to 1903, Stoker saw virtually hundreds of performances of psychological melodramas such as *The Corsican Brothers* and *The Bells* which alternated with revivals of Shakespeare and were the bread and butter of the company (Irving 532, 595).

In an essay in the book *Sexuality and Victorian Literature* (1984), edited by Don Richard Cox, I have shown that the novel *Dracula* is replete with references to the French psychologist Charcot, to dual personality, and to what the novel calls "unconscious cerebration" (*Dracula* 69, 191, 270), and I have argued that the novel's form is largely determined by its presentation of the vampire Count Dracula as a literary double for the unconscious or only partly conscious rebellious egoism experienced first by Lucy and then by Mina in reaction to the constraints and condescension which have been inflicted on them by their society, chiefly by the men around them and chiefly because the thinking of the society is dominated by anachronistic notions of social class and chivalry. Simple, conventional, upper-class Lucy is expected, especially by her class-conscious mother (95, 166), to marry the aristocratic but ineffectual Arthur Holmwood, but Lucy becomes restless and suffers attacks by Dracula. Mina is highly praised in chivalric terms by Dr. Van Helsing, her husband Jonathan, and the other men who gather around Van Helsing to pursue Dracula, but they protectively exclude her from the hunt—"a bitter pill" she reflects as they send her off to bed in Dr. Seward's asylum (242) while they go next door to raid Dracula's principal London hideaway, Carfax. Each woman develops what Van Helsing at one point calls a "dual life" (201)—a conscious, willing conformity to her society and a largely subconscious discontent. After the discontent develops to the stage of strong rebellion, Dracula appears and attacks. He is thus a symbolic double of each woman's rebellious feelings, and the literal vampirism which results from his bite represents the change in personality produced by these feelings. With reference to the women, his masculinity and aristocracy denote the kind of power they confront and want to wield.

Joined to the psychological allegory of Lucy's and Mina's rebellion is a *Bildungsroman* or education-novel structure in which the young men and their mentor, Van Helsing, learn to identify and eradicate their own masculine and aristocratic pride.[11] Dracula serves double duty as a projection of the women's rebellious egoism and of the men's oppressive egoism. As Carol Senf has said, "It is Stoker's genius that Dracula . . . means different things to different people. . . . [T]he key element . . . [is] his individualism" (47). Ultimately the link between the psychological allegory of female rebellion and the male *Bildungsroman* seems to be the mind of Mina. As soon as the men discover Dracula's attacks upon her, they readmit her to their confidence (290), but this act of respect fails to reverse her vampirism. The signs of her vampirism disappear only after the men pursue Dracula as he flees to Transylvania and slash his throat and heart with knives in the light of the setting sun. As I have argued in the "Dual Life" essay in *Sexuality and Victorian Literature* (35), the pursuit has all the earmarks of a journey by the men into their own psyches. In Geoffrey Wall's expansive phrase, "Transylvania is Europe's unconscious" (2). During the final pursuit of Dracula upriver toward his castle, Jonathan comments, "We seem to be drifting into unknown places and unknown ways; into a whole world of dark and dreadful things" (357). He and the other men can make the literal journey only by means of the information about Dracula's location which Mina provides when she uses a telepathic link Dracula has established between himself and her by forcing her to drink from the wound he opens in his own chest on one of the occasions when he attacks her in her bedroom at Seward's asylum. She discovers that the link can be used against Dracula if Van Helsing will tap her knowledge by hypnotizing her (311), and Van Helsing notes that she has won "this power to good" by her "suffering" at the hands of Dracula (343). Van

Helsing notes, too, that the usefulness of her knowledge depends partly upon his own "volition" (343)—that is, on his own willingness to use hypnosis to see into her mind and discover what she sees. The narrative suggests, then, that the men can locate and eradicate their own oppressive egoism, which has caused Mina's rebellion, only by seeing through the mind of their victim. Their reformation depends upon their volition and her knowledge of the cause of her rebellious feelings.

Now the precise act—Van Helsing calls it a "baptism of blood" (322, 343)—which establishes the telepathic link resonates with connections to earlier scenes. These all contribute to the single implication that, unlike the simple Lucy, Mina not only feels but understands her rebellion. The "baptism of blood" is described from two perspectives—first, Dr. Seward's, just after he and others learn from the injured Renfield that Dracula has entered Seward's asylum, where she is staying. Seward and his allies rush to the Harkers' bedroom and discover Mina.

> Kneeling on the near edge of the bed facing outwards. . . . By her side stood . . . the Count. . . .
> [H]is right hand gripped her by the back of the neck, forcing her face down on his bosom.
> (281–82)

Subsequently she herself explains that she had yielded willingly to Dracula's bite, but then he scratched a wound in his own bared breast and, she says, "seized my neck and pressed my mouth to the wound, so that I must either suffocate or swallow" (288). This is of course ground on which Freudian interpretation has a field day, and perhaps with perfect justification.[12] The context of the passage, however, is very important. Dracula prefaces his action with the explanation that the act is a punishment because Mina has presumed, he says, to "play your brains against mine. You would help those men to hunt me and frustrate me." The result of the act will be, he says, that "you shall come to my call. When my brain says 'Come!' to you, you shall . . . do my bidding" (287–88). Dracula aims to punish and control her mind. In forcing her to bend her head, he seems symbolically to be directing the attention of the mind it contains. By forcing her to swallow his blood, now enriched by her earlier submission to him, he forces her to "take in" and assimilate the fact of her willing submission. All of this suggests that Mina's rebellious feelings, personified in Dracula, are not merely rising to dominate her but are also gaining her intellectual recognition and understanding. Her reason does not necessarily sanction the submission but does identify the rebellious feeling and recognize that when it arises it will control her behavior.

This interpretation meshes with the sexual symbolism of nursing and of fellatio, if the latter is also implied. Dracula appears not only as the personification of Mina's rebellion but also as the force which her rebellion appropriates—

that is, the force of the men who are her oppressors. In the symbolic nursing, Dracula as the image of her rebellion teaches her to practice the men's own use of the world around them as what George Eliot in Chapter 21 of *Middlemarch* has called "an udder to feed [their] supreme selves" (156). Although the men have idolized Mina, their chivalry has denied her practical abilities and has promoted the men themselves to the superior worldly role of her protectors. Ironically, their chivalric presumption is an infantile act since it deprives Mina of her potential scope in order that they may enjoy that scope themselves, even while they expect to enjoy her gratitude, too. In the implicit allusion to fellatio, Mina's image of the oppressive men also teaches her to take life, not to give it. Her relation with the world around her will be the self-service that is symbolized by the substitution of alimentation for procreation.

The bending of Mina's neck recalls, first, Dracula's first attack on Lucy, which Mina witnessed in the Whitby parish churchyard on the evening of August 10. In this event, however, Lucy sat on a bench, "half-reclining with her head lying over the back of the seat" (90). There had been no struggle and no "baptism of blood" in addition to Dracula's bite. The implication is that Lucy was an unreflecting victim—at least at this point—as well as a willing one. However, the bending of Mina's neck also recalls Dracula's breaking of the necks of the old Whitby sailor, Mr. Swales, and of Renfield, the zoophagous patient in Seward's asylum. The attack on Swales occurs shortly after he has talked with Lucy and just prior to Dracula's first vampire attack upon her. Similarly Dracula breaks Renfield's neck after Renfield has talked with Mina and between Dracula's first vampire attack on her on September 30 and her "baptism of blood" on October 2. One may not expect complex structures of symbolic characterization in Stoker's novel, but Swales and Renfield seem clearly to function as literary doubles who represent the critical, reflective, reasoning faculty in Lucy and Mina respectively.

Swales enters the novel as a chatty old salt whom Mina and Lucy meet in their walks in the Whitby parish churchyard. Mina immediately describes him as "a very skeptical person" because he scoffs at the local legend that the ghost of a nun who was immured in the local abbey for disobedience is still to be seen there (63). Later, on August 1, Lucy meets him on a day when her nocturnal sleepwalking indicates that she is subconsciously resisting her impending marriage to Arthur and her mother's support of the marriage (64, 71–72). Lucy talks with Swales as she sits on a seat over a slab with an epitaph commemorating George Canon, who is buried underneath. To prove that epitaphs are usually untrue, Swales reveals that the monument was not "erected by a sorrowing mother to her dearly beloved son" who "died, in the hope of a glorious resurrection," as the epitaph claims. Instead, she was a "hell-cat" who insured the life of her sickly son in hopes of profiting by his early death, and he killed himself so as to prevent her from receiving an insurance payment. Lucy's response is revealing: "Why did you tell us of this? It is my favourite seat, and I cannot leave it" (66–67). Subsequently Dracula lands at Whitby, on the night of August 7, takes refuge in the grave (240), apparently becomes aware of Lucy when she uses the seat on the morning of August 10, and attacks her in it during the evening of that day. The fact that Swales is "found dead" in the seat in the early morning of the tenth indicates that he has been killed by Dracula as he made his way into, or out of, the grave. Swales's neck has been broken and his face bears "a look of fear and horror" (87). The train of events seems to symbolize an unconscious psychological process going on within Lucy. The events suggest that in her dreams she has been resisting her impending marriage, and this unconscious thought has transformed her unrest to rebellion by making her aware—albeit subconsciously—of the true relationship between herself and her mother. As the rebellion crystallized, however, her reasoning mind has resisted it and then she has been forcibly destroyed by it.

As Swales is to Lucy, so is Renfield in relation to Mina. Early in the novel Renfield appears as a patient in Seward's asylum and is characterized by "self-ishness, secrecy, and purpose"—specifically a desire for "life" which leads him to collect and eat insects and birds and makes him, in Seward's diagnosis, "an undeveloped homicidal maniac." He is also very methodical, keeping careful records of his dietary experiments (68–71). Later episodes show that he can be a keen logician and a cool debater (233, 243–47). When Dracula establishes himself at Carfax, Renfield meets and reveres him, apparently because Dracula promises greater feasts of "life" than Renfield has arranged for himself (e.g. 107). Mina meets Renfield shortly after her arrival at the asylum to aid Van Helsing and his young allies in the discovery and destruction of Dracula. Her interaction with Renfield and his behavior from the time of their first meeting on September 30, until her "baptism of blood" on October 2, strongly suggest that he represents the action of her own reason during that period.

After reading about Renfield in Seward's diary, Mina asks to see Renfield and "venture[s] . . . to lead him to his favourite topic." She has not yet been excluded from the confidence of Van Helsing and the young men, but she has experienced their courtly condescension, and apparently because of this she is interested in Renfield's odd theory of acquiring power. At this point he seems to become a symbol for her thinking about power. If so, then his immediate, direct advice, "[D]on't stay" (233), represents her own foresight—in contrast to Lucy's lack of foresight—that her thoughts may lead to uncontrollable and undesirable emotions. About three hours after this conversation, Van Helsing tells Mina that she is being excluded from the pursuit of Dracula and sends her "to bed" while the men prepare to raid Carfax (242). Although she does not complain openly, she regards the exclusion as a "bitter pill" when it is an-nounced, and she experiences Dracula's first attack upon her during the night of September 30, while the men are at Carfax. During the next day, October 1, she finds herself "crying like a silly fool" because of the exclusion and resolves to "put a bold face on"—that is, a cheerful face—for Jonathan. "I suppose," she says, "it is one of the lessons that we poor women have to learn" (257). Her discontent continues internally, however, as Jonathan observes a puckering of her forehead while she sleeps on the evening of October 2, "as though [he comments] she thinks even in her sleep" (267–68).

Mina's restless thought seems to be acted out in an expanded form by Renfield. After meeting Mina on September 30, he pleads with Seward to be sent away from the asylum. Apparently Renfield fears that Dracula will ask him for admission to the asylum and Mina. Seward's reply is a clear echo of Van Helsing's banishment of Mina to her bed while the men raid Carfax. Seward tells Renfield, "Get to your bed and try to behave more discreetly" (247). Thwarted by Seward, Renfield then gives in to Dracula's request for admission and his promise of "life" in the form of multitudes of rats, and Dracula drains Mina. On the following day, while Mina bursts into tears, Renfield is troubled by the thought that he may be destroying the souls of the creatures he eats or injuring his own soul, but he is buoyed up by the thought of his powerful "friend" Dracula (268–69). In the afternoon of October 2, Renfield asks to see Mina (259) and discovers that Dracula has "been taking the life out of her" (280). While Mina thinks in her sleep that evening (267), Renfield is resolved to resist Dracula's next entry into the asylum (280). In their confrontation, Renfield suffers what is described variously in the text as a broken back (275) and a broken neck (289), but Stoker's notes for the novel in the Rosenbach Library show that he drew upon precise professional information from his brother, Thornley, who was a prominent Dublin surgeon, for the diagnosis which is stated by Dr. Seward: "the real injury was a depressed fracture of the skull, extending right up through the motor area" (276; cf. Roth, *BS* 100) This resonates perfectly with the "baptism of blood" which Dracula inflicts on Mina for pitting her "brain" against him. That act of neck-bending gave her knowledge without power of resistance. Renfield's injury leaves him, too, with knowledge, but with no motor function. He can, however, inform Seward of Dracula's presence in the asylum, just as, in the book's final episodes, Mina's knowledge enables the men to locate and destroy Dracula despite her powerlessness to resist him herself.

The veritable harmony of bent and broken necks in the novel makes one refrain: the rebellion of the women is a reflex of the men's tyranny, and only through the mind of the intelligent, knowing rebel can the oppressors discover and eradicate their oppression. The motif of bent and broken necks also suggests that the novel's language may resonate with other, as yet unnoted, design.

If, for example, the description of the pursuit of Dracula into Transylvania suggests that "Transylvania is Europe's unconscious" and is, for the men, their own unconscious minds, then perhaps the language of the Transylvanian section at the beginning of the novel makes a similar suggestion. In fact, the opening section is replete with such suggestions. On the way to Dracula's castle, for example, Jonathan notes that he is "leaving the West and entering the East," where "every known superstition in the world is gathered into the horseshow of the Carpathians, as if it were the centre of some sort of imaginative whirlpool" (1, 2). As Christopher Craft notes (127), the fact that Jonathan sees "only myself" in his mirror at the castle although Dracula is beside him suggests that Dracula is to be understood as a double of Jonathan (25). Dracula draws upon Jonathan to perfect his command of English speech, geography, and business practices so that in London the Count will be "master . . . or at least none should be master of me" (20). Meanwhile on his vampire forays beyond the castle he wears Jonathan's clothing so that the local people will attribute the evil deeds to Jonathan (44–45). Finally, as Dracula leaves to become a resident of England, he leaves Jonathan locked in the castle to become a victim of the vampire women and thus a vampire himself. Because of this potentially double transformation, in the regal, predatory Dracula the newly qualified and newly affianced young solicitor seems to be encountering his own intimation of the role of imperious egoism he can choose to play as he begins his vocation and marriage.

A few words may suffice to suggest the unexplored range of design in *Dracula* which has apparently been neglected because of preconceptions that the novel must be "visionary," "volcanic," or sexually "Victorian." The seemingly "volcanic" quality of the novel is unmistakable in the episode of Jonathan's temptation by the vampire women in the opening section. Jonathan has been thinking of Mina as a housekeeper (1) and a stimulus to his professional ambition (15) and subsequently he thinks of her as "a woman" but in diametrical contrast to "those awful women" who seem to be "devils of the Pit" (53) as they dine on children and are "waiting to suck [his] blood" (39, 40). As every psychological interpretation points out, in the moments of temptation Jonathan is impelled by "burning desire" and repulsed by "deadly fear" (37). He has divided women into devils and angels, but his fear or virtue does not govern his behavior until the morning after the temptation. The agency which prevents the consummation of his desire is Dracula himself with his exclamation, "This man belongs to me!" just as Jonathan has slipped into a "languorous ecstasy" of anticipation (38, 39). Jonathan must not become a sensual beast until Dracula has become, as it were, Jonathan—an Englishman with all the native social abilities and business acumen. The pervasive design of the Transylvanian section with which the novel opens has been established by references to the young man at the beginning of his adult career and marriage meditating on the role he will play. Dracula's interference with the temptation suggest that the role symbolized by Dracula—that is, the sophistication of fundamental selfishness, the cultivation of hypocritical urbanity—requires a temporary restraint upon any engrossing but limited satisfaction such as lust. Later, apparently, when egoism has been thoroughly sophisticated and firmly controls the whole character, the urbane egoist will be able to manage mistresses, business, and a revered, repressed wife.

Subsequent events suggest that Jonathan does not "belong" to Dracula but vacillates uncertainly between acceptance and rejection of the total egoism he represents. Jonathan resists the vampire women and clings to his religious faith but flinches from destroying Dracula in his coffin (51–52) before the two depart for England. When Jonathan escapes to England, he suppresses his memory of the symbolic journey into his own mind, but he encounters Dracula again just after the death of Jonathan's employer and quasi-father, Mr. Hawkins, leaves Jonathan "rich, master of his business," and distraught at the responsibility thrust upon him (157, 171). It remains for Van Helsing, whose wife has very significantly gone totally mad prior to the novel's action (176), to use his own esoteric knowledge of human nature to assure Jonathan of Dracula's reality so that both men, with Mina's help, may advance to the self-knowledge of the final journey into Transylvania. In the context of his quest for sane adulthood, it is quite possible that various seemingly "volcanic" materials in the novel turn out to form a unique and unexpected design, and that Stoker turns out, apparently, to be a keenly perceptive, conscious critic of late-Victorian self-interest.

Notes

1. For bibliography see Dalby. For recent appraisals of Stoker's fiction, see Farson and Dematteis, Osborne, and Roth, *Bram Stoker*.

2. The Burne-Jones is privately owned. For other biographical details see Farson, esp. 233–35.

3. See also Bierman, "Dracula"; Craft, Leatherdale 145–75 (esp. 159, 175) MacGillivray, and Wall. Leatherdale's copious secondary bibliography is very useful; his discussion of critical approaches to *Dracula* including the psychological, refrains from evaluating the criticism or asserting a definitive interpretation of the novel.

4. Farson 212–14, 234–35. Ludlam, whose biography was written in concert with Stoker's son Noel (9), says nothing of all this; nor do Laurence Irving's biography of his father, Henry Irving, or reminiscential works by Stoker's contemporaries such as L. F. Austin (Frederic Daly), Hall Caine, and Ellen Terry. Personal inquiry leads me to conclude that Stoker's granddaughter has reversed her opinion of the marriage since the publication of Mr. Farson's book. A cartoon, "A Filial Reproof," in *Punch* 11 Sept. 1886: 126, suggests that Florence Stoker was a cool mother in public, more interested in her social presence than in her son, but not necessarily a cold wife to her solicitous husband.

5. Quoted from Roth, "Suddenly Sexual Women" 120; this essay appears substantially unchanged in Roth's *Bram Stoker* 111–23.

6. Griffin extends Weissman's view, noting that the women are provoked to sexual aggressiveness by their male admirers' "chivalric glorification of womanhood" (461), and Griffin theorizes that Stoker "subconsciously" alludes to menstrual blood (459).

7. See also Johnson for the "New Woman," and for other cultural contexts see Blinderman (Darwinism), Craft (homoeroticism), Fontana (Lombroso), and Hatlein (Marxist class structure).

8. Personal inquiry to Mr. Harry Ludlam and Stoker's lineal heirs leads me to conclude that they possess no material that is pertinent here, nor are such materials indicated in *Catalogue . . . Including the Library of the Late Bram Stoker.*

9. See Bierman, "The Genesis and Dating of *Dracula* . . . ," and Roth, *Bram Stoker* 91–102 and 145–46nl. For permission to use Stoker's ms. notes for *Dracula*, I am indebted to the Phillip H. and A. S. W. Rosenbach Foundation of Philadelphia and its assistant director, Mr. Walter C. Johnson.

10. For a recent example, see Maynard 124–26.

11. See Johnson, Byers and Hennelly, whose view is that the men learn vitality from Dracula.

12. E.G., Bentley 30: "Stoker is describing a symbolic act of fellatio." Cf. Craft 125–26, Griffin 459, and Roth (who adds male castration fear), "Suddenly Sexual Women" 119–20.

Works Cited

Bentley, C. F. "The Monster in the Bedroom: Sexual Symbolism in Bram Stoker's *Dracula*." *Literature and Psychology* 22 (1972): 27–34.

Bierman, Joseph S. "*Dracula*: Prolonged Childhood Illness, and the Oral Triad." *American Imago* 29 (1972): 186–98.

———. "The Genesis and Dating of *Dracula* from Bram Stoker's Working Notes." *Notes and Queries* 24 (1977): 39–41.

Blinderman, Charles S. "Vampurella: Darwin and Count Dracula." *Massachusetts Review* 21 (1980): 411–28.

Byers, Thomas B. "Good Men and Monsters: The Defenses of *Dracula*." *Literature and Psychology* 31 (1981): 24–31.

Caine, Hall. *My Story*. London: William Heinemann, 1908.

Catalogue of Valuable Printed Books, Autograph Letters, and Illuminated and Other Manuscripts Including the Library of the Late Bram Stoker, Esq., and Other Properties . . . Which Will Be Sold by Auction by Messrs. Sotheby, Wilkinson & Hodge. London: Dryden Press, 1913.

Craft, Christopher. "'Kiss Me With Those Red Lips': Gender and Inversion in Bram Stoker's *Dracula*." *Representations* 8 (1984): 107–33.

Dalby, Richard. *Bram Stoker: A Bibliography of First Editions.* London: Dracula Press, 1983.

Daly, Frederic [L. F. Austin]. *Henry Irving in England and America, 1883–84.* London: T. Fisher Unwin, 1884.

Demetrakopoulos, Stephanie. "Feminism, Sex Role Exchanges, and Other Subliminal Fantasies in Bram Stoker's *Dracula*." *Frontiers: Journal of Women's Studies* 2 (1977): 104–13.

Eliot, George. *Middlemarch.* Boston: Houghton Mifflin, 1956.

Farson, Daniel. *The Man Who Wrote Dracula: A Biography of Bram Stoker.* New York: St. Martins, 1976.

——— and Philip B. Dematteis. "Bram Stoker." In *British Novelists, 1890–1929: Modernists.* Dictionary of Literary Biography 36. Detroit: Gale, 1985.

"A Filial Reproof" [drawing]. *Punch or the London Charivari* 11 Sept. 1886: 126.

Fontana, Ernest. "Lombroso's Criminal Man and Stoker's Dracula." *Victorian Newsletter* No. 66 (Fall 1984): 25–27.

Griffin, Gail B. "'Your Girls That You All Love Are Mine': Dracula and the Victorian Male Sexual Imagination." *International Journal of Women's Studies* 3 (1980): 454–65.

Hatlin, Burton. "The Return of the Repressed/Oppressed in Bram Stoker's *Dracula*." *Minnesota Review* 15 (1980): 80–97.

Hennelly, Mark M., Jr. "*Dracula*: The Gnostic Quest and Victorian Wasteland." *English Literature in Transition: 1880–1920* 20 (1977): 13–26.

Irving, Laurence. *Henry Irving: The Actor and His World*. London: Faber and Faber, 1951.

Johnson, Alan P. "'Dual Life': The Status of Women in Stoker's *Dracula*." *Sexuality and Victorian Literature*. Ed. Don Richard Cox. Tennessee Studies in Literature 27. Knoxville: Univ. of Tennessee Press, 1984. 20–39.

Keppler, Carl F. *The Literature of the Second Self*. Tucson: Univ. of Arizona Press, 1972.

Leatherdale, Clive. *Dracula: The Novel and The Legend: A Study of Bram Stoker's Gothic Masterpiece*. Wellingborough, Northamptonshire: Aquarian Press, 1985.

Ludlam, Harry. *A Biography of Dracula: The Life Story of Bram Stoker*. 1962. Rpt. as *A Biography of Bram Stoker, Creator of Dracula*. London: New English Library, 1977.

MacGillivray, Royce. "*Dracula*: Bram Stoker's Spoiled Masterpiece." *Queens Quarterly* 79 (1972): 518–27.

Maynard, John. *Charlotte Brontë and Sexuality*. Cambridge: Cambridge Univ. Press, 1972.

Moglen, Helene. *Charlotte Brontë: The Self Conceived*. New York: W. W. Norton, 1976.

Moynahan, Julian. "The Hero's Guilt: The Case of *Great Expectations*." *Essays in Criticism* 10 (1960): 60–79.

Murphy, Brian. "The Nightmare of the Dark: The Gothic Legacy of Count Dracula." *Odyssey* 1 (April 1976): 9–15.

Osborne, Charles, ed. *The Bram Stoker Bedside Companion: Ten Stories by the Author of Dracula*. New York: Taplinger, 1973.

Richardson, Maurice. "The Psychoanalysis of Ghost Stories." *Twentieth Century* 166 (1959): 419–31.

Roth, Phyllis A. *Bram Stoker*. Boston: Twayne, 1982.

———. "Suddenly Sexual Women in Bram Stoker's *Dracula*." *Literature and Psychology* 27 (1977): 113–21.

Senf, Carol A. "*Dracula*: Stoker's Response to the New Woman." *Victorian Studies* 26 (1982): 33–49.

Spear, Jeffrey L. *Dreams of an English Eden: Ruskin and His Tradition in Social Criticism*. New York: Columbia Univ. Press, 1984.

Stoker, Bram. *Dracula*. World's Classics. Oxford: Oxford Univ. Press, 1983.

———. MS Notebooks for *Dracula*. Phillip H. and A. S. W. Rosenbach Foundation, Philadelphia, Pa.

Terry, Ellen. *The Story of My Life* 2nd. ed. London: Hutchinson and Co. [1910].

Wall, Geoffrey. "'Different from Writing': *Dracula* in 1897." *Literature and History* 10 (Spring 1984): 15–23.

Wasson, Richard. "The Politics of *Dracula*." *English Literature in Transition: 1880–1920* 9 (1966): 24–27.

Weissman, Judith. "Women and Vampires: *Dracula* as a Victorian Novel." *Midwest Quarterly* 18 (1977): 392–405.

Wolf, Leonard. *A Dream of Dracula: In Search of the Living Dead*. Boston: Little, Brown and Co., 1972.

Bibliography

Books

Auerbach, Nina. *Woman and the Demon: The Life of a Victorian Myth*. Cambridge: Harvard University Press, 1982.

Barclay, Glen St. John. *Anatomy of Horror: Masters of Occult Fiction*. London: Weidenfeld and Nicolson, 1978.

Boucher, Anthony. Introduction to *Dracula*. New York: George Macy, 1965.

Carter, Margaret L. *Shawdow of a Shade: A Survey of Vampirism in Literature*. New York: Gordon Press, 1975.

_____ . *Specter or Delusion? The Supernatural in Gothic Fiction*. Ann Arbor: UMI Research Press, 1987.

Dalby, Richard. *Bram Stoker: A Bibliography of First Editions*. London: Dracula Press, 1983.

_____ , ed. *Dracula's Brood*. London: Aquarian Press, 1987.

Day, William Patrick. *In the Circles of Fear and Desire: A Study of Gothic Fantasy*. Chicago: University of Chicago Press, 1985.

Farson, Daniel. *The Man Who Wrote Dracula: A Biography of Bram Stoker*. London: Michael Joseph, 1975.

Fiedler, Leslie. *Freaks: Myths and Images of the Secret Self*. New York: Simon and Schuster, 1978.

Glut, Donald F. *The Dracula Book*. New York: Scarecrow Press, 1975.

Haining, Peter. *The Dracula Centenary Book*. London: Souvenir Press, 1987.

Hurwood, Bernhardt J. *Vampires*. New York: Quick Fox, 1981.

Jackson, Rosemary. *Fantasy: The Literature of Subversion*. New York: Methuen, 1981.

Kincaid, Juliet Willman. "The Novel as Journal: A Generic Study." Dissertation. Columbus: Ohio State University, 1977.

Leatherdale, Clive. *Dracula: The Novel and the Legend*. Wellingborough, Northamptonshire: Aquarian Press, 1985.

_____ . *The Origins of Dracula*. London: William Kimber, 1987.

Lovecraft, H. P. *Supernatural Horror in Literature*. 1939; reprint, New York: Dover, 1973.

Ludlam, Harry. *A Biography of Dracula: The Life Story of Bram Stoker*. London: W. Foulsham and Co., 1962.

MacKenzie, Andrew. *Dracula Country: Travels and Folk Beliefs in Romania*. London: Arthur Barker, 1977.

McNally, Raymond T., and Radu Florescu. *Dracula: A Biography of Vlad the Impaler*. New York: Hawthorn Books, 1973.

_____ . *The Essential Dracula*. New York: Mayflower Books, 1979.

_____ . *In Search of Dracula*. Greenwich, Conn.: New York Graphic Society, 1972.

Punter, David. *The Literature of Terror: A History of Gothic Fictions from 1765 to the Present Day*. London: Longman, 1980.

Ronay, Gabriel. *The Truth about Dracula*. New York: Stein and Day, 1972.

Roth, Phyllis A. *Bram Stoker*. Boston: Twayne Publishers, 1982.

Summers, Montague. *The Vampire: His Kith and Kin*. London: Routledge and Kegan Paul, 1928.

Thornburg, Thomas R. "The Questor and the Castle: The Gothic Novel as Myth with Special Reference to Bram Stoker's *Dracula*." Dissertation. Muncie, Indiana: Ball State University, 1969.

Twitchell, James B. *The Living Dead: The Vampire in Romantic Literature*. Durham, N.C.: Duke University Press, 1981.

————. *Dreadful Pleasures: An Anatomy of Modern Horror*. New York: Oxford University Press, 1985.

Weissman, Judith. *Half Savage and Hardy and Free: Women and Rural Radicalism in the Nineteenth-Century Novel*. Mount Vernon, Conn.: Wesleyan University Press, 1987.

Wilson, A. N., ed. *Dracula*, by Bram Stoker. Oxford: Oxford University Press, 1983.

Wolf, Leonard, ed. *The Annotated Dracula*. New York: Clarkson N. Potter, 1975.

————. *A Dream of Dracula: In Search of the Living Dead*. Little, Brown, and Co., 1972.

Wright, Dudley. *Vampires and Vampirism*. London: William Rider and Son, 1914.

Articles

Astle, Richard. "Dracula as Totemic Monster: Lacan, Freud, Oedipus and History." *Sub-Stance* 25 (1980), 98–105.

Bentley, Christopher. "The Monster in the Bedroom: Sexual Symbolism in Bram Stoker's *Dracula*." *Literature and Psychology* 22 (1972), No. 1, 27–34.

Bierman, Joseph. "*Dracula*: Prolonged Childhood Illness, and the Oral Triad." *American Imago* 29 (1972), 186–98.

————. "The Genesis and Dating of *Dracula* from Bram Stoker's Working Notes." *Notes and Queries* 24 (1977), 39–41.

Blinderman, Charles S. "Vampurella: Darwin and Count Dracula." *Massachusetts Review* 21 (1980), 411–28.

Bonewits, Wanda. "Dracula, the Black Christ." *Gnostica* 4 (1975), No. 7.

Byers, Thomas B. "Good Men and Monsters: The Defenses of *Dracula*." *Literature and Psychology* 31 (1981), No. 4, 24–31.

Carlsen, M. M. "What Stoker Saw: An Introduction to the Literary Vampire." *Folklore Forum* 10 (1977) No. 2, 26–32.

Clements, William M. "Formula as Genre in Popular Horror Literature." *Research Studies* 49 (1981), No. 2, 116–23.

Coats, Daryl R. "Bram Stoker and the Ambiguity of Identity." *Publications of the Mississippi Philological Association* n.v. (1984), 88–105.

Craft, Christopher. "'Kiss Me with Those Red Lips': Gender and Inversion in Bram Stoker's *Dracula*." *Representations* 8 (1984), 107–33.

Davies, Bernard. "Mountain Greenery." *The Dracula Journals* 1 (1976–7), No. 1.

Demetrakopoulos, Stephanie. "Feminism, Sex Role Exchanges, and Other Subliminal Fantasies in Bram Stoker's *Dracula*." *Frontiers: A Journal of Women's Studies* 2 (1977), No. 3, 104–13.

Fontana, Ernest. "Lombroso's Criminal Man and Stoker's *Dracula*." *Victorian Newsletter* 66 (1984), 25–27.

Fry, Carrol L. "Fictional Conventions and Sexuality in *Dracula*." *Victorian Newsletter* 42 (1972), 20–22.

Griffin, Gail B. "'Your Girls That You All Love Are Mine': *Dracula* and the Victorian Male Sexual Imagination." *International Journal of Women's Studies* 3 (1980), No. 5, 454–65.

Hatlen, Burton. "The Return of the Repressed/Oppressed in Bram Stoker's *Dracula*." *Minnesota Review* 15 (1980), 80–97.

Hennelly, Mark M., Jr. "*Dracula:* The Gnostic Quest and the Victorian Wasteland." *English Literature in Transition* 20 (1977), 13–26.

_____. "Twice Told Tales of Two Counts." *Wilkie Collins Society Journal* 2 (1982), 15–31.

Hood, Gwenyth. "Sauron and Dracula." *Mythlore* 52 (1987), 11–17.

Irvin, Eric. "Dracula's Friends and Forerunners." *Quandrant* 135 (1978), 42–44.

Johnson, Alan. "Bent and Broken Necks: Signs of Design in Stoker's *Dracula*." *Victorian Newsletter* 72 (1987), 17–24.

_____. "'Dual Life': The Status of Women in Stoker's *Dracula*." *Tennessee Studies in Literature* 27 (1984), 20–39.

Johnson, Roger. "The Bloofer Ladies." *Dracula Journals* 1 (1982), No. 4.

Kirtley, Bacil F. "*Dracula,* the Monastic Chronicles and Slavic Folklore." *Midwest Folklore* 6 (1956), No. 3, 133–39.

MacGillivray, Royce. "*Dracula:* Bram Stoker's Spoiled Masterpiece." *Queen's Quarterly* 79 (1972), 518–27.

Murphy, Brian. "The Nightmare of the Dark: The Gothic Legacy of Count Dracula." *Odyssey* 1 (1976), No. 2, 9–15.

Nandris, Grigore. "The Historical Dracula: The Theme of His Legend in the Western and in Eastern Literatures of Europe." *Comparative Literature Studies* 3 (1966), No. 4, 367–96.

Oinas, Felix. "East European Vampires and Dracula." *Journal of Popular Culture* 16 (1982), No. 1, 108–16.

Phillips, Robert. "The Agony and the Ecstasy: A Jungian Analysis of Two Vampire Novels, Meredith Ann Pierce's *The Darkangel* and Bram Stoker's *Dracula*." *West Virginia University Philological Papers* 31 (1986), 10–19.

Raible, Christopher Gist. "Dracula: Christian Heretic." *Christian Century* 96 (1979), No. 4, 103–4.

Richardson, Maurice. "The Psychoanalysis of Ghost Stories." *Twentieth Century* 166 (1959), 419–31.

Roth, Phyllis A. "Suddenly Sexual Women in Bram Stoker's *Dracula*." *Literature and Psychology* 27 (1977), 113–21.

Seed, David. "The Narrative Method of *Dracula*." *Nineteenth-Century Fiction* 40 (1985), No. 1, 61–75.

Senf, Carol A. "*Dracula:* The Unseen Face in the Mirror." *Journal of Narrative Technique* 9 (1979), 160–70.

_____. "*Dracula*: Stoker's Response to the New Woman." *Victorian Studies* 26 (1982), No. 1, 33–49.

Shuster, Seymour. "Dracula and Surgically Induced Trauma in Children." *British Journal of Medical Psychology* 46 (1973).

Stevenson, John Allen. "A Vampire in the Mirror: The Sexuality of *Dracula*." *PMLA* 103 (1988), No. 2, 139–49.

Temple, Philip. "The Origins of *Dracula*." *Times Literary Supplement* 4205 (1983), 1216.

Twitchell, James. "The Vampire Myth." *American Imago* 37 (1980), 83–92.

Varma, Devendra P. "Dracula's Voyage: From Pontus to Hellespontus." Eighteenth National Convention, American Association of Slavic Studies. New Orleans, 21 November 1986.

_____. "The Genesis of Dracula: A Re-Visit," in *The Vampire's Bedside Companion*, ed. Peter Underwood. London: Leslie Frewin Limited, 1975.

_____. "The Vampire in Legend, Lore, and Literature." Introduction to *Varney the Vampyre; or, The Feast of Blood*. New York: Arno Press, 1970.

Wall, Geoffrey. "'Different from Writing': *Dracula* in 1897." *Literature and History* 10 (1984), No. 1, 15–23.

Walsh, Thomas P. *"Dracula:* Logos and Myth." *Research Studies* 47 (1979), 229–37.

Wasson, Richard. "The Politics of *Dracula." English Literature in Transition* 9 (1966), 24–27.

Weissman, Judith. "Women as Vampires: *Dracula* as a Victorian Novel." *Midwest Quarterly* 18 (1977), 392–405.

Index